THE

WESTERN

WORLD

the
development
of
modern
civilization

GENERAL EDITOR

BOYD H. HILL, JR.
University of Colorado

THE WESTERN WORLD

the development of modern civilization

James D. Hardy, Jr.
Louisiana State University

Arthur J. Slavin
University of California at Irvine

RANDOM HOUSE

NEW YORK

First Edition
987654321
Copyright © 1974 by Random House, Inc.
All rights reserved under International and Pan-American Copyright
Conventions. No part of this book may be reproduced in any form or
by any means, electronic or mechanical, including photocopying, without permission in writing from the publisher. All inquiries should be
addressed to Random House, Inc., 201 East 50th Street, New York, N.Y.
10022. Published in the United States by Random House, Inc., and
simultaneously in Canada by Random House of Canada Limited,
Toronto.

Library of Congress Cataloging in Publication Data

Slavin, Arthur Joseph.
The Western world.

1. Civilization, Occidental.   2. History, Modern.
I. Hardy, James Daniel, 1934–   joint author.
II. Title.
CB245.S57   910'.03'1821   73–16148
ISBN 0–394–31801–3

Manufactured in the United States of America. Composed by Cherry Hill
Composition, Pennsauken, N.J. Printed and bound by Kingsport Press,
Kingsport, Tenn.

Cover:
Design, Jeheber & Peace; illustration, courtesy Bettman Archive

Preface

Contemporary historians, in contrast with those of past years, often present the problems confronting mankind in a social and economic context. In the process of shifting their focus from traditional investigations of high politics to questions of social and economic significance, historians have more and more adopted the techniques of the social sciences. Their studies tend to concentrate more on mass crises and points of discontinuity than on the machinations of courtiers in the drawing room or the impact of dynastic marriages upon the shaping of political decisions. The difficulties of the modern age and the problems we now face tend to influence the work of historians who may be studying fifteenth-century Europe as well as those who specialize in the nineteenth and twentieth centuries. In short, mass movements, revolutions, the complexities of urban living, and the need to reconcile the good life with the demands for increased energy and greater industrial production have influenced the direction of present-day historical studies.

So much is this the case that we must begin this book by posing a fundamental question: Do the answers to our current political, social, and economic problems lie in the past? The answer is no if by "answer" one means that a careful study of the past will provide easy solutions to contemporary dilemmas. The past can indeed assist us in understanding our present condition, but "assistance" is significantly different from "solution," and we must be content to find in our present course of study many paths leading to understanding rather than one clearly marked road to the perfect society.

Various institutions—governmental, social, intellectual, and cultural—that characterize our own society can be discerned in their early form beginning with the fourteenth century and emerging more clearly during the course of the seventeenth and eighteenth centuries.

Yet undue worship of the idol Relevance and a narrow concern with the past only as it reflects our own society can lead to serious errors of judgment and can so distort the understanding of history that students become merely skilled polemicists and clever memorizers. To see only the germs of the modern English Parliament and of the United States Congress in the activities of similar bodies in the sixteenth century is a superficial approach that obscures the realities of past ages and prevents the raising of questions that lead to a better grasp of both past and present.

The authors of this text have taken pains to present students with recent discoveries of historical scholarship. Many of these discoveries focus upon population changes, food production, and health statistics, but to confront beginning students with the latest information on demographic studies without giving them at the same time an understanding of the major political and intellectual institutions would be impossible. Hence the authors have sought to combine some of the traditional topics with the results of more recent researches. The purpose of this volume is not only to familiarize students with the legends of their ancestors but also to introduce the more significant themes of change and transformation that characterize modern history. In other words, *The Western World* attempts to broach the study of origins as well as the theory of change within institutions.

The authors have severely limited their topics, choosing to present students with specific examples of various problems rather than to "survey" European history in the style of the older and heavier texts of the last thirty years. As a result, the following chapters represent a focus for reading and discussion rather than an encyclopedia of historical knowledge. It was felt that to present the countless facts of modern history regime by regime would achieve nothing significant for the student of Western civilization, since many comprehensive treatments of individual events are available in traditional format. Inevitably, certain favorite topics are missing, but the editor suggests that the gain in precision and subtlety is worth the curtailment of some time-honored characters and events. The advantages of such a radical editorial decision can be found in the uniqueness of content and the freshness of style in what follows.

Boyd H. Hill, Jr.
University of Colorado

Contents

THE WESTERN WORLD

the
development
of
modern
civilization

Chronology

1302	Papal Bull *Unam Sanctam*
1328	Start of Valois dynasty in France
1337	Hundred Years' War begins
1347	Black Death strikes Europe
1381	Russia defeats Mongols; English peasant rebellions
1410	Civil War in France
1417	Great Schism ends
1438	Pragmatic Sanction of Bourges
1453	Turks take Constantinople
1455	Bible printed by Gutenberg from movable type
1469	Union of Castile and Aragon
1485	Tudor dynasty begins
1493	America divided between Iberian powers by papal treaty
1505	Main creative period for da Vinci and Erasmus
1515	French forces victorious in Italy
1519	Charles V elected Holy Roman Emperor
1525	Imperial troops defeat French forces in Italy
1532	German Protestants organize Schmalkaldic League
1543	Copernicus and Vesalius publish revolutionary scientific works
1555	Charles V abdicates; Religious Peace of Augsburg
1559	Peace of Cateau-Cambrésis
1562	Englishmen open slave trade to America
1572	Dutch Revolt begins
1582	Russia loses access to Baltic Sea; calendar reformed by papal order
1589	Bourbon dynasty begins in France
1594	French Protestants granted religious toleration
1598	Peace of Vervins
1600	Bank of Amsterdam and British East India Company founded

PART ONE the first great transformation

1300-1600

In 1300 European society and Western civilization were nearly synonymous terms. The efforts of the crusaders to push that civilization into Moslem lands had clearly failed, and although Islam made new encroachments on Europe's eastern, Byzantine flank, there was in 1300 a certain poise, a balance between the desire for expansion and the fear of forced contraction.

But by the 1600s nearly all the world was Europe's. In an age of exploration and expansion the flags of the Atlantic powers had been carried into Africa, Asia, the Americas, and Oceania. Palestine remained beyond Europe's reach, however, since the Turks blocked the way. Yet there were compensations for the Turks' conquest of Constantinople and their threats to Vienna: Spain was now wholly Christian again, and exotic Japan had begun its "Christian Century."

Before 1300 a dramatic rise in Europe's population had forced a vast effort to bring new lands under cultivation to feed the hungry millions. By 1300 this phase of population growth and agricultural expansion had ended and decline began. Then the Black Death swept across Europe and decimated whole communities, and thus reduced the pressure on land and food supplies. Not until about 1450 did a new phase of growth begin which slowly gathered momentum and continued until 1600. Hence the territorial expansion of Europe which began about 1450 ran parallel to an upward surge of population.

The year 1300 also marks the start of a two-hundred-year decline in the power of the papacy. The 1400s witnessed the alienation of whole peoples from Rome. Then, by the 1500s, the Christian commonwealth shattered.

In secular government, the old axioms of rule had failed and a restless search had begun for new roots of authority and legitimacy.

A state system emerged and brought with it the language of diplomacy, sharpened by struggles for mastery. Not until 1598 was there a significant pause, as Spanish and imperial power proved inadequate to contain the Turk, Protestantism, the French, Dutch, and English in Europe and overseas. In the struggles for power the land empires of earlier times lost their central place to the new sea-borne empires.

These transformations had a great impact on thought and culture. In the Renaissance and the Reformation, Europe knew no single set of norms in art, literature, music, or philosophy, and various concepts of man, nature, and God multiplied.

This period thus contains two phases: one of decline from 1300 until about 1450, and a new expansive phase from 1450 on. The Atlantic became Europe's frontier; her economies, politics, and intellectual life were fundamentally reshaped.

ONE

The reshaping of rural society

There will be not enough men left to bury the dead; nor means to dig enough graves. . . .

Savonarola, *Sermons* (1496)

INTRODUCTION

Census Bureau clocks today count by the minute the daily addition to the earth's burden of people. Prophets of doom warn that men will drown in seas of their own offspring. Such attention to births reflects the belief that changing patterns of population have profound effects on the material and mental culture of our civilization. How and in what way are now matters of keen debate, but in the fourteenth century the study of population (demography) was not yet a serious concern of those who sought explanations for social changes. Moreover, among those who noticed changes in population, the anxiety was not that too many were being born but that too many were dying too fast. A terrible plague—the Black Death—had spread westward across Europe from Constantinople in 1347, followed by others at short intervals for more than a century. It seemed that an era of human development was ending in the charnel houses of Europe.

The decline in population consequent to the Black Death produced in both town and country some fundamental changes. Before the plague struck there had been a surplus of labor, with the results we ordinarily expect: Wages were low, conditions of employment on the land were often harsh, and people were in sharp competition

3

with one another to find a means of subsistence. But with the onset of the plague there was a long period of population decline which lasted from about 1350 to 1475. In eastern Europe the various monarchies had not developed the strength of their western counterparts, so eastern landlords were able to exploit the political power already in their hands and force the peasantry to accept serfdom, even in periods of labor shortage. In western Europe, on the other hand, it was a time of increasing freedom for peasants and profound social mobility for all the classes associated with the land. Most western monarchies were not as dependent on powerful aristocracies and did not surrender control of the peasantry to the feudal lords. There were also profound changes in the landscape, as the use to which people put land altered with the declining food demands of a shrinking population. Much land that had once produced cereals was given over to sheep and cattle grazing as well as other specialized uses in order to meet changing social needs.

This period with its catastrophic loss of life was paradoxically a good era for the survivors. Because population declined more rapidly than did the total output of goods and services, the smaller number of survivors enjoyed larger shares of the available wealth. The real standards of living for most rural folk rose, just as the freedom of persons under the law, or the absence of legal restraints on their position in society, also increased. When the long era of population decline and economic stagnation ended and a new period of growth set in, conditions worsened for the common people. Increased population pressure encouraged social and economic shifts opposite to those that had occurred during the period of decline, and by the early seventeenth century new problems for rural folk had emerged in the West.

PLAGUE AND POPULATION DECLINE

We do not know exactly how great was the slaughter caused by the plague, nor what the exact level of population was before 1347. Some facts are obscured by the imperfections of the surviving records. Such records as were kept disregarded whole groups: church records did not count Jews; roll calls made for military purposes omitted men in hospitals and jails; tax lists neglected the desperately poor. We are also generally ignorant about the proportions of rural to urban population and about the size of some towns.

Yet there is little doubt as to what the overall pattern of medieval population change was from about A.D. 1000 to 1600. From about 1000 to 1300 total population expanded rapidly in the West.

The evidence suggests a slower increase in the early fourteenth century and perhaps even a stagnation. Then the Black Death produced a dramatic decline and an enduring low level of population from 1347 to 1450. From about 1450 to 1600 there was a period of growth, slow at first, but very rapid from about 1510 on. The graphs represent these trends clearly.

In the general pattern of growth before 1300, urban populations apparently expanded at a faster rate than rural populations. The

POPULATION IN EUROPE ca. 1100–1640

Millions

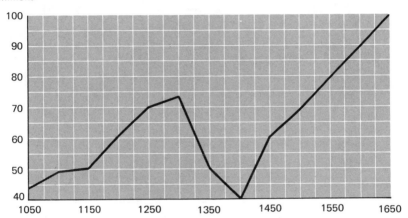

POPULATION IN THREE COUNTRIES

Millions

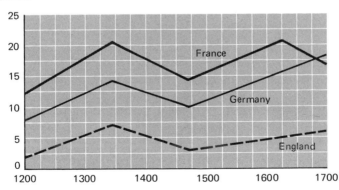

Source: M. K. Bennett, The World's Food (London, 1954), p. 9; W. Abel, Die Wüstungen des ausgehenden Mittelalters (Stuttgart, 1955), 2nd ed., p. 62.

5 The Reshaping of Rural Society

A detail from a fresco by Francesco Traini showing *Il Trionfo della Morte*
("the triumph of Death")as represented by the plague. *Alinari—Art Refer-*
ence Bureau.

evidence for this difference in rates is chiefly the more rapid expansion of urban church parishes over rural ones, as well as the mushroom growth of the areas enclosed by town walls as compared to
increases in the size of villages. So impressive had this growth been
that even after the onset of the Black Death urban officials were still
planning new expansions. A consequence of rapid growth, however,
was the inability of the towns to support adequately the enlarged
populations. The immediately surrounding countryside often could
not produce enough food for both its own people and urban consumers. Some truly great towns solved the problems of supply by
drawing on markets far away, even overseas; good examples were
Milan, London, Bruges, Barcelona, Cologne, and Oslo.

One consequence of growth before 1300 had been the development of such great towns as centers of consumption to support
specialized groups—lawyers, administrators, and so forth—not
engaged in either agriculture or urban trade. Many of these towns had
populations of more than 50,000 on the eve of the Black Death. In
Italy alone, Milan, Naples, Venice, Palermo, and Florence belonged
in this category.

Most towns, however, were on a smaller scale, and even the chief city of a region scarcely exceeded 15,000, what we today would reckon a small town.

Students of human population history differ in their estimates of the blow to population dealt by the plague. Some acknowledge that perhaps four out of every ten lives were lost; others tend to think the loss was not more than two in ten, or at the most twenty-five per hundred. It is hard to choose among them. One chronicle reports villages in South Tyrol losing 82 percent of their people. A 1350 census of victims in Bremen shows that 60 percent of the aldermen died, but "aldermen" are old men and we cannot generalize from the high mortality rate of this age group. In Salzburg, Austria, land rentals show a climb in vacancies to the 40 percent level almost overnight, and in Sweden and the Languedoc region of France similar evidence survives.

Apart from some isolated pockets in Lombardy, southern Flanders, south Poland, and areas of Christian Spain, the population decline in rural places was widespread and pronounced. The principality of Kiev had its *pustoshi* ("empty lands"), and Spanish landlords complained of vacant holdings. Europe experienced an extermination of whole settlements. Hundreds of villages were deserted in Britain and also in the German bishopric of Ermland. The Île de France (the agricultural lands surrounding Paris) lost half its population between 1346 and 1440. Where the plow once turned the ground, only sparrows played.

After the first wave of the plague (1347–1351) there was an attempted "natural correction" in the population. Those who survived were eager to marry earlier because vacant landholdings were available. Surviving women were abnormally fecund. Infant deaths shortened the lactation period, during which intercourse was normally taboo. This reduced the interval between conceptions, as did high rates of miscarriage and natural abortion. These circumstances also provided psychological incentives for new conceptions.

The attempted recovery failed. The 1361 epidemics inflicted especially high death rates on those children born after 1351, as they lacked whatever immunity resulted from exposure. The 1347–1351 plague had made especially heavy inroads against the young-adult, infant, and child groups, and one effect was to create a European population in 1360 lacking in adults of childbearing age. The long-range impact of this was to reduce the recovery potential and to increase the percentage of older adults among the survivors.

Other factors kept population down. Food shortages led to malnutrition; the dislocation of international trade curtailed food supplies; and the corruption of water supplies generated secondary epidemics. There was also a cult of continence: men believed intercourse weakened the body and made people prone to plague.

Detailed studies show that recovery was retarded and towns that had been small before 1350 grew even smaller. The plague still persisted chiefly in urban areas. There is dramatic evidence of this. Barcelona's population level in 1359 was 75 percent of the 1340 levels; in 1447 this level was diminished by half; and as late as 1497 the total had not climbed back to 60 percent of the 1340 population. In Siena the fall was more startling than in any other town in Italy: in 1348 only 37 percent of the previous year's population survived; in 1460 that level still held; and even by 1520 the rise had only restored population to 50 percent of the 1347 level. In 1357 the town

THE SPREAD OF THE PLAGUE, 1347–1350

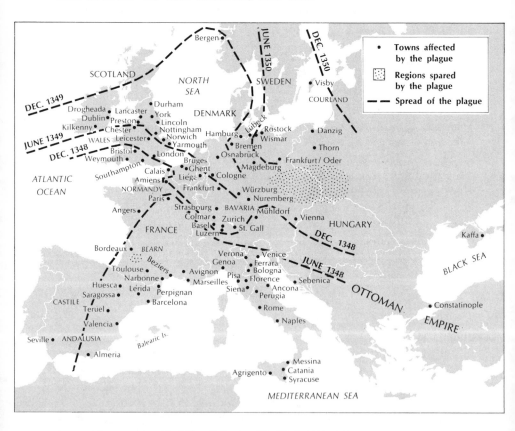

Source: Margaret Aston, The Fifteenth Century (New York, 1968), p. 18.

of Albi in southern France had only 47 percent of its 1343 total; its population hovered about a level of 50 percent of its previous maximum even as late as 1601.

The chronology in general shows that in some places the nadir was reached in the 1440s, in others not until about 1500. Thus it is safe to say that sustained recovery was long delayed, and that when recovery began it continued through the sixteenth century.

THE RECOVERY OF POPULATION

About 1450, population began a slow recovery to pre-plague levels (and beyond). One estimate places the total European population in 1450 at 60 million, with increases of roughly 10 million per half-century until the figure of 89,999,000 was reached in 1600.[1] Estimates for France, Germany, and England show the dramatic trend upward (in millions):

Year	France	Germany	England
1470	14	10	3
1620	21	16	5

Indices of prices of consumer goods and the wages of certain craftsmen bear out this trend. Prices shot upward, while wages were steadily depressed—developments that illustrate the increasing competition of consumers for scarce goods and the relative oversupply of labor.

Population figures for particular cities and countries give substance to this account. Between 1487 and 1595 the kingdom of Naples (without the city) grew from 215,127 to 540,000. Census data for Aragon show a change from 50,391 heads of households in 1495 to 70,984 in 1603. In the Low Countries, Brabant and Hainault experienced rapid growth between 1470 and 1540. The Swiss cantons had very little land upon which to support an increase from 600,000 to 800,000 between 1450 and 1530, and by 1600 the total had risen to a million. In Spain Philip II's inquest of 1570 showed that people were increasing faster than the houses to hold them. The situation was no different in France. By 1480 recovery, somewhat delayed by wars civil and foreign, had set in. Growth was especially pronounced in the cities of Italy and the Dutch northern provinces.

The evidence from Europe's peripheral areas is less detailed. It does appear certain that Norway experienced some growth

[1] M. K. Bennett, *The World's Food* (London, 1954).

throughout the sixteenth century and that Sweden expanded until about 1560. Finland had a largely stable population between 1400 and 1600. In Poland growth was pronounced after 1400, especially in the southern plains. For the Balkans the good census materials of efficient Turkish officials show rapid urban growth in all areas.

SOME CAUSES AND CONSEQUENCES

Just as people reacted to the disastrous decline of population after 1347 in sometimes violent ways (see pp. 24–25), so did men caught in the vise of a growing population and relatively fixed food resources cast about for the means to end their misery. We can point to new efforts to bring barren marginal lands under cultivation, overseas expansion, the Spanish expulsion of Jews and Moors, and the export of surplus men as mercenary soldiers. The German militant humanist Ulrich von Hutten advocated another way in 1518:

> There is a dearth of provisions in this age. What we all ought to have wished for—a foreign war, to relieve this pressure, has providentially come to pass. . . . War against the Turks is both warranted and necessary.

In the light of these attitudes and reactions, three questions seem especially pressing. How can we account for the changing patterns of population, apart from the ending of the great plagues? Was the keen anxiety about overpopulation realistic, since total population in 1600 was probably not above the level of 1300? And what overall impact did demographic change have on the West?

The wholesale decline of population in the 1300s marks the end of the traditional, feudal society of the West. The fifteenth century was a time of troubles out of which came a mixed agrarian-commercial society, traditional in many ways, but transformed in culture and technology in ways undreamed of in the age of Dante and Aquinas. There were profound alterations in land use between 1300 and about 1450, and in the 1500s came a mushroom growth of great cities. Social complaints, which had once been confined to lords and peasants, were now voiced about urban rogues. Picaresque novels showed in human terms the uprooting of the old and the planting of much that was new. All was flux.

No adequate total explanation for these demographic dislocations and recoveries exists. Even before the Black Death, decline had begun. Up to that time more and more marginal lands were being brought under cultivation, and poor yields may well have led to sustained local famines. Seaboard towns had come to rely in part on imports from great granaries in Prussia, Sicily, North Africa, and elsewhere. Landlocked towns had become completely dependent on surrounding farm areas. Any dislocations of trade or general failure of harvests produced instant crises.

Early in the 1300s crop failures were frequent, most notably between 1315 and 1317, when torrential rains and very cold winters ruined successive harvests. The problems multiplied in the 1320s, when epidemics among livestock further cut into prosperity and food supplies. Weather, famine, and epidemics have been shown to be mutually reinforcing in modern times. Overpopulation, poor diets, and very hard work had lowered human vitality and resistance to the plague in 1347. The fierceness of the Black Death was itself a commentary on the marginal quality of life for the masses in the West in 1347. In only a few years it had traced a wide path on the map—up from the Mediterranean into central Italy, Spain, and France, and thence into England, reaching the Germanies and Scandinavia by 1351.

We do know that the initial attempt at recovery failed. One reason may well have been the gradual emergence of a new psychology among survivors. Men did grasp that their standard of living rose with the lowering of population. They could enjoy more meat in their diets because more land was available (it took five or six times more land to produce one calorie of animal food than an equal amount of grain or other arable crop food value). The disasters thus promoted changes in agriculture and land use, increased individual holdings, and shifted taste and patterns of consumption. There is evidence of popular enjoyment of this prosperity: a Zurich tax register (1467) shows that only 50 percent of the men who were taxed were married, whereas 44 percent were bachelors and 6 percent were widowed and not remarried.

There was also a spectacular rise in prostitution. Luther complained of this in 1522: "Many . . . refrain from matrimony, because they cannot provide as well for . . . a family. This is the cause of whoredom." More grim are the reports of infanticide. Generally daughters were the victims, probably because they were thought an expense rather than a productive asset. The practice was widespread but we have no statistics. In a lighter vein, we have the conventional wisdom of folk songs and literature: Young men were to avoid marriages of passion and to bed prosperous widows past childbearing age. Also, some historians allege that both civil and foreign wars played a vital role in keeping population down until late in the fifteenth century.

Population Growth and Catastrophes

Contemporaries thought the growth of population after 1450 was the result of Providence, the abatement of plague and famine, and the cessation of wars. We know too little about the remission of epidemics, but what we do know suggests that "sweating sickness" in England, typhus in the Holy Roman Empire, and syphilis in Italy were all major new threats in the 1550s. What appears more certain is that epidemics became distinctly urban in incidence in the Renaissance. The great deaths of 1563–1566 and 1575–1577 were chiefly city plagues in England, Germany, France, Spain, Switzerland, and the Balkans.

War as a killer of men needs no explanation here. But there is no pattern that justifies talking of a cessation of war as having been in part responsible for the demographic upturn. England's population grew during the Wars of the Roses (1455–1485), Burgundy's during its wars with France in the 1460s and 1470s, and Austria's despite its conquest by Hungarians in 1477–1485. Moreover, only bad vision can obscure the bellicose character of the sixteenth century as a whole, convulsed as it was by the Peasants' War in Germany (1524–1525); the Hapsburg-Valois struggles[2] that sprawled over the whole century; the Wars of Religion in Switzerland (1529–1531), France (1562–1598), and Germany (1546–1555); the Revolt of the Netherlands (1567–1610); the Nordic Wars (1563–1570); and the continuing pressure of the Ottoman Turks on the southern flanks of the Holy Roman Empire after 1517.

Nor was there any disappearance of famines in Europe. There appears abundant evidence of their occurrence in various countries from the late fifteenth to late sixteenth century. The situation in 1600 seemed remarkably similar to the point of equipoise between growth and decline that was reached about 1315–1317.

The factors responsible for the sharp rise in population were too many and too deeply rooted in social and economic changes to be easily checked by wars, local famines, plagues, and even gross natural disasters. The structure of agriculture and trade in the last half of the sixteenth century had altered considerably since 1315–1317 and the 1350s. This may help account for the absence of panic in the later crises. Towns had adopted the policy of storing provisions in good times; so had territorial princes. The international grain trade in the Baltic and Levant had increased enormously (in 1560, Danzig

[2] The series of wars between the Hapsburg Holy Roman emperors and the French kings, chiefly fought over the control of Italy after 1494.

shipped ten times as much grain as it had in 1490). Yields of grain from seed had been increased. Overseas fisheries supplied new sources of protein. Stock raising of every sort had also helped reduce dependency on slender cereal surpluses. Hungary, Wallachia, Denmark, and England had significant meat export industries by 1600 where none had existed before.

In Protestant countries the abolition of cloisters and celibacy doubtless contributed to the population surge. Even in Catholic countries some writers espoused pronatalist policies and criticized clerical celibacy. The revolution in economy and society had produced physical and psychological buffers against disaster. The new evidences of population pressure could not restore the prudent restraints of the mid-1400s. Although the lot of many men in the lower orders of society fell seriously in the sixteenth century, in the articulate classes there was reason for confidence, even optimism. Against the pessimism of an old Dutch proverb that emphasized how children impoverished their parents,[3] many Europeans were already thinking of people as being synonymous with wealth. Europe had experienced a revolution in the agrarian bases of its society. Moreover, the commercial revolution in the towns was nearly complete. The remarkable imperialism that opened the world's resources to Europeans had begun. Life expectancy was growing in England, Denmark, and France, despite new population pressures. From demographic catastrophes a new Europe led the West out of its old confines and into the Age of Empires.

THE EUROPEAN LANDSCAPE

In any study of the shape of European society before the Industrial Revolution, the land first claims our attention. If land lent itself in different ways to human use because of soil, topography, and climate, it also shaped and was shaped by the societies of men living on it. The land responded to the density of population, to technology, to capital, and to the wiles of human inventiveness.

Heroic efforts were required to exploit barren countryside; villagers walked miles every day in short growing seasons to work the few good fields of their area. Where land was poor in character—hilly, mountainous, swampy—people could not depend on crops for their livelihood. They had to become cattle drivers and shepherds,

---

[3] *Luttel goets ende vile kynder/Dit brengt den meneghen in groten hynder.* ("Many youngsters will bring mankind to great harm.")

separated from their families as they tended their animals on whatever upland grass or hay existed, their seasonal movements giving noisy testimony to an ungracious nature. On high ground "high-pasture" farming was often the only possible way of life. The men who practiced it remained largely unaffected by the social and economic forces that gave to the European plains the vocabulary of feudal society—lord and peasant, demesne and strips in the open fields, chivalry and servility. In the upland regions there still survive in our time remote pockets where the pastoral economy bears a way of life closer to that of centuries ago than to the cities and farms of the plains then and now. Men who lived in these mountainous areas had little territorial sense or instinct. Conflicts were few; law was local custom; life was crude, often barbarous. Travel into such regions by outsiders was hazardous. Communities in the highlands remained immune to shifts of population and trade routes, and even in modern times "highland" in various European tongues is a synonym for strangeness, independence, and isolation—for people and communities out of the mainstream of life.

So when we talk of "typical" agrarian systems in Europe we mean primarily the peasant cultivation of enclosed and open fields in Europe's broad plains. They flourished in the Mediterranean grain basin of the south and in the huge flatland stretching from France through the Rhine valley and into the river courses of central and eastern Europe. These were the homelands of feudal society and seigneurial agriculture. There grew up in those areas between 1050 and 1300 an enormous system of cultivation, in which peasants worked land they did not own. Land was allotted in small parcels to dependent workers who enjoyed certain rights in common: grazing their limited stock, taking wood and water, and running their pigs in the stubble left behind harvested crops. In exchange for these rights and small areas in which they produced crops for their own subsistence, the peasants also grew cereals, pulse (peas and beans), and limited supplies of vegetables and fruits on the demesne lands of lords.

Although land was of necessity allowed to lie fallow part of the time, since land cropped too often in the absence of animal fertilizer quickly lost heart, what most affected the pattern of cultivated land was population change. Throughout the period from 1050 to 1300, population had climbed steadily. This climb pushed cultivation increasingly on to wasteland of poor quality and into redeemed forest areas, swampland, and marshes. There was a rise in highly specialized forms of agriculture, as represented by the vineyards of France and the dairy farms of England and Denmark. But for the most part until

1300 peasants worked the land in subjugation to feudal lords. Side by side with them were a number of free peasants who had escaped bondage primarily because they had helped their lords to colonize virgin land in exchange for freedom or because they had been among the few who had thrived while others had been forced to servitude.

February, **from** *Les Très Riches Heures du Duc de Berry.* **The earliest snow landscape in Western art, depicting medieval village life in winter, with the front wall of the cottage removed to provide an interior view.** *Photographie Giraudon.*

Evidence suggests that early in the 1100s there was relatively little demesne farming by wealthy aristocrats and church corporations. The repeated waves of invasions had left the nobles with little time for estate management. By 1150, however, there was a restoration of political stability and population growth which favored the lord who could put land under crops, and peasants competed eagerly for small holdings on the demesne. Competition for subsistence became a dominant factor of rural life. Since there were no great technical innovations that improved crop yields per acre, only the extension of cultivation alleviated hunger.

This extension ruled the 1200s. In most areas of arable land new manors grew up; the grants to lords of jurisdiction over peasants multiplied; and privileges in the form of market franchises and even the right to settle new towns appeared. Landlords waged vigorous campaigns to turn fallow land into working capital by attracting labor to it. It was common practice to grant freedom to peasants willing to settle virgin territories and undertake the backbreaking work of bringing woodland, marsh, and tangled waste under the plow. The pressure of expansion carried western peasants into wood and waste in their own countries and into the Slavonic lands of eastern Europe as well. Germany east of the Elbe was "colonized" in this way. Much of the land brought into cultivation, however, was only marginally productive. Many documents show that average per-acre crop yields went *down*.

There were many consequences of this expansion. Predictably, the landowning classes benefited from rising prices and profits. Population increases had tended to reduce the size of peasant holdings everywhere. Nearly all of the evidence indicates a decline in peasant fortunes. As yields fell and farm sizes among peasants shrank, it became harder to maintain animals over the winter. Since beasts were the chief source of soil nourishment, peasants, stock, and crops were linked in a reciprocal chain of poverty. Wages were fairly stable, yet wheat and other cereals increased in price nearly three-fold. Real wages therefore shrank. Peasant life about 1300 was uncertain, extreme poverty was common, and even the free peasants had only a precarious hold on subsistence.

THE DESERTION OF FARMS

The countryside of the West underwent a difficult time from 1300 to 1450 (and even to 1500). Every grain of wheat or flower that grew drew nourishment from the graves of men and beasts who did not survive the waves of catastrophe. Labor and capital changed their relationship, with the result that modes of production that had been profitable before 1300 either lost favor or were modified in order to survive. Village life itself was greatly altered, where it did not disappear altogether.

It is a notorious fact in agrarian societies that agriculture by itself creates little new capital. What is saved after meeting the immediate needs of consumption is often not left to the cultivators. In the society of the medieval West large parts of any crop went into unproductive hands: The clergy, the aristocracy, and the various secular governments exacted their tithes, dues, and taxes. Even had nature been more hospitable, improvements in peasant life would not have resulted from a more determined labor effort. Only the entrepreneurial classes had the freedom to react to the forces of supply and demand; hence their estate records show the drama of changes in the prices of wheat and other commodities, in wage levels, and in land values.

A diminishing labor force meant a shrinkage in the number of acres given to cereals. Because laborers were the heaviest consumers of crops, a decrease in their number lowered cereal prices, since the crops that were planted were plentiful in relation to the demand. The scarcity of labor made wages shoot upward. Manufactured products therefore advanced in price, since labor costs constituted most of the price of these goods. Furthermore, the falling demand for food (and its price) directly affected the basic return from land rent by reducing the margin of profit.

Various studies show the retreat of arable land. By 1419 one-fifth of the land in the hands of the Teutonic knights was unoccupied and out of cultivation. Less than twenty years later this proportion had risen to 40 percent in some areas and had reached as high as 80 percent in others. This took place in some of the richest grain lands of the eastern plains. Recent research on the areas around Oslo in the late Middle Ages shows conclusively the desertion of farms: Of the old small farms at least 79 percent were deserted between 1350 and 1520. In France many *villes neuves* ("new villages") settled before 1300 were lost.

Maurice Beresford's *Lost Villages of England* makes clear that hundreds of villages were populated between 1370 and 1480 and lost to arable production. Throughout Italy land once sowed with grain was abandoned. Over most of the Slavonic lands the recession of settlement left *pustoshi* ("empty lands") in the wake of the Death. Only the burial mounds increased in size.

Land did not fall out of use in exact measure to the fall in population, nor did prices drop in proportion. There had been a great backlog of demand for landholdings of every size, which had built up during the years of relative overpopulation. In most countries others were ready to take up the plow put down by their fellows. Prices for corn therefore remained high until the 1370s, and even when old demands for land were satisfied, prices did not permanently fall from their pre-plague peaks.

These reservations notwithstanding, the consequences of the plague did injure the prosperity of the seigneurial classes. Grains did soon collapse in price. Supply outran demand as the proportion of consumers shrank in relation to the total products. The towns were especially hard hit, with the result that their demands on the goods of countryside dropped very rapidly. One further factor driving down prices, and hence profits, was the unwillingness of peasants to work those lands most encumbered with feudal dues and services.

The reality of these changes struck the village of Buxeaul in

PRICES, WAGES, AND POPULATION IN ENGLAND, 1300–1550

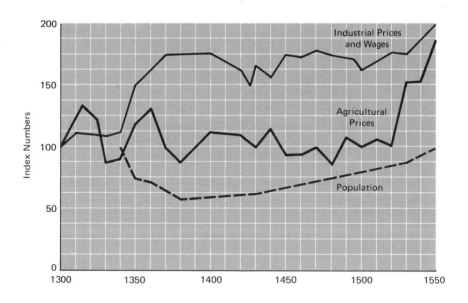

Source: E. Perroy, "Les crises de XIVe siècle," Annales, IV (1949), p. 173.

This graph shows clearly how the fall in agricultural prices quickly followed population loss, while wages and industrial prices reacted more slowly and inversely to the curve of population.

Burgundy in 1361. The lord of the peasants there was the king of France himself, Jean II. Plague and massacre by English soldiers had stripped his land of peasants. The king was unable to find tenants to work the land, so he made certain concessions. He offered leases with reduced dues, lower taxes, and limits on required services including plowing and road repairs. The king's agents were told not to claim these things from the people. In England, France, Germany, Poland, Norway, Bohemia, the Low Countries, Alsace, and Italy, there was a similar situation. Landowners experienced a sharp acceleration in the prices of industrial goods and labor, so that as their revenues from crops declined, their living costs rose abruptly. (The facts and their chronology can best be grasped in graphic forms.) In this context it is especially important to notice that *not all* farm prices fell: those for meat, butter, and animal by-products rose as steadily as cereal prices fell, which prompted landlords to think about changing their farming methods and orientation.

AGRICULTURAL ADJUSTMENTS

Landlords all faced the necessity of choice—whether to hold on to traditional values and enterprises, and so preserve the world in which they lived; or to adapt to the demographic and economic pressures in ways that would transform land use and with it the social and psychological bases of society itself. There were two extreme reactions. One was to use force to maintain dependent cultivation. The other was to turn to pastoral farming, with some surrender of the privileges and problems of seigneurial agriculture.

Peasant and Lord Relationships

In general, the European response to the demographic disaster was a "feudal reaction." Lords faced with holdings in danger of falling out of cultivation often tried to convert free tenements, created previously in the decades of expansion, into servile ones. By insisting on work dues, corvées (labor dues exacted for road repair), traditional rents, and services, the lords hoped to stand steadfast against the disruption of the milieu in which they ruled. They actually increased dues and services in new tenancies and in every way tried to get the most work for the least pay. They organized searches for fugitive serfs. They used their position in legislative assemblies to fix wages at pre-plague levels, to arrest the inflation of other prices, and to prohibit the migration of labor to less reactionary areas. Late in the fourteenth century, English parliaments, Norwegian Riksdagen,

German diets, and Spanish Cortes attempted to legislate the impossible. Town councils did the same, until it became clear that both lords and laborers had a vested interest in evasion.

One good example of this practice came from Italy. The town council of the commune of Florence passed a statute in 1348 that forbade plowmen to ask more than the pre-plague wages for work in cornfields. Violators were sentenced to a month in the town jail. And this law applied equally to those who offered higher wages and those who accepted.

The policy of restraint was soon abandoned in most of western Europe, although in some regions it remained, as, for example, along the upper Rhine where many of the great landlords were also petty princes with legislative power. This combination of economic interest and political strength occurred also in the Austrian Alps, Bohemia, and above all in the recently colonized areas of Germany beyond the Elbe and in Muscovite and Kievan Russia.

It was in eastern Europe that the feudal reaction triumphed. On the German lands, the decline of tenant populations coincided with the loss of military supremacy over the Slavic peoples so long under German domination. This meant that the warrior lords had difficulty in obtaining new labor supplies and that their income from war was shrinking. They thus had a maximum interest in taking up land cultivation and maintaining it by force. Lords in the Slavic lands shrewdly bargained for charters granting them legal power over peasants on their own lands, and in the fifteenth and sixteenth centuries used this power to develop a capitalist agriculture in which cereals were grown primarily to be exported to western markets.

The rise of capitalist farm production was especially pronounced in Brandenburg-Prussia, Pomerania, Holstein, Poland, and Russia. This entire great plains area had once been typical of the colonial regions of free peasant tenures. But now, east of the Elbe, lords became resident proprietors bent on survival through serfdom. The details and the chronology varied. In Poland it was not until 1491 that peasants were finally tied to the land and towns were stripped of their old right to aid fugitives. Ivan III's decree of 1497, which prohibited the abandonment of holdings, and the Prussian diet's 1494 decree, by which the Junker grain-growers gained the right to punish captured fugitive serfs without public trial, signaled the victory of reactionary lords. (The capitalist lords turned their backs on the native towns, which were often starved for grain and trade, in favor of foreign merchants and ports to absorb their products.)

Eastern Europe's large numbers of free farmers before 1350 had all but dwindled away by 1500. The region had become an area of large commercial farms specializing in grain for export. The feudal reaction rolled southwest to embrace much of Hungary and Rumania. Labor dues, which had been as minimal as one day per year in 1300, were by 1600 two and three days a week. Peasant mobility to other holdings became illegal, and even ordinary movements were restricted.

Political forces played a vital role in this transformation. In some monarchies the tax base was too slender to allow for state building. This weakness and the constant danger of foreign conquests (Teutonic knights, the Mongols, and Turks) provided a field in which the nobility gained at the expense of the crown. As early as the thirteenth century, bargains by the crown for support took the form of granting privileges that excluded the central government from extending its protection over peasants. By 1500 in some kingdoms rulers had surrendered jurisdiction over 90 percent of their nominal subjects.

The result was a vast and unchecked seigneurial regime resting on the exploitation of peasant labor. Perhaps the best analogy is the American experience of slavery in the South, where commercial capitalist agriculture based on export markets exploited the power of the states and the weakness of the Union to maintain the slave codes.

The Decline of Feudalism
in Western Europe

The lords in the west coped with the problem of labor in a different way, by modifying peasant obligations and by changing the entire mode of exploiting land. To attract new tenants they sometimes made periodic exemptions on annual rents. Rents in kind were exchanged for money rents, a distinct advantage in cases where the tenant could market a cash crop as prices recovered. Moreover, work in the lord's demesne was often abandoned or commuted. Odious dues, especially the obligation to mill grain or press grapes in the lord's facilities, gave way to freer arrangements. Poor peasants were given "stock and lot" leases whereby the animals and the farm tools were supplied by the lord in what amounted to a widespread system of sharecropping.

A good example is the French farm area of Provence in 1350. The landowner Raymond Béraud was a prosperous peasant who took advantage of the new conditions. He had from the seigneur William, lord of Bouches-du-Rhône, a farm at Cipierres. In exchange for certain rents, William provided Raymond with the land and half of all expenses involved in its cultivation. The expenses included, in fact, the wages Raymond gave to day laborers who did the harvesting, weeding, and threshing of the grain. In France this form of sharecropping was called *métayage*. Its Italian parallel was *mezzadria*, and after 1340 there were many instances in Italy where even oxen were provided. One Dino of Capella San Bartolomeo, "cultivator," got not only land, oxen, and tools, but a good cask of wine to boot; he promised in return only to faithfully cultivate and split a crop, giving so much to the monks of San Giorgio of Lucca.

One device to which peasants quickly responded was the lengthening of the rent contract. The incentive to work and improve land is never great where the effort involved is essentially short-term or subject to arbitrary termination. When labor had been plentiful such conditions had prevailed, but in the early post-plague generation, peasants demanded and got longer leases. In 1502 Maximilian of Austria granted hereditary leases on his Tyrol estates in place of revokable ones. "Tenants at will" (tenants without legal security of tenure) declined in number in England. There were contrary tendencies also, especially where townsmen bought land as investment and had sufficient capital to risk short-term losses.

From a social point of view the most dramatic transformation came in the legal and personal condition of peasants. Where lords had owned not only the land but the men who worked it, the promise of a release from bondage was an effective bargaining gesture. Villeinage receded rapidly in Scotland, many parts of England, France, Germany, the Low Countries, and in Scandinavia.

Thus, while in some areas changes in the nature and amount of rents and services enabled landowners to continue traditional farming patterns, in others only a change in the mode of exploitation could solve the problem of labor shortage and wage inflation. This change might take the form of a wholesale leasing of the demesne to farmers. In return for a sure rent the lord surrendered the privileges and anxieties of direct exploitation. Should the situation alter markedly, as it did with the great "repopulation" after 1480, lords could resume direct exploitation when leases lapsed. In the meantime, they became *rentiers*, paying professionals to administer their declining estates, and they shrugged off the burden of the large *familia*, or household. (One of the best examples is that of the archbishop of Canterbury in England, where between 1350 and 1450 the demesne was wholly leased.) In the northwest of Germany, the Low Countries, France, Italy, and Norway, leased demesnes constituted the majority of estate management shifts. This was as true on ecclesiastical estates as it was on those of secular lords.

In some areas another kind of change was to substitute one crop for another when to do so would mean better harvests, more efficient land utilization, or firmer market prices. Thus oats and barley came to dominate wheat lands in many places, barley gaining the most in countries where beer was a popular drink. Barley gave better yields, sold for more money, and was a good livestock feed. While root crops, legumes and fodder plants, industrial crops (wine and flax), peas, beans, and vetches provided money incomes and provoked changes in diet, they also replenished soil nitrogen and served admirably as winter cattle feed. Some of the foods—turnips, for example—were suitable for both human and animal consumption. Large plantations developed that specialized in grapes, flax, dye plants, and other useful or edible industrial crops.

But by far the most dramatic manifestation of change was the rise of livestock rearing, especially sheep. Even lambs required less labor than did crops, and in maturity they gave a variety of marketable commodities—meat, leather, and wool. Their price remained steadier than grain. Cattle provided meat and hides as well as butter and cheese. The increase in animal husbandry meant the enclosing of more and more arable lands and their use for sheep and cattle grazing; this exacted much hostile comment among contemporaries, but throughout much of western Eupore enclosure came by agreement between lords and peasants and was mutually beneficial.

Grazing became a dominant form of production in certain regions. The Italian, Flemish, and English cloth-making towns made a steady demand for fine wool. In Spain this demand led to the consolidation of a monopolistic association of cattle and sheep drovers, which since the thirteenth century had exclusive control over drove roads that linked northern summer pastures to the winter quarters in the south. In England grazier prosperity also illustrated the dominance of sheep, wool makers, and merchants. Whole rural economies were changed, and the English landscape became dotted with the houses of prosperous drovers, while the peasants in wool areas became spinners and loomers in lieu of working the soil. So also in areas of Denmark, Hungary, the Swiss valleys, and north Germany large-scale beef and dairy cattle farming replaced cropping as the dominant form of agriculture.

Intensive use of labor gave way to the drover and his dog, and where wheat once grew sparrows played on the backs of animals. The open fields farmed cooperatively by peasants and other communal forms of production surrendered to rural capitalism of one kind or another. Open fields survived only where the land was sufficiently rich and fertile to invite the plow even under the most adverse external conditions. But elsewhere peasant needs and seigneurial interests combined to convert old ways into new, and this could not but produce sharp conflicts in peasant society, where the meaning of life itself was bound up with cycles of work centuries old.

For over three hundred years before 1300, increasing the area of land under cultivation had the effect of minimizing conflict by giving to each partner in the rural economy a visibly greater share of income, and by allowing the adventurous and malcontent elements to settle the frontier areas. But after 1300 neither colonial areas nor the towns were able to absorb much surplus population, and immigration was not encouraged. What was especially annoying to the peasant was the mixture of freedom and liberty with servile tenures throughout much of the open-field area of Europe. Lords had gone far in abandoning customs that were harmful to serfs, but still maintained the old service dues on some holdings. These shifts happened at a time when central governments, hard-pressed themselves by the expenses of war, were vigorously taxing their subjects.

Peasant Revolts

Rebellions by peasants were common. One in Flanders in 1328 was led by a prosperous farmer named Zannekin, whose support came from solid peasants rather than the more depressed elements of rural labor. The rebels resisted seigneurial taxation and refused to pay a tithe to the church. Their goal was to deny to the *rentier,* be he gentry or clergyman, his former income. The *rentiers* rallied under common banners and a violent struggle ensued. The rural rebels had drawn support from the urban poor, and only the intervention of a French army in August 1328 led to their defeat.

In many ways the French peasant risings called the Jacquerie stemmed from the presence of English troops on French soil. Both invaders and defenders lived off the rich agricultural lands surrounding Paris, the Île de France, ruining production. In May 1358 spontaneous revolt against local lords triggered wider unrest. Nobles were murdered, castles and small towns sacked, and, as in Flanders, the town poor joined the peasants. Étienne Marcel was a leader of the Paris burgesses who tried to use the peasant rising for his own purpose, which was essentially to set up a program of government reform. In the south Charles of Navarre tried to use the rising as a springboard in an effort to usurp the crown of France. Faced with these two threats, the nobles banded together and made an all-out war on the peasants of the Île de France. Before the end of June over 20,000 peasants in the area had been killed. The resistance soon came to an end.

The English rising was precipitated by a series of unpopular taxes in 1377, 1379, and 1380. By 1380 evasions were common, and when Richard II's government tried to tighten the screws of collection, revolt came quickly. Wat Tyler of Kent led a march on London in June 1381 which resulted in the murder of many lawyers and officials and the destruction of much property. Tyler himself was killed under the flag of truce. All royal concessions previously granted were revoked, and severe repressive measures were taken against the leaderless masses. The English rising is of special interest because of the clear articulation of the peasants' program. Most striking was their request for the abolition of serfdom, the commutation of services for money rents, and the abolition of poll taxes. John Ball, a popular preacher, even advocated measures against the privileges of the clergy.

From 1400 on there was a rash of other risings—especially in France, but also in Catalonia, Jutland and Denmark, Finland, and the Germanies—which lasted from the late fifteenth to the early sixteenth century and climaxed in the great Peasants' War in 1524.

The impact of this unrest was a new scrutiny of social differences that, despite local variations, show some marked similarities. Most agrarian risings started in richer lands and were led by the wealthier rather than poorer peasant elements. In rural society dislike of the juridical aspects of serfdom and resentment of the privileges of gentry and priests weighed more heavily on ambitious men than in urban areas. These men feared the arrest of the general movement toward freedom. There was also a profound anticlerical sentiment throughout western Europe at this time, with hatred for the tithe and dissatisfaction with the poor performance of parish duties by local clergy. This theme was stressed by radical popular religious leaders. Finally, in each of the great revolts, the association between rural peasants and the urban poor and artisans is noteworthy: It seems likely that the struggle for particular peasant freedoms merged with the general trend toward greater personal freedom.

Lords learned to fear peasants, and peasant consciousness awakened to the wish to defy death rather than bear slavery. But that wish was not enough, for it did not father the political means which alone convert revolutionary protests into enduring achievements. The lords possessed the means for victory and could destroy all who challenged the leadership of society. Yet the fact of rebellion itself signaled to all with ears to hear and eyes to see that the conditions that ensured successful seigneurial control in the east were lacking west of the Elbe.

SOME SOCIAL CHANGES

The various lords had remarkably different long-range fates. Larger landowners suffered less than middling ones. They used taxes and other "aids" to compensate for lost revenues from the land itself. Many also formed permanent political alliances with princes in exchange for office, pensions, and other benefits. Some aggrandized their family fortunes by exploiting rural industry. Others combined one or more of these techniques of survival with that of marrying into rich bourgeois families.

All of these expedients were not available to every lord, however. Smaller proprietors had less capital reserves and so suffered more from declining revenues. Many of them found no royal patronage or bourgeois alliance, and most lacked taxing powers. Some were driven into careers as mercenary, or hired, knights, a life out of keeping with old self-concepts. Those who found no salvation by these means often settled into the demanding routine of the petty nobleman who farmed his estate for profit or, even lower in the scale of enterprises, engaged in industry, trade, or finance. Those who did nothing at all passed through a fixed pattern of decline, from debts to mortgages and, finally, to the sale of the estate.

The beneficiaries in the countryside, those who bought up the lands of petty noblemen and poor knights, were often from the middling ranks of rural society, that is, the lesser gentry and in some cases prosperous peasants. Others, chiefly administrative nobility, lesser officials, and bourgeoisie, acquired large holdings. But the crisis in agriculture had widened the basis of landowning by 1600. Rules that prevented the absorption of feudal holdings by bourgeoisie had been relaxed in most parts of Europe by 1450.

These developments do not mark the rise to power of the middle classes, however. The evidence of mobility makes it abundantly clear that these new-landed men quickly adopted country life styles and outlooks. What we see in the way of changes then is the reconstitution of landed aristocracies in western Europe, not their replacement in the social hierarchies.

Where the peasant population had been upwardly mobile in the golden age of rural labor before 1450, it suffered terribly in the new age of population expansion. As grass for grazing took the place of grain, there was no immediate sense of alarm. But by the 1480s a growing chorus of voices noted with dismay the erosion of peasant incomes and holdings. In Italy, Spain, parts of the Low Countries, and most of eastern Europe, the deterioration of peasant life was marked. Peasants of the middling ranks were poorer in 1520 than they had been in 1450. Between 1300 and 1450, real wages had advanced significantly, personal freedom had increased, and diets had altered for the better. Improvements in status were especially common, except in Italy and eastern Europe. But the growth of population and the startling increase in cereal prices after 1500 stood cheek by jowl with stationary money wages for labor. This combination worked against peasants whose real wages fell throughout the sixteenth century, as prices rocketed upward.

Population was the decisive factor. The pressure on cereal production was especially acute after 1510. Countries that had exported cereals in the fifteenth century—Castile, Andalusia, Sicily, and Granada—became dependent on grain imported from English, Dutch, and Hanse merchants. The conversion of arable to pasture in the preceding age meant not only less acreage for grain, but also that a larger share of that acreage went to produce fodder crops.

There were regional variations, of course. The price revolution struck Sweden late in the 1500s. In Italy, the great rise was a mid-century phenomenon. English, French, German, and Flemish sources show that by the 1530s and 1540s inflation was already spiking where population growth was most pronounced. The rise in the cost of living showed most dramatically in cereal prices, but other commodities were not slow to react. In decreasing order, inflation in western Europe affected arable farm products, livestock farm products, timber and woodland produce, building materials, metal goods, and textiles.

These trends are illustrated by some price indices from 1475 to 1620, drawn from English, French, and Alsatian data.

INDICES, 1475–1620 (1450–1475 = 100)

	England	France	Alsace
Food	555	729	517
Industrial goods	265	335	294
Wages	200	268	150

The clear meaning of the data is the loss of real wages, as everything tended to increase in price faster than wages. In one German town wages inflated nearly 300 percent between 1520 and 1620; but rye, wheat, butter, and meat rose 1500 percent, 1300 percent, 1100 percent, and 600 percent, respectively.

These differential increases had a depressing effect on peasants and wage laborers of every sort and they forced new shifts in agricultural priorities. Grass was no longer more profitable than cereal, since wool prices lagged behind wheat, butter, and meat. Thus in the late sixteenth century there was another desperate effort to increase the area of cultivated land.

There was also a great stimulus to plant a greater variety of crops, of which some were new. In the period after 1550 there was increased specialization in cereals, wines, olives (for oil), cotton, and sugar cane in the warmer climates. Where the sun was less beneficent, agronomists sought to widen cultivation of old crops or to increase yields. Land reclamation saved people from famine in Languedoc and Provence, in Brescia, and in the Papal States.

The period after 1480—especially after 1550 and before 1620—was favorable to landowners and harsh to dependent people. Grassland was plowed up and food production was increased, but prices pushed relentlessly upward. Peasants and rural artisans did not easily shift their diets from reliance on expensive grain to cheaper products. The need for lumber for urban building resulted in deforestation, which inhibited supplies of pork, the cheapest meat, since pigs were raised chiefly in forest areas. And as the industrial wages of towns rose faster than agricultural wages, farmers were encouraged to seek town markets for their produce. Thus while many local food crises persisted in rural areas, the grain grown there was exported to distant towns. These facts appear often in sixteenth-century literature of protest, where the advocates of agrarian innovation marched hand in hand with the chroniclers who recorded the poverty, famine, and death from starvation of many Europeans.

Contrasts Between East and West

Thus the record of agrarian society between 1300 and 1600 is that of forced adaptation to changing relations between land and labor, between capital and the men who commanded it and those whose labor transformed it into usable wealth. The manorial system itself survived, although its people experienced sharp changes in status, wealth, and the nature of personal relationships. The contrast east and west of the Elbe was striking, as the shifts in modes of production strengthened the lords in the east and weakened them in the west. Eastern European societies after 1450 were characterized by greater exploitation of the peasants. West of the Elbe, the bondage of peasants to the demesne was shattered. The lords no longer relied on the old pattern of estate management. Peasant liberty grew—in the legal sense and also in an important personal sense. Yet modifications in tenures and the details of agreements did not give safety against the brute ravages of economic factors in the burgeoning rural capitalism of the west.

It is one of the chief facts of history between 1300 and 1600 that the weakening of the manorial system did not establish forever the security of peasants, much less their freedom. The ways in which this was true varied east and west of the Elbe, as we have seen. This difference was thus part of the process that separated east and west, for the consequences of transformations in agrarian systems manifest themselves in social, political, and cultural realms far removed from crop patterns and tenure relations. When we talk of state government, towns, social classes in various countries, and even the Renaissance and Reformation, the significance of the land and its people will assume an important place.

TWO

Towns, trade, and the expansion of Europe

As many of our citizens have been utterly ruined by the violence and injuries inflicted on them . . . it is high time to find some way of avoiding such violence.

Preamble, League of the Rhine (1259)

[It is hard to get cloth] . . . at great and excessive prices and serve it out again in the craft of fulling at so low a price that we can in no wise live thereupon.

The London Fullers' *Complaint* (1488)

[America:] The Refuge and haven of all the poor devils of Spain, the sanctuary of the bankrupt, the safeguard of murderers, the way out for gamblers, the promised land for ladies of easy virtue, a lure and disillusionment for the many and a personal remedy for the few.

Cervantes, *El Celoso Extremeño*

INTRODUCTION

As rural Europe changed dramatically in character from 1300 to 1600, so too did urban Europe.

Perhaps the most visible alteration was in the patterns of trade by which townspeople lived. Under the impact of changing demands for urban-produced goods in rural Europe, the methods, sites, and purposes of manufacture and commerce underwent rapid alteration. After a period of trade depression, running roughly parallel to the demographic crisis, European merchants faced the future with new confidence. This was partly a result of changes in commercial technique—the use of new methods of credit and new forms of business associations. The Italian merchants pioneered the use of contracts, partnerships, and banking systems on an international scale, and where they led, others tried to follow.

The shape of towns also changed socially. There were sharp challenges to the former system of economic control as new methods and markets made their impact. Apprentices and journeymen in the many craft guilds—shoemakers and butchers, carpenters and tinkers—sought a share in decision making. And this struggle for control of the guilds had a basic effect on urban politics, for although the franchise varied widely from city to city, it was almost always linked in some way to property ownership or status in either a craft or mercantile association.

In this period too there was a decline in the power and independence of towns as new nation-states began to emerge. The struggle for law and order within the old communes was mixed with the larger struggle for urban liberty.

Another major chain of events that changed the urban face of western Europe was overseas expansion. Earlier the rise in population had led to a vast campaign of internal colonization within Europe, pushing settlement onto new virgin lands. As the population expansion of the fifteenth century gathered momentum, the tentative efforts of the Spanish, Portuguese, and Italians to settle small colonies in Africa and throughout the Mediterranean gave way to emigration on a grand scale. Benefiting from great advances in cartography and navigation techniques as well as shipbuilding, the Iberian powers pushed the European frontier into America, south and east Africa, and Asia. Then, in the sixteenth century, the French, Dutch, and English joined in the expansion. The goods from the New World and the two Indies, often exotic beyond belief, transformed cities, their sights and sounds, and the nature of urban life and commerce.

This movement outward from Europe gave Western civilization a global, rather than a merely European, influence. The Western hegemony had begun.

TOWNSMEN

Men in towns derive their incomes from a bewildering array of economic activities. Yet in the west towns have been historically of two kinds: groups of consumers whose resources are not industrial, and groups of consumers who are mainly industrial producers. Rome was primarily a political and religious center whose inhabitants derived incomes from the profits of empire or from the lands and taxes of churches. Our interest centers not on Rome, but on the industrially mature cities of the west between 1300 and 1600 where craftsmen were more predominant than administrators.

By 1300 the European walled towns were places with men commanding huge aggregates of capital. They had won privileges from lords and kings with regard to lands, taxes, the freedom of their citizens, and economic affairs. Their constitutions were, in most late medieval communes, hierarchical: Certain merchant groups had consolidated their social and economic control to the point where they formed a closed and privileged ruling class. These merchant elements dominated politics, production, the control of urban and suburban lands, and they tried to prevent the newly rich from sharing in their monopolies.

The government and military organization of the towns were based on merchants' guilds and those of the larger crafts. Before 1300 there had already been contests for power. But the contraction of the economy in the fourteenth century produced great social and political upheavals. Indeed, the era of regression in the economy was one of democratization in town government.

Before 1300 the most difficult problems for towns to solve had been those of feeding, housing, and ordering the swelling numbers within the limits of available resources. When the trend reversed from growth to decay, policies altered and the towns defended themselves against the countryside. It is therefore important for us to explore the whole range of adjustments in town activity consequent on the dramatic fall in population after 1300.

TRADERS

From the seventh through the tenth century in Europe the exchange of goods was never wholly absent, but it was dependent on itinerant merchants trading luxuries to the rich. In Mediterranean areas trade was given impetus by the Crusades, as merchants in Latin colonies in the eastern Mediterranean moved ceaselessly with their goods. And by 1200 Italians had established supremacy in European commerce.

Beyond the Mediterranean, trade was also in the hands of wandering merchants. Flemish, English, German, and Italian traders vied there, but Italians came to dominate. Sienese and Florentine merchants pioneered the transformation to the counting house. The wandering traders gave way to agents, factors, correspondents, and bankers with fixed places of business.

Thirteenth-century records make it abundantly clear that merchants had at their command sophisticated commercial contracts that tied traveling partners with investing partners who remained at home. The deal linked those with capital and those who took the risks of sea voyages. These forms of trade organization allowed the rise of daring men: Those too young to exercise power in their cities or to have substantial capital of their own could find opportunities in trade.

Even before 1300 therefore, notwithstanding the risks of piracy and nature, increased voyaging for luxury goods and grain was a common response to the pressure of demand in Europe. Seapower was highly organized and in the hands of merchants whose capital investments spurred the establishment of commercial colonies throughout the Mediterranean. Commercial treaties became an entry wedge by which Europeans began penetrating non-Western societies. Men from the Italian centers met Arab and Asian traders to deal in caviar, spices, and slaves. The Europeans traded silver, cloth, metal goods, furs, amber, and sometimes grain as far afield as Syria and China.

In the fourteenth and fifteenth centuries, Italian merchants consolidated their dominance over rivals from German and Scandinavian towns. Their victory was partly determined by the geography, since they were closer to the sources of western trade. But in large measure it was also the result of the Italians' devotion to matters of business procedure and technique: rates of exchange, bookkeeping in terms of cash transactions, the forms of letter-writing necessary to long-range trade, and other things that minimized wasteful traveling. The early postal services in private companies illustrate the resourcefulness of the Italian commercial houses.

By 1350 the Italian companies had branches throughout western Europe. Their factors, or salaried employees, labored under branch managers. Policy was made at home by the major partners, whose purpose was to insulate the whole structure from the effects of failure in one or more branches. The most successful were the Medici of Florence. The Medici bank, founded in 1397, not only had branches outside Italy but also controlled Italian manufacturing enterprises. Raw materials went to the homes or workrooms of numerous craftsmen who were dependent on Medici capital for their supplies.

Whether on a small scale to accommodate local trade or on a grand scale, Spanish, Flemish, and German merchants followed the Italian innovations. The most significant competition involved the Hanseatic merchants of northern Germany who ruled the Baltic. The Hanseatic towns joined in a single powerful league, and the resulting political and naval power enabled the towns of the league to build a vast trade. Led by Lübeck, places as far afield as Bergen and Riga were part of a huge trade network that also embraced London and Novgorod. This commerce had in part a colonial character: Riga, Stockholm, and other towns were colonies of German merchant families with close ties to their native cities.

The most typical form of Hanse activity, however, was partnership. A partner in Novgorod would sell his consignment at the same rate of profit as his partner in Bergen. This was convenient, since there was neither central bookkeeping nor authority, and confidence and integrity were the essentials of the trade. Sometimes merchants used factors, but more often traveled in person with their goods.

The technique of the Hanseatic merchants was generally simple. They had no banking centers, and they did not use commercial paper. Gold and silver coins were sent in consignment to pay bills in Poland. Hence the original nature of the Hanse as an association of traveling merchants was more perfectly reflected east of the Elbe than in the more elaborate colonies of London and Bruges. Yet the fellowship of merchants became a league of cities powerful enough to defeat England in a naval war (1469 and 1474).

The Fuggers

The one region in which commerce escaped Italian and Hanseatic control was southern Germany. There, international exchanges were tied to Venice, Milan, and Geneva. Finance, however, lay in the hands of local merchant-bankers whose companies rivaled Italy's both in scale and sophistication. The Great Company of Ravensburg had thirty-eight partners in 1497, and partnerships of lesser scope existed elsewhere. The Fuggers of Augsburg rose to great importance in imperial politics and papal finance, as well as in trading ventures on a wide scale. The family fortune grew out of commercial and banking interests. In the Fugger economic empire silver mines had been acquired as security for loans to various princes, chiefly Holy Roman emperors. Once in possession, the Fuggers operated some mines directly and contracted out the others, while reserving for themselves the final control over processing and selling the silver. Every specific aspect of production and distribution was geared toward the maximum profitability of the mines. And toward this end the family introduced into mining many techniques of standardization, ranging from the three eight-hour-shifts day to the division of labor.

In the time of Jakob the Rich (1459–1525), the Fuggers used the mines to support a vast banking empire in which the original family weaving business was only a tiny element. Just as cotton profits had financed banking, so did mining wealth enable the Fuggers to bankroll some of the most important political maneuvers of the Renaissance: wars, papal elections, even the election of Charles V as emperor in 1519. Kings confessed that they could not execute policy without the approval and support of Jakob Fugger!

No other "national" communities shared the prestige or power of the Italians and Germans. English firms were large in scale only in parochial terms. The Italians maintained control of English banking and of much of the import of spices and wine well into the sixteenth century. English Baltic trade was closely connected to Hanse privilege throughout the period.

TOWNSMEN AND TRADE: PROBLEMS OF POLICY

Merchants, whatever the nature of their techniques, were living in commercial centers in large numbers from the eighth century on. Whether the traders congregated at an old administrative center, at a convenient wharf, or at some count's fortified palace grounds, there soon grew up communities of men engaged in making and selling goods. By the 1100s it was almost universally the case that craftsmen and sellers settled within walls and made a town of producers, consumers, and merchants the focal point of economic and social life. Merchants were no longer a species of wanderers forced to sell goods at specified times in marketplaces. They were inhabitants of towns enjoying liberty to come and go and buy and sell as they wished.

The economic policies of towns, despite their differences in scope or scale, soon showed a common responsiveness to events beyond the walls. Policies shifted in response to the development of sea trade, changing commercial techniques, and changing patterns of population.

Both merchants and citizens depended on trade. So too did those capitalists who had invested in production and distribution or who owned the workers' tenements and shops for master craftsmen. Moreover, the population relied on commerce for food and other necessities. The government relied on taxes and tolls to supply the ordinary amenities of town life: water supplies, police force, street lights and drains, refuse dumps, government administration, charity for the poor, hospitals for the ill and aged, and education for the children.

It needs no insight, therefore, to say that townsmen would resist elements in society that obstructed trade or threatened to reduce its volume, whether these were forces of feudal politics, natural disasters, the failure of credit facilities, or foreign policy. From the point of view of outsiders, therefore, policies in defense of trade were selfish, competitive, and monopolistic.

Economic Regulation and Its Impact

The men who lived by trade were more attuned to the problems of craftsmen and social classes than lords wholly outside the towns. Hence, the defense of trade was often burdened by contradictions beyond town controls. (Within the towns, there were also difficulties. The defense of trade became an internal problem as well as one of foreign relations.)

A policy of the townsmen was what nowadays would be called consumer interests. This involved not only the importing of food supplies, but also the regulating of wages and prices. The concept of the public good, what some liked to call the common weal, was matched against the vested interests in control of town government.

The protection of food supplies led to the policy of free trade in grain and laws against such artificial restraints as engrossing, regrating, and forestalling. These were techniques of purchasing basic commodities outside the urban market for resale at high profits in times of scarcity. Such practices were combatted by rules which regulated markets, prohibited grain export, allowed the seizure of grain caravans near hard-pressed cities, and instituted political control over the surrounding countryside. Through such policies townsmen were immunized against famine, while farmers and peasants actually growing grain often starved in lean years.

The defense of trade and food supplies was designed to give the merchants and consumers of a town a practical, beneficial system of exchange. The idea was to provide cheap raw materials and food of high quality to craftsmen, but this was hard to reconcile with policies that excluded foreign goods imported at lower prices, for the concentration and regulation of markets might rob the general town population of its expectation of cheap, competitive products.

These incompatible concerns showed in a variety of concrete measures. Great grain merchants secured the ousting of rivals, and the result was that the price of grain rose rapidly. Some larger towns succeeded in monopolizing certain kinds of trade, forbidding dependent towns in the adjacent countryside from entering into them, and punishing offenders with military force.

The cities of the west thus developed a foreign policy based largely on economic considerations. This was especially true in the Mediterranean. The rival trade empires of Genoa, Venice, Pisa, and Barcelona struggled for hegemony over the rich routes to the East and the products of the Levant. In the north the League of the Rhine warred with feudal lords who interrupted the flow of goods or exacted too high tolls. The Hanseatic League was at war repeatedly with Denmark. Policies of monopoly were often policies of militant expansion.

This warring led to town laws restricting the freedom of alien merchants. Such laws increased profits for a few, while militating against cheap and plentiful imported supplies. One special form of legislation restricted the import of finished goods and the export of raw materials. The chief motive supposedly lay in the recognition that foreign products robbed domestic labor of employment, and the loss of employment was a source of social unrest.

Allegedly, the welfare of the city as a whole was behind these restrictions. Yet monopoly trade generated higher costs for some materials. Privileged groups claimed to advance the common wealth through restrictive trade practices. This was contested by consumers and producers who saw merchant rule as a form of exploitation. It was simply not always the case that control of the volume of trade and control over the price and quality of goods were compatible. The hunger for goods and the hunger for profits collided.

By the time of the Black Death, towns were powerful social entities divided along economic and political interests. For example, London artisans looked favorably upon Baltic grain shipments, since cheap bread meant more money available for domestic consumption of craft products and therefore extra money to artisans for living quarters. London millers and bakers, organized in powerful guilds, looked askance at both foreign suppliers and domestic fair-price legislation. Thus demand for low prices, which was the essence of the consumers' interest, meant a struggle against middlemen and monopolists in general.

This fact set the stage for the major conflict in Europe's towns between 1300 and 1600. The shock of population decline and the disruption of trade further called into question the role of the merchant guilds, the leagues of great families, and commercial companies. It ushered in a period of profound change in the assumptions by which urban communities lived.

THE DISRUPTION OF UNITY

By the middle of the fourteenth century, towns were highly regulated communities with elaborate policies of freedom, trade, and consumption. This regulation of urban life had produced a sense of community as well as a sense of opposition: Freedom in towns had come to mean that outsiders were excluded from town privileges and duties and also that the community inside the walls was hierarchically divided. Certain areas of civic life now fell for the first time under scrutiny of the law.

Already in the thirteenth century the merchant rulers had begun to make urban social mobility more difficult. The merchants controlled both the marketplace and the shop, but all groups were enjoying an increasing share of community wealth with the decline of population growth. Prosperity had reconciled diverse interests. Then the onset of the plague led to over a century—from 1350 to 1475 —of stagnation and commercial depression.

The response of merchants was to maintain the old margin of profit by force. This took three characteristic forms: the restriction of entry into the trade and craft guilds; a permissive attitude toward price increases in consumer goods; and the forcing down of wages as a way of controlling the price of the wares merchants carried elsewhere to sell. It was a period in which we can legitimately say that town policy gave way to class policy. Town life remained, but the sense of community was broken.

Craftsmen were excluded from the merchant guilds, and this exclusion closed off one of the major avenues of upward social mobility. Since wages were driven down and prices up, the loss of real income among poor artisans and day laborers was acute. Where they tried to organize their resistance, antiunion laws imposed severe penalties on them. When craft guilds tried to force wages up, there were clashes with the merchant guilds. The poorer urban consumers found little to applaud in either craft or merchant manipulations. In one way or another these drove up the prices for many goods, and the tempo of unrest increased.

Demographic changes were not the only reason towns lost power and fought bitterly for a share in the declining trade. Within the towns themselves class strife, riots, and strikes severely disrupted production and hence trade and consumption. Also, the rapid growth of restrictive practices proved inimical to production and often encouraged clothiers to locate industry beyond town walls. The countryside also attracted capital for technological considerations. The swift rivers of the hill country were necessary for operating power mills used in industrial operations: fulling of cloth, metal working, and iron making. An example was the movement of cloth and iron industries from the flat southeastern areas of England to the upland regions of the north and west.

Other factors contributed to the crisis, and the expansion of the Turkish Empire hastened the deterioration of the Levant trade. The wars in western Europe proved seriously disruptive. Historians aware of ecological issues have recently argued that the vast pressure of population before 1350 had hidden consequences. Pastures were overstocked and timber cut too rapidly to permit new growth and reforestation. This seems to have been the case especially in parts of England and Scandinavia. Mineral deposits near the surface were worked to exhaustion. Herrings off Skane in southern Sweden were overfished. Some cities emerged from the era of adjustment in superior positions (London, Bristol, Lübeck, Ghent, Milan, Mantua, Florence, Paris, Lyons), depending on differing adjustments to geographical and social factors. As we shall see, dynastic rivalries promoted certain (cloth) towns over others, and the association of some towns with princes in a so-called national policy caused trade to decline.

Effects of Economic Changes

There was a marked shift in the character of consumption in the wake of population decline. Falling grain prices were a general trend, which made it possible to spend more on meat, wine, spices, and dairy products in urban diets, and among the survivors of the Death there was a marked upsurge in personal fortunes. While moralists condemned unseemly and conspicuous consumption, the survivors seemed to revel in splendid dress, objects of art, and lavish buildings. This was a psychological reaction to the shock of disease and death on a massive scale. Economically, however, the significant result was investment of capital in enterprises that cushioned the disruption of trade and made many cities centers of growth even in the worst periods of general slump. There was a diminution of prudence, of the wish to save, perhaps even of the hope for posterity. Money was invested in culture and luxuries, and the church benefited through vast endowments and programs for decoration of church buildings.

It would be wrong, however, to leave the impression that the rise of art patronage and luxury industries was an effective counterbalance to the long-range disruptive consequences of plague. As the price of grain fell, that of manufactured goods rose sharply along with wages. As a consequence, the countryside, which had been a debtor region in regard to cities, was bankrupted. The agrarian sector of society had always had the bulk of the population, and it had generated vast demands for basic goods. Reduced agricultural markets and the price gap worsened an already bad balance of payments. This shrank the money resources of country people and undercut their demand for urban goods. Hence the sustained urban prosperity described above was superficial. While some areas grew and sustained that growth, most towns could not prosper on exotic demands and the bankruptcy of the countryside.

The cause was simplicity itself. The plague at first destroyed people but not wealth, so that some urban economies spurted. But the industries that catered to the basic needs of the population in the countryside fell on hard times. The market for woolen cloth declined dramatically. More important, the premium on labor in the countryside had encouraged the shift from grain to pasture and animal products. Therefore supplies of raw wool increased in amount, and this increase eventually meant overproduction for a diminishing market. The woolen textile industry showed the strain immediately, as a crisis set in and remained through much of the fifteenth century. The western economy in wool and its textiles had nearly collapsed.

The information we have on the international economy in the fourteenth and fifteenth centuries shows that port activities and trade volume steadily declined. This is true for Genoa, Marseilles, and England. During the period 1400–1465 all experienced a sharp decline of trade volume. The combination of plague, warfare, and a changing technology of production and distribution contributed to this recession and depression. And the money markets showed the effects. By 1364 English production of coins to facilitate trade was only 28 percent of what it had been in 1344. French money demands were similar in decline, as were those in Flemish mints.

The trade balance between north and south in Europe was controlled by the Italians. Italian bankers and merchant companies financed the papacy, the trade of western Europe, the Eastern luxury trade, and a good share of the conspicuous consumption industries: silk, spices, jewels, palace building, and war. The bank of the Medici and others like it grew rich and powerful early in the fifteenth century. Some maritime states in Italy declined—Genoa for instance—but Venice built its strength. War and luxury trade were the bases of Venetian growth. Venice was in effect supporting military artisans, seamen, silk workers, and fustian makers at the expense of her neighbors in Europe. Her affluence was thus symptomatic of the misery of others, a triumph of the luxury trade over necessities and a contributing cause of the general crisis.

What freedom the towns had to adjust to the crisis was itself partly a function of their relation to the strong monarchies that emerged from the collapse of the feudal system. In England and France, towns were circumscribed in their actions by the economic policies of the states. The towns of Germany and Italy, however, suffered no such checks: the Holy Roman Empire collapsed as an effective political unit in the north, and so did the papacy as a pretender to control of Italy in the south.

Guilds

Furthermore, the internal situation of the towns—their social structure and their politics—entered into a period of adjustment. Usually guild membership and citizenship ran together, and in many towns, the civic authority itself was a body of guild representatives. The crucial question was often one of a challenge to merchant guilds by craft guilds. It was generally the case that the craft guilds succeeded in challenging the oligarchy of merchants, financiers, and urban *rentiers,* but this should not be hailed as a victory of liberty.

Indeed, wherever the old patriciates collapsed, the policy of protection triumphed. Protection could be just as militant an ideal as trade expansion. Men bitterly aware that demand was falling and raw materials harder to find were no champions of freedom. Leiden tried in 1449 and 1469 to make sure that its wool merchants could not carry wool to competing clothiers. In 1393 Florence enacted guild legislation that forbade the sale of cheap cloth not made locally. English towns like Bristol and Winchester tried to crush the nascent industry in surrounding villages in the early 1400s.

But nowhere were the guilds able to resist forces against which even political power was inadequate. Labor scarcity drove wages up, and newly affluent consumers conspired to evade rules against cheap foreign wares. The guilds' desire for strength through monopoly may well have promoted brotherhood, but it did not reduce the appetites of men who desired to be free of regulation. Moreover, different guilds often had sharply divergent views of town interests, and unguilded workers resented guild control.

In places where craft guilds were weak, merchant rule often went unchallenged. This was especially true in many English towns and those of northern France, Germany beyond the Elbe, Castile in Spain, and in Italian cities. Other towns belonged to the category of local trade communities. If there was little democracy in them, there was little oligarchy either. Wealth was not sufficiently concentrated to sponsor elaborate social divisions. Many English and French towns were of this sort. In them guilds often contained producers as well as sellers in complex trading associations; and a wide latitude was given to artisan and retail organizations also. Various formulas existed, but what each did was to allow a certain play of forces in the town. While assuring oligarchic control, such a play of forces also reduced the dissatisfactions of other urban classes. This situation allowed for the development of town power over craft guilds and legitimately forestalled revolutionary tensions.

The town of Coventry in the English Midlands is a convenient example of yet another aspect of the relationship of guilds to the wider theme of urban history. The great food merchants and those dealing in cloth were equally sworn to the old notions of fair prices and honest products. But they controlled licensing, the courts, and the power to punish through fines. These powers were used to break the businesses of small dealers, through repeated fines for short measures or the sale of corrupted meats, breads, and beers. Meanwhile, the monopolists gave light-weighted bread and sold corn in false measures. The result was riots and reform agitation.

These actions of guildsmen in power remind us that their role in shaping the order of western cities socially and economically was not altruistic. Their self-concept was that of a community or society or fraternity sworn to advance the common well-being. But in practice, the commonwealth they advanced was often only that of the members. Their actions often inflated prices and certainly restricted the labor choices of men within the towns and from the country neighborhoods. The metal workers, butchers, high-quality leather craftsmen, and workers in precious metals were especially active in such things. Where they failed it was not for a lack of effort.

The freedom of craftsmen was not quite the same as abstract freedom for all townsmen. A wide variety of evidence about iron workers in England, metal workers in France (nails and armor), farm-tool producers in Germany, smiths in Italy, wood workers in London, and bakers nearly everywhere, shows citizens and the urban poor in sharp conflict with guilds over price policy. Bread prices and riots over them were the most common aspects of the problem, and in the monarchies special laws and proclamations fixing prices were designed to preserve social order. The cost of bread was a barometer of rebellion.

Everywhere guilds practiced restriction toward labor and the basic use of skills. This took the form of the apprenticeship system, where youngsters were exposed to a regime that was often cruel and capricious and rarely based on any recognition of childhood as a distinct process of physical and psychological growth toward adulthood. Most guild statutes about apprentices treated youngsters wholly as an abstract commodity. Records of runaways are frequent enough to throw light on the grim evidence of higher than normal death rates among adolescent apprentices.

Not even the oppressive system of apprenticeship was sacred, however. Relaxations in guild ordinances were made voluntarily, but sometimes relaxation came in less agreeable ways. John the Good of France (1319–1364) issued royal orders relaxing labor-restrictive rules in the shoemakers' guild in 1351, and Charles V (1337–1380) licensed Rouen cloth workers who had not served apprenticeship. In England and Germany the period of apprenticeship was voluntarily shortened. The revival of slavery was very widespread in the Mediterranean lands. Enslaved pagans, Slavs, Turks, and blacks, figured prominently in "solving" the labor problem.

Social solidarity was the lot of masters. This was true especially in towns where the various guild hierarchies dominated large-scale export production. Where guilds in small towns produced for local trade only, their power and pretensions were smaller, closer to the life of ordinary townsmen, and less likely to be a source of strife.

It is possible to overstress guild conservatism. But it is true that in the age of contraction craft guilds were a deeply conservative force. Cartel policies, strict control over entry, the harsh use of migratory rural day laborers adrift in towns, and hostility to rural industry did not help recovery in most places.

There were also the friendlier aspects of guild power: the establishment of schools, burial societies, agencies to distribute labor efficiently, and religious and charitable foundations; contributions made to developing the political processes of representation; and the dumb shows and dramas on holy days and feast days—all of these marked more benign rhythms in the social life in the towns.

THE QUALITIES OF URBAN LIFE

Between the precepts of the Gospel and the policies of the men who influenced the development of town life, there was often a large gap. There grew up in towns under pressure a distinctive culture, an urban view of society and its activity. This view was being developed in western Europe at a time when it failed to grow significantly east of the Elbe.

As town life matured it constituted a revolution in the shaping of Western society. This was only partly the result of contacts that brought men in the West to a more exact knowledge of other civilizations. The expansion of trade and the growth of industry forced on men in the West a fundamental reexamination of attitudes toward wealth and property, their unequal distribution, and the relationship of law to society. Town life created pressure to redefine traditional notions of status, family, and stability in society at large.

The Gospel of John warned, "The poor we have always with us." Yet misery lived too close to luxury in towns to foster the psychological distance that separated most seigneurs from their serfs in rural areas. Despite the insistence of lawyers and theologians that God had nothing to do with property or its regulation, the towns were troubled by the disposition of goods in crisis. They often practiced community of property in times of famine, which was a radical extension of the policy of provision.

Although many scholastic thinkers argued that unequally distributed property mirrored in social life the hierarchy of life in eternity, some were critical of the inequalities. Wealth was not an end in itself. Charity was a virtue beyond thrift. The virtue of poverty did not often recommend itself to the struggling urban poor. Even the defense of property made by theologians and secular writers did not lead them to deny that wealth was the outcome of work. Radicals criticized the way that value created by labor went chiefly into other hands. Food supply problems sometimes prompted townsmen to notice the conditions of labor in the countryside.

Thus a variety of forces in the daily lives of townsmen led them to begin questioning the norms of conduct that were prescribed by churchmen to preserve the social order and political elites. What constituted a just price, a fair profit, a lawful income, a legitimate interest on principal, the proper employment of capital, or the right relationship between masters and men? These were matters too important to be left in the airy realms of theology. The urban order was manifestly not the world in which Alfonso the Wise of Spain (1221–1284) had proclaimed the division of society into priests, knights, and peasants.

Economic life was giving the lie to earlier views of society. It was already changing the conception of the family under the stress of labor conditions in cities. It was altering the idea of marriage and of a woman's legal status and her right to property in her own name. In some guilds the urban franchise was inherent, and we have records that show there were women with the vote! Men were more upwardly and downwardly mobile than they had been in generations.

As noted earlier in this book, the culture of chivalry and the church appeared to be widely separated from the concerns of most of the agrarian peoples who dug crops. The same separation may well have existed for the large masses of the urban poor. But city culture had a wider popular base than that of feudal society. And its characteristic forms expressed this popularity. Nowhere was this more true than in Italian society, where politics and culture often seemed twins. For in towns the masses were exposed to innovations in thought and expression. Moreover, the gentry, the nobility, and the princes of Europe were themselves profoundly influenced by urban developments.[1]

One result of urban economic and social conflicts was the rise of principalities. This was not surprising, since towns were sympathetic to centralization. Even the political ideas of republicanism stressed the concentration of power for beneficial purposes. Vernacular literature and the secular domination of religion in the Italian towns had helped to fuse urban loyalties in an intense patriotism. Much the same thing happened in the great imperial cities of Germany, in Chaucer's London, and in a multitude of towns in the Netherlands.

Yet political power inimical to republican traditions produced a remarkable outpouring of concern for the fate of republican liberty, first in Italy and then, in forms suitably altered by the different scale of political life, nearly everywhere north of the Alps and west of the Elbe.

Italians had a great heritage of Roman law, which the towns had always nurtured, along with the ideal of political life,[2] which in the twelfth and thirteenth centuries meant some form of commune. The legal bases of towns were not feudal, but were embedded in the idea of voluntary associations. Naturally, political ideas reflected the divisions between the resident nobility, merchant oligarchies, and the lesser people. By 1200 power had been won by the communes from the papal agents and imperial regents. Magistrates ruled town councils in which mercantile and noble groups divided power. The struggles of the lower classes encouraged magnates and merchants to appeal to the craft population in the troubled atmosphere of the

[1] The general problems of humanist culture are dealt with in Chapter Four, especially in relation to reform ideas after 1400. Here our concern is narrowly political.

[2] The word *political* itself derives from the Hellenic *polis,* or city-state. So, too, civilization comes from Latin *civitas,* or city.

period from 1300 to 1450. Democracy was a stratagem of oligarchy!

The result was the triumph of the most monarchical elements over the popular ones. The communes yielded to oligarchies that in turn fell before the *signoria,* the control vested in a man and his family. The trend went further in Lombardy than in Tuscany, but the expansion of certain powerful men at the expense of others was common in both regions. And in the fifteenth century despots were as well known in both regions as free communes had been earlier. The contentions for supreme power over wide areas produced conditions that proved ultimately destructive of republicanism after 1492.

Culture in Italy

During the two centuries of conflict that ended in calamity, Italy was paradoxically the maker of a libertarian Renaissance culture and the leader toward a wider Western secularism and concern for freedom. Long before princes limited clerical privileges, commune law ruthlessly made priests subject to the common law. Moreover, Italy led in other ways. A peninsula that was utterly devoid of political unity nevertheless unified thought about law and politics.

Literature and art reflected every aspect of Italy's internal struggle and her expansion as the west's commercial center. In the 1300s Lombard artists began painting the monumental portraits that showed in naturalistic ways the *signori* who dominated politics. These magistrates enhanced their power by attracting popular support—at least at first. But power destroyed factional balances, resulting in lists of banished enemies, in civil wars, and finally in tyranny. The other side of the coin of secular portraiture was therefore the celebration of exile in the literary monuments of the losers. Dante's political writings and those of Machiavelli stood more than two centuries apart, but the attitudes they expressed were in a sense contemporary.

Thus Renaissance culture in the widest sense was the product of strife. Petrarch, Boccaccio, and Giotto were early giants whose roots are obscured by our ignorance about early fourteenth-century Italian developments in most places. Yet it is clear that Italian high culture was a product neither of cathedral schools nor of the castles north of the Alps. It was instead civic in nature and often in themes. Law was a more dominant university faculty than theology. Legal education and the high place of lawyers in public life symbolized a general orientation toward politics and commerce rather than toward less practical and concrete things.

The great development of the theme of service to the commune

The Deposition of Christ, **one of Giotto di Bondone's frescoes in the Scrovegni Chapel of Padua, painted between 1303 and 1305. Like other painters of his time, Giotto integrated every element of his work into a rational pattern.** *Alinari—Art Reference Bureau.*

and republican liberty came later, however. Petrarch's rediscovery of Cicero's *Letters to Atticus* in 1345 was more basic to the revival of Roman civic spirit than other classical recoveries. For the *Letters* showed greater concern for citizenship than for elegant Latinity. Cicero wrote as an exile from politics; he had surrendered office after Caesar's victories doomed the tottering Roman republic. Petrarch drew from his model a reproach to political meddlers. But in the next two generations others reflected more actively on the parallels between the decline of the Roman republic and the present dangers to republican liberty.

In Florence especially, the great merchants and their partners among craftsmen and smaller traders produced a conscious republicanism. Magistracies were of short duration. Elections were by both lot and ballot, techniques of rule encouraging to faction as well as to active concern for preserving liberties from the intrusions of despots. Against the forces of churchmen and nobility Giovanni Boccaccio (1313–1375) inculcated the value of secular, nonaristocratic politics and literature. The great Florentine chancellor Coluccio Salutati (1375–1406) developed these themes.

Salutati was both an eminent scholar and an active administrator of Florentine affairs. Trained as a notary, he early turned his thoughts to the critical investigation of man's life in political society. He produced a series of moral treatises and a voluminous correspondence with the leading scholars of his age. As chancellor of Florence, Salutati had led the resistance to despotism and foreign encroachments on his city's liberty. His writings, elegant Latin attacks on Florence's enemies, were more effective than an army, according to the Visconti rulers of Milan.

We can see what promoted this respect by a glance at Salutati's essay *Concerning the Secular Life and Religion*, which condemns the artificial division of human activity into contemplative and active spheres. The life worthy to lead is a fighter's life, he says. No true happiness lies in retreating into a monastery. A man must struggle within the world, must fight against the enemies of one's fatherland, family, and friends. The end of human work is the secure establishment of free men in a free state. For Salutati civic participation was a vocation as worthy as the life of the professed religion. Even monks would benefit their souls by taking as a guide Socrates, "the chief of our martyrs."

This supremacy of action over contemplative retreat was in fact an elevation of human will over intellect detached from citizenship. Salutati was thus a civic spokesman, a civic humanist committed to the view that the best truths were political ones. Christians had to buttress the treasure of revelation with philosophy and philosophy with the humility of St. Francis of Assisi. But they must always commit themselves to the highest forms of human action. In *On Fate* and *The Labors of Hercules* Salutati returns to the same themes: the supremacy of will over reason and the necessity of participation in civic life.

Elsewhere, a new "Tribune of the People" led a Roman revolt. Cola di Rienzo (1313–1354) championed a wider notion of citizenship, however, and was an Italian more in Dante's mold than in that of the great Florentine republicans. This wider political sentiment was reflected in the painters, almost entirely under northern influences until well into the 1400s. Only in the generation of Salutati's spiritual descendants did there flower the cult of man in the arts and republicanism in literature and social theory.

The spectacular rise of the Milan Visconti to a dukedom in 1395 challenged the idea of civic freedom. The expansion of Milan provoked defense of both political independence and self-government. This liberty was in fact oligarchic in character. But the chief works of three great chancellors—Salutati, Gian Francesco Poggio Bracciolini (1380–1459), and Leonardo Bruni (1369–1444)—localized liberty, made of it a Florentine thing, and put its themes forward in elegant dialogues and treatises rooted in civic pride.

Along with the celebration of freedom went its thoroughly bourgeois basis: the praise of wealth, the condemnation of monkish retreats from the world, the emphasizing of the corporate nature of family and privilege, and the importance of the tangible show of fame in splendid books, libraries, paintings, buildings, statues. Thus was an intellectual justification given for a style of life rooted in town experience and antithetical to both chivalric codes and those of Christian morality.

There is no room to treat here in detail how each Italian artist of the Renaissance incorporated in his work the concerns for human life in its natural setting, which we have observed in the writer Salutati. We may, however, look at one painter, Masaccio, the younger contemporary of the greatest architect of the age, Filippo Brunelleschi (1377–1446), and the greatest sculptor, Donatello (ca. 1386–1466).

Masaccio was a native of a small village deep in the Tuscan countryside. Born in 1401, he went to Florence in 1422, drawn perhaps by the desire to learn about painting and allied arts from Brunelleschi and Donatello. For seven years Masaccio worked in Florence, before going to Rome, where he died in 1428, on the verge of what might have been a great period of creative work under papal patronage.

Only four works of undoubted authenticity survive by Masaccio. Yet in them we can see how the new interests of the humanists were given content in artistic terms. The young painter borrowed the artistic technique of perspective from Brunelleschi, which enabled him to create illusions of depth on a flat surface through the use of simple geometry. By referring all objects to a single point and by using foreshortening and other devices, Masaccio was able to break with the tradition of flat and merely decorative renderings of the body. Masaccio adopted another element from Donatello, who had insisted on showing his figures in vigorous action; people appeared in direct and natural poses, less formal and abstract in their employment than was usual with the fourteenth-century masters. Masaccio combined this naturalness and dynamism with depth in his *Trinity,* which may stand as a signpost along the road to the art of humanism.

Artists quickly adapted in their own work the ideas evident in Masaccio's synthesis of tradition and innovation. Like Masaccio himself, his followers were eager to put men and women into natural settings in a natural way. Just as Salutati was concerned to explore man's life in its political setting, so the fifteenth-century artists broke with the Gothic tradition, which had emphasized man's symbolic place in the otherworldly settings of religion. Even religious painting assumed a direct and natural quality as the style of the Renaissance clarified into an art that was centered in human concerns and emotions.

Donatello's *lo Zuccone* **("pumpkin head"), an example of the sculptor's unrivaled realism and a departure from the conventional image of a prophet (as a bearded old man holding a large scroll).** *Alinari—Art Reference Bureau.*

Piero della Francesca's depiction of an ideal city, representative of the early Florentine Renaissance, in which the use of perspective aided the search for new architectural harmonies and enhanced the notion of the city as a perfect setting for social man. *Scala—Art Reference Bureau.*

Good examples abound. Masaccio himself used light to define the human shape in *The Virgin with Saint Anne.* Brunelleschi revealed the concern for proportion essential to the art and architecture of humanism in his great revisions of the cathedral at Florence and in other churches. Donatello, who was in the circle of humanists gathered about the writer and politician Poggio Bracciolini, dedicated his sculptural genius to revealing the human body with a fidelity and realism unrivaled even in the Roman models he studied. This is especially evident in his statues of saints in the Florence Cathedral— *Mark,* for example, which he did in 1411–1412. His bronze *David* is also epoch-making in its effort to characterize an individual, and the same is true in his groups of figures illustrating biblical scenes, where even perspective is distorted to render the emotions of John the Baptist and Mary Magdalene. The painter and sculptor Lorenzo Ghiberti (*ca.* 1378–1455) consolidated the new ideas, not only in his magnificent carved doors for the Florence baptistery, but also in his writings (*Commentaries*), which set forth the new style. Leonardo da Vinci (1452–1519) created drawings, paintings, statues, and other works embodying the Renaissance interest in man in nature. And he illustrated the entire body of ideas in his vast *Notebooks* as well as in the celebrated *Mona Lisa, Madonna of the Rocks,* the sculptural *Sforza Monument,* and numerous other works. But none shows more clearly what Leonardo was heir to than his simple drawings of embryos in their mothers' wombs and his close studies of human musculature and skeletal parts.

A CHANGE IN DIRECTION

What Petrarch could not anticipate, Cervantes and other anticolonial Spanish writers regretted. Before Cervantes died in 1610, urban landlords, industrialists, merchants, financiers, and even princes took part in ordering a Spanish imperial society that he bitterly criticized and utterly detested. Its most significant feature was that, like other commercialized societies, Spain had finally outgrown the legacy of the Death. New employment of commercial capital that had accumulated was sought within Europe and in the wider international economy of the West.

In the communes and *signorie* of northern and central Italy the social and political struggles between classes led to expansion within the peninsula. To a lesser extent, crises similar to the Italian ones took place in urban societies in Iberia and beyond the Alps. These transformed the old communes into towns where rival power blocs and ideologies shattered unity. This social stage in the growth of capitalist urban societies was in turn closely connected to the expansion, differentiation, and contraction of commercial activity.

Yet the new era of expansion came at a time when princes, rather than municipal authority or the authority of the church, were the chief governors of the process as well as its agents. The great classes of merchants and financiers no longer dominated the scene, as the progress of navigation, the discoveries, and the great struggles for supremacy in Europe and in empires were waged by monarchical states. The emergence of the western state system from its time of troubles destroyed one of the conditions in which merchant princes, guild oligarchs, and town nobility had grown to greatness and contested power among themselves. The victories of Castile and Aragon over warring factions in 1479 provided a Spanish symbol for the general flow of power.

Meanwhile, by 1500 new organizations dominated production and commerce, the directions of which had clearly altered. There was also a rise of new industries. The inflationary impact of population growth and the influx of precious metals into widened markets and Europe's great wars encouraged economic speculations and adventures.

THE AGE OF DISCOVERY

It is impossible in practice to separate voyages of discovery and the expansion of Europe from the technology of sailing. The intrepid captains who sailed before the technological revolution of the 1400s had inherited from the past a crude compass, the astrolabe, a tradition of poor maps, and the great galley ship of the fourteenth century. The galley was built with the calm Mediterranean in mind; it was not robust enough or broad enough in the keel to adapt easily to the Atlantic.

Before Portuguese sailors coasted Africa's western capes in 1415, vital advances in navigation had taken place. Compasses were improved, as were astrolabes. Together with log lines, these made possible the rough calculations of latitude and longitude that were essential to success on any large body of open water.

Even the advances in the technology of sailing and navigation would have been of little use without the revolution in cartography. Europeans knew little about the world in 1300, or even in 1400. Before 1375 the maps showed no good scale relationships between Asia, Europe, and Africa. Even in 1459 Fra Mauro's famous planisphere still put a verse from Ezekiel[3] before the certain knowledge that Jerusalem was not the center of three continents! Even Columbus' charts were not complemented by a globe, at least in the early voyages.

Portuguese Exploration

That the first circumnavigator of Africa sailed for Portugal depended on the Portuguese development of ships, especially the caravel. This was primarily a sailing ship. The Portuguese had also pioneered the heavier carrack, able to sustain the force of the Atlantic. Portuguese voyages before the time of Prince Henry the Navigator had reached the near Atlantic waters. Like Spain, Portugal had a long crusading history and thus a religious zeal to expel the Arabs from Europe and its adjacent islands.

Henry the Navigator was the key to Portuguese initiative. He wanted to spread Christianity to central Africa and also flank the Arabs and attack them from the south. There was in him an alliance of piety and commerce. He also possessed abiding scientific curiosity. Under his aegis and that of his successors, the grasp of world geography increased rapidly. It is enough to summarize the widened horizons: landings on the west African coast (1434); Dias to the Cape of Storms (1486–1488); Vasco da Gama's trip around the Cape of Good Hope in 1497 and his arrival in 1498 in Calicut, India; Cabral's voyage to Brazil (1500); and a variety of sailings to Arab trade stations on the east African coast.

Vasco da Gama brought back fantastic misconceptions of India. And his fabulous reports of wealth encouraged two things: Cabral's

[3] Ezek. 5:5: "This is Jerusalem: I have set it in the midst of nations. . . ."

voyages to the "orient," which in fact took him to Vera Cruz in Brazil and then on to Madagascar, Calicut, and Cochin; and the decision to send European gold and silver to exchange for Eastern goods. The grand objects sought by Westerners were spices.

The great problem of this trade was clearly the drain it represented on precious metals and the uncertainty of reception Europeans experienced in Africa, Asia, and the Spice Islands. The fact that the Indian Ocean and its border seas harbored no great sea powers soon encouraged Manuel I to take a step fateful for both East and West. Neither trading posts nor factories for trade gave security to the new commerce. Hence in 1505 Francisco de Almeida left Portugal with the title of "Vice-Roy" and with the command that he build forts in Africa and India to protect friends and punish enemies. The transition from an empire of trade to an empire of conquest had begun.

Spanish Exploration

The Spanish, meanwhile, had not been sleeping. Although they did not rival Portugal in the East until the seventeenth century, in 1565 they had already occupied the Philippine Islands and tapped the Chinese trade, as the English were to do after Drake's circumnavigation (1577–1580) and the Dutch after Cornelis de Houtman's voyage to Java, at the end of the sixteenth century. The Spanish made their main mark in the New World, however.

Columbus, a well-educated Genoese captain born about 1450, had sailed for Portugal early in the 1480s. In 1484, however, he went to Spain. There he secured the dramatic conversion to his cause of Isabella of Castile. She was one of the two rulers of the united monarchy of Aragon and Castile that had emerged victorious from the civil wars.

The admiral's luck in getting Spanish backing was a piece of good timing, but it was also the signal of a shift in the focus of Spanish commercial history. Catalonia, the great Mediterranean trading state of Iberia, had for generations centered Eastern trade in Barcelona. Castile's voyages had focused on the Atlantic, however. And the experience of subduing the Canarian aborigines had created a class of conquistadores anxious to combat the Arabs. Thus the proposal for voyages of western discovery meshed well with Castile's western orientation.

Thus an experienced sailor became the herald of the Spanish invasion and conquest of America. The voyage Columbus began on August 3, 1492, was intended to get him to Japan (Cipango) and south

China (Manzi). His intention upon arriving in the Orient was to govern all the lands he might discover. This was in fact the commission given him. Since the admiral carried no vast army, it is likely that his government was intended only for the lesser Japanese islands, perhaps as a base for trade, exploration, or even conquest.

Whatever we make of these intentions in the East, after Columbus' landfalls in America the establishment of a colonial empire was at once contemplated. Columbus founded Navidad near Cape Haitien on Hispaniola and warned the Spanish that to forestall the Portuguese they would have to settle in America in strength. A papal award of Alexander VI in 1493 provided the basis for an empire.[4]

The Spanish voyages and settlements can be quickly chronicled. Columbus explored the Bahamas and the Antilles. The admiral's brother founded Santo Domingo, the oldest continuous American colony of European settlement, on Haiti in 1498. The 1502 voyages brought parts of Central America into the expanded orbit of European geography and ambition. The journeys (1499–1503) of Vespucci and his letters to the cartographer Waldseemüller led to Amerigo Vespucci's name being adopted for the New World by 1507.

The process of further exploration, settlement, and conquest brought startling news to all of Europe. Balboa saw the Pacific from American soil in 1513. Ponce de Leon found gold in Puerto Rico in 1508. Before the conquest of America was undertaken, however, Magellan, the greatest of explorers, began to circumnavigate the earth in 1519 on a voyage he did not live to see completed in 1522. Cortez started the reduction of Mexico and the Aztec empire in 1519. Between 1528 and 1531 Pizarro subdued the Incas. In the 1530s and 1540s the Gulf of Mexico was explored, and De Soto went from Florida up the Mississippi to what is now Tennessee. Coronado worked his way westward from Mexico and discovered the southwest from Arizona and New Mexico to Kansas. By 1575 the Spanish in the New World had founded 200 towns; relieved their domestic population pressure through the emigration of 160,000 settlers; controlled and converted 5 million Indians; introduced over 40,000 black slaves into America; and laid down the basis of a great empire, with missions, presidios, pueblos, and vice-royalties.

French Exploration

The French got into the race only in 1523–1524, with the voyages of Verrazano. He coasted North America from Cape Fear in modern

[4] The Treaty of Tordesillas (1494) formally divided the oceanic world between Portugal and Spain.

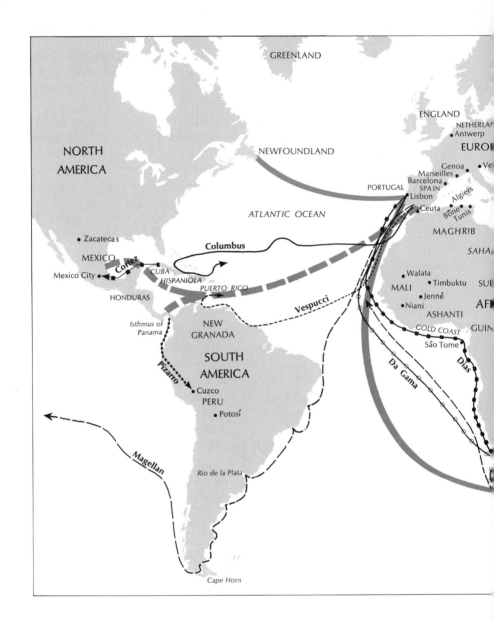

SPANISH AND PORTUGUESE EXPLORERS AND TRADE ROUTES IN THE FIFTEENTH CENTURY

Source: Eugene F. Rice, *The Foundations of Early Modern Europe, 1460–1559* (New York, 1970), p. 30.

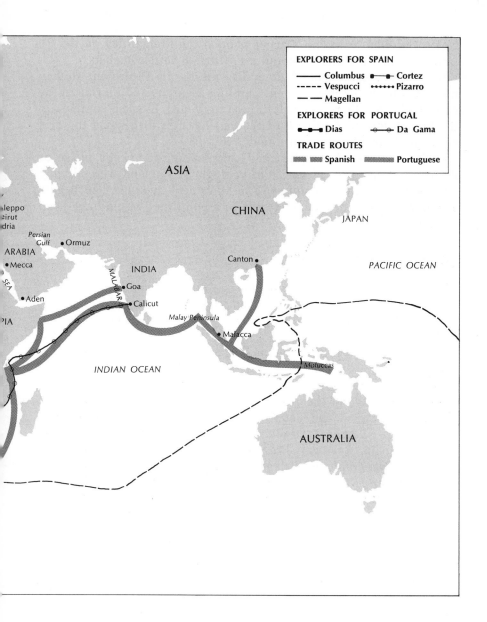

ASIA

CHINA

JAPAN

Aleppo
Beirut
Alexandria

Persian
Gulf   ● Ormuz

ARABIA

● Mecca

INDIA

Canton ●

PACIFIC OCEAN

SEA

● Aden

MALABAR

● Goa

● Calicut

Malay Peninsula

PIA

● Malacca

INDIAN OCEAN

Moluccas

AUSTRALIA

EXPLORERS FOR SPAIN

———— Columbus   ●—●— Cortez
- - - - - Vespucci   ●●●●●● Pizarro
—— —— Magellan

EXPLORERS FOR PORTUGAL

●—●—● Dias   ⊙—⊙— Da Gama

TRADE ROUTES

▨▨▨ Spanish   ▨▨▨ Portuguese

North Carolina to Maine. Cartier planted the French flag on the St. Lawrence in 1534 and explored and tried to settle Quebec in 1541. Efforts to settle French religious dissenters—the Protestant Huguenots—led to the explorations in Carolina, Georgia, and Florida in the early 1560s, but there Spanish forces intervened. Blocked southward, the French moved north. Nova Scotia (Port Royal) became the first permanent French colony in America in 1605.

The process of conquest and colonization ended the phase of discovery. Europeans in search of gold, glory, and God were already well launched toward empires. The movement overseas had begun. The horizons of Europe had grown to a point that would have been incomprehensible in 1300.

THE NEW TRADE ROUTES

The immediate consequence of the age of discovery was a shift in the routes of commerce as well as its cargoes. This development reflected but dimly the revolutionary impact of foreign lands and technology in the West.

The old Eastern trade routes had been the life of commerce for generations. Distribution from Italy to the northwest of Europe had been via the great Flanders fleet since 1317, thus linking the Italians with Europe beyond the Alps. The future held Venice, Genoa, and Barcelona in pawn. The last Flanders fleet went to England in 1532. The growth of oceanic trade in the hands of the five seaborne empires—Spain, Portugal, France, England, and Holland—rewrote commercial geography as well as the history of towns.

The great sixteenth-century trade routes centered on Iberia and the Spanish-dominated Netherlands and were in four main groups: the Mediterranean trades; the northern European trades; the Atlantic trades; and the great ocean trades to the east.

The spice trade in the inland sea continued to flourish, however, in the 1500s. The Venetians especially competed with the Portuguese, although after 1570 the wars with the Turks disrupted Levant commerce seriously. But increasingly the trade of the south lost its character as the hub of the West's world trade. This became evident in the early 1600s when Dutch and English commerce destroyed Venetian power altogether. The great trade other than spices was grain. The western grain trade reoriented itself northward chiefly because of a series of disasters to southern crops and the increasingly vigorous competition of Prussian grain. Moreover, as the prosperity of the Italian cities waned, densely populated cities had to import textiles as well as food. The great cloth guilds could no longer compete with Flemish and English goods, and neither the flourishing commerce in animal products nor that in silk compensated for the losses. Nor did the small mineral trades.

The northern invasion of the "Italian lake" was at first a boon to the Hanse merchants and shippers. Most northern goods were high in bulk—grain and timber—but low in price relative to spices. Big cargoes made for heavy ships, able to carry grain, fish, timber, and minerals. And the north was better supplied with raw materials of every sort. By contrast with the Mediterranean lands, northern soils were not eroded nor too intensely cultivated or overpopulated. The capacity to feed Europe's expanding millions was greater in its broad plains of wheat and on its dairy farms than elsewhere. The fisheries were the richest then known in the world. These ensured that the chance for commercial profits on a great scale existed.

But by 1500 the merchant fleets of the Netherlands were about equal in size to those of the Hanseatic League. There was in the making a duplicate of the Iberian challenge to Genoa and Venice, from the same nations who by 1600 had also come to the Mediterranean. The Dutch, with the English trailing to the rear, came to the fore in the northwest and northern trades a full century earlier than they did in the Levant and East. They were aided by the decline of Bruges and the fact that the three great Iberian routes ended in Antwerp.

Even the increasing Danish tolls, which tripled in the sixteenth century, could not offset the advantages of the Dutch. They came to dominate completely the carriage of fish, coal, English cloth, and the transshipped wares of America and the East. Dutch cities became the centers for refining and secondary or finishing industries.

Antwerp's rise also derived from the pattern of coasting trades and the use Spain made of the Netherlands. The Spaniards were by 1550 the second greatest shipowning nation in Europe; in 1580, after the Iberian kingdoms had been unified, Portuguese and Spanish merchant ships were the equal of the Dutch and larger than any other. Biscayne shipping had grown on the wool of northern Castile, sent by packtrains to Bilbao. The destination was the Spanish Netherlands (part of the inheritance of the Hapsburg Emperor Charles V) and the great textile towns there. Seville and Cádiz were the points from which Europe got spices, exotic foods, sugar, dyestuffs, drugs, cocoa, tobacco, and the fine wool and precious metals of America and Asia.

Seville's trade had since the fourteenth century been oriented toward England through Flanders, with winter fruits and Bordeaux wines carried north in Spanish bottoms, or Flemish, Dutch, and English ones. The multiple treasures of the coastal trade and the ocean trades thus fed the maw of northern industries and enriched its burghers. When the revolt of the Netherlands began in the late 1560s, the Dutch moved from the Baltic and coastal trades directly into competition for empire in America and Asia and Africa.

Thus trade concentrated in northern marts. This naturally implied inland distribution on the river systems linked by the Rhine, the great artery of German commerce, which met the ocean in Holland. The goods that came to Europe from America, Asia, and Africa were part of a complicated inland exchange throughout Flanders, Germany, England, Scandinavia, and the Baltic east. The mainland routes relied on rivers and mountain passes; and this made the south German cities of Augsburg and Nuremberg the main links of Italian trade with that of the Netherlands. Switzerland connected the upper Rhine to Italy for northerners. This promoted urban life in the Rhineland, southern Germany, and the Swiss cantons. Especially after 1530, North African piracy made the land route preferable to the way via Gibraltar and the Netherlands. The pack carrier was a harbinger of prosperity, at least until climate changes and the excesses of the Thirty Years' War disrupted Germany's commerce.

THE CAPITALIST ECONOMY

The trade of Europe had once focused on the central and north Italian towns, from which a rich network of radial lines spread over the west. In the sixteenth century all roads led to Antwerp! She was the queen of commercial capitals.

Antwerp

The centralization of the spice trade there by the Portuguese in 1499 represented Antwerp's triumph over Bruges. Before the troubled 1550s, the fabulous returns from spices and its allied trades had advanced the fortunes of south German bankers and those merchants of Dutch, German, and English origins who mastered Antwerp's exchanges. When wars and economic change wounded Antwerp, supremacy shifted to Amsterdam. After a struggle of great intensity in the 1600s that supremacy was to leap the gap of water separating Holland from England and rest in London for two centuries.

Until politics, religion, and commercial crises ruined Antwerp's hegemony, the English, Germans, and Italians poured millions into the city. Between 1500 and 1560, in the so-called golden age, rapid expansion marked the first two decades. A dizzy spiral upward distinguished the 1540s. And then the era of violent fluctuations in the 1550s produced the collapse of the wool trade in 1551–1552 and the banking failures of 1557–1558.

The impact was felt not only in the foreign communities but in Antwerp's own industrial society. Flanders and Brabant were the most densely populated parts of northern Europe. Perhaps 2 million lived there in 1550. Antwerp herself had by 1550 doubled her 1500 population of about 50,000. The masses of craftsmen and laborers engaged in sugar refining, fish curing, cloth finishing, metal processing, and soap making. The armaments industry also flourished there, with artillery the great specialty. There was also a solid consumer-based prosperity, which saw the increased utilization of good furniture, draperies, glassware, paper, foodstuffs, and books by the burghers.

Thus Antwerp's economy had many of the characteristics of a fully developed urban society based on commercial capitalism and colonialism. There was a mixture of trade in raw materials, manufactured goods, and refined goods. A large domestic bourgeoisie grew powerful, and the settlement of foreigners in large numbers promoted an increasingly cosmopolitan atmosphere. The "freedom of the towns" made Antwerp a melting pot of Spaniards, Portuguese, Germans, Scandinavians, Italians, and Dutchmen. A whole range of commercial service groups sprang up or enlarged. The society and culture of Antwerp were definitively bourgeois. Many who came to trade stayed and made Antwerp their home. And people who were only adopted sons became giants, competing with such men as Erasmus Schetz, "the Copper King," and Gillis Hooftman, "the Sugar King." These men patronized the arts and financed the wars of France and the Hapsburgs, the king of Portugal, Henry VIII of England, and the Netherlands government itself.

The simultaneous declarations of royal bankruptcy in 1557 by Spain, Portugal, and France were followed immediately by that of the public authorities in Antwerp. This spelled the doom of many small-scale capitalists, spreading the shock wave downward into the society as a whole. Thus there began the rapid dislocation of trade so common in the last half of the sixteenth century, exacerbated by the Spanish-Turkish wars in the Mediterranean, the religious wars in France, Germany, and the Netherlands, the great Hapsburg-Valois struggles for mastery in Europe, and the crisis within Europe's towns themselves.[5]

---

[5] For the nature of the major wars and their theaters see Chapter 3, where the subject is treated in the context of politics and political institutions.

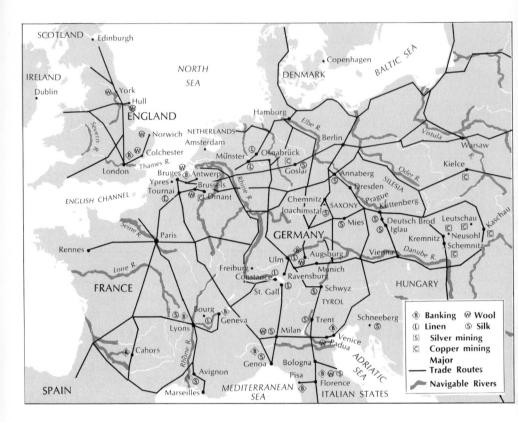

INDUSTRY AND TRADE IN EUROPE, ca. 1500

Source: Eugene F. Rice, *The Foundations of Early Modern Europe, 1460–1559* (New York, 1970), p. 42.

Growth of the Cities

In the more provincial urban societies the late fifteenth and early sixteenth centuries were marked by frenetic change on a smaller scale. As the face of Europe was altered by expansion, so too were its cities. Naples had grown to over 200,000 by 1600, in the face of a declining commerce, and became crowded and slum-ridden. Venice reached her maximum population—about 170,000—in 1563, and Milan reached 180,000 and Paris 200,000 by 1600; Marseilles grew to be a metropolis of 100,000. The cities facing the oceanic routes and a sounder commerce experienced the same sort of surge Antwerp had: London in 1600 had reached about 110,000; Lisbon about 100,000; Seville nearly 125,000. Far to the east Moscow had grown to about 200,000 by 1570, and Constantinople had reached perhaps 250,000.

Among smaller cities the growth was proportional. Florence, Vienna, Augsburg, and Danzig ranged in size from about 70,000 to perhaps 45,000. Madrid, a small town in 1500, was by 1600 the capital of an empire and groaning under the strain of about 60,000 inhabitants. Cities had broken a barrier of scale and style.

The degree to which the West became urbanized between 1450 and 1600 can hardly be exaggerated. As more effective central government and agrarian improvements combined with wealth from new sources overseas, the cities were increasingly able to sustain their growth, even if they could not improve the quality of life for common men.

Below the level of the ruling groups, towns in the West were places with pyramid-shaped social structures. In Coventry, England, for example, 2 percent of the citizens owned 45 percent of taxable wealth. Other English towns were similar in distribution of incomes. Property distribution in Flanders, Brabant, and northern Italy corresponded to the same pattern. The maldistribution of wealth created slums of vast proportions in which proletarians rubbed elbows with thieves, murderers, whores, and "conycatchers," the confidence men of popular literature who took advantage of the "dumb bunnies" from country villages newly arrived in the city. Nearly 50 percent of all western townsmen were living in poverty. Their poverty deepened as the inflation between 1500 and 1600 quadrupled food prices. Overseas voyages and mercenary service vied with colonization late in the 1500s as forms of permanent relief from urban misery.

The cities suffered not only from their population growth and inadequate technology. Their political relationship to the countryside around them was experiencing a sharp change. In most places this was the product of the growth of territorial powers inimical to town liberty and to internal divisions, which made it harder to sustain privileges in the face of princely pressures.

The solutions of the political problem were often profoundly determining of urban character, of urban civilization in general. Most cities that struggled to maintain independence were defeated. Where adaptation was practiced, in avoidance of direct conflict with growing monarchical power, great successes were won. Some leagues or groups of cities became the nucleus for republican states—the Swiss Confederation and the northern United Provinces of the Netherlands. Others flourished by openly embracing royal power, with the result that they rose to metropolitan dominance of their countries. Paris and London are the best examples, with their concentration of royal courts, high culture, finance, social life, representative institutions, lawyers and judicial systems, and powerful merchant corporations.

Antwerp was the representative par excellence of the city whose growth stood by a combination of new developments in trade and the alliance of its interest with those of foreign countries (the Portuguese spice staple and that for English cloth).

Rome alone was a great anachronism. In 1450 a provincial place containing not more than 20,000 inhabitants, by 1600 Rome had become that rare thing, a successful city without commercial or industrial importance! Her 100,000 people lived in the center of Catholic Christendom. She was a service city, anticipating the character of modern government towns (the Hague, Washington, Bonn), with art dealers, tailors, caterers, and sellers of religious trinkets giving emphasis to her character as a tourist center. Thousands lived by providing taxi and rooming services to pilgrims, charlatans, and the vast entourages connected with the revived papal government.

There town planning reached its apogee, when Michelangelo's devices were accepted by Sixtus V (1585–1590) and the radial boulevard system was laid down. It is today one of Rome's glories. In its layout, great architectural facades, monumental spaces and arrangements of buildings, in planned perspectives, Rome, the Eternal City, became also the city of the future. The alliance of aesthetic and functional aims took hold there centuries before Baron Haussmann was commissioned to rebuild Paris or the city fathers in the West generally concerned themselves with the reduction of urban sprawl and the redemption of urban ugliness.

INFLATION IN EUROPE

There is yet another sense in which the expansion of Europe was a concern of all Europeans. The sharpened pace of economic growth had fostered changes in the framework of economic, political, and social organizations. Beyond new techniques of using capital, new organizations of property, the revival of slavery, the growth of colonies, and the relegation of Italy to a secondary role in the drama she had hitherto dominated, beyond all the shifts in the economic balance of the West or those in politics, there was a shift in the balance of society.

The chief result seems clear. The classes that organized and lived by commerce became wealthier relative to landowners, producers,

An engraving of St. Peter's in Rome, where town planning reached its apogee. *New York Public Library.* ▶

and wage earners. Moreover, the degree to which prices ran away from the costs of production, especially wages, was a contributing cause to the aggrandizement of those already wealthy and powerful.

If English mints began to take some silver out of shillings—a debasement of the real money—foreigners would not give as many of their real coins in exchange. Another way of expressing this would be to say that the English money, silver pennies in fact, would be devalued on foreign exchanges. In point of fact, every European money of account was devalued between 1440 and the seventeenth century. Less silver could be gotten for them. The price of silver, of money itself, then, had experienced a steady rise or inflation in our period. And where monies were not devalued in terms of bullion they were often "cried up," or enhanced. That is, the value on the face of coins was arbitrarily increased while the silver content was not. Debasement and enhancement were equally popular devices of debtor governments for paying off creditors in artificially inflated money.

Every change in silver content or price was reflected in the price of other goods. When more clipped or debased coins circulated, as in England in the 1540s, merchants tended to demand more of them in exchange for goods; prices tended to rise as supplies of coins increased. And the supply of coins in the sixteenth century rose because of debasement and reminting, the increased output of Euro-

COMPARISON OF CEREAL AND ANIMAL HUSBANDRY PRICES

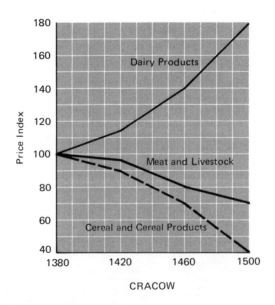

CRACOW

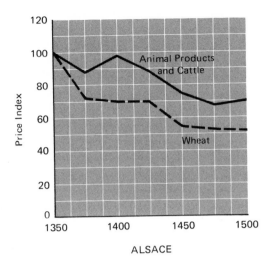

ALSACE

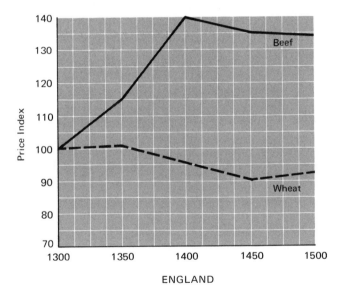

ENGLAND

Source: The Cambridge Economic History of Europe, II, 208; Ibid., I, 687;
J. Pele, Ceny w Krakowie w latach, 1369-1600 (Cracow, 1935), pp. 127-136.

pean mines, and the importation of Spanish silver and gold from Mexico and Peru. Under these conditions and the increased demand for gold and silver in a growing population, the charts and series reflecting commodity prices constitute a history of spiraling, unchecked inflation.

67 Towns, Trade, and the Expansion of Europe

Wheat prices are the best barometer of the inflation that took bread out of people's mouths, since people dispense with every other commodity before they abandon food. Prices assembled for European cities between 1400 and 1600 show the general crisis of food demand; wheat prices in Europe quadrupled between 1450 and 1600. The trend shown in wheat can be supported with other data: wine prices rose steadily between 1440 and the 1620s, while beer prices show similar inflation; meat increased in price but not as sharply as bread and beer. This suggests a certain backwardness in diet. Our sixteenth-century ancestors raised the proportion of bread in their diets, except above the line marking the boundary between existence and affluence. The difference in demand appeared in prices at Strasbourg. Between 1400 and 1600 rye prices rose 350 percent there, but the price of meat rose by barely 200 percent.

The prices of commodities other than food tend to confirm the trend in wheat, although at various levels. It seems clear that construction materials rose sharply. So too did the prices of tallow candles, firewood, textile fibers, processed dairy products, fish, and metal rise. Where combined indices of consumer prices have been made, these show a steep rise, often as much as 400 percent, from 1520 to 1600.

Wages, on the other hand, were fairly stable. In this context wages are in reality only prices of a special kind. The result of superimposing data about wage prices and other prices is to show that men were compensated badly for their labor between 1450 and 1600, and were driven to "prefer" poor products; those who failed even in that adjustment might starve. The regularity with which this happened in town and countryside can hardly be exaggerated.

The gains of entrepreneurs were reflected in the deaths of ordinary men, women, and children. Real wages declined throughout Europe by about 50 percent. This was in fact the social price paid by the profit inflation of the sixteenth century. The collapse of worker and peasant living standards was the reward most people got for increased labor. The majority of Europeans first tasted the progress of capital in the bitter bread of hardship, impoverishment, and dejection. Research shows clearly the relentless deterioration in the life of poor townsmen. Few things better repay study than the graphic barometers of social conditions printed here.

Theories of the Price Revolution

The lot of men in any locale might be explicable in the era of expansion with reference to local peculiarities of harvest, war, pestilence,

THE REAL WAGES OF DAY LABORERS, FARM HANDS, AND CARPENTERS

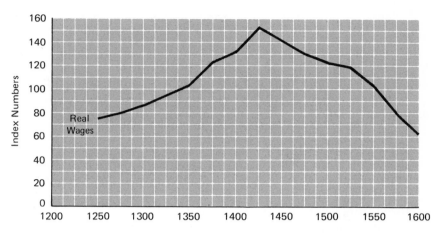

Source: See B. H. Slicher Van Bath, The Agrarian History of Western Europe (London, 1966), p. 103
We lack complete wage series. This doubtless makes any graph a distortion. But such real wages as can be calculated show the trend, especially as compared with cereal prices.

and population. But wage-price cycles are not adequately accounted for over the whole of the West by these circumstances, nor is the general character of the trends illuminated by reference to this or that place. Hence historians have been inclined to fall back on more general explanations of the price revolution. These have been mainly of two kinds: monetary shifts and real economic changes.

The monetary theory holds that prices are determined by the amount of money in circulation and the velocity with which it moves. Proponents of the theory point out that European expansion quickened old and new markets and fantastically increased the quantity of coins circulated.

Some historians have pointed to weaknesses in both the data and theory of this view. They have asked whether the expansion of the Iberian frontier and bullion imports were not the result of needs to increase economic activity in response to a rapidly expanding population after 1450. The upward movement of prices was already well advanced by 1520, before the first gold and silver from America had even arrived in Seville or Toledo!

Moreover, great shares of Spanish silver never circulated in ordinary commerce. It went to finance Hapsburg wars and diplomacy, as well as the colonization of America. Silver circulation on a grand scale was not characteristic of Spanish policy until very late in the sixteenth century. This gives no help at all in explaining why prices doubled in the West between 1510 and 1540, or why they almost doubled again between 1540 and 1570.

These observations have promoted the view that the demographic expansion itself created an inflation of demand in Europe. Since no industrial revolution quickened the production of goods, consumer competition forced an upward revision in prices before any other factor intervened to provide new momentum for inflation.

This emphasis on real economic factors has the advantage of explaining inflation in terms that relate it to the great movements of men and ideas we normally comprehend in the phrase "the growth of capitalism." For capitalism was the structure of economic and social life in which the discovery of America played a vital role and in which the establishment of sea routes to the Far East and the Indies was so prominent. In this way the price revolution can be removed from a narrow context and put in the wider one of the long-term transition in Europe, that which was to bring a commercial-industrial society out of the traditional, agrarian society of Dante's time.

Expansion was a concern of all Europeans in yet another sense. The lag of wages behind prices enlarged the margins of profit for merchants and bankers. It facilitated the concentration of capital, without which the later Industrial Revolution and that which consolidated the territorial state system would not have been possible. That is why wheat prices, town privileges, new trade routes, and the social struggles of classes melt together with agrarian social history and that of agriculture itself. The development of capitalism in the West is one of the central movements of our history. And in that process, the transformation of economy and society we have told of in the preceding pages was the midwife at the birth of new forms of political association, new notions of authority, and a new awareness of the world among Europeans.

THREE

The governance of society

It is very obvious and no more than natural for princes to desire to extend their domains.

Niccolo Machiavelli,
The Prince

According to wise men and writings of the past, each province is sufficient unto itself, so laws and ordinances ought to be appropriate to the province, and not all uniform and identical. . . . For this reason . . . in order that the laws should benefit . . . each province individually, Cortes and *procuradores* should be summoned. . . .

Article I, Cortes of Castile,
The Urban Capitulos (1506)

The most important task that confronts your Majesty [Philip IV], is to make yourself king of Spain. . . . Your Majesty should not rest content with the titles of King of Portugal, King of Aragon, King of Valencia . . . but should labor . . . to reduce all these realms of which Spain is now composed, to the fashion and laws of Castile, without any difference.

Advice to Philip IV (*ca.* 1624)

INTRODUCTION

The political institutions exported from the West to the newfound lands in the age of empire inaugurated by Columbus had also been transformed in the wake of the Black Death.

In 1300 a report on the political scene in Europe would have begun with the Holy Roman Empire and the Roman Catholic Church as the fundamental structures of the West. The various monarchies and republics would have come in for perhaps equal attention. It was not then clear that the political future belonged to the emerging dynastic states of Europe, rather than to the great communes of Italy, Germany, and the Netherlands, and the various leagues of cities formed for political purposes and also commercial ones. It was certainly not clear that either the great land empire of the Germans or the spiritual empire of the Roman church would suddenly decline.

Two hundred years later, however—or rather two hundred and fifty years later, say in 1550—a political reporter taking the European pulse would have this to say. "The age of the Holy Roman Empire is over. Spain has replaced it as Europe's greatest power, with France not far behind in leadership." Moreover, our reporter would have to confess that the Catholic Church had been struck a terrible blow by the Reformation, perhaps not fatal, but damaging enough to allow survival only in an altered, weaker form, and in command of no allegiance from millions of men and women. Not only had the church been thrust from the top rungs of the ladder of power and authority; so, too, had the Italian cities and the Hanseatic League. The two dynastic states of France and Spain had made a cockpit of Italy, where they fought for supremacy in Europe. And the traders from the Netherlands and England were cutting deep wounds into the commercial empire of the northern cities of Germany up and down the Baltic coast.

Indeed, an intelligent observer would report that by 1600 the dynastic state based on compact control over a coherent land mass had emerged as the victor over cities, empires, and churches in the European power struggle. In their political bases, these states were not yet nation-states; they were not based on the popular principle of the sovereignty of the people. They were instead the "estates" of their dynastic rulers, men and women who governed in cooperation with certain corporate bodies called parliaments and by means of councils and secretaries responsible only to the prince. In these states power and responsibility seemed to be flowing toward the prince; and, as we will see, it is false to suppose parliamentary bodies existed independently, rather than as parts of the essential structure of royal government.

In short, by 1600 the age of great republics and supradynastic states was over, practically speaking. The great cities were less independent communes than political, social, legal, and educational capitals of the new states. Protestants and Catholics and Calvinists picked over the still-warm body of the Holy Roman Empire. The principles of politics in the new age had undergone a revolution; and the new principles were already shaping colonial life in Spanish America.

POLITICS AND POWER

Politics and government are rooted in power. It now is our business to say what we mean by power in its political sense and to talk about the principles of politics.

The familiar landmarks of the medieval Holy Roman Empire and the independent communes lay in ruins by 1500, brilliant facades behind which no sound buildings stood. A political tourist in 1600 would require guides to identify new monumental structures: republican city confederations exercising hegemony over a wide countryside; a group of potent monarchies, the Iberian of which had developed empires thousands of miles from Europe; a system of relations among sovereign states often divided not merely by old appetites for territory and dynastic ambitions, but by ideologies of religion as well.

Concretely, this means that the principles of medieval politics were overturned. No matter what the survival value of certain ideas —James I and Louis XIV exercised the miraculous healing powers of semisacred thaumaturgic medieval monarchs—the mental habits of politics were profoundly different in 1600 from what they had been in 1300. Conflicts, and the disequilibrium they sprang from and engendered, were parts of a changing social history. The needs of new communities constantly broke through the crust of old customs of government. The rise of the concepts of "commonwealth" transformed the bases and purposes of some political actions. Old ways of viewing political action as the result of the balance of force between the powerful and powerless impose on Renaissance and Reformation Europe a useless dichotomy. The world of Henry VIII of England (1491–1547) was not merely one of *oratores, bellatores et laboratores.*[1] The structures of politics were changing, and with them the nature and distribution of power.

THE FAILURE OF TOWN AUTONOMY

The collapse of the fourteenth-century economy was matched by the disintegration of authority. After the demographic crisis, laws remained everywhere as they had been in 1300, except of course that they had been added to by men frantically trying to compel a halt in those processes of change we have already chronicled. Yet ready obedience to them was lacking. So too did kings, thrones, and aristocracies remain intact. But peasant rebellions and the doctrines of radical intellectuals challenged the legitimacy of their powers. Who or what is the source of law, and by whom do laws stand in their place, binding men to acts and also to passive obedience, became the capital questions of politics.

Populist ideas of government had shaped the institutions of the communes before 1300. Power had been ascribed to the community, or at least those in it had been given active citizenship by means of the franchise. It is enough to say that power and authority reached their apex in the governing councils and boards of magistrates who were elected in wards or districts, or in accordance with the distribution of the franchise through guild membership. Wherever such constitutions were threatened by the consolidation of oligarchies or the rise of despots, we meet the clamor of critics whose writings recall the virtues of the ancient Roman republic.

The cities, then, were continuing an old tradition that had not survived strongly in the feudal countryside. Their failure to maintain their corporate character and independence was complete by 1600. The exceptions prove the rule. For in the Swiss cantons and the Dutch republic the liberties of the cities were sustained only by their combination in political arrangements that were ultimately monarchical in character. Truly popular power existed on the microscopic level, in village communes where Cossack hetmen or English mayors disposed of local business in "committees of the whole." And there were of course some greater free towns, unions, fraternal associations, heretical sects, schools, and professional corporations in which populist assumptions ruled.

But on the macroscopic level, by 1450 most independent towns had ceased to hold real political power; guilds had fallen under the

[1] The threefold scheme of so many medieval texts: priests, knights, and peasant laborers.

regulation of extramural authorities. Only in legislative assemblies of the territorial states did the ideal of representative government survive. The north Italian republican models survived chiefly in literary laments—Machiavelli's *Discourses* and the numerous fifteenth-century writings of the civic humanists.[2] In the 1400s and 1500s the processes were well advanced that were to make men more conscious of their nation than of their town.

What was changing was not the central significance of political life but the units capable of organizing power and using it successfully. The constituent parts of states and cities were equally human beings; but in cities they were not able to successfully order their affairs. City law proved unable to cope with the consequences of demographic, economic, and social changes, which were European in scale; incapable of resolving tensions; and impotent when faced with the power of longer associations for political purposes.

The despots and oligarchs who had consolidated their rule by 1500 yielded in few places. The bulk of town inhabitants were legally free. But throughout the sixteenth century, town patriciates resisted popular parties and succeeded in subordinating the craft guilds. The situation was such that the great cities became predators in regard to the smaller ones. Venice, Florence, Milan, Genoa, and others subdued their neighbors. Ghent, Bruges, and many English towns practiced a different form of tyranny; they exploited local labor which was thoroughly subordinated to town cloth working. The German free imperial cities were unable to bring other towns under their control. But the Swiss exercised power over a large area, with the canton city becoming in effect the capital of a series of rural republics.

Florence is a prime example of the instability even of large city-states. Faction fights and class struggles brought despotism under the Medici. The same fate awaited Milan under the Sforza, Mantua under the Gonzaga, and Urbino under the Montefeltre. Machiavelli's *Prince* and *Discourses* show the tension of republican and authoritarian ideas, especially where strong nobilities and large proletariats favored monarchy (Naples and Rome), or where republican forces struggled unsuccessfully against the power of despots (Florence).

[2] Machiavelli was notable as a politician at Florence, but he is more famous as a writer about politics. In his *Discourses on the History of Livy,* Machiavelli explores the nature of republican institutions, just as in his more famous *Prince* he describes and analyzes despotic power in realistic terms. He was thus the heir to the tradition of vigorous interest in civic life we saw in Salutati. Like the earlier civic humanists, Machiavelli's works and letters constantly fuse the knowledge of classical history with a search for understanding of contemporary events. Machiavelli was different chiefly in his clinical studies of one-man rule, where realism triumphed over moralism.

Even when despotic lines failed, as in Florence in the 1530s, the rule of the many gave place to the rule of renewed oligarchies.

Far to the north, Lübeck attempted the oligarchic pose Venice used effectively in the south. After a series of defeats in the 1530s, however, the great Hanse town declined politically and became subject to Danish influence. So, too, the greater German cities were under severe imperial pressure, as Charles V struggled to limit their freedom.[3] The politics of religion split the evangelical cities of north and central Germany from those of the south. This made all of them less able to withstand the pressure of local princes whose territorial power expanded about in proportion to the decline of imperial power.

In France, Spain, and the Netherlands, towns had never had the autonomy enjoyed by German and Italian cities. What liberties had survived the ducal and royal attacks in Burgundy collapsed under the massive weight of Spanish oppression in the southern Netherlands after 1550. The French monarchy had subordinated its cities by the 1560s. The towns of Castile, however, provided the great theater of conflict between nascent monarchy and urban privilege. The *communeros* (urban political groups) had before 1500 aided the princes against the feudal magnates. This alliance was upset by the triumph of the monarchy. Ferdinand of Aragon and Charles V tried to subordinate the parliament (Cortes) and then placed unpopular royal officials *(corregidors)* over town governments. By 1520 the revolt of the *communeros* had begun, and the crown believed it to be aimed at communes on the medieval Italian model. The social revolution implicit in this notion drew the dissident nobles to the royal course and broke the revolt in 1521. Towns in Castile were wholly subordinated to the crown by 1600.

To the east, as we have repeatedly stressed, the failure of townsmen had been a feature of the triumph of the lords and princes early in the 1400s. The great cities of Prussia, Poland, and Russia were symbols of the general decline. By 1570 Ivan IV had completely subordinated all Russian towns. And nowhere in the east did the

---

[3] This prince was heir to Burgundy, the united crowns of Aragon and Castile, the Spanish empire in the New World, and also the hereditary lands of the Hapsburgs in the Germanies. In 1519 he was elected Holy Roman Emperor, chiefly because of the importance of his German connections, lands, and jurisdictions. He reigned until 1555, when he resigned power, splitting his inheritance between two heirs, Philip II of Spain and the Emperor Ferdinand. It is commonly assumed that Charles did this for two reasons—because he was shocked by his failure to suppress the Protestant reformers and because he saw the burden imposed on his other dominions by the emperor's involvement in German religious politics.

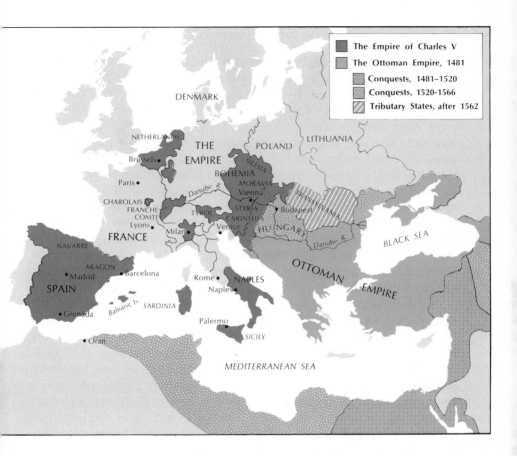

TWO SIXTEENTH-CENTURY "EUROPEAN" EMPIRES

Source: H. G. Koenigsberger and G. L. Mosse, *Europe in the Sixteenth Century* (New York, 1968), p. 177.

bourgeoisie develop the legal and social character of the western European classes whose life style and ideas were so pregnant with the revolutionary notions of freedom that were to distinguish urban civilization in the West.

EMPIRES: WEST, NORTH, AND EAST

The Holy Roman Empire failed to maintain its claim to power in the fourteenth and fifteenth centuries. This failure was significant in a variety of ways, especially for the character of political life in the German heartland of Europe.

The Weakness of German Imperial Power

The German emperors of the fourteenth and fifteenth centuries were in fact the feudal suzerains of a loosely knit confederation of small and large lordships, principalities, and kingdoms. They were not able to rule effectively any appreciable part. The reasons for this inability were many and the consequences legion, but one central fact must be stressed. Whereas the decline of feudal and theocratic monarchy in most of the west produced an answering growth of powerful dynastic states, in the German case the inability of emperors to rule in their own or some wider public interest created a situation in which no one territorial state was strong enough to rule the others. The failure of imperial power cast the Germans into the hell of particularism, the assertion of the supremacy of the small states over the Empire, until Prussia and Austria grew strong enough to vie for supremacy in the eighteenth and nineteenth centuries. This fact shaped central and western European politics for centuries.

The limitations of the imperial monarchy had been clear enough before 1300. Apart from any theoretical challenge to the *Dei gratia* (by the grace of God) doctrine or any recollection of the elective nature of the imperial monarchy,[4] there was the fact that this monarchy had been shared between 1272 and 1486 by four families: Nassau, Wittelsbach, Luxembourg, and Hapsburg. This sharing of the crown was solidly anchored in facts less pretentious than the claim to be monarch of all Christendom. The history of the late medieval Empire was one of disunity, corruption, and disorder. Moreover, "Empire" itself was an ambiguous expression.

"Empire" actually denoted an area as well as a mode of government. The area had expanded steadily eastward, until early in the 1300s Slavonic state power and Bohemian (Czech) strength marked a halt in that direction. Westward, the growth of French royal power at the expense of feudal dynasts and the rise of the Burgundian state drew a line across the Rhine's course. By 1450 the Holy Roman Empire was in fact the claim to rule the "German nation," even though reactionary authors might say that "Empire" and "Christendom" were synonymous as late as 1439.[5] How inconsistent these aims were with the power actually in the imperial hands can be grasped easily enough.

---

[4] Old Germanic tribal kingship was elective within the closed circle of the male members of the royal family. The medieval emperor was elected by the seven electoral princes, three ecclesiastics, and four secular rulers; Mainz, Cologne, Trier; the Palatinate, Saxony, Bohemia, and Brandenburg.
[5] In the famous *Reformatio Sigismundi,* or "Reform of the Emperor Sigismund."

Emperors faced a bewildering array of challenges to their power to do or to get done and to their authority over the princely nobility, the towns (free and imperial), the service or ministerial nobility, and the hordes of knights of the petty aristocracy.

The strong expanded the territorial base of their own power, while the weak leagued together to ensure their survival. The leagues of Protestant cities against Charles V in the 1530s and 1540s were familiar enough, repeating as they did for religious politics what the Swabian knights had done for secular causes in 1426. Sigismund had admitted he had no power to satisfy the grievances of Cologne burghers against their electoral prince, Archbishop Dietrich of the powerful Mörs family.

Yet even powerful electors were not the true focus of effective power in Germany. Physical strength inhered chiefly in the territorial princes. The period from 1300 to 1600 is distinguished by the fact that the greatest of these gained power over the lesser nobility and the cities. Their rise was a reminder that power was a relationship between what a government wanted to do and what it had resources to do. Direct rule over large areas was impossible at a distance, once the limitations of technology and communication were exposed. The emperors had not the income or the machinery to master the local concentrations of people and wealth in the age of population growth; and they lacked utterly the means to hold together their *imperium* in the chaotic conditions that prevailed after 1350.

They were not able to give succor to oppressed peoples in rural society. Their edicts against murderous lords who exploited their peasants lacked *potentia et vigore* ("power and force"), as Nicholas of Cusa said in 1433. The lower classes constantly took the imperial insignia and the five wounds of Christ as their badges in rebelling against their lords. But their appeal to imperial power gave no salvation, however successful they might be with God. The struggle between them and the great and small landlords merely mirrored in its lack of equilibrium that which was being waged between the emperors and the combined princes.

The emperors were too weak to spread peace and justice in the areas nominally subject to them. Even the right to rule was the result of electoral bargains. The mighty Hapsburgs often secured their dynastic interests in exchange for a certain princely freedom granted to other rulers. Late medieval emperors were also debtor kings. They depended on the revenues of the imperial towns at a time when commerce was disrupted. In 1422 the emperor was unable to raise an army to suppress the nationalist religious revolt of Bohemian Hussites. In 1475 Frederick III was unable to enforce a sentence against his vassal, the powerful Burgundian prince Charles the Bold. And in 1495 Maximilian's efforts to rescue his finances through a new tax program was rebuffed in the imperial diet, or parliament.

The Emergence of German Territorial States

The dynamic of German politics and governance was increasingly that of the princes. By 1450 several leaders had emerged to consolidate territorial states, thus bringing to Germany the development so fateful for the west nearly everywhere else in Europe. Among the greatest of these men were Albert Achilles in Brandenburg, Frederick the Victorious in the Palatinate, Eberhard the Bearded of Württemberg, George the Rich in Bavaria, and Dietrich II of Mörs. Their rise was beset by adversities of fortune. The conditions peculiar to their territories made a patchwork of victory and defeat their common history.

What was especially significant in these cases was the victory of the centralizing force of a prince over feudal collections of rights and privileges. Princes slowly gathered territories and administered them as single units. Their councils were made into instruments of their sovereignty. Princes took as advisers and administrators able men without regard to rank and birth. Bureaucrats trained in civil law made professional careers, often in more than one territory.

The focal points of adjustment in the political process became the estates, which were meeting at their own initiative. There princes met parliaments and exchanged privileges for taxes. The idea of the public interest slowly emerged from the welter of events. Thus in the newly integrated territorial states, authority took a form in which the competing principles of medieval politics merged. There was a diffusion of authority, with the theme of declining monarchical power in close conjunction with the notions of greater participation and representation and more popularist sentiment.

This development gave strength to the courts in their administration of justice, to the tax collector in his impositions, to the armies in their aggressions and in their defense of home soil, and to the root idea of central power. The genius of the territorial states in Germany lay precisely in its reconciliation of feudal, popular, ministerial, manorial, and urban interests.

Not even the new prosperity of the late fifteenth or sixteenth centuries could in fact rescue a true German kingship. When Charles V gathered together the Hapsburg lands, the empire, and the Spanish and Burgundian inheritances, Germany was poised on the brink of religious war. The Turks threatened to dismember the empire in the southeast, as they had already done to Byzantium. And between 1555 and 1556 the great Hapsburg king was to recognize the impossibility of his task. He split Spain from Germany, leaving the former free to fight great battles for empires overseas and against the Valois in Europe. He recognized that in Germany the territorial states had triumphed, a bitter admission for the great Catholic monarch, since among them were Lutheran and Calvinist powers.

The Decline of North European Empires

The fate of the medieval supranational political units elsewhere in the West was a similar dissolution. The English empire on the mainland vanished in the defeats and stalemate of the Hundred Years' War with France. By 1453 the vanity of reviving the Angevin empire was clear to most politically articulate Englishmen. They began to attend to the tasks closer at home, the suppression of quasi-feudal anarchy and the formation of the kingdom of Britain out of the English, Welsh, and Scottish territories. Henry VIII might hear tunes of glory and so struggle to conquer lands in France again, in 1513, 1523, and 1544. But even Calais was lost to the English in 1558; and future incursions on the Continent were to have as their reason supporting brothers in Christ of the Protestant persuasion: in France in the 1560s and 1570s, in the Netherlands in the 1580s, and in the Rhineland in the 1620s.

A far more interesting example is that of the falling to pieces of another of the fringe empires—Scandinavia.[6] In 1300 the Scandinavian peoples were wholly engrossed in trying to settle and integrate the areas of Norway, Sweden, Denmark, and Finland. Norway maintained relations with Scotland, while its more powerful neighbors, Sweden and Denmark, focused their energies on the Baltic. The crowns were elective, serfdom hardly existed; but the aristocracies were still powerful farming interests and managed to survive the impact of depopulation. Feudal power remained great. To a certain extent political arrangements resembled those in the weak eastern states of Poland, Hungary, and Bohemia. Towns were few and small. The bourgeoisie had little weight in the diets (Riksdagen) of the north. Commercial life lay in the hands of the Hanseatic League cities.

Then, late in the fourteenth century, a combination of marriages, good fortune, deaths, and wars brought to fruition the schemes of

---

[6] It is an important fact that the powerful late medieval empires existed on the far western, northern, and eastern edges of Europe.

Margaret of Norway, regent for her son, Prince Olaf, after the death in 1380 of Haakon VI, her husband. The Danish throne of her father had fallen by election to her young son in 1375. Margaret's son thus became king of both Denmark and Norway in 1380. When Olaf died in 1387, she continued to rule in both countries. Meanwhile, in Sweden, the German house of Mecklenburg had alienated aristocratic support by its favor to German courtiers. A rebellion in the early 1390s deposed Albert, and the rebels offered the Swedish regency to Margaret. By 1397, a complicated series of negotiations between the Hanse, German interests, and Margaret ended in the Union of Kalmar. Her adopted son Erik of Pomerania (in fact her nephew, the grandson of Ingeborg) was given the crown of the three kingdoms.

The union was controversial from the beginning, however, because of the marked hostility between Denmark and Sweden and the favor the Danes were shown over both Norwegians and Swedes. Throughout the fifteenth century factionalism threatened to destroy the union, as did peasant revolts and foreign interventions. The result was a fragile northern empire in which Denmark continued to dominate Norway until 1814 but conceded the fact of Swedish independence. The royal power was no proof against the support the Swedish nobility gave to one of their own number, Gustavus Vasa, and in 1523 he began the long reign (1523–1560) during which he consolidated in Sweden a Reformation territorial state very much on the model of others in western Europe. Christian III (1533–1559) did the same in Denmark. These political facts should not disguise another fact, however. In the northern limits of the West hereditary Protestant monarchies in Sweden and Denmark-Norway grew out of the collapse of a tenuous empire, despite bonds of language, religion, general culture, and a similarity of institutions.

Imperial Shifts in Eastern Europe

Far to the east, in Byzantium and Russia and its borderlands, an old empire disintegrated and a new state was being built. Byzantine power was feeble and often dependent on Muscovite wealth. Basil I of Moscow had sent men and money to relieve the Turkish blockade of Constantinople. The Ottoman Turks had been established in Europe by 1350 and by 1390 were in possession of most of the territory of the eastern empire, including Bulgaria and Serbia. Only satellites in Greece and the Aegean remained under Byzantine rule.

The "gathering of the Slavic peoples" into powerful, rival political systems had begun. One nascent state had its center in Moscow, the other in the grand duchy of Lithuania. Biding their time, slowly building their power through alliances with the boyars (landed aristo-crats),[7] buoyed by the support of the Greek and Russian Orthodox churches, the Muscovite princes unified eastern Russia and then defeated the Tartar power in 1380.

This first victory in the war to liberate European Russia from Asian domination gave Moscow incredible prestige. Until the fall of Constantinople to the Ottomans in 1453, Byzantium played its few cards well enough to avoid becoming a Russian client. The prestige of Constantinople mattered in eastern Europe and was used as a weapon by Moscow in its struggles with the Polish and Lithuanian princes who held sway in western and southwestern Russia. Impetus to this development had derived from the fall of Kiev before the Mongols in 1300. The primate of the Russian church had fled to Moscow. By 1453 he was recognized as "Metropolitan of Kiev and of all Russia." Threats by Polish and Lithuanian emissaries failed to convince the Byzantium patriarch to translate the center of Slavic Christendom from Moscow.

The importance of this development can hardly be exaggerated. When the Turks captured Constantinople, a centralized Slavic church power was already lodged in the hands of the most powerful of the emerging Slavic states. Over a century of maneuver and ruse after 1750 had given to the Muscovite dynastic leader Prince Dmitri and his successors, Basil I and Basil II, the pretense of a challenger for authority over Orthodox Christendom. The Orthodox teaching, that there was one empire and one church, was in fact the legacy of Byzantium to Moscow in 1453. The Byzantium patriarchs themselves had championed the idea that it was "not possible to have the Church and not to have the Empire." Hence in the eastern empire the Russian authorities were quick to respond to the catastrophe of 1453 with a new claim. If Constantinople had been the "second Rome," ordained to carry on the civilizing mission of the embattled western empire of Rome, then Moscow was the "third Rome." She would carry the standard of Christian culture for the embattled peoples of the east.

As the "gathering" progressed, as peasants were enserfed, as boyar privileges were reduced, as town liberties were crushed and power was enlarged at the center, the traditions of *Tsargrad* (Con-stantinople, the Imperial City) were translated into Russian idioms. The 1439 Council of Florence had reunited the Greek and Latin churches, but Moscow had rejected union with Rome in 1439 as decisively as its princes had defeated Slavic challenges to Muscovite supremacy.

---

[7] In exchange for aristocratic control of the peasantry; see pp. 20–21.

The centralizing, autocratic Muscovite monarchy after 1453 imposed its power on most of Russia. It made little difference that the fall of Constantinople rendered void the decrees of Florence and gave back to Constantinople orthodoxy. Turkish political leadership of the center of Christendom was no more acceptable in Russia than papal religious leadership. In 1459 the Muscovite metropolitan blamed the fall on Byzantium's turn from God in 1439, when the besieged patriarch of Constantinople sought aid from the Latin West by agreeing to terms to end the religious schism begun in 1054. Others pointed out that Muscovy defeated its enemies and was righteous in the sight of the Lord. Throughout the sixteenth century these nationalist and religious ideologies continued to merge. On the eastern flank of Western civilization a new land empire had risen to claim the inheritance of Rome and Byzantium.

Empires there were in the West, then. But they existed on Europe's eastern and northern fringes only. That of the north was a mere facade. Russia's was on the pattern of the territorial state. The Turkish Empire was not so much a part of the West as it was a threat to it. Where in fact imperial aspirations and accomplishments did exist in the West, these were new creations, colonial empires far from Europe's shores. And in them white men subdued and humiliated men of other colors: in India, Malaya, the Indies (East and West), and the great pre-Columbian Aztec and Inca realms of America.

THE RISE OF THE DYNASTIC STATES

Power in the West, meanwhile, was flowing in the direction of dynastic, secular nation-states. In a sense this trend had appeared first in Italy, where religious radicals led by popes had broken the feudal ties that held the church in thrall to the emperors. The Italian communes had been the spearhead of a political revolution, and their task was at first to smash the power of imperial barons, pull down their castles, force the nobility into towns, and subject them to a common law. They ended by stripping their ecclesiastical partners, the bishops, of their secular powers. Well before 1300, when power everywhere else still hid behind the mask of quasi-sacramental kingship and the complexities of feudal arrangements, in the cities of northern and central Italy purely temporal power of a popular nature had been a fact of life.

The central fact of political life in the west about 1300 was that the feudal monarchies were decadent.

Wherever national monarchies developed at the expense of

feudal particularism and ecclesiastical independence, there were common elements. Kings resumed certain rights that had once been widely distributed among the seigneurial classes of society and the enfranchised bourgeoisie. This was especially true with regard to the administration of justice, military organization, the regulation of economic life, and the collection of taxes in support of the expansion of royal government.

The provision of adequate finances was central. Money was the nerve of power and its muscle. The ambition to rule required that monarchs assume functions once performed elsewhere. Revenue in staggering amounts was necessary to the centralizations of court systems, the employment of paid armies, the maintenance of salaried administrative cadres, and the pursuit of economic policies of a national rather than a provincial character. Finally, money was also the sinew of war and diplomacy; and as the state system of Europe developed, wars became greater in scale, more intense in their capital requirements, and longer.

It is impossible to sketch in any detail these developments in each of the emergent territorial states. Nor would the mere accumulation of such facts represent particularly well the nature of the accomplishments or their chief consequences. A more satisfactory way to illustrate the processes lies in a comparative approach to Europe.

The first object before us is simply to point out the evidence for the roughly simultaneous consolidation of the states, the resumption of jurisdiction over subjects and the notion of power over them.

The Emergence of National Monarchies in Western Europe

In the Iberian Peninsula, consolidation was a triumph of war and dynastic marriage. Aragon (Valencia, Catalonia, the Balaeric Islands, and Aragon proper) and Castile married in 1469. This was part of the process by which the wars of reconquest won back the peninsula from Islamic domination and subordinated the *ricos hombres* ("great nobles"). The Moors and the nobility had prevented strong central rule, and the kings of France and Portugal had tried to prevent the union of the two crowns. But nuptial diplomacy created a unit that combined Aragon's trading empire and Castile's powerful military orders.

France had been kept in a divided state by incompetent kings, the chaos of English campaigns in its countryside, and the rivalries of the various independent princes in control of whole segments of the country. This was especially true under Charles VI (1380–1422), when the dukes of Orléans, Burgundy, Berry, and Anjou fought more effectively among themselves than against the English. The victories of Joan of Arc and Charles VII (1422–1461) marked the beginning of royal recovery. Charles' long reign began the crucial phase in which agreements with the church and armed campaigns against the grandees reversed the flow of power, but it remained for his son, Louis XI (1461–1483), to establish mastery through an alliance with the great towns, especially Paris. Louis' reduction of Brittany, Anjou, Maine, Armagnac, and Burgundy in 1477, despite the League of the Public Weal among the factious nobility and Swiss and imperial mercenary aid to Burgundy, allowed the formal consolidation of power in the unified territory between 1483 and 1547 under Charles VIII, Louis XII, and Francis I.

Civil war and marriage alliances were also characteristic features of unification in England and Burgundy. In 1400 England was weak and divided. Great feudal lords in the north and in the Welsh borderlands tried to partition the kingdom in 1403. And the house of Lancaster provided three kings—Henry IV, Henry V, and Henry VI—who proved either incompetent administrators or warrior kings fatally addicted to the lure of empire in France. Henry V married the French Princess Catherine and won notable victories, but his son was first a feeble infant and then a mature imbecile. The English counterparts of Iberian *ricos hombres* and French appanage princes constantly resisted the corrupt Lancastrian regime of favorites, and in the 1450s the loss of France combined with civil war and threatened the destruction of the medieval kingdom. Edward of March, son of Duke Richard of York, successfully rallied the aristocracy to his usurpation of the throne, and between 1461 and 1483 he provided the strong leadership necessary to subdue the regional aristocratic factions. His real successor in this work was not his brother, Richard III (1483–1485), but the Tudor earl Henry Richmond (1485–1509). Henry VIII (1509–1547) married a Yorkist queen to unite rival factions at home and also arranged marriage alliances with Scotland and Castile to secure English interests within the island and in western Europe.

The duchy of Burgundy, which had been created out of the unification of the provinces of Brabant, Burgundy, Flanders, Holland, and Zeeland, was in danger of falling apart as a consequence of the French defeat at Nancy in 1477. Burgundian forces of particularism were entrenched in the various estates of the duchy's component parts. The Grand Privilege of 1477 spelled out the rights of the territories of the Netherlands, in order to prevent any further princely illusions of sovereignty. It was in fact a feudal document in which territorial self-sufficiency was proclaimed, and in that climate France was tempted to reduce Burgundy to a province of its monarchy by conquest. Marriage saved the Burgundian Netherlands in 1477, when Maximilian, the duke of Austria and the Hapsburg heir to the Holy Roman Empire, married Mary of Burgundy, the daughter of Charles the Bold, who had been killed in battle at Nancy.

The alliances of England and Burgundy with Spain and Austria drove home the point. While the Hapsburg role could not prevent the loss of Burgundy to France in 1482, it did ensure that the main provinces of the Netherlands would pass to Spain as an integral part of the Hapsburg empire early in the next century. Charles, the grandson of Maximilian and Mary and future emperor, began a restoration of the integrity of Burgundy in 1514, and this state was always a chief component of his power in the larger world of Reformation Europe. England was able to use the Spanish (and then the Hapsburg) shield as a counterweight to French ambitions, especially in Scotland. The fate of both states depended on dynastic marital diplomacy, as had that of Spain in 1469.

The Efforts to Create Territorial States in Eastern Europe

The political patterns of the West's most distant eastern fringe were strikingly similar to those of the western monarchies. Russia was in the midst of the great gathering. This state, which was some day to absorb all of eastern Europe, survived the successive waves of Mongol and Turkish assault. The Grand Duke Basil II (1425–1462) passed an integrated territory to Ivan III (1462–1525), who quickly expanded what were to be the hereditary holdings of the tsars. To the east there was no opposition, and Russian pioneers pushed to the Pacific under him and Ivan the Terrible. The Muscovite state also took in the rich Volga steppe lands of the southeast, thus embracing Armenians and Cossacks.

The western flanks were, however, another matter. Ivan III had to wage long wars to conquer the independent territories of Tver and Novgorod. The latter was especially resistant, since it enlisted the aid of the Hanseatic powers in the interest of their trade depot there. Hence this brace of victories was in fact more significant than is sometimes realized. It opened Muscovy's first "window on the West," more than 150 years before Peter the Great's creation of St. Petersburg. Ivan III also fought successful wars in the Lithuanian-Polish and Ukraine provinces of what was to be Russia.

Elsewhere east of the Elbe the two most important general developments were the successful building of an Ottoman state in southeastern Europe and the failure of the territorial state in most other areas of eastern Europe. The contest between Russia and the Turkish Empire would take place in a power vacuum created by the failure of monarchy in Poland, Hungary, and the Balkans. We cannot detail this failure, but we can state what its general conditions were. For the contrast in developments in politics was itself a good example of how the same general problem, the great fourteenth-century crisis, produced remarkably different effects in various parts of the west.

The European east was poorer than the west, in soil, climate, and geography, as well as in commerce. Yet between 1300 and 1500 agriculture between the Elbe and Dnieper prospered, as lords won power over the peasantry. A dozen struggles[8] took place between local magnates, towns, and the greater feudal lords on the one side and would-be monarchs on the other. The results were fatal to territorial integration. Towns never became strong enough to supply the revenue base that might make kings less dependent on feudal service and land revenue. Instead, princes were forced back on semifeudal alliance systems in return for financial and military aid against external enemies. The domestic consequence was the elaboration of a social order in which public authority turned its back on the peasantry, allowing them and the land to pass under the private jurisdiction of the greater aristocrats.

Only on the extreme edges of Europe did the territorial state prosper: Muscovy, Prussia, Sweden, and the Ottoman segments of the Balkans. Elsewhere a line dividing Slavic and Germanic areas was drawn from the Baltic to the Adriatic, allowing for the enclave of Bohemia.

Far to the north the Finno-Ugric language peoples (Finns, Estonians, Livs, and Cours) lived between the forces of Slavic and German expansion. Toward the south their Hungarian cousins suffered in much the same way. The Baltic Finns became Swedish or German dependents; and the Hungarians waged long struggles against incorporation, finally succumbing to the Hapsburgs after successfully resisting the Mongols and the Turks. The Poles and Lithuanians, after defeating the Teutonic knights late in the fifteenth century, fell gradually into the great Russian orbit.

After the formation of kingdoms in the fourteenth century, the

[8] In Bosnia, Serbia, Wallachia, Moldavia, Hungary, Bohemia, Poland, Lithuania, Prussia, Courland, Estonia, and Livonia.

high point of independence was passed. Poland could not defend the achievements of Casimir the Great (1333–1370), who had codified the law, extended a welcome to Jews, and allied the Piast dynasty with its Hungarian neighbors. The Jagello dynasty of Lithuania for a time united the two kingdoms, but the upshot of this was to draw the Poles into the competition against Muscovy. The victory over the Germans (Peace of Thorn, 1466) was to prove a force that released the provincialism of the nobility. By 1505 the diet had forced on the crown the decree *Nihil novi* ("Nothing New"), by which the seigneurial veto power over centralizing legislation was recognized.

The Czech monarchy of Bohemia split apart on the rock of religious war. Brilliant achievements under Charles IV (1346–1376) and his son, Wenzel (or Wenceslas, 1378–1419), were followed by the Hussite heresy and the civil wars of religion, dividing the kingdom into religio-political factions in which ethnic lines were also drawn. The dominant German minority faced a moderate national Czech and a radical Hussite opposition. The triumph of the native aristocrat George Podebrad (1458–1471) was short-lived. His death brought the ambitious Polish-Hungarian Jagellos to power in 1471, and fifty-five years later another foreign house, the German Hapsburgs, began their long career as Bohemian rulers.

So, too, had Hungarian power fallen into foreign hands by a combination of exhaustion and biological accident, after the expansion and success of Louis the Great (1342–1382). First the German house of Luxembourg and then the Polish Jagellos came to power. The nobility escaped royal ambitions by electing as their king Ladislaus Jagello of Bohemia. The ambitious contender had promised to renounce the absolutist designs of the great Matthias Corvinus, king (1457–1490) of Hungary. Neither he nor his heirs could prevent the disintegration of the kingdom. The Turkish victory over Ladislaus Jagello in 1526 set the seal to the testament of the monarchy. The Hapsburgs became protectors in western Hungary. Petty Magyar princes soon were semiautonomous in the center (Transylvania) and the southeastern fringes. A great medieval kingdom was dead.

On their borders, the newly powerful western states saw Ottoman power poised for further campaigns against their civilization. It had already dismembered and absorbed Byzantium, most of Asia Minor, and the Balkans.

The eastern areas of Western civilization had thus diverged from the path of development prevalent between the Atlantic and the Elbe. There was not only the Muscovite "third Rome" with its nascent despotism and the mature despotism of the Turks. There was a permanent legacy of territorial fission everywhere else in the east.

There was the appalling poverty of the Balkans; the aristocratic excesses of power so inimical to sovereignty in Poland, Hungary, and Bohemia; the lack of resources with which to pay agents in future campaigns to defeat particularism; a wholesale failure of urban society to consolidate mercantile techniques, capital, and bourgeois ideals of liberty. There was above all else the ethnic, linguistic, and religious chaos of the eastern areas. This specter haunted Europe beyond the Elbe. Soon it took shape in the German heartland itself.

PRINCELY GOVERNMENT

The territorial consolidation of monarchical states in the West reached its apogee between 1450 and 1600, when states developed the characteristic political institutions of sovereign powers.

As kings became masters in their kingdoms, commentators on politics were especially aware that princes were wholly transforming the bases of politics. Medieval writers on kingship had focused on what rulers did to be good; Renaissance theorists and practitioners of kingship dwelled on the idea that the test of kingship was action rather than a state of being. Efficient government was the legacy of a good ruler. His business was to elaborate the structure of government. This was true in France, England, Spain, Moscow, the Turkish realms, the several German states, Scandinavia, and the major Italian states. Only in Switzerland and the Low Countries, where mercenary military power and religious magistracies usurped the place of the state, and in the Low Countries, where mercantile power was supreme, was this note of monarchy not struck.

The practical implication of efficiency was that princes sought ceaselessly to monopolize power and justice in their states. To do so meant to shape institutions directly subject to royal will and capable of mobilizing the resources of power.

Councils as Tools of Centralization

The characteristic instrument of royal power, at least in the western European monarchies, was the council. Royal domination through them had a long past history of conflict, in which opposition might seek to limit royal power by controlling the choice of councillors and the scope of their action. By the early 1500s kings in western Europe chose advisers bound only to themselves. These men were often neither aristocrats nor high churchmen. Councils in France, England, Spain, and other monarchies achieved their own institutional life in the 1500s, with clerks, records, and procedures peculiar to them. In each case judicial functions fell to offshoots of the parent body. The most effective exploitation of councils took place in Charles V's Spanish dominions, where a variety of councils existed for special tasks—finance, state affairs or diplomacy, war, even the colonial administration of New Spain. Every region and realm had its own governing council. In a similar manner, the Tudors made councils to help subordinate the recently assimilated Welsh area, the western borderlands, and the marches against Scotland.

This development was especially prominent in the more successful German territorial states. The greater princes marched toward full autonomy. Their jurists and professional administrators steadily enlarged the scope of conciliar reach into towns, ecclesiastical domains, and aristocratic franchises. Inner circles of privy councillors existed in electoral Saxony by 1574, Bavaria by 1582, and Brandenburg in 1604. Their rise was speedy in every part of Germany not too burdened with thickly spotted towns, although even in the Rhineland the elector of the Palatine was an effective state builder, despite contentious Calvinist opposition.

The elaboration of councils wholly dependent on royal initiative did not take place east of the Elbe, with the great exception of Russia. Ivan III and his successors were not content to be the "first among equals," on the Hungarian or Polish model. Victorious over the boyars and dissidents within the royal family and successful in territorial acquisition, they elaborated a "service nobility" based on conditional holdings of estates (pomestya). Slowly but surely Ivan, Vasily III, and Ivan the Terrible centralized administration. Even during the troubled period of the 1540s, a "chosen council" carried on reforms, among them a tightening of control over territorial governors, the augmentation of crown revenues from land, and the centralization of military command. These movements were capped in the 1560s and 1570s in the famous terror against the old nobility, the *oprichnina,* or special administrative court of loyal administrators in the control of the autocratic ruler.

Compare these developments with those in Hungary, where the monarchy was all but extinguished between 1480 and 1520. There, Corvinus' reforms were dismantled, and by 1507 the crown powers reposed in aristocratic hands. Perhaps the best symbol of this was the 1514 decrees, which constituted a council determined by the nobility and prelates and designated sixteen of the lesser nobility to govern with four high officials, four magnates, and four bishops. The crown could do nothing without the consent of this body. The same had happened in Poland by 1505, when the famous constitution *Nihil novi* gave to the council of aristocrats all executive power.

In the councils themselves great ministers emerged on the basis of the king's confidence rather than other bases of power. Such men lacked security of tenure; their power turned on the effectiveness and loyalty of their service. They enabled the king to do what was necessary, working through the corps of satellite ministers and administrative cadres further removed from power. The most significant of conciliar governors came to hold the office of king's secretary, and the office rapidly developed into a true ministry of state in the sixteenth century.

Wherever such governors came to prominence—and there is evidence they did in Scotland and Saxony as well as in the great monarchies—they concentrated royal power and became leading councillors. To them fell the tasks of coordinating local government with the center and handling financial and military affairs and even problems of heresy. Thomas Cromwell in the 1530s in England is perhaps the best example of an omnicompetent secretary. In 1535 he gained the power to exercise royal authority over the emerging Reformation church, as the king's vice-gerent and vicar-general in spiritual affairs. Yet in 1540 his king's wrath was his death warrant, as if to underscore the final truth: that a councillor's life and power lay wholly in his master's trust.

The problem of every prince was to make effective at a distance in his kingdom the control he exercised in his capital, where court and council made his power visible and immediate. The effort was made in a variety of ways. But one thing shared in common by the Castilian *corregidors,* English justices of the peace, French *lieutenants du roi,* German *Ministeriales* and *Kammermänner, oprichniks* in Russia, and Ottoman *kullar,* was the fact of their appointment by the crown and their subordination to the council's directives. Loyal local officers were expected to govern for the crown and be loyal to it. Rewards there were in plenty.

But in every case steps were taken to prevent the growth of entrenched local magisterial classes. The monarchs had to struggle relentlessly against the sale of the local offices of the establishment of patronage lines between the local aristocrats and the professional administrators. Ownership encouraged independence, and the degree to which local governing classes became independent was a measure of the failure of centralization. But even this caveat cannot obscure the striking way in which esprit de corps developed among royal servants in the emergent territorial states or the degree to which the rise of these classes was an adjunct of royal power at the expense not of the crown but of old nobility, clergy, and town corporations.

Law and Royal Power

The proliferation of administrators was matched by the growth of royal law officers and institutions. The era when the prerogatives of justice had been parceled out to feudatories was ending. Only England had a common law, one code of uniform jurisdiction for all regions, and there the development of other institutions of royal justice furthered centralization. In the 1500s especially, courts immediately subject to royal control or that of royal agents grew: chancery, requests, Star Chamber, the conciliar courts in the north, and the Welsh marches.

The development of new judicial bodies out of the council was not peculiar to England, however. The basic function of late medieval government was to enforce law and adjust disputes. Hence, acts of government had the form of acts of justice. What we call executive and judicial power were not separated sharply, if at all. The two French superior courts, the Parlement de Paris and the *grand conseil*, or great council, showed their conciliar origins in their procedures. French kings used the great council to subdue the many laws and jurisdictions existing in the country. The parlements were high courts that had won independence of the crown, and one of the central patterns of Valois politics was the royal attempt to rob them of that freedom.

Across the mountains in Spain, Charles V was more able than his Valois rivals to subordinate rival provincial codes and courts. Toward that end he used older institutions in preference to new creations, turning the *chancellarias y audiencias*—the system of royal courts—to the business of better and faster justice. He added judges and multiplied sessions, always in the royal interest. This tactic often raised the question in Spain that haunted the centralization of justice elsewhere: Was better royal justice compatible with the once immune, privileged elements of the polity?

Wherever aristocracies retained the upper hand, there were sharp limits set to codification, the multiplication of royal agencies of justice, and the idea that was so central to sovereignty—that the right to make law and enforce it, with strict sanctions, was the essence of power. While Ferdinand I, the Hapsburg heir to the Bohemian monarchy, was able to make effective these conciliar and curial institutions—the court council (*Hofrat*) and the privy council (*Geheimrat*)—elsewhere in eastern Europe only the Muscovite tsars and Ottoman sultans duplicated this "western" feat. Wherever the great and petty nobility triumphed in local diets, local privilege inhibited the development of anything like a national system of legal administration. In fact, over most of eastern Europe, neither royal councils, cadres, nor courts were the dominant organs of government. That place fell to the parliaments or great diets or estates, and their composition favored landlords over every other element.

That this was not the fate of the western monarchies was in large measure due to a certain conjunction of facts. Kings in the west became independent of aristocratic military service and found adequate revenues.

We have already shown how the eastern and western reactions to demographic change and its socioeconomic implications were sharply different. While peasant restraints declined rapidly west of the Elbe, serfdom grew steadily more oppressive in the eastern areas. Eastern aristocracies and churches avoided the forced transition to the different social basis of power that prevailed over feudal privilege in the west. This transformation had facilitated the growth of royal authority in the chaotic and often anarchic fifteenth century in England, Spain, Burgundy, the German territories, France, the larger Italian powers, and the Dano-Swedish area. Bohemia under the Hapsburgs was a border area in which the variant forces met. But to the east, victory went to the landowners, except in the Turkish and Russian fringes. Vast concentrations of power were built on the base of peasant labor, but this power was seigneurial rather than royal in character, and it was all the greater because of the failure of town independence vis-à-vis the aristocracies. The lords concentrated both fiscal power and military power in their hands in the eastern lands.

Monarchs and Money

In the western states power was concentrated too. There, however, it took forms other than the oppressive power of the exploitative feudal regimes. Parliaments in the western monarchies expressed this fact well, since in them the struggle to contain arbitrary force marked out the path walked by monarchs. They had to compound with their subjects for taxes; they lacked large standing armies but were independent of aristocratic levies; and while they commanded administrative staffs, courts of law, and councils, their sovereignty avoided the defects of Polish "election" and the enormities of Ivan IV's terror. They made the law, while being bound by it rather than being above it. And they had discovered in the process that their strength lay in their people's willing adherence to the royal government.

Every step on the road to power had cost money. A more ambitious government was a more expensive one. The wars in which princes consolidated their nations were fought by hired soldiers at prices inflated by new technology and the general economy. The attacks so many of them made on the independence of the church made them responsible for footing the bills of ecclesiastical government. The growing problem of poverty in the sixteenth century soon surpassed the relief capabilities of mere charity and ushered in the "poor laws" of Europe. Diplomacy itself proved a costly thing, since states were known by the "state they kept abroad." The salaries of royal officers, pensions to noblemen, the splendors of Renaissance courts, and the patronage processes by which the nobility were domesticated and changed from an aristocracy of blood to one of educated service were all expensive.

Most monarchs found traditional resources inadequate to pay sharply escalating costs. These resources consisted of profits of justice (the fees and fines paid by litigants), revenue from the crown's own estate, indirect taxes (the customs on wool, wine, meat, and cloth), and the profits of foreign treaties, or the accidents of births and death, such as direct inheritance or the wardship or escheat of aristocratic lands.

Some governments experimented with special indirect taxes: a French salt monopoly (*gabelle*), a Spanish tax of 10 percent on commercial transactions (*alcabala*), a dominant role by the English crown in the marketing of wool and wool products (the staple system at Calais), and a Muscovite policy of wholesale confiscation of aristocratic estates and their conversion into "service farms" (*pomestye*). When these did not suffice, loans were common: from native bourgeoisie (Louis XII), Antwerp bankers (Charles V), the nobility, town corporations, bishops, and Italian bankers (Henry VIII). There were also sales of government bonds in France and special government issues in Spain.

Yet none of these practices did more than disguise the fever that was a symptom of deep malaise. The way toward solvency in the monarchies led through the pockets of the ordinary subjects. Expenditure was greater than income on a scale that necessitated direct taxes. The view of ordinary subjects was, however, the traditional one, that kings should practice good economy and "live on their own." Hence to go to the estates and parliaments for money required some weighing of royal needs versus private interests. Or else how should a king put his hand into subjects' purses? The people were averse to helping make themselves poorer, and the king lacked the authority that might compel them to do so. The lack of telephones, printing offices, rapid transport, and a standing army made the royal power seem remote and unreal in many regions. In peacetime, Francis I (1515–1547), the greatest of the French Renaissance kings of the Valois dynasty, had fewer than two modern divisions under arms. His subjects were not disarmed relative to his strength by advances in the technology of war. The German and Swiss mercenaries, along with Poles, Greeks, Italians, and Englishmen who made up Holy Roman Empire, French, and some English armies were often unpaid, unfed, and unreliable.

It was thus both necessary and politic in the western monarchies to meet gentlemen and merchants to discuss money. The evidence is strong that the pressure of finance had pushed developments towards what we may well call dualism in France, Burgundy, Castile, Aragon, England, Brandenburg, Saxony, Bavaria, most of Italy, Scandinavia, and the western Slavic kingdoms by 1500. Rulers augmented their power in representative assemblies by making concessions to the liberty of their subjects—or rather liberties, since no abstract idea of freedom was meant—and so winning their loyalty and their consent to taxation. Sometimes the assemblies, or estates, were general, as in England and Brandenburg. Sometimes there were several provincial estates, as in France and Spain. No matter. Taxation simply required the consent of subjects. The American colonists who said so in the 1760s and 1770s stood in a very long line of those who looked askance at any unfettered royal claim to the private property of common people.

Parliamentary Government Versus Sovereignty

Thus the English Parliament, Spanish Cortes, French Estates General and provincial, boyar dumas, and various diets and Riksdagen became vital sources of power and instruments of monarchical growth. In time the principle of consent was practically defeated in Spain and France. In England it triumphed, as it did in some German parliaments for decades, even generations. Where its demise was absolute, monarchy sailed the clear waters of greater royal power, as for example in France, Muscovy, Spain, and Portugal. When the idea of consent became a basic part of the disposition of power, the tide ran more toward very limited forms of royal power. Where the triumph over the taxing power was absolute, states could not flourish.

Clearly, it would be simple-minded to hail the victory of the Slavic diets as victories for law, order, social welfare, and popular government. It would also be wrong to think that English bourgeois liberty derived from the triumph of consent over royal arbitrariness. The record seems clear that the rise of territorial states was part of a long process in which liberty and tyranny were possibilities arranged in a variety of ways. Parliaments were not, in origin, enemies of royal power. And royal power in its advancement was often vital to the development of subjects' rights and protections against the most selfish and oppressive forces of town and countryside.

In the English, French, Spanish, Netherlands, and German representative assemblies, deputies of the towns, gentry, and upper aristocracy, both lay and spiritual, assembled. The same happened in Scandinavia, the Italian kingdom of Naples, and in the Slavic lands. The gentry and nobility often usurped town seats wholesale. Yet it was generally true in western Europe that urban interests met rural ones on a better footing than was the case elsewhere. And in the assemblies of the West deputies held what was in effect full power (*plena potestas*) to give political advice and also judicial consent to motifs of government brought forward by the royal councillors in their midst. What in England became a permanent feature of political life at the center—the struggles between deputies of the communities and the king on a national stage—in France, Spain, and the Netherlands took place at another level. It was in fact the crown's wish in every major state to see the power of deputies increased rather than belittled. For if the assemblies so empowered could be open to persuasion, then the real power of the monarchy might be enhanced by their bargains.

Thus town and country became the focus of international political fights that reflected the efforts of rulers to procure tractable assemblies. Unscrupulous or weak deputies might sell the interests of their communities, whether for personal rewards or merely out of fear. Yet parliamentary bodies in many states in the sixteenth century —Spain, the Netherlands, England, France, Brandenburg, and Saxony —became the center of a movement that, even within the framework of politics, was revolutionary. Struggles were waged about financial matters, of course; but there were also great battles about general political, economic, and religious affairs. Where the crown preferred finally to abandon parliaments altogether, this was as much a sign of political failure and the diminution of royal power as it was a harbinger of the rise of a royal absolutism. Elizabeth I of England was a stronger monarch than was Charles I; she preferred to compromise and have the crown's needs met by Parliament rather than the sort of costly victory won by her Stuart successors, for their tyranny of rule without Parliament made them pauper kings. And pauper kings were weak kings.

Whenever subjects had fundamental rights and reasons to distrust their rulers, debate became a sure token of the advance from dynastic monarchy and its politics to those of national monarchy and national politics. This experience was the bitter fruit of every Hapsburg governor-general in the Spanish Netherlands, before the revolt and in its various stages. Don John of Austria, the duke of Parma, the spokesmen of the Catholic southern provinces (the Union of Arras), and William of Orange were aware of the powers of the deputies as advocates of the welfare of their provinces and towns. When they agreed on a major issue, that of resisting Spain's economic and religious policies in the half-century from 1560 to 1610, the greatest monarchy in Christendom was unable to put down their "common weal."

Few parliamentary spokesmen anywhere tried to connect their powers to a theory of sovereignty. But their stubborn survival in the western monarchies imposed limits to the sovereignty of dynasts. The estates of Holland made a formal notice of their sovereignty in 1621, long before the English parliamentarians did so or the French *frondeurs* ("plotters against the crown") of 1648–1653. They did so in the name of the authority and power of the "people," however limited that nebulous term might be in application. And this act was symbolic of the vast gulf dividing the nature of governments in the Atlantic communities and those of eastern Europe, where the triumph of the estates was narrowly aristocratic and a reflection of the power of a feudal, landed class. In the west, even in France, the term *absolutism* is misapplied to royal government. There was too much of consent in the disposal of power. In the east, however, where popular power failed, the choice proved to be between absolutism and a lack of governance. There, no parliament elaborated the modern "state" theory enshrined in the preamble to the English "Act prohibiting appeals to Rome" in 1533:

> This realm of England is an Empire . . . governed by one Supreme Head and King . . . unto whom a body politic compact of all sorts and degrees of people . . . by the names of Spirituality and Temporality be bounden. . . .

FOUR

The reformation of Christian society

> I am bound by the Scriptures I have quoted and my conscience is captive to the Word of God. I cannot and will not retract anything. . . .
> Luther, at Worms, April 18, 1521

> For it would be a great shame to me and to you . . . if in our time not only heresy but suspicion of heresy . . . should through our negligence dwell after us in the hearts of men. . . . I am determined to proceed against him ['_uther] as a notorious heretic . . . for that reason I am absolutely determined to stake on this course my kingdoms . . . and my body and blood, my life and soul. . . .
> Charles V, at Worms, April 19, 1521

INTRODUCTION

The Reformation in the sixteenth century was another aspect of transformation in Europe. The various movements of reform cannot be understood outside the wider context of Western ideas and values, however. In this chapter, therefore, the central issue we will deal with is that of the combination of events and movements that to us seem to account for the alienation of millions of people from their own cultural heritage.

Again, it is basic to our view that the crisis of the fourteenth century produced pressures to transform thought and expression as well as economic, social, and political structures. Thus we begin our account of the Reformation not with biographical sketches of leaders—Luther, Erasmus, Calvin, and others—but rather with some aspects of the mental life of the masses, of the followers, without whom leaders preach only to open space. And in order to get at what was characteristic of the spiritual life of the masses, we look at the impact of religion on some very ordinary things. How, for instance, did the doctrine of the sacraments work psychologically? This seems to us a more basic question for society than what obscure lecturers and writers finally decided which titles in church law might lawfully be dispensed by the pope.

Because painters and poets as well as preachers reflect changes in mental climate, we often look at familiar works more for what they tell us about popular culture than for what they tell us about the history of style, while commenting on style in passing. In a sense, our treatment of the humanists from Petrarch to Erasmus has a similar orientation. We treat more fully themes connecting Christian values to secular life than topics in the history of literature and philosophy. The extensive study of Lorenzo Valla illustrates this perspective, as it also ties his work to our general theme of alienation and the urge to reform. Erasmus is viewed from the same perspective: to discover in him what was common in the mental life of reformers and those multitudes who shattered the unity of Christendom after 1517.

Our discussion of the Reformation is therefore rooted in a sense of malaise in the church and in the often grotesque practice of religion against which Luther and his spiritual peers raised their protests. Since our purpose is to convey the nature of the mental life of the age, not a capsule-sized encyclopedia of its events, we use broad themes and prefer some treatments in depth to a universal survey.

Our hope is always to convey the view of the past from a social perspective that brings into view the totality of an age, with emphasis on what were the transformative elements. This hope makes it necessary to employ generalizations and to treat the character of society as a whole, rather than to suppose this character is only the sum of the narrative histories of Britain, France, Germany, Italy, and the other political divisions of modern Europe. Nowhere does this seem more important than in the discussion of the loss of spiritual unity in the West.

ON THE EDGE OF THE ABYSS

Before 1300 the publicists serving the church had developed a theory of papal sovereignty. Popes exercised full power and their office had at its disposal the administrative and executive instruments of a powerful court and council. In theory at least, papal authority over Christendom still was absolute.

Boniface VIII most clearly reiterated all of this in his great dispute with the kings of France. His bull *Unam sanctam* (1302) admitted no departure from the claim to wield temporal and spiritual powers. The papal monarchy had been forced to compromise its claims in fact, as it did over taxes in the bull *Clericis laicos* in 1296. For it needed money as much as any government did. Hence its political history in the later Middle Ages was like that of the centralizing territorial states.

Even in the fourteenth century, however, the facade of papal monarchy had cracked. Germans put down papally inspired bishops' elections. The English used parliamentary laws to blackmail priests into resisting papal assertions of rights. French kings in effect made the popes "annexes of France" during the long period when popes lived at Avignon. This "Babylonian captivity" (1309–1378) culminated in the spectacle of rival popes. French and Italian papal candidates secured election simultaneously and their controversies during the Great Schism (1378–1417) eroded the authority of the church itself.

Yet it would be an error to conclude that the Reformation was merely the last stage of a revolution to divide Christendom and cast down its old monarchy. The church was more than a state. Cardinals and popes patronized letters; most of the great Renaissance painters and sculptors held important papal commissions, as did theologians and lawyers who worked in the magnificent papal libraries. The church was in so many respects the center of civilization in the 1300s and the 1400s that its failure must inevitably appear to be more than a constitutional revolution in Christendom.

The late medieval church was sick in spirit as well as body. Europe in the fourteenth century fell prey to growing disorders. We have studied the struggles of princes and estates, merchants and craftsmen, peasants and lords. The contests between popes and princes, or ordinary people and their priests, were simply another manifestation of the endless strife of the era. Society itself seemed unstable, violent, lawless. The condition was common in Germany, where the lack of an effective central political system gave scope to unbridled power.

Italians in 1500 found northern Europeans religious to a fault. They took the sacraments in excess. They built churches and monasteries without visible limits to their zeal. They bought more indulgences and made more pilgrimages than did Mediterranean Christians. They collected relics more avidly, and their piety was proverbial.

Popular piety did not exhaust itself in buildings or in their gorgeous decoration. Preaching had risen steadily in importance since 1100 A.D. Many saw in the Word of God a Christian duty second only to the priestly administration of the sacraments. Yet there was more censure of the church's enemies in most sermons than summons to battle with those devils within the church. In the fourteenth century, drawing on the Gospel to urge reform through an active preaching ministry was not popular with high authorities.

Radical Reformers

John Wycliffe (d. 1384) in England and John Huss (d. 1415) were deemed heretics in their time and after their deaths. Huss was a Bohemian (Czech) academic from the University of Prague. He was condemned for a variety of teachings deemed heretical and touching questions of papal power, the eucharist, the nature of the Trinity and of sacramental grace, the powers of the priesthood, and the exercise of temporal wealth and power by clergymen. Many of Huss' views were developed long after they were first expounded by Wycliffe, whose work Huss knew. Both men reacted against excessive formalism in religion and abuses of power by princes of the church. Each reached toward the goal of a reformation of religion and churchmanship. Wycliffe and Huss shared a desire for a religion purged of gorgeous spectacle and gross superstition and abstract doctrines beyond the comprehension of believers. Wycliffe was never in his lifetime successfully convicted of heresy, but he was silenced and forbidden to teach certain doctrines at Oxford. He was posthumously condemned, however, in 1414, when Huss was convicted at the Council of Constance of maintaining heresy. Despite the fact that the Czech reformer had gone to Constance under an imperial safe-conduct, he was seized, tried, and executed. The same fate overtook the Florentine radical reformer Savonarola, who early in the 1490s had introduced a furious puritanism among the citizens of the wealthy Italian city. Thus the thrust of radical reform was blunted.

Wycliffe, Huss, and Savonarola were feared by those in authority because radical reform seemed always to involve a bid to under-

An anonymous painting by a sixteenth-century artist showing the Piazza della Signoria on May 23, 1498, when Savonarola was burned at the stake. The large dark structure, which is the town hall, typifies the medieval fortress-like style of public buildings before the classicizing features of Renaissance architecture. *Scala—Art Reference Bureau.*

mine the structure of all authority. This was demonstrably true in Florence, where Savonarola was a major political force. Wycliffe was associated with the political programs of the popular rebels and dissenters called Lollards in England. And their repeated risings early in the fifteenth century provoked savage acts of repression by the government. In Bohemia, Huss' more radical followers were basic to the revolutionary movement called the Hussite Rebellion, which fanned the flames of civil war in Bohemia for five years before giving rise to even more radical splinter groups (Taborites) who preached the overthrow of all authority then established in the kingdom.

Political disrepute alone does not explain the failure of the radical reformers. Wycliffe and Huss appeared before the advent of printing from movable type. Savonarola was a successful propagandist in print, but the facts of technology limited earlier advocates of thoroughgoing reform, who made little headway against the conformist manuals written for the benefit of parish priests. Luther complained he had never heard the Gospel preached plainly in a church.

Popular Religion

The sort of gospel religion associated with Protestant churches had a weak hold on popular audiences. Far more potent were the flamboyant varieties of religious culture; anticlerical religion of the humanists;[1] the religion taught children at their mother's knee; and the pious devotions used among the Brethren of the Common Life. This last was a late fourteenth-century pietistic sect of men and women, city folk in the Netherlands, who had property in common and who exercised control over education through their own schools. The Brethren spread a simple popular religion of prayer and devotion in emulation of Christ's humility. Luther recalled learning the Lord's Prayer and Ten Commandments from his mother. She also gave him a love of the simple hymns that flourished well before his break with Rome. He edited texts of the mystic tradition. He went to a Brethren school.

Devotional forms of popular religion were given new life by Gutenberg's invention. In the early history of printing, humanist tomes and heavy books of theology were not as widely circulated as were hymn books, collections of psalms, prayers, creeds, with translations and paraphrases. Wherever people could read or listen to the readings of friends, especially in the towns, these books found eager audiences.

Simple people who turned away from visiting shrines, making pilgrimages, and buying indulgences found comfort also in certain pious associations. Lay associations for devotional ends had long ancestries. Men who believed in Rome and accepted its clergy had for centuries also struggled against clerical pretensions and the holy monopoly of education. Some had given an eager reception to ver-

---

[1] On the humanists who preached a biblical religion centered in the forgiveness of God rather than His vengeance, see pp. 111–119.

nacular Scriptures. Subject to strong persecutions, these fraternal cells were never wholly rooted out of cities. They were often helped by such men as Rulman Merswin of Strasbourg and John Ruysbroeck of Brussels. By the 1380s Ruysbroeck was closely associated with Gerhard Groote, who shaped a community of laymen and women into the Brethren of the Common Life in 1384, in Deventer, Holland.

These Christian communist societies expanded rapidly in the Netherlands, Alsace, and the western German territories in the fifteenth century. They maintained a school system through which the "new devotion" was taught to new generations. They also formed a connection with the Windesheim Augustinian monks. The Windesheim Congregation itself became a powerful second spearhead of reform, spreading throughout western and central Germany by 1480.

Perhaps even more important is the evidence that the various Brethren groups seemed to be generating a nonconformist religious society on a European scale. Bohemian sectarians, the Waldensians of Savoy and France, the Brethren of the German circles, and some English Lollards used a common catechism at least as early as 1498. Editions of it in French, German, Italian, and Bohemian dialects survived into the 1530s. There also floated freely in such circles a number of mystical treatises, fragments of a vernacular Bible, some sermons, and other writings. Even *The German Theology,* edited by Luther in 1521, was a part of the underground literature.

The Idea of Death

These varieties of religious life, however, were not the ways of the masses. To grasp mass culture we must remember death was the most immediate experience of every man. Quite apart from the hazard of disease, daily life itself was violent and uncertain. Whole generations of survivors grew to maturity in constant fear of starvation or the collective memory of mass death. The marginal nature of life produced in people a longing for the security denied by everyday experience.

The violence of life was thus both personal and public. The contrast between pleasure and pain was absolute and direct; joy and suffering were near neighbors. Life had a frightening passion and excitement now being restored to the realm of immediate experience. In the twentieth century, death has come back to us through television. We live with genocide, the bomb, ideological war, mass starvation, ceremonial public executions, demonstrations for and against ultimate truth, patriotic war cults, and peace cults, each with its shrines and pilgrimages.

It may not surprise us, then, to find in the popular religious culture of the two centuries before 1500 solemn and impressive rituals making sacred the facts of ordinary life. Formality and benedictions hallowed journeys, work, birth, marriage, copulation, death, the processions of lepers, executions, the processes of justice, and acts of war.

Examples of the consecration of ordinary things reveal the character of popular religion. Early in the sixteenth century, burghers were called by bells to the celebration of a special mass in commemoration of the flight from Egypt by Mary and Joseph. The mass was capped by audience responses of brays and the celebrant's three brays at the elevation of the sacrament, in place of the familiar bells and the "sanctus, sanctus, sanctus." This, by way of honoring the ass that gave transport to the mother of Christ!

Richard the Preacher, a noted fifteenth-century Parisian friar of the Franciscan order, preached on death, judgment, heaven, and hell for ten consecutive days in the Cemetery of the Holy Innocents, from 5 a.m. until nearly noon. The story is told of the Dominican Saint Vincent Ferrer stopping a sermon on Christ's Passion to draw attention to an adulterous couple being led to their death-by-burning. He had the couple seated beneath his pulpit, the more effectively to teach them and his flock the justness of the sentence. His words charred the couple, leaving only bones in their place; and the people thought the reputed saint had saved the illicitly passionate couple by the holy passion of his words.

If punishments were cruel and sins great, there was also in spectacle the hope of Christ's compassion for man. In 1500, in a German village four blind men caught begging were forced to try to beat a pig let loose in their midst. The beggar lucky enough to kill the pig got it as a check on hunger. And the point could not be lost on men who were themselves constantly moving from joy to despair. The fate of beggars was their fate too, in a world that often seemed an endless calamity of bad government, clerical oppression, war, pestilence, and every misery of the spirit attendant on the obsessive fear of hellfire and damnation.

The popular religion had its fundamental capital invested in death. The mendicant preachers specialized in it. Christian thought

A woodcut by Albrecht Dürer entitled *Apocalypse.* **The violence and uncertainty of daily life in the fifteenth century helps to account for the prevalence of death in Renaissance art.** *Marburg—Art Reference Bureau.* ▶

about sin and its deserts was being compressed into a frantic, gloomy vision of life. Woodcuts on the dance of death theme outnumbered every other fifteenth-century motif. The advent of printing merely extended the impact of the sermons. Prints were new guides to a holy life, like those "bibles of the illiterate" drawn on the walls of churches. Their purpose was to press the complexity of death in its relationship to human life into the framework of contempt for the natural and the perishable. Men were directed to think about their mutability, the vanity of beauty, and the unrelenting will of Death to drag them off unprepared to meet God.

Much of Renaissance painting, poetry, and sculpture was devoted to death, despite the habit we have of looking at the gaiety and optimism in those works and at the pastoral and idyllic elements in culture of the period. After 1350 the imagination of Christian artists and writers perfected the *memento mori* in a spate of enthusiasm that lasted until the late sixteenth century. Depictions of countless crucifixions vied with horrible tomb sculptures; hideous, naked corpses with devastating literary images of perdition and the living representation in dramas like *Everyman*. Bucolic themes in art were less familiar to ordinary men than were some of the macabre prints of Dürer. For each new play on man's dignity there was more than one performance of the dance of death. The result of this was to take attention away from every religious idea stressing compassion and joy. The trouble was not that popular religion was ethereal. Rather, it was earthbound in a hideous way, as priests and faithful alike responded to the massive psychological pressure of disaster in human affairs.

Those responses were saturating the religious environment with fears that were expressed in public ceremony and church ritual. The reaction of the church policy was to direct every action toward earning salvation through the church's monopoly of grace.

Materialistic Aspects of Religious Faith

In the economy of salvation men were taught to merit their wage by the character of their work, which meant the sacraments—from which Christ's grace flowed to men—and also the hallowing of ordinary life. Pierre d'Ailly warned that there was a great danger inherent in making physical presentations of holy things. Men might find in the mechanical dispensation of grace in the sacraments no relief from the anxiety induced by excessive morbidity. And they might sharply confuse their observances, images, relics, and the works of men for the redeeming work of Christ's sacrifice.

That the danger was real may be seen in the dominance of the saints. Cults, pilgrimages, and shrines brought men face to face with saints as part of a vast system to augment the power of churches and churchmen. There were too many holy days, vigils, and mass demonstrations of faith marred by superstition. Religious orders competed for people's loyalty. Pierre d'Ailly's *De reformatione* deplored all of this. He wanted to limit the mendicants, because they took alms from the truly poor and those not physically able to work. He wished to ban the sale of indulgences, or letters that promised the remission of penalties for sin for those who did good works.

The practice of granting indulgences had grown up in the twelfth century, perhaps to some good, in that it gave men the hope of drawing on Christ's endless treasury of merit. But in the 1400s it seemed to suggest nothing more than that merit was for sale. The idea militated against the inward reformation of life that d'Ailly and others made central to faith and salvation. Luther made the doctrine of the treasury of merit and its associated sale of indulgences into the first battleground of the revolution of 1517. Briefly stated, the idea of the treasury of merit was that Christ's death had piled up all the merit necessary for human redemption. The critical question was how this massive treasure might be assigned to people. How might they draw on this bank? One answer, which became increasingly popular in the fourteenth century, was through the performance of good works. A pilgrimage or pious deed might encourage God to remit part of the penalty—especially time in purgatory—imposed for sins. However, this notion lent itself to corruption easily. Money gifts became a common substitute for the hard acts of contrition. Thus it was said that God's indulgence to sinners could be bought, and hawkers did sell letters of indulgence promising the remission of penalties to eager givers. To the reformers this seemed a crass commerce in Christ's gift, which He had himself paid for with His terrible Passion on the Cross.

The church had encouraged other strange practices. Men debated in public whether the Virgin had taken an active sexual role in the conception of Christ. Some thought it important to ask the faithful to ponder whether the body of Christ would have decomposed had He not been resurrected. People kept statues of the Virgin with panels that opened to show a miniature Trinity inside. Even the sacrament of the altar was profaned by speculation. Some men went to numerous daily masses because they had heard they could not grow old in the presence of Christ's Body and Blood.

The priesthood itself, or rather the idea of the character given to men in the sacrament of holy orders, became the object of base humor. The father of the Dutch humanist Agricola, a monk, received news of his son's birth after he said his ordination mass. "God's blessing on it! Today I have twice become a father," he said.

Within the church buildings themselves the danger of profanation from approved practices showed in those not sanctioned. Audiences at mass were noisy, often uncomprehending of the Latin bawled at them. Prostitutes used churches as rendezvous points, and lovers for trysts. Pilgrim places were famous for their debauchery, as we are reminded by Thomas a Kempis: "Those who go on pilgrimages rarely become saints!"

Thus it was that toward the end of the fifteenth century great familiarity with holy things and the flamboyant character of popular religion masked discontents. There was both an unexampled religious emotion in the people and an unhealthy, nervous climate of fear, anxiety, and despair. These mixed attitudes encouraged superficial piety and mechanical celebrations. Holy things, rituals, acts, ceremonies, and popular practices were given as a sop to people in need of apprehending the reality of a saving grace.

The Search for Spiritual Assurance

The psychological function of assurance was necessary. But it was increasingly questioned whether saints' images and shrines would lead to any but the crudest, most manipulative kind of religious life. People desperately needed protection against the forces of a hostile nature and social predators. Yet it was increasingly doubted that safety lay in a wild, animistic practice. Erasmus, the great Dutch scholar and humanist propagandist, the so-called Prince of Humanists, put it clearly when he said of saints that they must be more malevolent in Paradise than ever they were on earth. Rumors did feed a popular belief that the saints who patronized the human body and its parts would send horrible maladies if the saints were not suitably honored. One hundred years earlier, Jean Gerson had urged the Council of Constance to reform and keep a simple faith.

The connections between popular consciousness, mass events in society, modes of thought and expression, and spiritual directions are difficult to establish. Yet Millard Meiss' great book on Florentine and Sienese painting between 1350 and 1375 shows how the Black Death transformed the social basis of life. Meiss says the transformation is reflected in the town annals and contemporary literature, such as the work of Boccaccio, who was one of the first great vernacular literary figures of the Italian Renaissance. His *Decameron* was set in the context of a flight from plague and took the form of a series of bawdy stories told by the fleeing gentlewomen. It was against the same background of slaughter sketched by Boccaccio that Saint Catherine of Siena wrote of mystical experiences. Artists, writers, and saints showed their quick sensitivity to a shift in the religious climate, as Siena's population shrank from 42,000 to 15,000 in two decades.

Painters in the 1350s showed the restless violence in the fierce brutality of gestures and techniques. Life was agonizing. Barna of Siena, who flourished in the second half of the fourteenth century, fixed the transformation in the fresco cycle at San Gemignano that is attributed to him in Ghiberti's *Commentaries* (1447).

Escape from calamity lay in a closer reliance on the church. Violent scenes invoke the horror of life, and men were directed toward a God remote, austere, superhuman. This artistic attitude both anticipated the maturity of a shifting popular culture and religion and reflected its origins. Stylistic changes moved painting away from the humane grace and ease of Giotto, and it quickly became nonnaturalistic in scale and spatial relations; the figures were somber, without emotions of softness, and always frontal in presentation. The subjects reflected a deepened religious sense, often mystical, detached from the gentleness of cultivated life, but always showing to patrons and the common people their own cataclysmic experience.

When the later Renaissance painters and writers overwhelmed bleakness and anxiety with joy and their revival of a softened naturalism, in the age of da Vinci, Raphael, and Michelangelo, when God appeared more accessible to Adam on the Sistine ceiling, Luther was bringing to Christians another religious view as well. The new buoyancy of the period after 1475 made the hoary, guilt-ridden popular religion of the 1400s less effective and less necessary. And it had at its command the humanist tools of a century of doubt and criticism.

HUMANISM AND REFORM

That criticism, schism, and heresy would flourish in the mental and physical environment of the era we have described seems predictable. That its chief forms were fantastic millennarian sects, pietistic associations, and the calmer speculations of humanists is a matter of fact. About the fraternities we have had some say; the sects will occupy our attention in another context. Now we will look more closely at what was certainly the most important general cultural achievement of the fifteenth century—the rise and spread of humanism. Its central concern was for the quality of human life, its relation to both nature and God. The humanists were constantly in quest of the highest of human goods—wisdom.

The development of humanism marked a stage in the triumph of a lay culture over the ecclesiastical culture of the earlier medieval centuries. To know something of how this happened, it is necessary to look once again toward Italy, where the "new learning" took root and grew earlier than elsewhere. There it assumed the character it was to have in its migrations: informed by the study of history and philology, rooted in the classics, concerned with human dignity, profoundly influencing the arts, determined to alter the culture of the West by the institution of educational reforms, and deeply committed to reconciling man with God.

There were "humanists" well before the noun *humanista* was in common use to designate a group of teachers and students in the "humanities" (*studia humanitatis*). Humanists were concerned to know "how life might be humanely lived," a rallying cry borrowed from Cicero. They believed that the culture of classical times, based on rhetorical and historical studies, formed the character of men in a certain way.

Humanists had varied ideas about what cultural ideals should prevail. They were Platonists, Stoics, Aristotelians, Christians, or even skeptics. For humanism was less a philosophy than it was a method of approaching the classical past. The stress was on the fact that the application of historical and philological techniques to texts revealed the true sense by anchoring them in their time.

This conviction remade intellectual life and refashioned the arts and scholarship. It transformed not only secular literature but sacred literature as well. The historical bent of humanist thought provided a rallying point for law reform, the criticism of morality and religion, and the demand for a return to "biblical" values and modes of Christian life.

Humanist consciousness was profoundly historical. Early figures like Petrarch (1304–1374), Giotto (1266–1337), and Boccaccio (1313–1375) were aware of the gulf that separated classical learning from the inheritance they had received from their immediate ancestors. This they explained by sharply marking off antiquity from the "dark" and "barbarous" age that fell upon the West in the fourth century. They felt themselves to be "modern." They rejected the "middle ages" that separated them from antiquity. This historical stance brought into being the familiar Western view, that our own history has had ancient, medieval, and modern phases. The transformation of mental perspective was startling. Pagan antiquity became the essence of what was good in culture, while the Christian Middle Ages were condemned as decadent, deficient in aesthetics and wisdom, truth and God.

From Petrarch's revival of the classical poets to the insistence of Erasmus (1467–1536) that monks and scholastic theologians had lost the understanding of Christ's doctrine and mission, that theme was constant. The humanists hailed Aristotle, Paul, Cicero, and Augustine as their contemporaries, while looking at scholastics alive in their time as relics, representatives of barbarism, and enemies of elegance.

Their archaeological enthusiasm exhumed works of classical literature, philosophy, science, art, architecture, history, and theology. Yet their rediscoveries were less important than the way in which they approached texts and relics. They abandoned the habit of making Christian symbols of classical materials. And they sought through a knowledge of classical language, through philology and criticism, to uncover the original meaning of the works. They were in short no longer intent on making the masters of the distant past servants of a "medieval" vision of the universe. Some humanists, such as Marsilio Ficino (1433–1499), did attempt to make a Christian out of Plato. Most, however, used the tools of linguistics, archaeology, and historical criticism to gain an unalloyed understanding of ancient arts, law, philosophy, ethics, political ideas, and the nature of early Christian institutions and thought.

The Attack on Religious Tradition

In no area of endeavor were the efforts of the humanists more unsettling than in that of religious thought and organization. This was true in at least three significant senses: humanists sharply questioned the authenticity of papal pretensions; they cast doubt on natural theology, preferring instead a relentless search for the pristine Christianity of Scripture; and they constantly turned against the religion of tradition, especially in its flamboyant, mechanistic varieties. Thus their intellectual preferences came sharply to reinforce the simpler biblicism and pietism of dissident popular religion. Their emphasis on moral freedom and human dignity was unsettling to authority.

This we can perhaps dramatize by looking briefly at Lorenzo Valla's attack on papal authority, the rise of the "positive" theology of revealed truth, and the use made of biblical and patristic materials by Erasmus and kindred spirits north of the Alps.

Valla (1407–1457) ransacked the papal library in a humanist pursuit of philosophy and Christian ethics. He also clearly elaborated ideas that led to charges of heresy and the enmity of powerful churchmen.

His dialogue *On Sensual Pleasure* seemed too favorable to the notion that virtue was not its own reward, while saying openly that monkish mortification of the flesh was against nature. He castigated those who introduced philosophy into problems of making sense of difficult scriptural passages in *On Free Will*. The implied attack on scholasticism was made sharper in his *Dialectical Disputations*. He condemned blind followers of Aristotle who knew only "treacherous" Arabic translations and who used syllogisms instead of a practical dialectical approach based on simple language.

In his *On the Profession of the Monks*, Valla bitterly opposed those who followed human "rules" in preference to the divine one given to the Apostles by Christ. Every Christian, lay or clerical, had to follow the one sure way to moral perfection. Love became for Valla the force drawing Christians to Christ. Love was the dynamic of God's sacrifice and also of each man's orientation toward God. Valla does not draw the "Protestant" conclusion, that all believers are priests without need of priestly intermediaries. But he does say bishops should be teachers of their flocks rather than wielders of temporal power over them.

Valla's most decisive attacks on traditional Christianity came in his proof that the document preserved among the pseudo-Isidorian *Decretals* of A.D. 840, purporting to be Constantine's donation of spiritual and temporal authority over the western parts of the Roman Empire, was a forgery. A document used repeatedly to assert papal control over territory was a precious thing.

Opponents of papal power had attacked it for centuries. Legists in the emperor's service from the twelfth century to the fourteenth considered it spurious. Dante, who used humanist techniques of criticism, argued against it in terms of political theory.

What Valla did that was utterly shattering was to apply historical and philological criticism to prove a host of anachronisms in it. Its confessional clauses used doctrinal theses about the Trinity, the Incarnation, and iconoclasm elaborated at councils held in A.D. 325, 451, and 787, well after the conversion of Constantine and his grateful "donation." The word *fief* was used in the donation clause, a term created only after Constantine's death. *Lorum* was a term wrongly used in a description of Constantine. The emperor would hardly have worn a mule harness in place of a shoulder strap! Valla's curse, "May God destroy you, vulgar scribe, who attributed barbarous language to a cultured age," showed both his self-delight and the affront to his sensibility.

If Valla's ideas focused and clarified a tradition of humanist criticism already a century old at his death, others extended it in different directions and met nonhumanist critics on the common ground bordering their own. This was especially true among humanists concerned to know the relationships between philosophy and theology.

Wisdom and Religious Truth

Scholastics, reformers, and humanists agreed that wisdom was the highest good. Yet there was not so great a distance between Luther and Aquinas in their definition of wisdom as there was between them as to what instruments, if any, brought man toward it. How were divine wisdom and human prudence and virtue related? How was man's world of nature related to the supernatural world of grace?

Since St. Augustine's time Christian wisdom had embraced both divine and natural things. This tradition made it important for Christians to ask whether there was not confusion about the "scientific" and "spiritual" dimensions of "Christian wisdom." The humanists stressed in their reading of Cicero, Seneca, and the Fathers the notion of wisdom as an "art of living." This was especially true among the German humanists concerned with practical piety and the character of popular religion. Their emphasis led them to distrust what they took to be the scholastic emphasis on the "scientific" aspects of wisdom. Thus the great theologian Alexander of Hales seemed to perpetuate errors of the "dark ages" in teaching that men were moved toward God because of the knowledge they had of Him. Scholastics had elaborated a theology and a doctrine of the sacraments in keeping with the idea that the helps required to strengthen men depended in some sense on a scientific and systematic approach to the religion of Scriptures. Against this "scientific" concern, with its elaborate apparatus of rational theology and mechanistic faith, Petrarch, Erasmus, and Luther railed.

They agreed that wisdom came to men through participation in God's grace. But they were concerned to drain Christian truth of the adulterating fluid of philosophical theology and scientific speculation. Theologians like Wycliffe exhibited a radical skepticism that man could know God through the study of the natural order. The "biblical" humanists insisted that revelation alone was central to right religion.

All relied heavily on Scriptures. One favorite text was 1 Corinthians 1:19–24: "For it is written, I will destroy the wisdom of the wise, and will bring to nothing the understanding of sages. . . . Hath not God made foolish the wisdom of the world? . . . Greeks seek after wisdom, but we preach Christ crucified, unto the Jews a stumbling block. . . ." Tertullian in the second century had noted the ending of the text, "But unto them which are called . . . Christ the power of God [is] the wisdom of God," and put his famous question: "What has Athens to do with Jerusalem?" The humanists understood Tertullian's question in the context of their spiritual-academic revival of Athens and Rome. The humane studies were required to strip away the vain clothing given to cover God's naked truth. Christian wisdom lay in no rational ascent from the world of senses to that of grace on the logical ladders of the scholastics. It required a leap of faith in the souls of men stunned by the vision of Christ revealed in Scripture. Faith, hope, and charity were not intellectual achievements; they were not gifts produced by the use men made of the world of things—cults, pilgrimages, indulgences, and self-inflicted wounds. True faith took form in the believer through the simple act of his exposure to God's redemptive promise in the Gospel.

Humanists claimed to find this compact idea in certain patristic writings. John Colet (1467–1519), Jacque LeFèvre d'Étaples (1460–1536), Guillaume Budé (1468–1540), Valla, Johann Reuchlin (1455–1522), Konrad Celtis (1459–1508), and Erasmus led the way in the early sixteenth-century elaboration of it. The attack on the several "scientific," metaphysical traditions was thus a truly international movement.

One special contribution of fourteenth- and fifteenth-century scholastics of the so-called modern way (via moderna) was vital. William of Occam (d. 1347) and Nicholas of Cusa (1401–1464) had insisted that religious truth was exclusively found in revelation. They were the philosophers of Christian positivism. All self-knowledge and all knowledge of being that was not material, especially of God, lay outside of man's investigative capacities. Occam rejected entirely arguments from analogy in theology, leaving only room for an unknowable God, except insofar as He manifests himself to men in revelations. Only by our faith in His word do we "know" Him. That was the stern, forbidding sentence, exiling "natural" theologies and putting in their place what was positive, what stood by revelation. Occam said explicitly that theology was not a science, had no demonstrable propositions, and could not be taught. The truth of God's existence stood sola fide, by faith alone.

The teaching of Cusa perfected the idea of buoying up faith by stripping it of the life jacket of reason. He celebrated "learned ignorance" and attacked Aristotle's hegemony and the "scholastic

A drawing by Hans Holbein for Erasmus' *In Praise of Folly,* **showing Erasmus at his desk. The notation above, in Erasmus' hand, comments that were he as handsome as this, Erasmus would not be without a wife.** *Oeffentliche Kunstsammlung Basel Hausaufnahme.*

sect of metaphysicians." His aim was less to humble reason than to elevate Scripture and man's openness to divine illumination.

The literary fusion of humanist criticism and positive theology was the work of Erasmus (1466–1536). His early education took him to a Brethren school, where he was the pupil of Hegius, Agricola's friend and disciple. He early imbibed Dutch pietism, and humanist influences attracted him in the Augustinian monastery at Steyn. In 1493 he left Steyn under a bishop's dispensation to study at Paris. He quickly entered the humanist circle of Robert Gaugin and Jacque LeFèvre d'Étaples. There he also met the young English aristocrats, who later introduced him to the English humanists John Colet and Sir Thomas More.

In 1499 Erasmus' journey to England proved as much a "conversion experience" in his life as Luther's discoveries in 1513 were in the career of the Reformer. He made a decision to devote his life to biblical texts, purified by humanist criticism, and the reform of Christian life through a cultural revolution.

In the years between 1500 and 1517 Erasmus elaborated a humanist, Christian culture pervaded by classicism. He was determined to purge Christian devotion and its literature of abstract and formal language and to make of prayer and devotion a thing of common speech. The first monument of his reform was his *Manual of a Christian Soldier* (1503). In form it is Erasmus' spiritual guide for an illiterate knight. Erasmus announced in it the program of purifying doctrine by a return to the fountain of Scripture. He advocated Christian social responsibility as the true good work. A year later his discovery of Valla renewed his allegiance to the critical task. He vowed to edit the whole New Testament, using as guides Paul, Jerome, Ambrose, and Augustine.

After his second English stay (1502–1506), Erasmus went to Italy, where for the next three years he gave himself to the unremitting labor of putting his works through the Aldine Press. He was in this respect a revolutionary, showing the way Luther followed. The Reformer was to publish a quarto every two weeks for nearly thirty years! But Erasmus was the first critic of the church to work entirely for the press. This gave him a public role unmatched among his contemporaries and without parallel in the past. It made him "The Prince of Humanists." Over the next dozen years, he produced dozens of books—volumes of letters, texts, and commentaries. The best known of these were *The Praise of Folly*, the fruit of his third English residence (1509–1514); his celebrated antipapal satire, *Julius Exclusus;* the manual for princes, *Institutio Principis Christiani;* the heroic edition of St. Jerome's *Opera Omnium;*[2] and his Greek New Testament.

Beneath the satire, the friendly banter, and the frivolity of humanist jokes, his books spoke plainly about their central theme. "Civilization" as it was maintained by princes and popes was a plague. Their deluded "wisdom" was pure folly, when contrasted with the healthy and life-giving wisdom of fools made wise in Christ.

Through satire Erasmus criticized prelates and monks for their vices. They were to be defeated or converted by classicism of style and the advocacy of a biblical Christianity in which lay initiative, simplicity of worship, and faith in Christ were central. Centuries of the cults of saints and other practices had done nothing but turn men's minds from God. What was required was only that Christ

---

[2] We may translate these titles as *Pope Julius Excluded from Heaven; The Education of a Christian Prince;* and St. Jerome's *Collected Works.*

be deeply printed in the hearts of men. This meant bringing to them the pure truth of Scripture. The work on texts was a step toward Scripture in the European vernaculars. When he spoke of the rebirth of Christ in men, Erasmus passed to the correction of the church, from scholarship to reform.

The peak of Erasmus' career was the publication of the New Testament in 1516. On the eve of Luther's explosive anger over indulgences, Europe lay at his feet. His correspondence constituted the main link in an invisible European university dedicated to reform. Yet reform, when it came, would not be veiled in his elegant Latin. Between men and Luther no barrier of ancient diction stood to inhibit populist sentiment.

THE LOSS OF UNITY

Some men better incarnate their time than others. Luther was such a man. In a world sick with longing for spiritual food, he was—in the formulation of the Danish philosopher Sören Kierkegaard—both "the weightiest patient" and the chief physician.

The broad-jawed, small-eyed Dr. Martin Luther proclaimed at Leipzig in 1519 that there were certain "articles of John Huss . . . which are truly Christian." Luther stood where Huss had stood more than a century earlier, under sentence of papal condemnation for his writings. By September 1520 he was under the papal ban, and in 1521 found himself a hunted enemy of the emperor and Christendom's most famous revivalist preacher. He had moved on the road to reformation.

How he came to be on that road is not obscure. His family was one of the rich central German peasantry. But his father was a youngest son and so was forced off the land by inheritance customs. Hans Luder and Margaret Ziegler Luder left Thuringia and settled in the mining frontier town of Eisleben, near Mansfeld, soon after the birth of their first son Martin (1483–1546).

Luder's four sons and four daughters claimed a solid bourgeois life. Martin, the eldest, had had a good education. His father had ambitions for him to become a lawyer. This might carry the family into the imperial bureaucracy, or that of the Saxon duchy. Martin was schooled by the Brethren of the Common Life at Magdeburg. Further education at Eisenach (1497–1501) exposed him to gifted teachers, pious family devotions, the learning of a good vicar, John Braun, as well as the orderly religious life of the Franciscan fathers there. Luther early committed himself to their urban pietism.

The choice of the university at Erfurt for further studies was significant. Martinus Luder de Mansfeld lived and studied in the small hostel of St. George's from 1501 to 1505. In four years he took both his bachelor's and master's examinations, stood second in his class, and was suitably devoted to Aristotle's physics and metaphysics, philosophy, and theology. But the dominant school at Erfurt was that of Occam and the *via moderna*. Beyond that, philosophy there was strongly ethical in its orientation, reinforced by a preference for the humanities. Luther acquired in Erfurt the view that religious truth was positive in character. Also, he bought his first Bible there.

Between 1505 and 1510 Master Luther was transformed into the monk of Wittenberg. Disappointing his father, the arts lecturer abandoned law and took vows. The order he chose was that of the Augustinians at Erfurt, since 1473 affiliated with the Windesheim Congregation. He turned to mastering the rule and its attendant rites. Both his dedication and his learning earned the respect of his superiors. In 1507 he was ordained and set to study theology in the House of General Studies. His mentors were Occamists. Luther was then a successful, if troubled, young scholastic. His studies centered especially on biblical theology.

In 1508 this adherent of the *via moderna* was called to a professorship in moral theology at Wittenberg. It was the capital of electoral Saxony, where Frederick the Wise had a castle church whose twelve galleries housed 17,433 holy relics in 1517! Indeed, the chief business of the town was the tourism associated with the elector's collections. Luther longed for the Bible, however, and rejoiced in his recall to Erfurt in 1509. In 1511 he was in a delegation sent to Rome to consider the resolution of certain disputes within the congregation. A year later, a new doctor in theology, he went back to Wittenberg, this time in the congenial chair of biblical theology.

Few teaching assignments in Western history have had such great consequences. Between 1512 and 1518 Luther preached in the parish church of the university, served as overseer of eleven monasteries, and lectured on Psalms (1513–1515) and Paul's Epistles to the Romans (1515–1516), Galatians (1516–1517), and Hebrews (1517–1518).

The pastor and lecturer had grave doubts about the central doctrines of his church. He was suffering a revolution in his mind in his efforts to attain personal assurances of grace and salvation.

Luther first collected his thoughts about the doctrine of unearned justification because of his specific abhorrence of the "cheap grace" sold by indulgence preachers working in Germany. The specific occasion of his attack on Johann Tetzel, a Dominican priest, was this. In 1514 Albert of Brandenburg had obtained election to the archbishopric of Mainz. He owed Rome enormous sums, the "first fruits" or income of the benefice during a single year, the papal tax on high-level promotions. To get money to pay for his promotion, Albert arranged to have preached a large-scale indulgence campaign, with half the profits for himself and his agents, the Fugger bankers. Tetzel was its chief instrument, a friar who had preached indulgence since 1502, with convenient jingles to prompt compliance: "As soon as gold in the the basin rings/Right then the soul to heaven springs."

Efforts to keep Tetzel's troupe out of Saxony failed. In 1517 Luther posted his Ninety-five Theses on the Wittenberg parish church door as a challenge to perverse teachings. They were in effect a pastor's warning to his flock. They were also the occasion to continue a long and bitter dispute between Luther's Augustinian order and the Dominicans. By 1519 Luther's charges and the countercharges of the pope and Charles V had made of the Saxon monk a major political problem in Germany.

Luther turned to the press and put his ideas before the people in three great pamphlets: the *Address to the Christian Nobility of the German Nation; The Babylonian Captivity of the Church; The Liberty of a Christian Man*. In these works, written in 1520, Luther made his private struggle a public one.

The German *Address* devoted itself to religious, social, and ecclesiastical problems. It embodied the idea that secular power alone was adequate to the demands of reform. The princes of expanding territorial states listened with interest. The Latin *Captivity* exhorted the clergy to reform doctrine, the sacraments, and the tyranny of Rome over the faith of men. Priests, aware of the alienation of lay support and the rise of a dangerous anticlerical sentiment, gave heed. The German work on Christian liberty was a book of popular edification, simple in language, strong and earthbound, earnest in its plea that men join in the struggle to win a new freedom in their pursuit of Christ's message. The bourgeoisie, hungry for such food, swallowed it whole, while peasants got drunk on the strong spirit they mistook for a worker's call to throw off their shackles.

The achievement of these three books was great. In them Luther distilled for public consumption both the essence of his personal theology and its practical consequences. He also showed in them that his problems were those of his people and his solutions adaptable in public ways rather than being merely the private remedies of a sick conscience. In them he showed his concern for the family, the congregation, and the state.

Luther's motto might well have been his famous saying: "Ein Worthlein kan ihn fahlen." ("A little word may fell the Devil!") His success in using words to convey the oppression of his own conscience by the doctrine of good works belied his expectation, however:

> After I had pondered the problem for days and nights God took pity on me and I saw the inner connection between the two phrases "The justice of God is revealed in the Gospel" and "that the just shall live by faith." I began to understand that this "justice of God" is the righteousness by which the just man lives through the free gift of God, that is to say by faith.

This putting together of his own efforts and God's gift drove a wedge into the heart of his problem and the doctrine of the church.

Historical theology and doctrine, ritual and worship, were grounded in the belief that human effort earned some part of the merit of Christ's sacrifice and made men just in God's sight. Thus justification sprang from works, especially the sacramental channels of grace. The kingdom of grace and that of nature were joined by human initiative, and God was in a sense obliged to redeem men of "holy practice."

Luther's theology rested on a contrary experience. Anxiety, rather than assurance, was his lot when he sought salvation by works and through adherence to the law of Scripture. His sins were too enormous. *Nit Aufgabe aber Gabe*—"Not works but the Gift," not the law but the Gospel—that was his "discovery" in 1513.

There is the crucial thought. Men are saved not through ritualism, good works, indulgences, but by faith alone—the "Gift." All men are therefore equal before God, each is a priest to himself. No papal or priestly mediation is necessary. Salvation has nothing to do with this earthly visible city of man: flesh, works, reason. Its realm is God's invisible city of the spirit; faith and grace. And within that city there is no room for the whole unreformed religion of cults, relics, the sale of indulgences, or the other "degenerate paraphernalia" that made of God's grace a bargain basement sale!

"On the tree of genuine faith good works shall grow." So said Luther. This reversed traditional teaching, in which good works strengthened men in faith. And it held out the hope of salvation as a revolutionary transformation. Luther's church was a Christian way of living in one's own calling, after the inward change derived from "surrendering to Christ." The means of that change—its passivity and its impact on the condition of life—show clearly Luther's relationship to Erasmus, the theologians of the modern way, St. Augustine, and expositors of the Bible, who stressed man's helplessness. What saved Luther from more ideology was his understanding that theory was simple, reality complex.

Lutheranism and the State

After his condemnation at the Diet of Worms in 1521, Luther had to consider the political implications of his protests. Peasant leagues had been in revolt continuously since the 1470s. Great millenarian prophets had arisen out of every such movement.

The Saxon priest Thomas Münzer (ca. 1489–1525) had followed Luther for a while and then become his leading critic, condemning the Reformer as a mere scribe and upholder of authority. Münzer was the archetype of the sectarian feared by Luther, a believer in visions of an earthly paradise and a reviver of natural theology. He taught that ordinary Christians familiar with the Gospel were naturally good and able to live in a hallowed relation to nature. He preached revivalism at Zwickau, before going to Prague to raise the old spirit of Bohemian religious and social revolution. By 1524 he was back in Saxony, at Allstedt, where he urged peasants, miners, and artisans to form a league and force the New Jerusalem to birth. He asked the duke of Saxony to be his secular arm against the ungodly, and when that failed he joined the Peasants' Revolt, and suffered execution after the collapse in 1525. His colleague Karlstadt (ca. 1480–1541) escaped, however, and continued to link Luther's teachings with a puritanical Old Testament prophecy that condemned music, images, and secular authority,[3] sometimes under Luther's gift of asylum.

Luther's difference with the peasants and the prophetic spiritualists was deep. Abolishing sin required responsibility and authority —power—as he had clearly taught in the *Address*. "Salvation is a free gift . . . [but] obedience is God's command." The justice of God revealed in the Gospel meant an order taught by the state. Justice lived by faith, but in Luther's mature teaching this justice came to men passively; and their passivity in obtaining divine justification was matched in the world by their obedience as citizens.

---

[3] He had been Luther's defender at Leipzig (1519). In the late 1520s and 1530s he worked chiefly in Switzerland, for Zwinglian reform. He profoundly influenced other sectarians.

Hence for Luther the struggle was not only against wrong authority in the Roman church but against the abrogation of right authority in the masses. Simple people had no organized means of pursuing either ecclesiastical or social reform. The state was therefore necessary. And in reliance upon its shield in electoral Saxony and elsewhere as the Reformation spread, religious and social revolutions might be worked. The alliance of a powerful doctrine with the power of expansive states became the seat of God's activity in the world. Sectarians who sought to escape from history in millenarian fantasies were, in Luther's view, rejecting Christianity.

The problem of maintaining in their place both the Gospel and the law accordingly occupied Luther steadily after 1521. The Reformer became the builder of a German church and the patron spirit of national churches elsewhere. He elaborated his idea of worldly authority. He sought to guard against wrongful readings of his eagerness to cast down the law in the economy of salvation and make of it a force exiling the law from society. Duty and obligation were declared "right by law," in all areas where the law is not related to salvation. Laws had nothing to do with that justification.

The political alliance was "a glorious ordinance of God," functioning in the world as a security measure. "Every realm must have its laws and statutes; without them no state can exist, as experience daily demonstrates." For if the law reveals the bondage from which the Gospel liberated men in their spirits, it also reveals the limit beyond which conduct is transgression in civil affairs. The reorganization of the church was in fact a matter of ecclesiastical politics in which magistrates must take a hand. Luther called princes magicians and healing heroes, just as Lord Bacon styled Henry VII of England, Louis XI of France, and Ferdinand of Aragon "magi-kings" for their labors as state builders. Thus did he marry a radical theology and the politics of the territorial states.

Luther's call for a governmental role in reformation strengthened an already strong secular power in the sixteenth century. And between 1520 and roughly 1560 new Caesars became the political beneficiaries of the religious and intellectual revolutions of their time. Though Luther counseled peace, wars of religion between nations and within them characterized the century after his death. Not that such wars lacked other causes; but they included an ideological element not previously present among Christians.

The Reformation was in this respect not only a reform of the forms of doctrine, ritual, and worship—in which sacraments were reduced in number; saints' days cast into limbo; vernacular Bibles made available; pilgrimages and shrines abandoned; great religious art often destroyed; and monks, monasteries, cardinals, and popes cast out of whole countries. It was a stage in the emancipation of lay life from clerical control and the secular state from ecclesiastical power.

The Spread of the Reformation

A mere table of chronology shows this with respect to the Lutheran phase of this revolution. It spread quickly from its German base in three directions: toward the southwest, the north, and the northwest. In Switzerland it underwent sharp alterations in the 1520s under the leadership of Huldreich Zwingli (1484–1531) and his successors. Yet by the late 1530s it was secure in Zurich, Basel, Bern, and their countrysides. In the Rhineland and Alsatian cities it took a strong hold, with Strasbourg as a center. The sects thrived in the southwest especially, and there was also a constant struggle against Protestant clericalism there, as in the northern Netherlands around Leiden. The movement leaped the channel separating England from the Low Countries and quickly merged with old domestic dissent, especially Lollardry, to produce a powerful Lutheran movement in the southeast of England. In the late 1530s, and especially in the years of Edward VI's short reign, 1547–1553, the Reformation there assumed a Protestant character.

Far to the north, Denmark was led into the Lutheran camp by 1527, through an alliance of native Lutherans and Kings Christian II and Frederick I. The German colony at Bergen radiated reformed teaching in that country as early as 1526, and the final triumph of Denmark over Norway in 1537 (the Union of Kalmar was resisted intermittently until that year) consolidated the new religion there. Resistance among the Swedish hierarchy was strong, but King Gustavus I threw his support to the religious radicals, perhaps as a technique in building state power at the expense of old and conservative Roman supporters. When he died in 1560, his power and Protestantism had advanced together. Finland absorbed religion from Sweden as Norway did from Denmark. That completed the separation of north Europe from Rome. In Poland, Hungary, Lithuania,

Breugel's satirical statement about the Reformation and the Counter-Reformation, entitled *The Battle between Carnival and Lent*. The artist's choice of the daily life of the common man for his subject matter, rather than traditional religious themes, is characteristic of Netherlandish painting in the sixteenth century. *Kunsthistorisches Museum, Vienna.* ▶

France, Iberia, and northern Italy Protestant evangelists found stony soil for their seed. The political powers there found no need to use religion, either because state building had earlier consolidated power through papal concords or because the often urban-inspired German movement had a weak base easily attacked by a strong eastern landed aristocracy.

Greater interest attaches to the failure of Lutheran Protestantism to establish itself over vast areas of Germany and to the development of a second generation of reformers impatient with Protestantism's moderate character.

Wittenberg had become a center of missionary activity in Germany in the 1520s. When Frederick the Wise was succeeded by John (1525–1532), Luther had a prince frankly "Lutheran," one who turned the church in Saxony into a Lutheran state church. This pattern, initiated throughout Scandinavia and in England especially, took hold also in some other German territories. The Reformation supported the princes against rebels and reaped dividends in East Prussia (1525), in Hesse (1526), and in 1528 in Brandenburg-Ansbach, Schleswig, Mansfeld, and Brunswick. The rulers imposed Protestantism from above on the Saxon model.

In the 1520s magistrates in certain towns gave strong support. There were also urban reformations that were popular in character, in Nuremberg in 1524, and soon after Strasbourg, Ulm, Augsburg, all in the south. Between 1528 and 1531, many of the greater northern cities followed suit, led by Magdeburg. Over two-thirds of all imperial cities became Protestant, with only Regensburg and Cologne remaining loyal to Rome, or rather in awe of the Bavarian Catholic princes of Wittelsbach and the archbishop-prince of the electoral city. Throughout the towns Protestantism rose from below, promoted by the craft-guild workers and pietistic fraternities demanding the secularization of church lands, evangelical pastors, and doctrinal changes, often over the objections of the oligarchs. Despite various efforts of Charles V to keep the Empire together in religion and politics, the revolution went forward, spurred by deeply anticlerical sentiments among the lay faithful.

In some areas, however, at Zurich for example, where Zwingli led the reform, and in the poor peasant republics of Zurge, Clarus, Uri, Schwyz, and Unterwald, suspicion of the urban oligarchies and their "guild" Protestantism ran deep. Yet Zwingli's objections were wholly religious and theological in character. Luther had not gone far enough in elaborating the idea that the church consisted of God's chosen few gathered in a disciplined body still at odds with the unredeemed many. To Zwingli a more complete break with the past seemed warranted, as well as a more rigorous social separation of the faithful from the fallen. Elsewhere, in the poor forest and mountain regions, acute poverty, the relative excess of population, and absolute political chaos inhibited the spread of the Saxon model.

Thus even in the Protestant world of the 1530s, there was a growing restiveness of radicals who wanted further reform. This often cast them into conflict with princes and magistrates content with the break from Rome and Luther's doctrine.

Calvinism

Jean Calvin gave shape to the yearning for new departures. This Frenchman began his education with humanists, continued it under nominalist[4] influences in philosophy and theology, and gave early promise of academic distinction. Calvin had pursued legal studies at Orléans and Bourges. He persisted in them longer than Luther did, only to give up in 1531, upon his father's death. He then went to Paris, where he resumed classical and biblical studies and honed his Latin and French style. He turned toward Protestantism in 1533, when he became involved in disputes in theology on behalf of some friends who embraced Luther's doctrine of justification by faith. For the next two years he was underground after a precipitous flight from the inquisitors of the Sorbonne. Calvin reached Basle in February 1535 and remained there for more than two years. He then resumed his migration and reached Geneva, which proved to be the scene of his great Reformation ministry.

His first sojourn in Geneva (1537–1538) gave him a taste of the further risks of reform advocacy. The Protestants were there caught between Catholic Savoy, the power of the Empire, and the weak support of Berne and other Swiss cities. The Reformation was also endangered there by sectarians and conservative magistrates, who forced Calvin and Guillaume Farel (1489–1565) to seek refuge in Strasbourg. From 1538 to 1541 Calvin worked as pastor of the French congregation in an atmosphere of international Protestantism in Strasbourg, which had become the gathering point of French, German, Dutch, and English reformers. Thus Calvin's formative Protestant experiences were those of a man exposed to danger. He was a refugee, a man without a country.

[4] The school of nominalism had insisted on setting Christian theology on a positive basis, by which was meant revelation in place of the speculations based on Aristotle's *Metaphysics* or other ideas from pagan philosophy. The nominalist masters argued that philosophy and theology had to be kept apart, lest doctrine be undermined by rationalism, especially the "natural" theology of the Dominicans who followed the ideas of St. Thomas Aquinas.

These wanderings and the persecutions he witnessed shaped doctrines that became the heart of what was revolutionary in international Protestant circles. Calvin fulminated against Catholics and the compromising Protestantism of the "state" revolutions. At Strasbourg, Martin Butzer strengthened Calvin's confidence in certain doctrines, especially predestination, and also in his views of church polity. So, when Calvin received a second call to a Genevan pulpit in 1541, he went back newly armed to that badly divided town. There he spent the rest of his life as the town's leading minister.

Among the things in his baggage on his travels, Calvin carried his six-part manuscript *The Institutes of the Christian Religion*. This book was a catechism in Latin. It was to be enlarged in 1539, translated into elegant French by Calvin himself in 1541, and then constantly revised until it achieved definitive form in 1559. But the first edition contained the kernel of Calvin's thought, distinguished chiefly by its rigor and by Calvin's expression of confidence that he was God's agent in the active reform of society. The book's biblicism and focus on God's will as terrible but just were fortified by great skill in the humanist critique of sources. The chief divergence from Luther followed from Calvin's legalism. He did not stress the Gospel as a total deliverance from the law of the Old Testament. His insistence was on a strong church exercising a rigorous scrutiny over man's fidelity to the law. This gave rise to the characteristic puritanism so marked in his austere followers.

The Divine Will dominated Calvin. If he was its instrument, his personal austerity and the regime he instituted in Geneva matched that of his vision of God. His "Sovereign Governor" of the world was wholly alien to man, unknowable. He called very few to salvation, and those few who were chosen had the heavy obligation of being the vanguard, the "elect" already assured of their place in the "community of saints" at Judgment Day.

Calvin's theocentric ideas did possess a softer side. The "Christocentric Calvin" stressed Christ's gifts of saving grace. His work at Geneva was marked by the production of tough revolutionary cadres. Yet it also produced the General Hospital of Geneva, a charitable trust distinguished for its radical attack on social problems when much moderate wisdom did nothing.

Calvin gave his pastors, teachers, elders, and lay deacons the idea that they were the cutting edge of a sword that must prevail against all opposition. That meant that Calvinists would in time constitute revolutionary "parties." Luther's more passive "reformed" churches were not totally purified of abuses of clerical power. Sixteenth-century Protestants complained of their lack of a well-

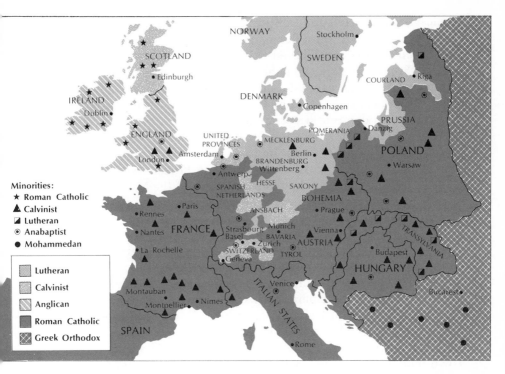

Minorities:
★ Roman Catholic
▲ Calvinist
◪ Lutheran
◉ Anabaptist
● Mohammedan

Lutheran
Calvinist
Anglican
Roman Catholic
Greek Orthodox

Source: H. G. Koenigsberger and G. L. Mosse, *Europe in the Sixteenth Century* (New York, 1968), p. 273.

RELIGIOUS DIVISIONS IN EUROPE, ca. 1600

educated ministry. Reformed churches had not been able to root out retarding influences of lay control over benefices and church office. Indeed, the argument was made by some discontented observers that second-generation Lutheranism was more retrograde than the vigorous Catholic Church, newly impelled by the reforms of the Council of Trent (1542–1563). Rome was busily founding seminaries; new social-service orders were springing up to teach the ignorant, nurse the sick, and relieve the poor, and Loyola's Society of Jesus was a counterrevolutionary salient better educated and more disciplined than any force in the Protestant world.

The Political and Social Impact of the Reformation

Calvin's followers stepped into that gap. They had to address new problems. They had to find ways to gain control of the levers of ecclesiastical, social, and political power in countries and cities but halfway on the road from Rome to Geneva.

Their efforts were based on a revolutionary appeal that convulsed France, Britain, and the Netherlands, as well as Swiss and German lands between 1550 and the Peace of Westphalia in 1648. Calvinism quickly showed its superiority to Lutheranism as an expansive force. Its doctrine was simpler and systematic. In France it was able to provide a rallying point for dissident nobility and upper bourgeoisie, as well as artisans, none of whom drew much hope from Luther's cheerful support of princes. The French Wars of Religion (1562–1598) and the Dutch-inspired "Revolt of the Netherlands" gave ideological coherence to factions otherwise sharply divided in their immediate backgrounds and social concerns. Geneva produced pastors actively antiauthoritarian and equally critical of Spanish power, the Valois kings of France—especially Francis I, Henri II, Francis II, and Charles IX, who exhibited open hostility to Protestant Reformation—and Queen Elizabeth I. And from the rapidly developing Calvinist center at Heidelberg sparks shot in every direction. By 1566 in France a synod of Calvinist churches—Huguenots—had attracted the Prince of Condé as their patron. In the Netherlands William of Orange played that role. Across the English Channel, Elizabeth's own moderation found itself circumscribed by the fact that both in Parliament and in her own Council Puritans and their sympathizers were on the rise after 1570.

The history of "Calvinist conspiracy" by 1570 was that of men whose real economic and religious grievances drew them together in democratic underground assemblies that were subversive of the established order. Town after town fell to their control in France and the Netherlands. In England they captured magistracies and councils, local offices, and seats in Parliament. The Dutch Sea Beggars— militant merchants and naval groups attacking Spanish forces— fomented revolution at home and negotiated with sovereign powers abroad fifty years before the Estates of Holland claimed popular sovereignty in 1621.

Although the ruling elements proved tough enough in England to prevent civil war—and pliable enough also—in France that was not the case. Nor was it true in Scotland or the Low Countries, where Spain's efforts to keep her empire could scarcely disguise the confessional split between the southern Catholics and the northern evangelicals. The Huguenots put Henry of Navarre on the throne in France in 1594, when he decided that "Paris was worth a mass."[5]

[5] A great massacre of Protestant leaders had taken place in 1572, on St. Bartholomew's Eve!

Early in the seventeenth century their Dutch cousins worked the miracle of beating Spain. And not too many years later English Puritans executed Charles I and made England a republic—sans king, lords, and bishops.

These triumphs proved short-lived. Calvinism failed to move a profound social revolution. Puritan London, Rembrandt's Amsterdam, and Louis XIII's Paris were ruled by oligarchies. In the Dutch future there were kings, and in the English one an aristocratically restored monarchy. Yet the world in 1600 was transformed by the religious revolutions and counterrevolutions of the sixteenth century. The Europe of the contending confessional states was in being. The Christian commonwealth was a pious memory. Catholics, Protestants, and "reformed" Protestants faced each other across shifting boundaries.

Beyond the seawalls of the Continent the struggle for empire showed itself religiously as well as politically, especially in the rivalries in North America, where established churches followed the flag. The mental world had been transformed. There still was authority, yet papal power in its old sense was shattered forever. The Holy Roman Empire had been dismembered. A new republicanism was rampant in Europe; and its seed was planted on the other side of the Atlantic. Monarchies contended with "parties" in a politics made national rather than merely dynastic as much by religious differences as by any other force. Economy and society in 1600 were increasingly commercial in the controlling northwestern European countries, and the traditional agrarian sector was in the midst of a transformation that marked the Old Regime off from the dying feudal world of 1300.

Europe was to remain as it was in 1600 until transformed by political revolution in France and the Industrial Revolution in England. The Old Regime already existed.

The English martyrologist John Foxe (1516–1587) traced the opening of his age to about 1300. He was intent to show in his *Acts and Monuments* (popularly known as the Book of Martyrs) that the Reformation in his time owed something to the denials of papal authority issued by Marsiglio of Padua and William of Occam. Foxe also recalled how Dante's canticle of *Purgatory* and Petrarch's *Epistles* had called the pope "the Whore of Babylon." He also traced the descent of Luther from Wycliffe and Huss. The fourteenth century was thus the start of "modern" history. Popes fought for dominion with one another and with kings. Bishops repressed the people. Yet these calamities heralded the advance of the spirit that revived Christianity in an urban, capitalist civilization. And in his own day,

Foxe could confidently say that the act of printing itself had brought the reformation of society to its consummation:

> The Lord began to work for His Church not with sword and target . . . but with printing, writing and reading. . . . How many printing presses there be in the world, so many block-houses there be against the high castle of St. Angelo [at Rome], so that either the pope must abolish knowledge and printing or printing at length will root him out.

The cultural revolution had driven home the point, that between the Word and the World there was more than one consonant's difference.

Bibliography

CHAPTER ONE

The modern literature on social and economic change in late medieval and early modern Europe has increasingly focused on the relationships that existed between land and labor and the changes produced in those relationships by population decline and recovery. The most basic reference is M. M. Postan, ed., *The Agrarian Life of The Middle Ages* (vol. 1, 2nd ed.), of the *Cambridge Economic History of Europe* (Cambridge, Eng., 1966). The fundamental data about population change may be found in *J. C. Russel, *Late Ancient and Medieval Population* (Philadelphia, 1958). Convenient summaries of the arguments made here about population level, land use, and the changing nature of rural society abound. At the most general level, see the relevant chapters in* Robert-Henri Bautier, *The Economic Development of Medieval Europe* (London, 1971); * Harry A. Mishkimin, *The Economy of Early Renaissance Europe, 1300–1460* (Englewood Cliffs, N.J., 1969); and * Gerald A. J. Hodgett, *A Social and Economic History of Medieval Europe* (London, 1972).

Three important and more specialized works by the late French master Marc Bloch are essential to a sound grasp of agrarian society and the feudal relations within it. * *Feudal Society* (2 vols., Chicago, 1961); *French Rural History: An Essay on Its Basic Characteristics* (Berkeley and Los Angeles, 1966); and * *Land and Work in Medieval Europe* (New York, 1969). Perhaps the best one-volume synthesis is that by Georges Duby, *Rural Economy and Country Life in the Medieval West* (Columbia, S.C., 1968). This translation by Cynthia Postan contains many valuable tables and documents, as does Olive Ordish's translation of * *The Agrarian History of Western Europe, 500–1850* by B. H. Slicher Van Bath (London, 1966).

The interesting nature of rural social history at the level of the material life of the common man is best appreciated from a reading of the recent work by the great Fernand Braudel, *Capitalism and Material Life, 1400–1800* (London, 1973), in the translation of Miriam Kochan. Braudel deals explicitly with the problems and methods of demographic historians and also with the ideas of decline, growth, and technical change. On this last subject there is much profit in reading * Lynn White, Jr., *Medieval Technology and Social Change* (New York, 1962). For an understanding of depopulation and its consequences for agriculture see * Maurice Beresford, *Lost Villages of England* (London, 1954). A more technical work on agrarian change to 1500 is M. M. Postan's new book, *Essays on Medieval Agrarian History* (Cambridge, Eng., 1973), which incorporates Postan's studies on population. Students who wish to follow in detail the development of a pastoral economy should read Julius Klein, *The Mesta* (Cambridge, Mass., 1920).

CHAPTER TWO

The general books mentioned above are valuable as introductions to commerce, city life, the overseas expansion of Europe, and capitalism. Pride of place belongs to Braudel's *Capitalism and Material Life,* however. A useful, brief book on the "recovery" is * J. Johnson and W. Percy, *The Age of Recovery* (Ithaca, N.Y., 1970), but it does not have the benefit of the splendid illustrations found in * Margaret Aston's *The Fifteenth Century* (London, 1968). For the sixteenth century perhaps the most interesting book is George Mosse and H. G. Koenigsberger, *The Sixteenth Century* (London, 1966). Useful for its integrated account of social change and expansion is * A. J. Slavin, *The Reorganization of Europe, 1300–1760* (Lexington, Mass. Xerox, 1973).

The literature on the city in Western history is vast. One of the most stimulating books on the consequences for civilization of urbanization is by the anthropologist * Robert Redfield, *The Primitive World and Its Transformation* (Ithaca, N.Y., 1953). The late * Henri Pirenne's *Medieval Cities* (Princeton, N.J., 1969) synthesizes the author's lifework in a slender book. Important for any grasp of the nature of cities and urban institutions is the social theory of urban life developed by sociologists. Especially valuable are two classic works: * Gideon Sjoberg, *The Preindustrial City* (New York, 1965), and * Max Weber, *The City* (New York, 1966). Both books examine the different theories of city origins and the relationships between economic activity and legal-political structures, especially patrician-popular conflicts. An approach to the city as a human environment is made by * Howard Saalman in *Medieval Cities* (New York, 1968), and * Giulio Argan in *The Renaissance City* (New York, 1969). Both these books are in the Planning and Cities series edited by G. R. Collins.

The experience of eastern European merchants and urban politics is scarcely treated in English. But good essays appear in * Peter Burke, ed., *Economy and Society in Early Modern Europe: Essays from Annales* (London, 1972), and in William H. McNeill's *Europe's Steppe Frontier* (Chicago, 1964). More important are two works dealing with the German and Baltic world: Fritz Rörig, *The Medieval Town* (London, 1967), and P. Dollinger, *The Hansa* (Palo Alto, Calif., 1970). Rörig's book, despite its title, covers our period as a whole on a comparative basis. Two other books worth reading are * J. H. Huizinga, *Dutch Civilization in the Seventeenth Century* (New York, 1968), and * J. C. Russel, *Medieval Regions and Their Cities* (London, 1972).

Books on the Italian cities and their commerce and institutions are legion. From a large literature the following may be especially recommended: * David Waley, *The Italian City Republics* (London, 1969); * Alfred von Martin, *Sociology of the Renaissance* (New York, 1973); * Anthony Molho, ed., *Social and Economic Foundations of the Italian Renaissance* (New York, 1969); * D. S. Chambers, *The Imperial Age of Venice* (New York, 1970); and * Brian Pullan, *Crisis and Change in the Venetian Economy* (London, 1968).

The general problem of the complex relationships between population, commerce, money, expansion, and industrial technique has preoccupied many scholars. A classic book on this subject is by * John V. Nef, *The Conquest of the Material World* (New York, 1967). This collection of essays stresses the period from 1450 to 1640 as fundamentally important in putting Europe on the road to industrial civilization. Without the exaggerations found in Nef's work, the books of * Carlo Cipolla also focus on changes in the character of commercial civilization after 1400: see especially *Money, Prices, and Civilization* (Princeton, N.J., 1955), and * *Guns, Sails, and Empires* (New York, 1966). This last book contains good information on the role of technological innovation, while banking is stressed by R. de Roover's *The Rise and Decline of the Medici Bank* (Cambridge, Mass., 1964).

The role played by overseas expansion in changing the shape of the West cannot be easily exaggerated. Again, from a vast literature it is possible only to select a few key works. The best brief book in any language is still untranslated from French: * Pierre Chaunu, *Conquête et Exploitation des Nouveaux Mondes* (Paris, 1969). The wealth of data found there is not matched elsewhere, but a very good introduction in English is * J. H. Parry, ed., *The European Reconnaissance* (New York, 1968), a volume of documents to be read in conjunction with Parry's standard text, *The Age of Reconnaissance* (London, 1963). The impact of Europe on America is the main concern of * C. H. Haring in *The Spanish Empire in America* (New York, 1963), which is a very good work on imperial institutions. On the general question of the impact of America on Europe there is a masterful essay by * J. H. Elliott in his book *The Old World and The New, 1492–1650* (New York, 1970).

CHAPTER THREE

For a general survey of the changing nature of politics and the state system from 1300 to 1600 the following are useful: * J. Russell Major, *The Age of the Renaissance and Reformation* (Philadelphia, 1970); * J. R. Strayer, *On The Medieval Origins of the Modern State* (Princeton, N.J., 1970); and * Eugene F. Rice, Jr., *The Foundations of Early Modern Europe*

(New York, 1970). A comparative treatment of political systems stressing the nature of competing power centers—cities, dynastic states, and empires—is found in * A. J. Slavin, *The Reorganization of Europe, 1300–1760* (Lexington, Mass., Xerox, 1973). A classic work on the state system as a system of relations between states is * Garrett Mattingly's *Renaissance Diplomacy* (London, 1955).

On papal politics, the papal state, and the impact of political ideas on papal monarchy see especially * Geoffrey Barraclough's survey in *The Medieval Papacy* (New York, 1968). The impact of the Babylonian Captivity is the subject of a masterful study by * G. Mollat, *The Popes at Avignon* (New York, 1965). Among the many books on the conciliar era the most concise recent one is by A. J. Black, *Monarchy and Community: Political Ideas in the Later Conciliar Controversy* (Cambridge, Eng., 1970). The question of representative institutions in the period embraces secular governments as well as ecclesiastical ones. Antonio Marongiu's *Medieval Parliaments* (London, 1968) treats Italian and western European systems in a comparative fashion. A valuable source book with commentary on government developments in the sixteenth century is Gordon Griffiths' *Representative Government* (Oxford, 1968).

Studies of government and politics within the framework of particular states abound. Some useful ones are J. Russell Major, *Representative Institutions in Renaissance France* (Madison, Wisc., 1960); * F. Graus and others, *Eastern and Western Europe in the Middle Ages* (London, 1970); * Speros Vryonis, *Byzantium and Europe* (New York, 1967); * Ian Grey, *Ivan III and the Unification of Russia* (London, 1964); J. H. Elliott, *Imperial Spain, 1469–1716* (New York, 1963); * J. S. Shennan, *Government and Society in France, 1461–1661* (London, 1969); F. L. Carsten, *Princes and Parliaments in Germany* (Oxford, 1959); and A. J. Slavin, *The Precarious Balance: Government and Society in England, 1450–1640* (New York, 1973).

CHAPTER FOUR

Among the most interesting and relatively brief introductions to the world of humanism and the age of the Reformation, three stand out: * Myron Gilmore, *The World of Humanism* (New York, 1952); * G. R. Elton, *Reformation Europe* (London, 1963); and * Hans J. Hillerbrand, *Men and Ideas in the Sixteenth Century* (Chicago, 1969). The period of the Counter-Reformation and the Wars of Religion has also been treated synthetically in brief compass: perhaps the best text is * J. H. Elliott, *The Wars of Religion, 1559–1598* (London, 1965). A well written, beautifully illustrated work is * A. G. Dickens, *The Counter-Reformation* (New York, 1969). The most remarkable essay on the moving spirit of Catholic reform is the posthumously published book by H. O. Evennett, *The Spirit of the Counter-Reformation* (Cambridge, Eng., 1968).

The general problem of the meaning of humanism and its relationship to the concept of "renaissance" has never been settled authoritatively. But for the views informing this book students may read profitably

* Paul O. Kristeller, *Renaissance Thought: The Classic, Scholastic, and Humanist Strains* (New York, 1961); * Denys Hay, *The Italian Renaissance in Its Historical Background* (New York, 1968); Eugenio Garin, *Italian Humanism* (New York, 1965); and the source book edited by * Paul O. Kristeller, Ernst Cassirer, and J. H. Randall, *The Renaissance Philosophy of Man* (Chicago, 1948).

The problem of Renaissance scholarship and its impact on Christian and secular ideas still perplexes students uncertain about what weight to attribute to ideas as "causes" of social change. Important contributions to the discussion are * J. H. Huizinga, *The Warning of the Middle Ages* (New York, 1954); * Federico Chabod, *Machiavelli and the Renaissance* (New York, 1965); * Peter Burke, ed., *The Renaissance Sense of the Past* (New York, 1969); and * Ernst Cassirer's classic *The Individual and the Cosmos in Renaissance Philosophy* (Pittsburgh, 1972), translated by Mario Domand. On the scholar as reformer see * E. Harris Harbison, *The Christian Scholar in the Age of the Reformation* (New York, 1956). There is also a great work by * J. H. Huizinga, *Erasmus and the Age of the Reformation* (New York, 1957), in which the case is made that Erasmus did not grasp the profound nature of the religious crisis and did not understand Luther's significance.

A quite contrary view informs the work of * H. A. Enno Van Gelder, *The Two Reformations in the Sixteenth Century* (The Hague, 1964); he argues that the Erasmian "reformation," secular and liberal, was more fruitful for the future than the narrower "confessional" ones made by Luther, Zwingli, Calvin, and their peers. A good survey of the various reformers is * A. G. Dickens, *Reformation and Society in Sixteenth Century Europe* (New York, 1966). Dickens favors the deep impact of the leading reformers in the Protestant tradition, as does * H. R. Trevor-Roper, *Religion, the Reformation, and Social Change* (London, 1967); see especially Chapters 1, 4, and 5. On the major "Reformations" the literature is so vast that any recommendation may seem eccentric. We value highly the following: * Hajo Holborn, ed., *On the Eve of the Reformation* (New York, 1964), which prints the infamous *Letters of Obscure Men;* also the general collection of documents in * Hans J. Hillerbrand, *The Protestant Reformation* (New York, 1968). For material on Luther see * Gordon Rupp, *Luther's Progress to the Diet of Worms* (New York, 1964) and * James Atkinson, *Martin Luther and the Birth of Protestantism* (London, 1968); on Calvin and Calvinism two especially goods books are John T. McNeill's, *The History and Character of Calvinism* (London, 1962) and the collection of essays by leading scholars entitled *John Calvin* (Abingdon, Berkshire, 1966). For the Reformation in England the best work is * A. G. Dickens, *The English Reformation* (New York, 1964). The most succinct one-volume presentation of Protestant theology is * J. S. Whale, *The Protestant Tradition* (New York, 1969), which has major essays on Luther, Calvin, and the "sectarian" leaders.

Chronology

1648	Treaties of Westphalia
1643–1715	Reign of Louis XIV of France
1681–1699	Long war of Christian powers against Turkey
1680–1790	The Age of the Enlightenment
1689–1725	Reign of Peter the Great of Russia
1739–1763	Great war for empire in which Britain defeated France
1740–1763	Prussia wars against Austria in which Prussia became a great power
1772–1795	Three partitions of Poland
1775–1815	Early Industrial Revolution in England
1789–1799	French Revolution
1799–1815	Wars of Napoleon and extension of the Revolution into Europe
1815	Congress of Vienna
1848	Revolutions occurring almost everywhere in Europe
1859–1871	Unification of Italy
1864–1871	Unification of Germany
1860–1914	General democratization of European society and government; general secularization of European thought and belief
1861	Emancipation of serfs in Russia
1870–1914	Height of European imperialism
1905	Albert Einstein publishes his Special Theory of Relativity
1914–1919	Great War
1917	The Russian Revolution
1929–1939	The Great Depression
1931–1939	Appeasement of dictators by Western liberal democracies
1933	Hitler assumes power in Germany
1939–1945	World War II
1945	First military use of the atomic bomb
1945–1973	Cold war, and occasional hot wars, between Russia and the United States and their client states
1957	Formation of the European Common Market

PART TWO the modern world

The historian of 1600, looking back over his heritage, would see a broad sweep of gradual, and, at times, nearly imperceptible change. Although, over the course of the centuries, some changes had been substantial, they, too, occurred very slowly. It took a millennium to alter the religion of Europe's peasants from paganism to Christianity. The Roman Empire in the West collapsed in stages over a span of three hundred years. The medieval urban recovery in the West was a lengthy process, covering most of three centuries. Even a cathedral took more than a hundred years to complete. Men lived in a stable society, where the things of the past lived on, where the ways of the fathers were a sure guide for the lives of the sons.

After 1600, however, this comfortable pattern began to break down, and the pace of change accelerated. Two major factors were at work in this process leading to modernity. The first to emerge was the development of the modern, bureaucratic state, an institution that became supreme over individual citizens and, to a high degree, began to control their lives. By the end of the seventeenth century the focus of political power reflected this development, for it was shifting, for better or for worse, from the churches, nobles, and towns to the state. By the middle of the eighteenth century a second factor had begun to catch public notice. The Industrial Revolution had begun, combining scientific knowledge, technological progress, and rapid and dramatic changes in the methods of production. The effect of industrialization was overwhelming. It changed every known pattern of personal life, work, leisure, education, social status, and consumption of goods; and, like the growth of the power of the state, it became an endless process.

Thus the modern historian, looking to both the past and the future, sees constant change where his predecessor saw continuity.

The world appears constantly new. The past, it seems, loses its importance, and the old ways are no longer the best ways. The perceptive student, however, sees more than just flux: the present is not divorced from the past, but different from it, and modernity means that the student must look more closely at his cultural inheritance than he has ever looked before, to distinguish the temporary from the permanent, things growing from things fading away.

FIVE

The Old Regime

Negotiations without weapons are like music
without instruments.
                                    Frederick the Great

Trade is the true and intrinsick interest of England, without which it cannot subsist.
                                    Slingsby Bethel
                        *An Account of the French
                        Usurpation upon the Trade of
                        England (London, 1674)*

The increase of any Estate must be upon the
Foreigner . . . for whosoever is somewhere
gotten is somewhere else lost. . . .
                                    Sir Francis Bacon

INTRODUCTION

The period from the great depression of the seventeenth century to
the French Revolution was the anteroom of the modern world. Virtually every aspect of the economy, political structures, and intellectual life underwent a vast change, moving away from medieval
patterns toward those conditions and styles characteristic of the modern world. By the end of the eighteenth century, Europe was becoming rapidly modernized and the medieval world remote and distant.

The great seventeenth-century depression completely altered the
economic map of Europe. The Mediterranean basin, prosperous since
the Neolithic revolution, was utterly ruined, and the center of economic strength completed the movement to the North Atlantic. In
political organization, also, familiar patterns and structures of government were slowly replaced by more modern ones. Personal mon-

archies collapsed under the strains of monetary inflation, prolonged war, and irreconcilable religious antagonisms. During the seventeenth and eighteenth centuries, a new bureaucratic or parliamentary state evolved to replace the broken political machinery. The new political structures centralized decision making with the king, or king and parliament, and greatly reduced the power of provincial, municipal, or manorial authorities. The new state was much stronger and more flexible than the old, so much so that even the upheavals of the French Revolution merely strengthened it further.

The world of the mind was marked by an abandonment of medieval modes of thought and philosophy. The Enlightenment was the first major intellectual movement that may be called truly modern. Enlightenment philosophers considered empirical and scientific knowledge to be far superior to the rather uncertain efforts of abstract reason and logic. The growth of modern scientific thought and the origins of massive technological innovation were also products of the Old Regime. The Enlightenment presented a strikingly secular and modern attitude toward religion—skeptical of the miraculous, contemptuous of superstition, suspicious of the clergy, and hostile to the organized church. The eighteenth century was a time of searching for the rights of man and the proper ordering of political systems. Man was seen as having certain natural and inalienable rights, and politics was best organized when the state possessed a written constitution. No country took these views more seriously than the emergent United States.

These decisive changes from medieval toward modern did not occur with the appalling speed that modern man has come to know and fear. The shift took two centuries. Not everything changed at once. The social structure inherited from the Middle Ages serenely survived all change during the Old Regime. Monarchy was unaffected by knowledge of the laws of gravity, or even by ruinous economic collapse. Institutions had not yet felt the implications of all the changes in thought, politics, and the economy that were already occurring; but they would. The Old Regime, ten generations ago, was a curious mixture of medieval and modern, of things dying and things being born. It was the beginning of the modern world.

THE GENERAL CRISES OF THE SEVENTEENTH CENTURY

It seemed like a little thing, at first. The Holy Roman Emperor, Charles V, asked his bankers and ministers for 600,000 ducats to besiege Metz. By 1552, however, bankers were running out of money to lend to kings. A tremendous credit inflation had been growing for decades, with both sovereigns and merchants competing for the available funds. No silver shipments from Mexico could keep pace with the insatiable demands of kings to finance their wars and governments. Charles' requests were impossible to fulfill. Loans to Henry II of France, to England and the German states, and to Italian princes, as well as the needs of commerce and industry, had exhausted the European money markets. In 1557 the European monarchs and bankers tottered into bankruptcy. Spain went first, bringing ruinous losses to the great Fugger and Welser banking houses and temporarily destroying the Antwerp bourse. The debts of Henry II of France, consolidated under the title of the "Big Deal," was repudiated in December 1557, destroying the banking and mercantile houses of Florence and Lyons. A wave of smaller failures swept over the bankers and merchants of Germany, the Low Countries, and Italy, following the bankruptcy of Europe's two greatest powers.

The credit crisis of 1552–1562 engulfed all Europe, bringing a shattering pause to the long spiral of growing prosperity that had endured for nearly a century. Bankruptcy halted the prolonged wars between France and Spain. Staggering though the fiscal crisis was, it by no means ended with princes' propensity to borrow or the merchants' desire for profits. Within a decade the credit pyramid was building again. Borrowing climbed, repayment fell off, funding operations were proposed. To no avail; by 1575–1576 France and Spain again defaulted. But so pressing were the demands of the state that the fiscal and credit inflation began once more.

By the last decade of the sixteenth century, however, the European money market was less able to supply the demands of both commerce and the state. In the vast domains of the Hapsburg imperium, the needs of trade and industry were ruthlessly subordinated to those of the king. The merchants of Spain, Portugal, Italy, and Belgium were sacrificed to the glory of the Hapsburgs and the Catholic faith. When the Spanish crown defaulted in 1595, and again in 1608, 1627, and 1647, it pulled into irretrievable ruin the towns and merchants of nearly half of Europe. The French did no better. The silk merchants of Lyons fell victim to an endless war. France defaulted again and again, until none could be found to lend. The state was eating its merchants and industrialists alive.

The monetary and credit crisis signaled the onslaught of a general economic depression unequaled since the Black Death. Trade routes established during the Crusades dried up. Towns long noted as banking, commercial, or industrial centers sank into ruin, bringing penury and misery to their citizens. Revolutions shook the social and political structure of the European kingdoms. Population declined or remained static in most European states. Wars of great ferocity and destruction completed the general picture of depression and ruin.

The general crisis spanned most of a century. It began in Flanders in the 1580s, when the Dutch closed the Scheldt River, choking Antwerp, which previously had been the economic and fiscal center of northern Europe. With the Spanish bankruptcy of 1595, the economic crisis deepened in the Mediterranean basin. Early in the seventeenth century the industrial towns of northern Italy slipped into profound and prolonged depression. For the rest of the Continent, the great depression began in 1619, coinciding with the beginning of the Thirty Years' War and renewed religious strife in France. Not until the 1660s was there much sign of recovery. Even then the upswing was not general. The Mediterranean area continued to decline, and from 1683 to 1725 France suffered a second, even more dreadful, slump. Real recovery was primarily restricted to Atlantic powers in northern Europe, England, Holland, and in the eighteenth century, France.

Economic crisis in Spain began with the fiscal policies of Philip II. The tremendous influx of colonial silver and the constant royal demands for money produced a vast wage and price inflation. Felt everywhere, it was most acute in Spain. Prices rose over 300 percent from 1550 to 1640 and were already high when Philip II ascended the throne. The wage-price spiral progressively drove Spanish agriculture and industry out of the market, first abroad and then ultimately, at home as well. By the 1590s it was cheaper to import. Inflation struck more than the royal finances; it crumbled the agricultural and industrial foundations of an entire region.

Spanish industry and trade never recovered from the depredations of royal bankruptcies and inflation. Seriously damaged at the death of Philip II, the textile industry collapsed utterly during the seventeenth century. The *Casa de la Contratación* of Seville, which controlled Spanish colonial trade, was unable to supply colonial needs by 1600, so scarce and expensive had Spanish goods become. The international trade fair at Medina del Campo closed. Peasants were driven from the land, which was turned from arable to grazing. Severe plague and famine from 1599 to 1601 completed the disaster.

The Iberian dependencies were equally affected. In Portugal, the spice trade that had made Lisbon rich was lost to the Dutch by 1620. In 1640 an attempt by the Spanish crown to increase taxes stung Portugal into revolt. For twenty years the horrors of war were added to the effects of depression. In 1668 Portugal emerged with her independence, but her countryside was shattered and her trade ruined. Recovery was painfully slow, and Portugal never developed an industrial base, nor even regained the commercial position of 1550. In Catalonia, depression was also a factor in rebellion. Public revenues sagged fully one-fifth from 1600 to 1627. Banditry became the scourge of the countryside, as impecunious nobles and dispossessed peasants joined forces to loot the agricultural economy. Finally, in 1640, disputes over taxation and provincial rights pushed the impoverished province into revolt.

The Italian states also suffered from a severe depression. Heavy taxes for protection against the Ottoman Empire hurt Sicily, whose economy could not support the war effort of Philip II. The silk industry of Messina declined dramatically during the seventeenth century. Sicily became an importer of foodstuffs in the seventeenth century, a reversal of previous conditions. The retail price level broke sharply after 1618, indicating that the island's economy was increasingly depressed. Banditry became a major rural profession. Sicily never recovered and remains a backwater of Europe even today.

Naples, Milan, Genoa, and Tuscany fared little better. Genoese bankers, staggered by the Spanish bankruptcy of 1595, were nearly ruined in 1608. Trade followed banking, and Genoa gradually declined during the course of the century. In Milan, the seventeenth century brought the collapse of the textile industry. From 1600 to 1705 Milan's commercial looms dropped from 2,000 to only 1. Economic stagnation in Naples culminated in Masaniello's revolt in 1647, triggered by high bread prices and no work. For all of Italy, the plague of 1657 simply added to the disaster, and the developed industrial and commercial economy regressed toward subsistence peasant agriculture. The great Renaissance towns were left idle, relics of past glory.

In France the seventeenth-century crisis followed a somewhat different course. Royal credit collapsed in 1619, and the accumulations of war and depression expanded royal repudiation into a general commercial decline. Prices dropped and trade fell off. War demanded increased taxation from a weakened economy. In the years before the revolt of the Fronde in 1648, peasant rebellions and bread riots were yearly events. The nadir was reached in the wretched conditions of the 1650s.

There was some recovery from 1660 to 1683. Colbert, Louis XIV's minister of finance, paid great attention to the industrial and commercial development of the realm. He fostered new industries, supported colonial enterprises, and tried to increase French commerce. However, the Colbert prosperity was not deep enough to survive the advent of new wars. England and Holland throttled

French trade, and the famine of 1691–1694 confirmed the disaster. Between 1709 and 1710 the worse famine in French history struck the nation. Grapes and fruit failed as well as grain, and animals starved for lack of silage. Cities shut their gates on bands of wandering peasants, and more than a million people died of starvation, exposure, or disease. Not until the 1720s did France begin to recover from the depression of the seventeenth century.

The economic crisis was equally severe in Germany and the Baltic. Two generations of state bankruptcies had driven the German banking houses to cover. German trade had depended on Italian cities, and their decline slowly strangled the German merchants. The decline was steady but gentle until the Thirty Years' War. Depression began in earnest in 1620. The movements of the armies disrupted trade on the rivers, which had served as the natural route of commerce in an age that was almost without roads. Looting spread destruction and starvation from Bavaria to the Baltic. Armies grew so large that they had to be kept marching in order to be fed. During its last two decades the war degenerated into a movable famine. In central Europe its impact was decisive.

Baltic trade was one of the victims. In the period before 1620 Baltic lords had reorganized their estates to produce grain for the export market. Dutch and German merchants had prospered, bringing wheat, iron, copper, and lumber from the Baltic ports to the west. In the 1620s this trade broke sharply. An impoverished and war-torn west was less able to buy Baltic grain and lumber. After 1650 trade slowly recovered. But the eastern powers were too weak and· poor to make the investments in shipping, mining, banking, or agriculture necessary for real economic progress. Eastern Europe remained economically localized, an exporter of raw materials to a recovering west.

In the British Isles the depression was considerably less severe than in most of the Continent. Although English trade was depressed, it did not suffer the severe damage common elsewhere. English manufacturers continued to grow, but more slowly than before. Iron and textiles profited from war, and the London money market was not rocked by royal bankruptcies. The crown borrowed sparingly, and the available capital went to satisfy the needs of trade. The reign of Charles I was a sort of mild economic slough, aggravated by the turmoil of the civil war.

But with the Restoration from 1660 to 1700 came a tremendous expansion of all phases of the English economy. Technological improvement accompanied increased markets. Overseas trade expanded, as did the English merchant marine. By 1700 England had surpassed the Netherlands as the leading carrier of European commerce. New colonies were acquired in America, Africa, and the West Indies, and new colonial products, such as rice, indigo, and sugar, added to British prosperity. London increased in importance as a money market. England recovered completely and rapidly from the general crisis, emerging with the strongest economy in Europe.

Only one European nation escaped from the depression. Although engaged in almost constant conflict from 1572 until 1648, the Netherlands managed to profit from the wars that ruined everyone else. The Dutch did much of their fighting at sea, where their naval superiority enabled them to prey on Spanish, Portuguese, Italian, and German shipping at will and thus pay the costs of war. The apex of commerce raiding was reached in 1628, when Piet Heyn captured an entire Spanish treasure fleet.

But more important than booty was the impetus war gave to Dutch trade. After the formation of the Dutch East India Company in 1602, Netherlands merchants were able to seize most of the East Indies from Portugal. Within a decade Amsterdam had become the center of the spice trade. The Dutch were equally successful in absorbing the Spanish commerce in slaves and colonial products from America. Fishing also fell to the Dutch, who made salted herring a staple of the European diet. In the Baltic the Dutch replaced the Germans in carrying grain, lumber, and metals. Even English and French coasting trade was dominated by the Netherlands during the first half of the seventeenth century. The Dutch profited enormously from universal distress.

Dutch income from commerce also supported the fiscal institutions of the new republic. The Bank of Amsterdam, the strongest fiscal institution in Europe, was founded in 1609. Dutch marine insurance was the best in the world. Dutch merchants had ample funds to invest, and Amsterdam commerce attracted funds from abroad. Nothing illustrated the strength of the Amsterdam money market better than the great tulip mania. In 1636, tulips began to increase extravagantly in value. A frantic curb exchange in Amsterdam dealt with the tulip speculation. In 1636 a single rare bulb sold for two lasts of wheat, four lasts of rye, four fat oxen, eight fat pigs, twelve fat sheep, two barrels of wine, four barrels of beer, two barrels of butter, one thousand pounds of cheese, one bed, one suit of clothes, one silver drinking cup. The inevitable crash came in 1637, but the Amsterdam money market, its banks, and its merchants survived handsomely. Not until the 1670s, under the relentless pressure of war with France, did the Dutch fiscal superiority begin to slip. Yet even then it was more the extraordinary expansion of the

English economy than the Dutch collapse that ended the Netherlands' preeminence.

The general crisis went beyond commercial and agricultural depression. It was also the occasion for considerable social and political unrest; a crisis of the organization of state and society. Incessant warfare, the gradual emergence of the bureaucratic state, the new political ideals of absolutism—all were unsettling in themselves. But the existence of the severe economic decline gave a sharper edge to social discord and added the agony of want to political conflict.

Hardest hit by revolution and civil war was the Spanish Empire, the most severely depressed area of Europe. Faced with endless war against France and the Netherlands, the Spanish prime minister, Count-Duke Olivares, searched for new sources of income. He decided to tax Catalonia and Portugal at the same rate as Castile, contrary to the privileges of those two provinces. This only produced revolt. In both areas, defense of local rights and privileges, sharp-

The Anatomy Lesson of Dr. Tulp **by Rembrandt van Rijn, the great master of the Dutch school. The painting, which established the artist's reputation as a portrait painter, is indicative of his power of dramatic characterization.** A. *Dingjan.*

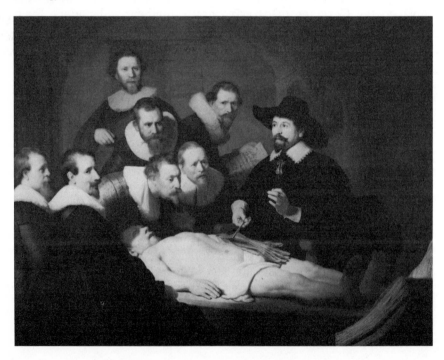

ened by a declining economy, was far more important than any notions of imperial responsibilities. This was equally true of the Italians. In 1647 Naples and Palermo flared into revolt, mainly over the high price of bread and lack of work. In 1671 a rebellion in defense of local privileges occurred in Messina that was repressed only after three-years of war. Depression aggravated the endemic conflict between royal centralization and traditional local rights.

A similar conflict between the powers of the crown and the privileges of subjects began in France in 1648. The Fronde lasted four years before the king could subdue the loose coalition of towns, law courts, nobles, and provinces that fought against him. The occasion of the revolt was a fourfold disaster: royal bankruptcy, the call for new taxes, a famine, and the Thirty Years' War. When the king asked for money, several sections of the nation rose up in revolt. The impoverished nation asserted with some justice that it could not pay. Ultimately, however, Louis XIV made his will felt, and local and class privileges fell before the advancing centralization of royal power. The Fronde was the prelude to French absolutism.

The most serious revolution was in England. The English civil war had constitutional and religious roots, as well as the discontent of depression. But in England, also, the immediate cause of rebellion was the king's need for money, in this case to liquidate a losing war with Scotland. Charles I was soundly defeated, and Cromwell's main support came from London and the commercial towns, depressed by the long economic slump. But the change in regime could not end the depression, and the English economy only began its rapid growth with the Restoration.

Recovery from the worst effects of the general crisis began in some areas of Europe after 1660. The population, level for almost two generations, began to climb once more. Trade increased, and new products such as coal, cottons, tobacco, and sugar became profitable staples of European commerce. Industry revived in France and England, where textiles, mining, and metallurgy made tremendous gains. Colonies showed a new prosperity—particularly the West Indies. The whole economic psychology of northern Europe in the latter part of the seventeenth century was one of expansion and profit. The Mediterranean basin, however, remained profoundly depressed.

Recovery was built on a number of factors. There was the end to an era of revolution and social unrest. Government became more stable after 1660. The great adventures of religious wars and Hapsburg domination of Europe were over. In central Europe, the basic fact was the end of nearly fifty years of exceptionally destructive wars. After 1660, war lacked the compulsive pillage of earlier conflicts. Finally, European governments paid increasing attention to their economies after 1660. Monarchs and parliaments strove mightily to establish new industries, foster and encourage trade, and develop colonies. It was the great age of mercantilism.

Yet, for all of its vigor, economic recovery was extremely uneven. The Mediterranean area continued to decline until the middle of the eighteenth century. Even after that, recovery was very slow. The relative economic supremacy of Spain, Italy, and Flanders over the rest of Europe was lost forever. In central Europe and the Baltic, recovery was more rapid. Exports of grain, lumber, iron, and copper grew, but central Europe remained an exporter of raw materials to the west. The attempts by eastern powers to industrialize generally failed. Thus the economic gap between east and west grew rather than diminished as a result of the general crisis.

In northern Europe, however, economic recovery set the stage for industrial revolution. England and France enjoyed a tremendous prosperity in the eighteenth century. In both states there was a substantial growth in population, in England after 1660 and in France after 1720. Commercial and industrial towns grew enormously, and London and Paris became the biggest cities in the world. A vast increase in trade provided an accumulation of capital and a market great enough to initiate and sustain industrial enterprise. In agriculture, the eighteenth century brought land reclamation, enclosures of waste and common, and the introduction of new crops. Yield increased, and peasant labor was released to the towns to work in commerce and industry. Particularly in England, economic growth moved beyond mere recovery from a depression toward an industrial society.

Thus the seventeenth-century crisis was more than a series of revolutions or a profound economic depression. It decisively changed the political and economic map of Europe. It completed the shift in the economic geography of Europe, changing the focus of wealth and productivity from the Mediterranean to the north Atlantic. The beginnings of industrialization in England grew out of the recovery from the depression. The era of the general crisis marked the faint beginnings of the patterns and structure of the modern European economy.

POLITICS OF THE EUROPEAN STATE SYSTEM

"L'État, c'est moi" ("I am the state") is an aphorism attributed to Louis XIV of France, the most dazzling and powerful monarch of seventeenth-century Europe. Nothing expressed so well the ideal of absolutism, the dominant political theory of the time. The powers of the crown were exalted over all local and provincial privileges, traditional rights, and class distinctions and barriers. Even the subjects' religion was at the disposal of the king. Royal sovereignty came from God, to be used for the purposes and glory of kings. As political theory, absolutism was neither complex nor profound. But it was adequate justification for the growing centralization of political power in the person and bureaucracy of the king.

In spite of the wide claims of absolutism, there remained, of course, substantial limits on royal power. Louis XIV failed to recruit fishermen for the royal navy. He could not eliminate the tax inequities among various provinces of France. He could never find enough money to pay for his government. He did not even dare try to dent the established class privileges of the nobles, bourgeoisie, and clergy. What the theories of absolutism granted the king, reality denied him.

The major trend of politics in France, however, was toward centralization and increased royal authority. Local, provincial, and class privileges were under constant assault by the state. A rational, systematic form of government must prevail. The remnants of feudalism, manorialism, and medieval government must bow before the rights and powers of the monarchical state. Louis XIV tried to live up to the claims that absolutism made in his name.

However, royal centralization did not always succeed. Portugal, Spain, and Naples, while not actually disintegrating, stagnated. There was also a third pattern of politics, confined to England and the Netherlands, where the national representative assembly became the focus of power. Although neither the English Parliament nor the Dutch States-General replaced the king, each did achieve a coordinate status in government. Politics in England and Holland extended to two fronts: the attempts to centralize the administration of the realm and the struggles between Parliament and the crown.

Royal Centralization in Western Europe: 1660–1740

The Old Regime state that most nearly achieved the ideals of absolutism was France. There the power of the crown appeared the greatest, royal income the largest, the army the best, and the glory of the king the most effulgent in all the Christian world. Louis XIV was the Sun King, the greatest monarch since Charles V. His victories, his realm, his wealth, the magnificence of his court, excited the envy and emulation of his royal contemporaries. Could anyone doubt that he was indeed God's representative to the French people?

Versailles, the great palace built for Louis XIV, became the focus of French life during the monarch's reign and a symbol of his absolutism. This painting, entitled *View of Versailles in 1722,* is by J. B. Martin. *Versailles Museum.*

Although frightfully expensive, the glittering facade of the royal court was vital to Louis' prestige and power. In an age when most people could not read, visual propaganda was the only method of impressing the world with one's position and greatness. Conspicuous consumption was an important element of statecraft. No one spent more lavishly or publicly than Louis XIV. He lived at Versailles, the greatest and most costly palace in Europe. He arose in the morning, retired at night, and passed his days according to the most exact and punctilious etiquette, all of it designed to emphasize the power and glory of the Sun King. No action of his public life was unplanned. All reflected the wondrous awe that one should feel in beholding the king. The spectacle of the king being menially served by the highest lords of the land impressed everyone: Louis' real power must be vast indeed.

Behind the facade of glory and magnificence, Louis XIV and his ministers worked hard to increase royal power. No activity received more of their attention and loving care than war, the duty and profession of kings. The Sun King and his ministers strove to make the army an obedient and dependable instrument of royal will. This gigantic task fell to the war minister Louvois, who argued and cajoled, demanded and persevered, and gradually broke the military to central control. A rank structure was invented, with promotion coming from the king. Civilian control was ensured by hordes of inspectors and auditors constantly dispatched from Versailles to watch the administration of army commanders. Military armament and fortifications were also improved. Cannon were made more reliable, less likely to explode and kill the gunners. A ring bayonet replaced the pike, adding firepower to infantry formations. Improvements in the pistol added a new weapon to the cavalry. Marshal Vauban greatly strengthened the fortifications on the frontiers of France and improved the effectiveness of French siege warfare. A map service was added to the French military staff, lessening the chances that the army would get lost. Not only was the French army better organized, it fought better.

Centralization of the apparatus of civil control was as important to royal power as a massive military machine. The government of Louis XIV moved toward the modern bureaucratic state in the areas of taxation, management of the economy, and general civil administration. The work of administrative centralization fell largely to Jean-Baptiste Colbert, the comptroller-general of finances from 1663–1683, who labored to perfect the new bureaucratic instruments of royal power.

This was not easy to do. Whole classes of royal officials, particularly those in justice, and finance, owned their offices. Royal offices had become property. Public service was a species of investment. Ministers had found the sale of offices a valuable fiscal expedient and had increased the privileges of the officeholders in order to continue the practice. The disadvantages of this were obvious. A caste of rich and privileged royal officials, who acted in their own interest and not the king's, had been created. Royal orders were ignored. The officials themselves were too numerous and powerful for the king to confiscate their property. The crown therefore simply had to work with the privileged officials as best it could.

The Sun King made great efforts to circumvent the vested interests of privileged officials. A new bureaucracy grew up around the ministers in Paris, run by men who did not own their office. The king's councils were staffed by councillors of state, removable at will. In the provinces, the position of intendant, which was not owned, became the major vehicle for local and regional administration of royal affairs. Intendants were given wide authority, particularly in the realms of justice, finance, police. They developed their own bureaucracy, and sent subdelegates throughout their jurisdiction to enforce the king's will and reduce the independent power of the towns and nobles.

Some intendants became legends in their provinces. D'Etigny in Basse-Navarre built roads, encouraged industry and agriculture, and greatly increased the prosperity of his province. Marillac in Poitou was such a ferocious persecutor of the Huguenots that Louis XIV had to relieve him. In Provence, Gallois de la Tour was a discreet and effective representative of local interests to the king's ministers. French government was not so bureaucratic that it excluded the personality of its officials.

The finances of the king also underwent major reform. Colbert destroyed many of the internal tariff barriers of France, forcing the central provinces of the realm into a customs union, the largest free-trade area in western Europe. He introduced a systematic royal budget and an audit of expenditures. Taxation was rationalized. The excise taxes for the whole realm were organized into one great contract, let to a single group of tax farmers, and carefully supervised by the crown. This Royal General Farm increased the yield to the king, and reduced somewhat the enormous social costs to the people. Control over the taille, the basic royal tax on peasants and their land, was slowly wrested from local officials. The amount the peasant paid was reduced and the amount the crown received enlarged. Under Colbert, royal fiscal administration was as efficient and just as it would ever be during the Old Regime.

In spite of the efforts of Colbert and Louvois, however, French government in the Old Regime retained grievous faults, which became more unpopular as the years wore on. Taxation remained regressive, falling hardest on the peasant, who was least able to pay or complain. No reforms could offset the enormous social costs of such a tax system, which lacked even the merit of providing the crown with enough money. Nor did the Sun King overcome the galling class distinctions of the Old Regime; nobles and the clergy retained their immense privileges over the common run. The provinces of Languedoc and Brittany retained their tax exemptions. A single system of justice or law did not prevail in all of France. Frenchmen continued to buy offices from a government too weak and too poor to refuse them. Finally the Sun King plunged France into a vicious campaign of religious persecution against the Protestants. The persecution, based on the theory that only Catholics could be truly loyal to the king, was a monstrous and dismal failure. It reduce the prestige of both the king and his church.

When one regards the spectacle of "absolute" monarchy in France, therefore, the dominant impression is one of paradox. On the surface, all was glitter, magnificence, and success. The court of the Sun King was a stupendous production, French armies marched all over Europe, colonies were established in every part of the world. At home certain real improvements were made in the form and administration of government. But deep and serious social and economic problems remained. Invidious social privilege was increased, and hideous poverty remained the lot of the peasant and artisan. The crown was strengthened and the royal government was centralized and improved, but both king and bureaucracy were placed at the service of social and economic privilege. In 1680 no one questioned this; a century later such a government would stand universally condemned.

Not all European kingdoms were undergoing the painful process of internal consolidation exemplified by seventeenth-century France. Several were falling apart under the increased pressure of competition with their neighbors. In the period after 1640 the Spanish Empire was the sick man of western Europe, suffering a series of major military defeats that only accelerated internal disintegration. Spain was plagued by the anarchy of feudalism and localism, an increasing vacuum at the center, and by the quiet despair of economic depression.

Peripheral provinces of the Spanish Empire claimed that the feeble attempts at political centralization in seventeenth-century Spain were unconstitutional and they replied to royal efforts by revolt. Royal officials in Madrid bewailed the lack of institutional and administrative reform. There was no real recovery from economic depression. Continual war from 1570 through 1659 destroyed royal finances and overseas trade alike. The growth of the institutional Catholic Church absorbed many of the energies of the people, while the Inquisition imposed a paralyzing and deadly system of thought control over Spain. The growth in status of the nobility turned the energies of Spaniards away from industry and agriculture to attempts to acquire social rank. Finally the government of the king, never a model of efficiency or honesty, became steadily worse after Philip II. During the seventeenth century, Spaniards suffered under a debilitating tyranny of inefficiency. Spain possessed an incompetent state mismanaging a decaying society.

So forcibly did the uninterrupted disasters of Spanish society and statecraft impress contemporaries that it pointed moral as well as political lessons on seventeenth-century observers. For Protestants, Spanish decadence was an example of the wrath of a righteous God upon the Inquisition and Catholic religious persecution. Spaniards themselves drew religious conclusions from the decay of their state and society, saying that Spanish sins were responsible for the disasters, which were a cross sent by God to test true Christians. Seventeenth-century Spain was a contemporary object lesson in catastrophe.

Representative Institutions in Western States: 1660–1740

Bureaucratic centralization and aristocratic decadence were not the only patterns of government in western Europe after the general crisis. In the Netherlands and England another pattern emerged— government by king along with a representative institution. In both countries the representative institutions had strong medieval precedents: the English Parliament dating from the fourteenth century and the Dutch States-General dating from the 1355 charter of privileges known as the "Joyous Entry." The English crown had not recognized Parliament as an ally, but saw it as a rival for power. Philip II of Spain viewed the Dutch provincial estates as his bitterest enemy, and Charles I of England went to war with his Parliament in 1640. National representative institutions in the early modern period, therefore, owed their existence to success in war. It was that very success that established the pattern of continued close cooperation between king and Parliament.

Old Regime Netherlands was unlike any other state in Europe. Primarily a commercial republic, it derived its income from trade and fishing. Along with commerce, the Dutch engaged in banking and marine insurance, and Amsterdam was the fiscal capital of seventeenth-century Europe. No other European state derived most of its gross national product from nonagricultural pursuits; the Dutch republic had an economy unique in preindustrial Europe. In such a state, power resided in the towns and the urban patriciate that ran them. Delegates to the States-General were normally from the cities and represented urban interests, with those of Amsterdam paramount. Both domestic and foreign policy of the Netherlands were directed toward the growth and safety of trade, fishing, and banking.

The government of the Dutch republic was extremely complex. At the head of the state was the *Stadtholder*, who possessed by right the supreme military authority. His power grew in wartime and faded in peace. Sharing the sovereignty of the state and holding legislative authority was the States-General, an assembly of representatives from the seven Dutch provinces. In this parliament the representatives of Holland were dominant, largely because of the immense wealth and power of Amsterdam. The States-General was extremely jealous of the *Stadtholder's* prerogatives and consistently maintained a policy of decentralization, states' rights, and legislative initiative. In its views the States-General was ably seconded by the estates of the seven provinces, which were also suspicious of any appearance of royal bureaucratic centralization. Within this loose system of interconnecting assemblies, one official provided some degree of continuity—the grand pensionary or advocate-general of the province of Holland. He drew up the agenda for debate at the provincial estates, represented Holland to the States-General and the *Stadtholder*, and put forth the views of the merchant oligarchy of Amsterdam. His position rested on his personal ability, the backing of the delegates of Holland, and the wealth of Amsterdam, rather than on any institutional base. In the periods of peace when the *Stadtholder* was powerless, the pensionary ran the country. In such a state the politics were bound to be complex, though the basic pattern is clear—a perpetual struggle for power between the *Stadtholder* and the grand pensionary of Holland representing the States-General.

In Great Britain the essential political question had to do with the terms under which the monarchy had been restored in 1660. Charles II quickly showed that he was not going to follow his father's sad example and indulge in a futile experience in absolutism. He called for the election of a Parliament. Charles' first Parliament met in May 1661 and quickly led king and nation into a program of religious repression against the Puritans, known as the Clarendon Code after the prime minister, the earl of Clarendon. As the memory of the Commonwealth receded, the Clarendon Code commanded less support, although religious passions were still strong enough to defeat an attempt by Charles II to decree religious toleration and to obtain passage in Parliament of the Test Act of 1673, which required all officeholders to be Anglicans.

In addition to religion, both king and Parliament were also

concerned with prosperity, which meant trade and colonization. The Restoration brought a remarkable growth in British wealth, a sustained interest in colonization, and passage of the Navigation Acts. Although the government was too poor to colonize directly, it was generous with grants to individuals willing to establish plantations, with schemes for privateering, and with plans for conquering the colonies of others. The growth in British trade and naval power made this policy work, and by 1700 the British were firmly established in North America and the West Indies.

Charles II was a clever and able king; his successor, James II, was not. Stubborn and tactless, James paraded his Catholicism in a land where it had been equated with treason. He appointed Catholics to ecclesiastical and university posts, to his ministry, and to his civil service. He also showed ominous signs of ignoring the powers and position of Parliament. The birth of a son in 1688, which raised the prospect of Catholic and absolutist succession, sealed James II's doom. In November 1688, the Protestant William of the Netherlands, who had married James' sister Mary, landed with an army, and James fled to France. So swift and sure had been the revolt that it was called the Glorious Revolution.

In January 1689 a Parliament was called to reorganize the government. James II was declared to have forfeited the throne, and it was offered to William and Mary, to rule jointly. This tender was accompanied by the Declaration of Rights, which set down the rights of the people and Parliament of England. These rights were quite extensive. Only Parliament could pass or repeal laws, levy taxes, or maintain a standing army. Elections and debate in Parliament were to be free from control by the sovereign. Monarchs were to hold frequent Parliaments. The rights of man were not neglected. No man was to be deprived of his property without due process of law. Englishmen were entitled to habeas corpus, trial by jury, and freedom from excessive bail. William and Mary swore to accept these conditions, and, by the large, they did.

The reign of William and Mary (1689–1702) and that of their successor, Anne (1702–1714), were mostly taken up by war with France. Parliament played an increasing role, and the effective power of the crown steadily diminished. In Parliament, fairly solid factions —the ancestors of parties—emerged, and the ministers could not rule for long without a majority in Commons. Two factions quickly developed: the Whigs, led by Marlborough and Godolphin, and the Tories, led by Harley and Bolingbroke. Under Queen Anne, the Whig and Tory factions alternated in office, but after George I came to the throne in 1714, the Whigs ruled supreme. Parliament fell firmly under their control. In 1721 one of the early Whig associates of Marlborough and Godolphin, Sir Robert Walpole, became prime minister, a position he held until 1742. Walpole believed in peace abroad and prosperity at home, and his political motto was to let sleeping dogs lie. In Europe, he tried to maintain a balance of power,

Gianlorenzo Bernini's masterpiece, *The Ecstasy of St. Theresa.* **The artist's flamboyant and emotional depiction of Theresa of Avila, a saint of the Counter-Reformation, typifies the artistic sensibilities of the baroque period.** *Alinari—Art Reference Bureau.*

in the hope of keeping the peace. At home, Walpole concentrated on his majority in Parliament. He managed it by being an expert politician, always finding enough votes by bribing, promising, threatening, and persuading, and by cutting his program to fit the Members' needs. These were uninspiring methods, but they worked. The urban merchants and landed gentry who were the backbone of the Whig factions were reasonably satisfied, and Britain enjoyed a stable government.

In the century after the restoration of Charles II, England moved steadily toward the dominance of Parliament. Although the king retained a great deal of power after the Restoration, he was less and less able to use it effectively. Royal dependence on a parliamentary majority grew, and the king progressively lost control over his cabinet ministers. Under Charles II a minister needed first to keep his sovereign's confidence; under George II he had to concentrate on Parliament. This was partly the result of revolution. In the main, however, a powerful Parliament suited the merchants and most of the gentry and peerage by conforming to their notions of how England ought to be governed. A Protestant state church, with substantial toleration for Protestant nonconformists, also suited the English magnates. English kings could not ignore this weight of opinion. Noble Frenchmen might believe in divine right; the English magnates believed in Parliament and the rights of Englishmen. British political development reflected this.

Patterns of Old Regime Diplomacy in Western Europe: 1660–1740

In the years following the Peace of Westphalia (1648), there emerged patterns of war and diplomacy that existed almost unchanged until the 1730s. A dual diplomatic and military system developed—one sphere in western Europe involving Spain, England, France, Holland, and Austria; the other in the east, consisting of Sweden, Prussia, Poland, Russia, Austria, and the Ottoman Empire. The western powers fought over trade and colonies as often as they did over European territory, very little of which changed hands after 1660. The eastern powers fought exclusively over land, and huge provinces, with ill-defined borders and small populations, were continually shifted back and forth by various wars and treaties. Except for Austria—a participant in both diplomatic and military spheres—the eastern and western states played only the most minor roles in each other's wars. Geographical distance and divergence of interests were too great to be bridged by mere treaties.

Patterns of military affairs also remained relatively constant throughout most of the Old Regime. The armies of the seventeenth and eighteenth centuries were too weak and small to win total military victory over another great power. Good command helped, of course; Turenne, Marlborough, and Eugene of Savoy won more battles, took more towns, and pillaged more villages than their less talented opponents. But in the end, try as they might, they could not force a surrender. So the wars dragged on, always to be ended in compromise and diplomacy. In the Old Regime the most crucial battles were fought in the peace conferences.

It was the interminability of war, and not so much the intensity, that made it so ruinously expensive. There was not enough money in Old Regime Europe, which was an underdeveloped society, to pay for prolonged warfare. Wars devoured the resources of king and country, and the meager rewards of limited victory were incommensurate with the costs. Yet, ruinous or not, wars continued to be fought, often ended only by mutual exhaustion. Even in the more prosperous western diplomatic sphere, economic factors were as important as the military in determining conditions that would lead to diplomatic victory.

Finally, a diplomatic balance of power slowly emerged as the basic pattern of international affairs in the years after 1660. The balance of power arose from the increased authority of the newly centralized states, one of which—France—could reach for domination of all of western Europe. The smaller and weaker powers therefore banded together to survive and to balance the force available to their stronger neighbors. Thus the diplomatic tides swung slowly but inexorably against the strongest power, which until 1715 was France. In the years after 1660 the balance of diplomatic power sometimes operated without much conscious discussion in the chancelleries, but by the eighteenth century it had become a respected and venerable principle of diplomacy, and statesmen often appealed to it as an explanation for their actions. The balance of power had become one of the basic patterns of European diplomacy and war.

In western Europe after the seventeenth-century depression the strongest single state was France. French power had been achieved largely at the expense of the Hapsburgs, both in Austria and Spain. At Westphalia in 1648 France obtained Alsace, and in 1659 in the Treaty of the Isle of Pheasants, Spain surrendered the province of Roussillon. But this was only the beginning. Having weakened the Hapsburgs, Louis XIV was determined to make France the dominant power of western Europe. In three major wars—the Dutch War (1672–1678), the War of the League of Augsburg (1689–1698), and the War of the Spanish Succession (1701–1713)—Louis XIV struggled for hegemony in Europe against Holland, Great Britain, and Austria. Although France won some victories and annexed the province of Franche-Comté in 1678, the larger goals were lost. France was not strong enough to dominate Europe.

The drive for hegemony by France under Louis XIV was not the only element in western European diplomacy. There were also important commercial and colonial issues. In this instance, however, the state seeking hegemony was England, and the defensive powers were the Netherlands, France, and Spain. The objectives of war and diplomacy in maritime matters were colonial possessions and the domination of lucrative branches of trade. The spice trade was firmly in the hands of the Dutch, but commerce in slaves, fish, grain, textiles, ironware, sugar, indigo, and tobacco was sought in a fierce and unremitting competition. The penalty for failure was ruin, and the prize for success was wealth and power: In the mercantilist age, wealth and trade were held to be synonymous, and diplomacy in western Europe reflected this belief.

These patterns continued unchanged during the eighteenth century. British naval supremacy over the French, established at the Battle of La Hogue in 1692, was never relinquished. Although the Spanish were able to keep physical possession of their colonies, the trade and profits from them continued to fall into foreign hands. Steadily the English engrossed a larger share of the trade and wealth for themselves, eclipsing the Dutch and French. The Netherlands was too small to fight France on land and Britain on sea. By the middle of the eighteenth century, France and Great Britain were left to fight for imperial supremacy. In the great war for empire that lasted from 1739 to 1763, the British could not help but win.

During the Old Regime, in most places, the semimedieval monarchy of the Renaissance and Reformation was gradually and painfully supplanted by more centralized and modern governments. Such vast changes were hard to make. By the end of the seventeenth century, however, many European states were succeeding. States were developing their own support, their own constituency in the men whose lives were spent in state service. Bureaucrats, military officers, judges, municipal officeholders appointed by the king—all depended on the success of government policy for their prestige, status, rank, and income. Royal officials made the laws, enforced them, collected taxes, fought wars, suppressed revolutions, and directed the activities of the church. The king and Parliament could rely increasingly on its own men. In the past they had been too few; now they were not. The essential fact of state building and centralization was that the government, whether royal or parliamentary, had become self-sufficient.

THE EMERGENCE OF EASTERN EUROPE

In 1650, eastern Europe—the lands between the Elbe River and the Urals—was still medieval, hardly different from the days of the Mongol invasions. The population of this huge area was thin and scattered, living mainly in peasant hamlets. Nomadic tribes of Cossacks and Tartars roamed over most of western Russia, a constant threat to the settled peasantry. Banditry was a major recognized occupation. Localism was overwhelming, both in society and government; the village, its church, and château were the boundaries of the whole world to almost everyone. Central government was confused, poorly articulated, and usually powerless; lacking both bureaucracy and standing army, it often existed in only a formal, or feudal, sense. The huge provinces, which eastern monarchs claimed to govern, had impossibly vague boundaries, and many inhabitants did not know in what state they lived. Compared to the more urban and industrialized west, eastern Europe was incredibly backward. Indeed, it was another world.

Government in much of the east differed widely from western bureaucratic and parliamentary models. In Poland, Turkey, and the Swedish Empire, government remained incoherent throughout the Old Regime. Officials were semi-independent, armies more the property of their generals than the state, finance disordered, and civil administration was invariably rudimentary and inefficient. Such inchoate government made intelligent decision making unlikely and efficient reaction to problems impossible. The failure of the empires of Sweden, Turkey, and Poland to develop effective institutions and procedures of central administration was the biggest single factor in their decline or disappearance.

Not every eastern state was sliding into feudal decay. Kings in Prussia, Austria, and Russia introduced western methods of war and government into their domains. They extended the power of the crown into the countryside, encouraged towns and trade, built complex bureaucracies and effective armies, and made the power of the state a reality. Westernization became the fixed policy of progressive and successful governments in the east. Resistance was strong, especially from the nobility and clergy, but the monarchs crushed it when they could, circumvented it when necessary, and pushed ahead with reform. They met with spectacular success. Prussia under Frederick the Great set the standard for military and administrative efficiency,

Vienna by 1800 boasted a more brilliant culture than Paris, and the tsars of Russia so firmly established westernization that the policy has persisted until today. The basic thread of Old Regime history in eastern Europe was the progressive modernization of military and civil administration in Russia, Austria, and Prussia, something their fading rivals could not accomplish.

The Decline of Turkey and the Rise of Austria: Politics and Diplomacy from Westphalia to Karlowitz (1648–1699)

After the Treaties of Westphalia, three great imperial powers dominated politics and diplomacy in eastern Europe. Sweden, one of the main beneficiaries of the Thirty Years' War, had emerged with a substantial Baltic empire, which was enlarged by further conquests from Poland in 1660. South of Sweden lay the huge and diffuse kingdom of Poland, an immense conglomerate of feudal lordships and principalities. The Ottoman Empire dominated the Balkans and Black Sea, an incoherent state held together by a superb army. Hollow as these empires were by western standards, they were still huge and far outclassed their potential rivals. Yet, in the years after Westphalia, the power balance in the east was slowly and subtly shifting. The great powers were not so strong as they seemed. Economic depression and political malfunctions were sapping their strength. The smaller powers, particularly the half-western Austria and Prussia, were growing—less in size than in cohesiveness, but the result was to be the same. Inexorably, political dominance in the east began to change hands.

Although the various eastern powers fought among themselves during the last half of the seventeenth century, the main conflicts were a group of wars between the Christian powers and the Ottoman Empire. These were nearly continuous, and divided themselves into two distinct periods. The first, from 1645 until 1681, was composed of a series of rather disconnected conflicts, with Turkey rarely fighting more than one enemy at a time. In these wars the Turks won more often than they lost. From 1645 until 1670 Turkey fought Venice in the eastern Mediterranean and ultimately won the siege of Crete. The Turks did only a little less well in a short war with Austria. Although the Austrians won the major battle of St. Gotthard, the Truce of Vasvar (1664) contained no gains for them. In the Treaty of Zuravno, which ended the Polish-Turkish war of 1672–1676, Turkey kept Podolia and part of the Ukraine. Only in the Russo-Turkish war of 1677–1681 did Turkey lose any territory, part of the Ukraine, to the growing Muscovite power. Turkey was well able to hold her own against any single European enemy, in spite of a declining economy, an increasingly feeble sultanate, and an inferior military technology.

In the great Christian crusade against the Turk, from 1682 to 1699, these conditions changed. Instead of fighting a single front, the Ottoman Empire was engaged everywhere for nearly fifteen years. Imbued with a sense of purpose and cooperation that had eluded them earlier, Turkey's enemies waged a continuous campaign that finally inflicted crucial defeats on the Ottoman Empire. Indeed, it was Austrian preoccupation with her war with France (1689–1697), rather than Turkish military prowess, that saved the Ottoman Empire from an even more crushing defeat.

The war started well enough for Turkey, with the Ottoman armies pushing to Vienna in 1683 and laying siege to the city. A desperate defense led by Rüdiger von Starhemberg held the Turks at bay until the arrival of a Polish army under King John III Sobieski lifted the siege. Following the successful defense of Vienna, Austria and her allies took the offensive. Between 1685 and 1687 the Venetian general Morosini conquered the Peloponnesian peninsula and advanced as far as Athens, where an ammunition dump in the Parthenon exploded, nearly destroying the temple. Austrian armies advanced slowly down the Danube and in August 1687 defeated the Turks at Mohacs and cleared Hungary of Turkish forces.

After Mohacs, the Austrians paused in their pursuit of the Turkish armies and began consolidating their conquests in Hungary. Beginning in 1690, Leopold I settled thousands of Serbs along the southern Hungarian border in a continuation of military frontiers begun in the sixteenth century in Croatia. The Serbian peasants were given their land on the condition of military service against the Turks, making them almost the only free peasants in eastern Europe. Leopold also gave thousands of acres of land in Hungary and Transylvania to Austrian lords, such as the Esterhazy, in an effort to ensure the loyalty of the new territories to the emperor.

After 1695 the tempo of war increased. Capture of Azov in 1696 gave Russia a Black Sea port, and the immense Austrian victory of Eugene of Savoy at Zenta in 1697 gave upper Serbia to Austria and destroyed any possibility of Turkish recovery of Hungary. In 1699 the allies, victorious but exhausted, signed the Treaty of Karlowitz with the defeated Ottoman Empire. The treaty generally followed the military situation, with Russia keeping Azov, Poland keeping Podolia and southwestern Ukraine, Venice keeping the Peloponnesus, and Austria getting Hungary, Croatia, Transylvania, and Slavonia.

The Treaty of Karlowitz marked a virtual revolution in the power relationships of eastern Europe. Poland, whose brief flurry of activity under John III Sobieski ended by 1687, sank to the level of a second-rate power. The Ottoman Empire had suffered an irreversible defeat. Although her empire in Europe did not disappear until the Balkan Wars of 1912–1913, she never again regained the military or diplomatic initiative. Austria and Russia were the major victors. Austria, which had modernized her army and government to compete with France in the west, found these instruments capable of immense victories in the east. Russia, beginning her rise to world power, found the declining Ottoman Empire a victim for imperial expansion. Karlowitz clearly showed two of the new eastern powers, Austria and Russia, and two of the power vacuums, Poland and Turkey.

Politics from Karlowitz to Hubertusburg, 1699–1763: The Rise of Prussia and Russia

The Austrian victories in the Turkish war had been spectacular, but they were not as portentous as the single Russian success at Azov. The rise of Russia under Peter the Great was an entirely new factor in the politics of eastern Europe. When he became tsar in 1689, Peter inherited an Asiatic state that lacked the basic institutions of military and civil government common in the west. Without a ministry, a civil service, any educational system, a navy or an army, a system of law or taxation, the sprawling Russian state was governed primarily by the nobility and the church, under the general direction of the tsar when he was strong enough to make his will felt. Peter was violently hostile to all this. He nursed great ambitions, which could only be fulfilled by Westernizing his state. Peter began with himself, making his famous journey (1697–1698) in which he worked as a shipwright in Holland to learn about Western navies. When he returned to Russia in 1698 it was to crush the revolt of the palace guard, the *streltzy*, who opposed western influence. Thereafter, until his death in 1725, Peter labored to Westernize Russia and expand its boundaries. He built a new capital at St. Petersburg on Baltic land conquered from Sweden. He built a navy and modernized his army. He centralized the administration, abolishing the council of boyars and establishing a senate in 1711 and governing bureaus called colleges in 1718. He took control of the Russian Orthodox Church through a holy synod. He forced the nobility to do state service in the army or administration in return for their land, peasants, and privileges. His reforms were hasty and incomplete, and some were failures, but generally they had the desired result; Russia moved toward the West and the power of the crown was greatly enlarged.

The wisdom of Peter the Great's program of Westernization was vindicated in the Great Northern War from 1700 to 1721, which saw the destruction of Swedish power in the Baltic and the definite establishment of Russia as a great power. The war began as a coalition of Denmark, Poland, and Russia against the boy king of Sweden, Charles XII. Charles was an untried youth, and the allied powers thought now would be a good time to rob him of all he had. The allied monarchs had not anticipated that Charles XII would be a natural military genius. The young Swedish king raised an army, defeated the Danes in six months, and then turned on Peter the Great. At Narva in November 1700, he routed an immense Russian army in a battle fought in a snowstorm. Next it was the turn of Augustus II, king of Poland and elector of Saxony, who lost every battle and surrendered in 1706. Charles again turned against Russia, his only remaining foe. Peter the Great had modernized his army somewhat and had been busy conquering Swedish possessions in the Baltic. In a furious battle at Poltava in 1708 Charles XII was defeated for the first time in his life, and his army fell apart. Although war dragged on for over a decade, the issue had been decided. In the Treaty of Nystad in 1721 Russia received Livonia, Estonia, and part of Karelia, all taken from Sweden. Predominance in the Baltic passed to Russia, which took its place with Austria as a great power in eastern Europe.

The years after Nystad saw the development of an effective diplomatic balance of power in eastern Europe. The two great powers, Austria and Russia, gradually came to the conclusion that cooperation, not competition, was the rational and profitable way to settle eastern problems. Random warfare died down. Diplomacy became better organized. There was increasing recognition of the existence of the Eastern Question, which was seen as the disposition of the politics and territories of Poland and the Ottoman Empire. Both great powers began to coordinate their policies when dealing with the Eastern Question, and an Austro–Russian alliance became the lodestar of eastern diplomacy.

Until 1740, when the Austrian emperor Charles VI and the Russian empress Anna both died, the alliance between Russia and Austria had given a certain stability to the diplomacy of the area. In 1740, however, a new kingdom made a bid for great-power rank. Since the Treaty of Westphalia in 1648, Brandenburg-Prussia had been growing slowly and steadily. Frederick William, the great elector of Brandenburg (1640–1688) had nursed his state back to health after the devastation of the Thirty Years' War. He had encouraged trade, settled lands, reorganized the government, strengthened the army, and reduced government expenditures. He assumed the royal title of king in Prussia in 1701 and acquired more lands after the Great Northern War. Frederick William I (1713–1740), by careful management, built his state up still further. He increased the size of the army until it reached 83,000, the largest effective standing force east of the Rhine. He organized the civil administration, centralizing political control into a council of ministers responsible to the king. Although Prussia was poor, small, and underpopulated, it was a stable, well-organized state, better prepared for war than any of its eastern neighbors.

The new Prussian king, Frederick the Great, used these advantages. In 1740 he launched a surprise assault on the rich Austrian province of Silesia, taking it from the unprepared defenders. Prussian aggression brought the rest of the great powers into the war. France joined the Prussians, and Great Britain allied herself with Austria; thus the War of the Austrian Succession became a struggle parallel to but separate from the Franco–British war for colonial domination. When a general peace was signed in 1748 at Aix-la-Chapelle, Prussia kept Silesia, and a new diplomatic equation existed in eastern Europe. Austro-Russian hegemony had been replaced by a tripartite balance; Prussia had become a great power.

The Austrian empress, Maria Theresa, refused to accept this balance. Outraged by Frederick's treachery, she declared that she would rather lose her petticoats than Silesia. After the war, therefore, the Austrian government was strengthened, the army enlarged, and a systematic search for allies began. By 1756 two had been found —France and Russia. The "abominable" Frederick found himself isolated, facing three of the most powerful armies in Europe.

Frederick the Great could see this as well as anyone, and he began the Seven Years' War in August 1756 by invading Saxony and driving the Austrians back on Prague. Once again a war involving balance of power in eastern Europe became merged with a Franco-British colonial struggle. In eastern Europe, however, the Seven Years' War narrowed to a single question: Could Prussia keep Silesia and remain a great power? Although Frederick won a number of tremendous military victories and drove France practically out of the war, the superior manpower of Austria and Russia gradually wore him down. In 1762, with Frederick all but finished, the Russian empress Elizabeth died. She was succeeded by her son Paul, a great

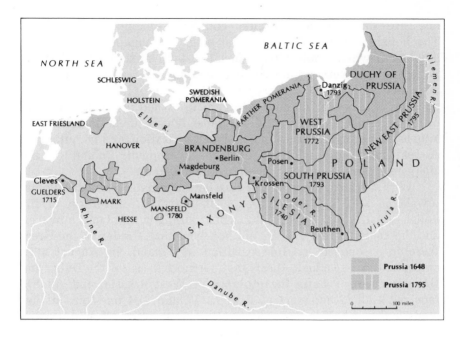

THE EXPANSION OF PRUSSIA, 1648–1795

admirer of Frederick. Paul took Russia out of the war and saved
Prussia. Maria Theresa, furious at being balked at the threshold of
victory, tried to continue the war alone. But the Austrians did not
have the strength to finish Frederick off. The Treaty of Hubertusburg
in 1763 provided for a mutual restoration of conquests and a return
to the prewar situation. Seven years of terrible and exhausting conflict had confirmed the rise of Prussia. After 1763 the cooperationist
diplomacy of the years before 1740 was gradually restored, and the
Seven Years' War was the last general conflict between great powers
in eastern Europe until the Great War of 1914–1918. The Treaty of
Hubertusburg established a stable diplomatic balance in the east.

Devouring Poland: Politics and Diplomacy from
Hubertusburg to the French Revolution: 1763–1795

After the end of the Seven Years' War, the main political and diplomatic problem in eastern Europe became the fate of Poland. Poland
in the course of the eighteenth century deteriorated steadily as an
effective government. The elective kingdom was a sort of aristocratic
republic in which the nobles counted for everything, while every-

one else—bourgeoisie, peasants, and king—amounted to nothing. The Polish diet, which elected the king, was composed of nobles, any one of whom could block legislation by a single vote. All of the Polish nobles were permitted to attend the diet, whether princely magnates such as the Czartoryski, Potocki, or Branicki who owned millions of acres, or landless gentry who owned nothing. The great princely families were virtually independent in their domains. The king had no army, no taxes, no civil administration, and no authority. A vast rural land without form or government, Poland by the eighteenth century lay at the mercy of its neighbors.

With the accession of the Russian candidate, Stanislas Poniatowski as king in 1764, there began stirrings for reform of the Polish constitution. Real reform would strengthen Poland, however, and the eastern great powers did not want that. Frederick the Great therefore proposed a triple partition of Poland. In August 1772 agreement was reached. Russia took territories east of the Dvina and Dnieper rivers, Prussia the province of West Prussia, and Austria received Galicia and part of Podolia. Poland lost one-third of her lands and one-half her people, and the great powers found a satisfactory formula for settling Polish affairs.

The partition was an immense shock to the Polish nobility, and it greatly spurred a reform movement. A genuine Polish national spirit grew in strength, supported by the king and his party. Unable to act because of Russian pressure, the reformers waited until the Russo-Turkish war of 1787–1792 before calling a reform diet in 1788. For two years the diet debated while the Russians and the Turks slugged it out. Finally, late in 1790, the diet began to make decisions. It banished the landless nobility from the regional assemblies, thus depriving the conservative magnates of their most raucous and numerous followers. In April 1791 the diet passed the Statute of the Cities, granting the bourgeoisie limited political participation and making generous provision for burghers to become nobles. Finally, on May 3, 1791, a new constitution was proclaimed, making the monarchy hereditary and adding to its strength and authority.

Satisfactory though the new constitution was to the Poles, in that it provided a real political revolution, it greatly irritated Russia, Prussia, and Austria. The eastern powers mobilized against Poland. Aided by dissident Polish magnates, who formed the Confederation of Targowica, Russia and Prussia invaded Poland in the summer of 1792 and soon routed the reformers. In January 1793 a second partition was arranged, with Russia getting the western Ukraine and Podolia, while Prussia took Danzig and Poznan. The Austrians were left out. A year later, Polish patriots led by the hero of the American

Revolution, Thaddeus Kosciusko, began a desperate national uprising against the foreign powers. Russia and Prussia invaded Poland at once, crushed the rebellion, and decided on a last partition. In October 1795, Russia received the rest of the Ukraine and Lithuania, Prussia took Warsaw and central Poland, while Austria took the Cracow region. By eighteenth-century standards the Polish problem had ended.

By 1763 the patterns of politics and diplomacy in eastern Europe were clear and fixed. In dealing with the Eastern Question, the great powers attempted to cooperate with each other, a tactic that worked spectacularly most of the time. This understanding did not break down until the Serbian crisis, which began the Great War in 1914. In dealing with their own subjects, monarchs in Austria, Prussia, and Russia continued to follow the road of bureaucratic autocracy copied originally from Louis XIV. But it was no longer called divine-right monarchy. For a time it was "enlightened despotism." Then it became "defense of the monarchical principle." In Western history most things never go away; they just change their names.

EUROPEAN COLONIAL EXPANSION
AND THE GREAT WAR FOR EMPIRE

By the middle of the seventeenth century Europe's monarchs and ministers could look out on colonial empires of fabulous extent and wealth. In the years since the Portuguese conquest of Ceuta in 1415, European states had established naval and commercial superiority in the East, conquered native tribes and empires in America, and colonized much of the New World. The most diverse sorts of men—Malaysians, Indians, Aztecs, Algonquins, and Arabs—had fallen under European sway. Imperial expansion had brought unimagined wealth in gold and silver and even more from trade. Nothing else in European history had been so profitable or had made kings so powerful.

Kings and ministers therefore looked upon colonial expansion and overseas trade with great expectations. Savage wars had been fought to establish colonial empires; even more brutal struggles would be waged to defend and enlarge them. Colonial and commercial considerations were an essential element of statecraft and strategy. Colonial promoters were given the most solemn hearing, no matter how preposterous their schemes. Finally there emerged from European countinghouses and chancelleries a notion that colonial affairs had the transcendent importance a previous generation had given to religion.

Mercantilism

The complex of economic and political notions that justified the feverish colonial expansion of the early modern period was termed mercantilism. By no means a systematic hypothesis of political economy, or even a group of coherent theses, mercantilism was a galaxy of miscellaneous ideas, maxims, and prejudices that the rulers of European states had come to believe. What mercantilism lacked in consistency, however, it more than made up in moral authority, for its axioms were piously intoned by everyone. That many mercantilist notions were pure rubbish had little effect on their overwhelming popularity. Hard-headed merchants and practical politicians believed in them, for Old Regime Europe was mercantilist to the core.

There is a fairly simple explanation for the ready acceptance of mercantilist doctrines. It was basically a question of political values. Old Regime monarchs were struggling with towns, feudality, and churches to centralize the administration of their states and increase royal power. Mercantilist theorists accepted state building as a positive good and bent their efforts toward devising ways this might be accomplished. Mercantilists were sworn enemies of feudal power, municipal privilege, and clerical immunities. Mercantilists had no doubt who ought to run the country. They were, par excellence, kings' men. Therefore kings responded in kind, repeating mercantilist slogans, appointing mercantilist ministers, and supporting mercantilist projects.

Mercantilist doctrines were basically rather simple. It was the king's duty to make the nation prosperous, a responsibility inherited from the medieval city. The economic interests of the realm consisted of supporting merchants, artisans, and manufacturers in three basic ways: encouraging and subsidizing industry; trade legislation; and the acquisition of colonies with a navy to defend them. Equally pervasive was the view that all states were engaged in constant economic warfare. People believed that there was only a fixed amount of trade, and a gain at home meant a corresponding loss for some other state. Further, there was also only a finite amount of money, and each mercantilist king had to corral as much of it as he could. Such doctrine, of course, subordinated the goal of commercial profit to the objectives of royal foreign policy, but it did ensure state intervention for the benefit of the merchant and manufacturer.

Nowhere were mercantilist precepts so honored, or mercantilist ideas so assiduously practiced, as in the France of Louis XIV. The Sun King's finance minister, Jean-Baptiste Colbert, used every administrative resource to foster national prosperity and royal power according to mercantilist writ. Like many mercantilists, Colbert thought luxury products designed for the nobility were more profitable than the goods consumed by common folk. He took special pride in fine French silks, lace, furs, glass, tapestries, and china, all renowned for fine quality and high price. Limoges china received government subsidies, as well as monopoly privileges and prices. The Gobelin tapestry works produced cloths that were works of art as well as commerce. Alençon point lace also obtained grants and privileges, as did the manufacture of French fur hats and capes. Furs ideally exemplified Colbert's mercantilist theories; they were purchased by the aristocracy, and the furs themselves came from French Canada. Colbert also fostered production of glass with considerable success, for French glass ultimately took much of a market that had traditionally belonged to Venice. Lyons silk received similar preferential treatment, for it had long been a major staple of French export, and Colbert did not want it to decline.

Along with subsidy and monopoly privileges went considerable royal regulation. Colbert wished French products to have consistent quality, size, and weight, and the old medieval market regulations were transferred to the national level. The results were bad. The hordes of inspectors needed to enforce the minute royal regulations were venal and corrupt, and they cost producers large sums in graft. The regulations themselves were rigid and inflexible, and industrialists could not produce what their customers wanted. Even worse, the rules were occasionally enforced, and cloth was burned and glass and china were broken because they did not conform to the exact specifications. The cost of such nonsense was enormous, but Colbert persisted. The honor of the king was at stake.

Colbert was equally interested in commercial legislation. He and his successors organized monopoly companies to exploit Canadian furs, Caribbean sugar, African slaves, and the Mediterranean trade. All failed—some several times. The most ambitious of these schemes was the Mississippi Company, established in 1717 by John Law to exploit the wealth of Louisiana. Since a major Louisiana export turned out to be Spanish moss to stuff sofas, the company collapsed in one of the most spectacular crashes of the Old Regime. Mercantilists listed its demise as death by misadventure and continued to boost the merits of giant commercial monopoly companies.

Other European states were more fortunate with commercial companies. The British East India Company dominated India until the Sepoy Mutiny in the nineteenth century. The Dutch East India Company, founded in 1602, established an empire stretching from

Ceylon to New Guinea. Dividends of 20 percent a year were not uncommon until the 1640s; after that they were smaller, although the company always made money. Here, at least, the mercantilists' dreams were realized.

Commercial encouragement embraced more than monopoly companies; it required legislation and regulation on a national scale. These laws were called navigation acts and were most fully articulated in England. The basic aims of the English Navigation Acts were four: (1) the colonies were to have a monopoly of the English home market; (2) English merchants were to have a monopoly of colonial trade; (3) all shipping was to be English; (4) the colonies, not England, were to pay the customs duties. Refinements were added to this basic system, notably the exclusion of Scotland and Ireland from colonial trade, until the great Navigation Act of 1696. This law contained the institutional establishment of mercantilism. The Board of Trade was created to oversee colonial policy, and customs and vice-admiralty officers were sent to the colonies. A marine registry was begun to aid in the identification of English ships. In this basic form the English navigation system survived until the free-trade movement after 1820. It was the most successful mercantilist attempt at general commercial regulation.

Yet mercantilist policies of encouraging industry and regulating commerce were generally failures. They did not bring the promised prosperity. French industry survived the regulation mania of Colbert and his successors, but only barely, for there was a profound economic slump from 1683 to 1720. Navigation acts were equally ineffective. In Spain, efforts to restrict colonial trade to natives only drove prices up, compensating for the risks that foreigners took in trading with Spanish America. Mercantilist exclusion only helped drain wealth from the Spanish Empire and increase the profits of foreigners, exactly the reverse of its purpose. In England, the trade patterns naturally followed, rather than defied, the intent of the Navigation Acts. Great Britain could supply the necessary quantity of cheap textiles and dependable ironware that the colonies needed. The British home market was large enough to absorb colonial products at reasonable prices. Britain and her colonies had the merchant fleet to sustain colonial trade. In the British Empire, unlike France or Spain, navigation acts did not contradict economic reality.

Equally dramatic evidence of the failures of mercantilism could be seen in the economic history of seventeenth-century Holland, which subscribed to a minimum of mercantilist notions and enjoyed a tremendous prosperity. The key to this economic growth in the midst of nearly universal depression was a strikingly modern fiscal and commercial policy. The Dutch excelled in volume bulk trade. Their ships were efficient and their prices moderate. Moreover, in the early years of the seventeenth century the Bank of Amsterdam established itself as the strongest fiscal institution in the world. Both trade and banking assured a steady flow of capital into the profitable and nonmercantilist Dutch commercial economy.

In one of its primary functions, however, mercantilism did not fail. It provided support for monarchs who were centralizing the administration of their kingdoms. The general acceptance of mercantilist notions helped monarchs to break down economic provincialism, to destroy internal tariff barriers, and to tax cities hitherto exempt. None of this could have been done without the ideological and political support of mercantilists. For kings and ministers, and many a mercantilist as well, this was enough.

The Development of Colonial Empires: 1660–1740

The years around 1660 were a time of considerable change in the tenor and patterns of European colonial expansion. The end of the seventeenth-century depression in England and France gave great impetus to a lusty colonial expansion. For the Dutch, however, the decade around 1660 was the end of colonial expansion. The Netherlands conceded the loss of Brazil to Portugal in 1661 and in 1664 lost New York to the English. In the years after 1660 colonial initiative passed to England and France.

The Spanish Empire, despite a sustained decline in wealth, retained great areas of strength after 1660. The Catholic faith and Iberian culture were so strongly rooted that nothing could shake them. The loyalty of both Indians and colonists to Spain remained firm, even in the face of piracy, war, corrupt and inefficient government, and poverty. Aside from Jamaica and Haiti, Spain retained all her colonies, in spite of the most appalling military and naval weaknesses. Spain could not exploit her empire, but she did not lose it either.

The Spanish Empire was most seriously threatened by the English and the French in the Caribbean, the legendary Spanish Main. In the years after 1660, a vast increase in English and French shipping cut into Spanish trade and increased the privateering and piracy that nearly all merchants were prepared to practice at the slightest opportunity. Attempts in Europe to reduce Caribbean piracy and privateering failed utterly. The time-honored rule of no law on the high seas prevailed, and there was constant war on the Spanish

Main. Between 1655 and 1671 Henry Morgan sacked and destroyed the Spanish gold towns of Panama and Porto Bello, butchered the inhabitants, and carried off vast quantities of loot. Although Morgan sought steadier work as lieutenant-governor of Jamaica, the call of crime was too strong, and he reverted to piracy. Against this concentrated plundering the Spanish were helpless. Their ships were too slow, their navy too weak, and their merchants too ready to buy from the smuggler. Spanish decadence at home was more than matched abroad.

English colonial expansion, in stark contrast to Spanish decay, achieved success in defiance of mercantilist doctrine and practice. English colonies were the result of individual initiative and private financing, whereas the role of the king was minimal. New York, captured from the Dutch by the duke of York, had the character of a royal appanage. Pennsylvania, the Carolinas, and New Jersey all had lords proprietors, who had rights over land and government and obligations to colonize, independent of the crown. Georgia, begun in 1733 by a committee of philanthropists, was a private undertaking in which the powers of the crown were severely circumscribed until the expiration of the charter. The reasons for colonial enterprise were equally varied, the hope of profit and religious freedom being the most prominent. Until the pressures of imperial war forced it upon them, the English ministers were not guided by any general strategy of expansion, and the colonies retained their local differences.

English colonial expansion after 1600 was rapid, extended into many areas of the world, and was a varied experience. In India, English control took the form of widely separated commercial bases, supported by treaties and having native rulers. Very few Englishmen settled there. In North America the Hudson's Bay Company, founded in 1670, exploited the fur trade and resembled French colonization. Colonies such as Jamaica, Virginia, and the Carolinas had plantation economies—run with slave labor and producing rice, indigo, sugar, and tobacco, which were in great demand in Europe. The northern colonies, from Pennsylvania to Massachusetts, evolved an economy and society much like those of England, increasingly urbanized, oriented toward trade and manufacture. The slave stations in West Africa were indistinguishable from the neighboring French pestholes. There, both Briton and native alike lived in squalor and degradation, the result of the disgusting brutality of their profession. English colonies represented all types known to Western imperialism.

After 1660 France emerged increasingly as the major imperial rival to England. French colonial expansion was conducted according to the best principles of mercantilism. All French colonies were the result of government initiative. Royal control was extremely tight, with even the most trivial questions being sent to Paris for decision. France enacted navigation acts, of course, but French control over colonies was more institutional than commercial. Religious toleration was unknown; and the established, privileged Catholic Church was everywhere in evidence. French colonies were a department of state.

In the years before Colbert's accession to power in 1661, the French had made a small beginning in colonizing Canada. Most of the settlers were Jesuits, fur trappers, government officials, and there were a few peasant farmers; trade in beaver skins provided a cash crop. Colbert decided to expand the colony. He ordered the legalization of the brandy trade with the Indians, over the most heated protests of the Jesuits and bishop, who maintained that liquor corrupted and debased the noble savages and made their conversion to the true faith impossible. Efforts were made to find mineral resources, establish a shipbuilding industry, and begin trade with French possessions in the Caribbean, all without success. Beaver skins remained the only marketable export. Canada remained a forest—an Indian empire, exploited by fur traders, ruled by soldiers and officials, and converted by Jesuits. More successful were three sugar islands in the Caribbean: Haiti, Guadeloupe, and Martinique. The slave and plantation culture of the islands fitted well into the absolutist and mercantilist patterns of French colonialism. French sugar was better quality than English, and by the 1730s, it dominated the Continental market.

Although French imperial power and colonial trade were considerably inferior to those of England, they nonetheless made steady gains after 1660. The system of central control from Paris gave the appearance of a grand imperial strategy, so greatly at variance with the manifest anarchy of the English. Moreover, the spectacular growth of French trade after 1720, particularly in tropical products, ate seriously into British markets. Franco-British hostility, concentrated in the seventeenth century on questions of Continental hegemony, became predominantly imperial in the eighteenth.

The Great War for Empire: 1739–1763

British victory in the War of the Spanish Succession did not lessen mercantile and political tensions in the Caribbean Sea. The profits from tropical products were so great that France, Spain, and Great Britain all gave the highest priority to controlling the West Indian trade. Spain had never abandoned the theory of a closed commercial system, and the new Bourbon monarchs once again sent fleets from Spain to the American fair towns, bringing manufactured products and returning with specie, indigo, dye woods, tobacco, and sugar. Spanish authorities also licensed a fleet of coast guard vessels to enforce mercantilist regulations. Paid out of condemnations, the coast guards preyed indiscriminately on foreign shipping, outraged British public opinion, and created a diplomatic rift between Spain and Great Britain.

The British view of West Indian trade was somewhat different from the Spanish. British merchants wished to force Spain into a recognition of commercial reality, and open ports on the Spanish Main to free trade. They used the *asiento*, a privilege giving the English limited commercial rights, as an opening wedge for fairly extensive smuggling in slaves, grain, and manufactured goods. British merchants in the House of Commons put tremendous pressure on the ministry for protection from the West India squadron, and, after 1735, talked increasingly of war. Fear of growing French competition, a contempt for Spain, and an outburst of chauvinism drove Britain into war. On October 19, 1739, the great war for empire began.

The critical element in the imperial conflict was the sea. The war would be won by the strongest naval power, regardless of any local successes by the other side. French victories in India or raids in Pennsylvania or New York depended on French ability to keep the sea lanes open. Spanish colonies, with their strong religious and cultural cement, were less vulnerable, but they too were ultimately dependent on sea power. At sea the British had immense advantages, although these were not used very effectively in the early part of the war. By 1747, however, the Royal Navy had turned the tide in favor of Britain, having captured 2,457 French and Spanish merchantmen and driven enemy commerce raiders from the seas. In May 1747 the Western Squadron, commanded by Admiral Anson, destroyed a French fleet off Cape Finisterre and gobbled up much of its attending convoy. In October the same year, Admiral Hawke led the Western Squadron to a second victory over a French fleet at Cape Finisterre, destroying another convoy. These two decisive naval victories shut France off from her Western colonies. In the islands, the West India Squadron blockaded the French sugar islands of Martinique, Guadeloupe, and Haiti. Had the war not ended in 1748, the French islands would have been forced to surrender without firing a shot, for the slaves were starving and the sugar was rotting in the harbor.

By 1748 all the participants in the great war for empire were near exhaustion. The British ministry, timid in even the fairest breeze, was terrified of bankruptcy, having a national debt of £76 million sterling. They were equally despondent over the dramatic French victories in Flanders. Despite total victory at sea between 1747 and 1748, the British government merely wanted peace. For France—near bankruptcy, her empire in tatters, her trade destroyed, her ships captured or blockaded—peace was vital and came just in time. Under these conditions negotiations were rapid and smooth. Britain and France simply agreed to return to the status quo ante-bellum, with mutual return of conquests. The British blockade was lifted, and French ships once again put to sea. The French colonial system had survived.

The treaty of Aix-la-Chapelle in 1748 brought only a respite in the great war for empire. War in North America started in 1755. The French were too weak to hold a forest empire stretching from New Orleans to Newfoundland, and in five years the British completely conquered Canada. They were equally successful in the West Indies. The basic British strategy was to blockade French trade, destroy French slaving stations in Africa, and force the capitulation of the French sugar islands, thus opening them to British exploitation. Both Guadeloupe and Martinique were captured, and after 1762 no ships but British sailed in the West. In India the British took Calcutta and destroyed the French native allies at the decisive battle of Plassey in 1757. After Plassey, India was British; neither the Indian nor the French could resist.

As in the previous war, the decisive element was sea power. With graceful sarcasm the French marine minister, Maurepas, had observed that one could not make war on a maritime power without a navy, and the truth of that remark soon became evident. In 1759 British naval victories at Lagos and Quiberon Bay destroyed the French fleet. There was nothing left to protect the Mediterranean trade or the sugar islands. France again resorted to the use of privateers; those from Martinique alone took nearly 1,400 British and colonial ships. After 1759, however, commerce raiding fell off to nothing. The French coasts were blockaded, the sugar islands captured, and French ships swept from the sea. By 1763 France was again bankrupt, her trade ruined. She had lost more merchant ships than the British and could no longer fight. France had lost her empire.

A second reason for overwhelming British success was to be found in the direction from London. In the previous war the government had been timid and incompetent, but from 1757 to 1761 the ministry was dominated by William Pitt, who was neither. Pitt infused energy and direction into British policy. He aimed at the total destruction of French imperial power, and his means was control of the sea. While a series of French ministers were torn between trying to avoid an imperial disaster or save a blundering Continental policy, Pitt beat France to bankruptcy and surrender. Although the minister fell before the war ended, his victories were the basis of peace.

When the Peace of Paris was signed in 1763, France was on the verge of collapse. Skillful diplomacy by the duke of Choiseul might save something; eagerness for peace shown by the British prime minister, Lord Bute, might save more. Considerations of the balance of power would help, but France paid the price of peace: Canada went to England, Louisiana to Spain, and only the sugar islands of the West Indies were retained. In India, France lost everything except Pondichery and Chandernagor. Great Britain was now mistress of the seas and arbiter of the non-Western world.

The Peace of Paris not only ended the great war for empire; it also ended an era of colonialism. There were no rivals left to Great Britain; there was no possibility of another European state establishing new colonies. Only the Dutch East Indies and Latin America remained beyond British possession, and Spanish American trade was largely in British hands. In the very moment of triumph, however, the victorious British Empire began to come apart. During the years from 1763 to 1775 it slid into civil war between home and colonial aristocracies. The first phase of European expansion ended with the American Revolution.

THE LADDER OF SOCIETY

It took the family of Jean Bâtard of Toulouse seven generations to ascend the ladder of Old Regime society. Beginning in the early seventeenth century as fish peddlers, the family rose through the positions of merchant and lawyer to magistrate, from petty bourgeoisie into the nobility. Finally, toward the end of the eighteenth century, the count Bâtard-d'Estaing became first president of the parlement of Toulouse, an important member of the great nobility of southern France, prominent enough in politics and high enough in status to end his life on a revolutionary guillotine.

The society through which successive generations of the Bâtard family climbed was extraordinarily stable. The social hierarchy was distinct and traditional. The social classes had remained in roughly the same relationship to each other since the high Middle Ages, and individuals normally remained in the same class, even the same profession, as their fathers. Mobility was slow—a matter of generations, not years. Stability was further assured by the belief that the social order was not merely inevitable but right, a part of the natural order ordained by God and, as such, unalterable. Finally, social stability was maintained by the relatively primitive state of European technology. The lack of any source of power beyond wind, water, and muscle condemned millions to the endless toil of peasant farming, or the lengthy processes of handicrafts. Since each peasant produced so small a surplus, if any at all, the peasant class remained on the land out of necessity long after the legal bondage of serfdom had ended. It was the same in manufacturing, in which the techniques of medieval Europe persisted into the Old Regime. Technological requirements, as well as social pressure, assured the stability of the ladder of society.

Old Regime society was organized into a distinct and complex hierarchy, in which public social distinctions enjoyed the approval of nearly everyone. No notions of equality disturbed the repose of the social theorist in early modern Europe. By common agreement the nobility were the visible summit of the social hierarchy. No matter how rich a merchant or lawyer was, he saw the nobility above him in honor and status and the artisans below him. Within the great social classes there were infinite gradations. In France, in the legal profession, a long social and economic trail wound upward from the provincial notaries, through the bourgeois ranks of solicitors and barristers, to lawyers licensed to practice before the king's bench. Above those were the noble magistrates of the king's courts, great royal officials, full of wealth and status. All were lawyers, but what a difference there was among them. There were similar distinctions everywhere. No one would confuse the self-sufficient English small yeoman with an impoverished cotter, yet both were peasant farmers. There was a vast difference between the country hidalgo of Castile and the princely grandee who lived at court and counted thousands of servants in his entourage. Yet both were nobles.

For most people of the Old Regime, life had a strong corporate element as well as a hierarchical one. The family itself was a legal corporation under the control of a father who directed the lives of his children. The whole family, uncles and cousins as well as parents, contributed to the dowry of a daughter, the education of a son, the purchase of a royal office or a piece of land. The whole family sacrificed to advance the fortunes of one of its members, in whose person and position the whole family would share. Those in authority practiced nepotism on an awesome scale. Consider the practices of Guillaume de Bochetel, secretary of state in France from 1547 to 1556. He placed one son-in-law, Claude de l'Aubespine, in office as a secretary of state in 1547; another, Jacques Bourdon, became a secretary of state in 1556. These in turn found places for their progeny and relations. Claude de l'Aubespine placed his son as secretary of state in 1567 and his nephew in the same office in 1570 and married his daughter to a third secretary of state. In eighteenth-century England the same system prevailed. Viscount Barrington put one son in the army as a general, another in the church as a bishop, a third in the navy as an admiral, and a fourth in the House of Commons, while the eldest got the title and the estate. Barrington was well thought of for his efforts.

Marriages were equally important in advancing the fortunes of the corporate family. Marriage created expectations, such as Claude de l'Aubespine's hopes for promotion when he wed the daughter of a secretary of state. Marriage customarily included a contract, specifying the wife's dowry, the husband's property, and even the land and moneys coming to the happy couple upon the death of their relatives. Thus the 1722 marriage contract of the Marquis de Fourquevaux and Demoiselle Catellan enumerated the gifts that made the bride's contribution to the new family. Included were bequests payable on the death of the wife's relatives, arrangements for disposition of the dowry on the death of either partner, and the wife's rights and income if she became a widow. The contract specified that the eldest son would inherit half of his parents' property, thus preserving the family status and wealth intact. Marriage was a civil as well as a religious contract, for everyone thought that the corporate family was necessary to the well-ordered society.

A strong sense of corporate identity also characterized units larger than the family. The guild framework continued until the era of the French Revolution, despite increasing objection to its regulation of commerce. The towns of Europe retained a corporate identity long after the monarchical state had absorbed their powers of government. In the countryside, corporate manorial jurisdiction and responsibility far outlived serfdom. The peasant village was collectively responsible for its taxes to the king; the upkeep of roads, fences, and ditches; and the support of the church. Some villages collectively pastured their animals and defended themselves at law as a unit against the threats of enclosure. Corporate organization also provided an important element of social security. In times of famine the landed peasant and the urban citizen were fed, while the casual laborers starved. The guild guaranteed a place for the son and support of the window. The corporation provided its members with considerable protection against the often arbitrary and capricious activity of the government. Finally, upward mobility in the Old Regime meant more than acquiring more money and personal power. It meant entering a higher corporate group and sharing its status, welfare, and position. It meant acquiring new privileges.

Privilege was essential in the structure of the corporate and hierarchical society. The Roman idea of citizenship, with its rights and obligations shared equally by all, was foreign to the Old Regime social order. People conducted a grim and endless search for privilege, which more than anything else denoted one's exact rank in the social hierarchy. The possession of privilege was almost a requirement for survival; in a society without clearly defined rights, privilege alone enabled one to prosper. Corporate entities, guilds, towns, families, social classes, the clergy, and nobility sought privileges as eagerly as any individual. Those who lived outside the protective cover of privilege, whether individual or corporate, were truly the meek, the poor, and the humble of this world.

Some forms of privilege were basically honorific, though nonetheless sought after. In the procession in Paris commemorating the entrance of Henry IV into the city, the Parlement walked in front of the Chambre des Comptes and engaged in fist fights to protect this privilege. In most parish churches, the local nobility had separate pews with their arms emblazoned on the side. Other privileges were more substantial. The bourgeoisie in France, Spain, and Italy generally paid no tax on the wine they sold in the cities; peasants did. Nobles everywhere were exempt from most forms of direct taxation. Commissions in the armed services in all European states except Holland and Britain were almost exclusively reserved to the nobility. In most European towns, only the rich merchants and lawyers of good family were eligible to hold municipal office and to reap rewards therefrom. Privilege was a form of wealth and property, as well as of social status. It was the envy of the poor and the pride of the great.

By its very nature privilege could be the possession of only a few. The social pyramid of the Old Regime rested on a very broad base of peasants and workers, vagabonds and soldiers, and servants. These were almost completely without privilege and certainly without rights. They paid the costs and bore the burden of the status and privileges of others. The unprivileged masses comprised about three-quarters of the population in wealthy England and Holland, and about 95 percent of it in rural Russia and Poland. Above them were the privileged few—the guildsmen, merchants, nobles, clerics. and kings—who owned most of the land and nearly all the wealth and were confirmed in that wealth by their social status and corporate privileges. At the narrow peak of the social pyramid stood the nobility of Europe. First in honor, and usually wealthy as well, they dominated the social psychology of Old Regime Europe and determined the style and standards of life.

The gathering places of the noble society were the royal courts of the European monarchs. Increasing royal power required that kings occupy a splendid stage. There they posed and strutted about marvelously, surrounded by their servants, courtiers, attendants, and families. An elaborate etiquette emphasized their grandeur. Almost constant dynastic wars magnified their importance and glory. Kings were the fashion; medieval barons and Renaissance cities had had their day. The Old Regime was preeminently an age of monarchs.

Under the stimulating gaze of their subjects, many monarchs developed rather decided eccentricities. Tsar Alexander I of Russia died thinking he was the second coming of Christ. George III of England was possessed of a more modest lunacy; he thought an oak tree was Frederick the Great and spoke to it accordingly. Louis XIV of France developed an elaborate daily ceremonial that stopped just short of proclaiming his divinity. Charles II of England led his court in lively and ribald entertainment, as did the regent Philippe d'Orléans of France. Louis XV of France liked the ladies also and seduced as many of them as he could, but in this pursuit he was far surpassed by August the Strong, elector of Saxony and king of Poland, who was reputed to have sired 365 illegitimate children. Whatever the exact figure, there were many, and one of them, Maurice de Saxe, became a marshal of France and the most celebrated soldier of his age. By contrast, Empress Maria Theresa of Austria was a model housewife and mother. Frederick William of Prussia made his mark as a martinet; he would arise at dawn, sneak out of the palace and berate the royal postmasters when they opened their stalls two minutes late.

The flamboyance of kings was not intended to demonstrate individuality, but to display their preeminence in power and privilege. Consequently they were always accompanied by their royal court and household, which was as colorful and expensive as could be managed. The chief adornments of the royal court were the great nobility, who attended the king, basked in his glory, and devoured his pensions and gifts. Those who lived at court were the greatest nobles in the realm, possessed of proud names and, occasionally, massive geneologies. The Roman family of Colonna boasted several medieval popes, the Mendozas owned large tracts of Castile, the Rochechouarts in France traced their family back to the ninth century, and the Roman Massimi claimed descent from Fabius Maximus.

The great families—peers in England; grandees in Spain; dukes in Austria, Naples, and France; cardinals in Rome; bishops and generals everywhere—were the chief and indispensable adornments of the royal court.

Residence with the king, however, did not necessarily mean that the great nobles ran the government; indeed, most European monarchs made special efforts to keep them out of positions of power. Having them at court curbed their authority in the provinces, where they held huge estates. The Schwartzenburg family owned 400,000 acres of Bohemia; how much better for the crown for them to be at Vienna than at home! But the great noble families were not devoid of influence. The honor and prestige of their names ensured at least a hearing for their views. They were close to the person of the monarch, his wife, his son and heir, his mistresses. In the Byzantine politics of the court, great nobles often could make their opinions felt.

The personal influence of the nobles, great though it might be, was different from control of the administration of the state. This, too, was in the hands of nobles, but nobles of a different type. The latter nobles had a legal and administrative background, not a military or feudal one. Their families in most cases had reached the nobility during the period from 1500 to 1650. In Portugal, Spain, Italy, France, and the Holy Roman Empire, thousands of new men filled the growing royal bureaucracies and claimed noble rank as part of their new position. They had received it from monarchs too poor to refuse. During the course of the Old Regime, these nobles came to be recognized as a distinct type, the *noblesse de la robe*, to designate them in French, the dominant language of the European aristocracy.

In Spain and France the robe nobility filled up the royal councils and provincial administration, in Austria they formed the bureaus, and everywhere except in England the administration of justice fell completely into their hands. Legal and administrative posts paid well. Almost everywhere, office provided a larger income than land, as the opportunities for profit given to officeholders were enormous. The administrative and legal nobility were the richest in the realm, if not individually then as a class. Consequently the older but poorer landed and military nobility lost few opportunities to marry into the rich families. By the middle of the eighteenth century the taint of dishonor that once attached to the robe had been erased by the effective solvents of money and power.

Most of the European nobility, of course, were not grandees living at court or judges in royal and provincial capitals; they were country gentry, living on their land, serving in the army, or enjoying a modest position in the provincial clergy. In England the gentry controlled local government, but on the Continent these positions were in the hands of the robe nobility. So the country nobles went into the lower ranks of the army or the middle levels of the clergy or stayed on the land. Some were well off, but many were quite poor, living at subsistence level in shabby châteaus, quarreling with their peasants, importuning the crown for a military commission, perhaps scheming to marry a daughter to a wealthy bourgeois. Not surprisingly, the country nobility were frequently the most revolutionary elements in the realm. The mid-seventeenth-century revolutions in Catalonia, Portugal, England, and France were in large measure the work of the petty nobility.

But the country gentry, even the poorest hidalgos in northern Castile, were more securely established in their noble status than the rising bourgeoisie. The legal fact of nobility was clear, but the social composition of the nobility was not. If a man bought a noble fief, received a royal patent of nobility, or purchased a noble office, was he a noble? It was not easy to answer these questions. Voltaire was lord of a manor and village and collected seigneurial dues from his peasants, but he was considered to be bourgeois. The playwright Caron de Beaumarchais purchased a patent of nobility from Louis XVI; most people grudgingly conceded his new status. The exact lines between noble and bourgeois were quite unclear. Throughout the Old Regime, in every country but England, a constant stream of merchants, landowners, lawyers, and officeholders were in the process of becoming noblemen. It took time, often generations, but the prize was great and the families persevered. They were often the most active and enterprising of the middle class, yet their attitudes and ambitions and style of life clearly marked them as noble. In the Old Regime, except for ordination into the clergy, one did not suddenly leap over class barriers; one oozed across.

While the boundaries of the aristocracy were blurred, those of the clergy were clear. Vows and ordination created a cleric, no matter what his social background. No order or profession cut across the class lines as dramatically as did the clergy. The church contained modest as well as important positions, callings of poverty and want as well as those of magnificence and luxury. There were rural parishes to be filled, frontier missions to be staffed, and churches in urban slums that needed pastors. Hospitals and almshouses demanded nuns and monks to run them. There were also, of course, churches of pomp and power. Cathedral canons, abbots, mother superiors, vicars-general, bishops, archbishops, princely cardinals—

all lived a life of pride, affluence, and authority. Bishops were greater than most barons, and cardinals ranked with princes of the blood royal. But they were a minority within the church. There were far more country priests than bishops, more friars, monks, and nuns than canons and abbots. In the Old Regime such numerical inferiority hardly mattered. The importance of hierarchy exceeded that of numbers. In a more revolutionary age, the large numbers of the lower clergy was to become a factor of surpassing importance.

The organized church had great wealth and privilege. It did not matter if the denomination was Greek Orthodox, Roman Catholic, Lutheran, Anglican, or Reformed. The established church was the greatest privileged corporation in the state, the firm ally of the throne and aristocracy. Invariably, the church paid very little tax, though it taxed its people, receiving tithes and fees as well as income from its property and the gifts of the faithful. The church owned vast tracts of land—perhaps one-fifth of France, considerably more in Spain, Portugal, Naples, and Sardinia. It could greatly affect public policy. Nowhere did dissenters from the established faith enjoy much more than a grudging toleration, and they often were actively persecuted. England, Prussia, and Holland were notable eighteenth-century exceptions, but the rest of Europe continued in the hallowed traditions of the Inquisition. Education was in the hands of the church, which controlled universities as well as seminaries. Books were burned along with people at the behest of clerical authorities. The vital statistics of the state were kept in the parish registers, and the king's laws were read to the people from the pulpit on Sundays. Power, wealth, and privilege were the hallmarks of the established church.

These desirable things were distributed very unevenly within the churches. The poor parish priest had very little of the power or privileges or wealth of the church. Often he had barely enough to eat. He saw the tithes and income from his parish going elsewhere while he and his flock did without. The timber, thatch, and rough stone of the parish church compared unfavorably with the marble, stained glass, and grandeur of the cathedral. The special status of the clergy was mainly enjoyed by prelates and abbots, while the priests and nuns shared the social and economic condition of their flocks, patients, and students. The clergy were recruited from the same social level as the people they served. Everywhere the pastor was overwhelmingly from the peasant class. The bourgeoisie and gentry sent their sons and daughters into the better convents, monasteries, and cathedral chapters, which were steps by which a family might move into nobility or rescue a sagging fortune. The European aristocracy regarded the upper clergy as a preserve for their sons and nephews. Bishoprics became almost hereditary in certain noble families. The Roman princely houses of Colonna and Orsini had a cardinal nearly every generation. The Richelieu controlled the see of Lucon, and the bishop of Paris for four generations was a Gondi. Obviously this system gave small hope for advancement through the ranks of the ecclesiastical administration. The church faithfully reflected the stable, hierarchical society that it served and that it sporadically tried, by fire and sword, to save.

The wealth of that society was concentrated in the towns. The vast country estates of the gentry and peerage certainly produced an income for their owners, who normally spent most of their money in town or at court. The bishops, resident in the cities, drained off the income from the rural churches. Kings lived in town, where their courts were a major industry. Universities, law courts, and the royal administration were all centered in the towns. The markets, where the countrymen sold their produce and bought their handicrafts, were in the towns. Overseas trade was conducted from the city. Administrative, religious, commercial, and social factors all combined to concentrate the liquid wealth of the Old Regime in the city. This was strikingly clear in the more heavily urbanized west, but the phenomenon of the wealth of towns was true everywhere, even in rural Austria and heavily depressed Spain and Sicily.

Physically, the towns of the Old Regime retained a medieval appearance. They were still surrounded by walls and battlements. The streets were unpaved, cluttered with garbage, and lined with houses whose upper stories jutted out above the lower, almost blocking out the light. Peddlers crowded the streets and markets. Shops opened directly onto the narrow sidewalk. The wealthy, in carriages or sedan chairs, preceded by servants and lackies, pushed through the confusion. There was noise and bustle everywhere, for the cities were small and densely populated.

But more than noisome alleys and the babel of the markets, the great cities were filled with such monuments of a glorious past as cathedrals, squares, palaces, public buildings, all of which gave a distinctive flavor. Kings, nobles, and prelates continued to embellish their towns with impressive and beautiful buildings. The great London fire of 1666 was the occasion for the rebuilding of the city, and the plan included the beautiful churches of Christopher Wren. In Paris the Palais-Royal, the Place des Vosges, the avenue of the Champs Élysées, and the Place de la Concorde were built during the Old Regime. Rome saw the building of the Vatican colonnade, numerous baroque churches, the Trevi fountain, Piazza Navona, and Piazza del Popolo. The Belvedere and the Schönbrunn palaces in Vienna, the bishop's residence in Würzburg, were eighteenth-century creations. Kings and their people felt that palaces, parks, public squares, and churches were important and valuable, adding beauty, spaciousness, and magnificence to the crowded and inconvenient cities. The commercial and industrial values that predominate in the twentieth century, emphasizing building mainly for immediate monetary profit, were relatively unimportant in the Old Regime. Before the Industrial Revolution, magnificent buildings and public squares were their own justification. Old Regime cities were crowded and dirty, but they were not, as so many cities are today, artistically squalid.

The chief class in the Old Regime city was the nobility. Although there were a few exceptions, such as Glasgow and Amsterdam, most cities were still socially ruled by bishops, canons, aristocratic magistrates, royal officials, and the wealthier of the resident gentry. They, not the merchants, dominated the towns, particularly since the local government had long since passed from the merchants to the king's officials.

The bourgeois urban patriciate, although often snubbed by the nobility, was affluent and privileged. Cities were organized for the economic advantage of the local merchants. Though royal government had sapped the political authority of the merchants, it had also provided opportunities for wealth. Urbanization, the expansion of colonial trade, the steady movement of wealthy nobles into town— all by-products of absolutism—greatly stimulated trade and commerce. The tobacco market of Glasgow, the Atlantic commerce of Bristol, the slave trade of Nantes, and the sugar trade of Bordeaux were instances of commercial and mercantile prosperity in the eighteenth century. The recovery from the seventeenth-century depression chiefly benefited the merchant class, and the commercial policies of both king and town worked to see this prosperity continue.

But for most merchants, mere wealth was not enough. The aristocratic ethos of Old Regime society was alluring. All too often they invested their wealth in titles, land, or office, withdrawing their capital from the economically productive enterprises of commerce and industry. Merchants strove to become nobles. In some cities, such as Toulouse, entrance into the upper levels of local administration automatically gave noble status to the fortunate bourgeois merchant. As a class, the bourgeoisie were not rising to displace the nobility from their urban prominence; indeed, since 1600 the urban merchants had been steadily losing political control over their own towns. But individually more and more merchants and lawyers were able to rise into the noble class. And they did. Upward mobility was easier in town than in the country.

Upward mobility was not so easy, however, for those with less capital to invest. The artisans, members of the craft guilds, found it much harder to move upward into the more privileged levels of society. The craft guilds were not organized to make their members rich. They were designed to provide everyone with a living, a fair living, and to see that all the guild members earned approximately the same income. In the smaller towns, which served primarily as administrative and ecclesiastical centers and farm markets, these guild restrictions could be effectively enforced. In such cities as London, Bristol, or Paris, the population was too large and the guilds too weak to regulate the trades. Thus some artisans became rich and some went bankrupt. But these circumstances were exceptional. Most guild artisans simply could not accumulate the capital necessary to buy an office or enter large-scale commerce. Thus they remained the urban middle class.

Below the shopkeepers and artisans were the servants. The largest nonfarm occupation in the Old Regime was personal and domestic service. Not only were hordes of servants feasible for the wealthy and privileged, they were also necessary as an indication of status and importance. The great were surrounded by maids, valets, stewards, and footmen of all description. Great lords lived in a crowd, sometimes a large one. The Cardinal Rohan was reputed to employ 5,000 servants of all descriptions, and the Guéménée family threw nearly 3,000 people out of work when it went bankrupt in 1788. In eastern Europe, Poland, Russia, and Austria, the personal entourage of the great princes reached even more fantastic size. Personal privacy was not yet the prized possession of the rich; it was still the curse of the sick and lost.

Many servants were, of course, virtually unemployed. They stood around in livery, occasionally opening doors, or not even doing that. Even servants with jobs—maids, cooks, or gardeners—were normally underemployed. This prodigal use of manpower, unchanged since Old Kingdom Egypt, was socially desirable in the Old Regime, when there was too little land for the peasants and too few jobs in industry and commerce. Service absorbed much of the surplus productive population. This system was closed out by the labor demands of the Industrial Revolution, though remnants lasted until World War I. But in the Old Regime, the social uses of manpower were still infinitely more important, rewarding, and spectacular than any mundane values of mere productivity.

At the bottom of urban society were the casual laborers, some of whom were agricultural workers, who worked at odd jobs in town in winter and left during the summer for work in the fields. There were often vast numbers of such people. Paris contained nearly 250,000 of them in the middle of the eighteenth century. They left the city in droves late in June, harvesting the crops in a wide circle of farms from the Loire valley to the Somme. By October, they had returned. Some took up jobs as street cleaners or water carriers or construction laborers. Others turned to crime or begging. Some went on relief or entered domestic service. The Paris authorities could not possibly keep up with all of these people and made no attempt to do so. They merely tried to keep food prices low enough so people would not starve.

The urban proletarian lived a precarious existence. The physical squalor of his surroundings exposed him to disease. Cholera, dysentery, typhus, plague were endemic in the poorer sections of town. The itinerant worker was utterly dependent on the markets, and even a slight price rise for bread or fish might bring him to the edge of starvation. Work was hard to find, the skilled occupations were closed, and a living wage was often only a dream. Many of these people were recruited into the countless legions of crime, which was a major social problem in Old Regime cities. Barbaric and public penalties did nothing to discourage an endless chain of violence and crime. In Paris, prostitutes were whipped nude through the streets to discourage the others, but the usual result was to advertise the charms of the victim and thus enhance her profession. Public executions were supposed to be dire warnings to felons, but the populace regarded hanging day as a festival, and the gallows were scenes of hilarity and holiday spirit. Branding, the stocks, or cropping of ears, and other measures failed to discourage the criminals or impress the public. For crime, in truth, was the high road to social mobility for the very poor, and it is hardly surprising that famous criminals such as Dick Turpin or Cartouche became folk heroes.

The poor were despised by their betters—and also feared. Wandering proletarian laborers were regarded as an element of social unrest and revolution. Modern historians have amassed a great deal of information proving that the very poor were much more concerned with survival than revolt. But Old Regime authorities did not know this. They proceeded on the simple assumption that those who were the most deprived were the least contented, and occasionally an event would occur that gave credence to their views. On Corpus Christi Day, 1640, the *segedors,* itinerant agricultural laborers of Catalonia, rioted in Barcelona and touched off the great Catalan revolt. But this event was exceptional. The Old Regime urban proletariat was an individualist class, and their discontent took the form of felonious assault rather than social revolution.

The city contained the human debris of society. Almshouses, hospitals, and conventual establishments tried to minister to the hopeless, the sick, and the lost. But the needs were too many and the help was too slight. Scenes of starvation, begging, disease, and death in the streets were common, and the privileged were hardened to them. The leper's bell evoked fear, not compassion. Cities tried to keep out the poor and the sick and closed their gates on them when they could. But no amount of policing, legislation, or pious exhortation could keep the crippled from the city. Confusion and fear drew as many people as ambition and opportunity.

In spite of the political and economic domination of the town over the countryside, nearly 90 percent of the people of Old Regime Europe lived on the land. The countryside was much poorer than the city. A primitive agricultural technology tied people to the soil and was the dominant factor in their way of life. Antique methods of farming, lack of fertilizer, inferior seed, broadcast sowing, inadequate pasture—these condemned the peasants to a subsistence level of productivity. Frequently near starvation, the peasants worked at an unending task. All were underprivileged; many were serfs. Old Regime rural society was only partially on a money economy, and the vast majority of its inhabitants lived on a subsistence regimen. The most salient characteristic of the Old Regime countryside was its poverty. Yet everyone was not equally poor. Within the huge society of peasants there were numerous gradations of status, position, and wealth.

At the bottom of the rural hierarchy were the itinerant laborers, people who were half vagabond. These wandered from place to place, following the harvest, working a day here and a day there. In good years they barely ate, in bad they starved. They eked out survival by living off the land, particularly in the wastes and woods. Poaching, petty crime, and brigandage were part of the endless routine of the wandering rural laborers. They were the true rural proletariat, both despised and feared by their betters. The existence of this class helps to explain the prevalence of brigandage in Italy, France, and Spain and the French Revolution cry of "The brigands are coming."

Above the itinerant laborers were the serfs and sharecroppers. Serfdom was a dying institution in Europe west of the Elbe River, but in the east, from Brandenburg through Russia, serfdom was alive and growing. Though the lords oppressed the serfs to the barest subsistence level, and sometimes below, serfs at least had their land. Next year's crop had to be sowed, animals had to be kept alive over the winter, fences and buildings had to be maintained. The land held the serf more firmly than the lord's law or power ever could have. The land was the supreme value of the peasant's life, and its possession and use gave even a serf a certain status, perhaps even a little security. It was not a good life, but it was better than vagabondage.

In western Europe, the lowest person on the social ladder of the stable rural society was the sharecropper. In northern Italy, France, and the Rhine valley the sharecropper might own some land, but not nearly enough to support a family. So he was forced to rent the rest of what he needed, but on terms so unfavorable that the whole profit went to the lord. The most serious danger to which a sharecropper was exposed was his situation as a short-term leaseholder. Normally, he leased the land for a three- or five-year period, and sometimes from year to year. He was utterly vulnerable to rent-racking, in which the lord raised the rent to the highest level he could get, regardless of the peasant's welfare. A common enough practice today and applauded as economically progressive, rent-racking was widely condemned during the Old Regime. It drove peasants to starvation, pushed them off the land, and swelled the number of urban laborers. In spite of condemnation and even royal prohibition, rent-racking was very common; combined with taxes, it left the sharecropper with almost nothing.

By a miracle of thrift, some sharecroppers did inch their way into the tenant class. Established tenants still paid taxes to the king, the town, and the seigneur, of course, but they were protected from the worst abuses of rent-racking. They held their land on an extended lease, sometimes for life. The long-term copyholders in England and the tenants of northern France and Catalonia held their land on almost indefinite tenure. Any rise in the value of the crops or the land went to them, not the lord. Nor could they be dispossessed without long and arduous recourse to law. So they enjoyed the security of established position, and growing prosperity during the eighteenth century brought the long-term tenant a considerable rise in living standards. When one considers that many established tenants owned some land of their own, it is clear that some were sufficiently well off to accumulate the capital necessary to rise in the social hierarchy. It was in the tenant class that the possibility of upward mobility became a reality. Below the tenants, mobility was a mirage.

The peasant aristocrat of the Old Regime was the landed proprietor who owned enough land to feed his family. He was fairly rare and barely exceeded one percent of the total peasant population. Nearly thirty acres were needed for a peasant to live from his own property. But for the fortunate few the advantages were enormous. The proprietor was free from rents and, frequently, from seigneurial dues as well. He had enough local status to avoid the full force of many royal taxes. He had enough capital to hold part of his harvest off the market until prices were at their peak. He hired the labor of itinerants and sharecroppers and rented his horses and plow to his poorer neighbors. He might well obtain the powerful position of estate manager to an absentee lord and become a rent-racker himself. He could purchase an office for his son, thus advancing the family into the bourgeoisie.

This huge society of peasants, so varied within itself, was viewed with distaste by the privileged orders. The nobility and bourgeoisie thought of peasants as the natural servants and laborers of society. They were the social beasts of burden. Cardinal Richelieu considered poverty their natural state and thought that if the peasants grew rich they would get above themselves and stop working. But the great also feared them. Bread riots, peasant uprisings, and aimless rural violence were annual events. The countryside was never completely secure. The Russian imperial army took three years (1773–1775) to suppress Pugachev's Rebellion. The French bread riots of 1775 spread through three provinces in less than a week. Peasant guerilla warfare in Spain took a savage toll of Napoleon's armies. The privileged orders were never safe from the anger of peasant discontent.

The peasants themselves thought of their betters as one more cross to bear. They were only sporadically radical, however. The peasants' entire vision was directed toward the land. With a constant and terrible intensity they hungered to own land. Peasants passionately resented noble and bourgeois ownership of the land. Nothing—not war, famine, oppression, or taxation—could destroy that elemental desire. The nobles and gentry never really understood the awesome force of this emotion, which was to play such an important role in the great French Revolution.

Viewing Old Regime society as a whole, one is constantly impressed by the overwhelming moral value given the idea of stability. The social ethic reserved its approval for tradition, continuity, and hierarchy. There was no emphasis on personal mobility, growth, or development. Society rested on a narrow aristocratic base of power, magnificence, and distinction. The European aristocracy utilized their social privileges. They were great patrons of the arts and letters. Bernini and Rembrandt; Voltaire and Newton; Mozart, Haydn, and Handel all created for a small aristocratic audience and constituted an essential part of Old Regime society. But ultimately even the achievements of such genius could neither save nor justify the social structure of the age. Society was fantastically wasteful of its human resources. Most people were condemned to the endless toil of simple survival. As the eighteenth century wore on, the social fabric began to bend under an increasingly sophisticated technology that demanded more productive use of people than was permitted by subsistence farming or handicrafts. But this bending was also due to a change in the intellectual climate, to the ideas of the Enlightenment, which put forth the notion—incredible at the time—that all men were created equal.

AN AGE OF ENLIGHTENMENT

During the Old Regime, Western thought underwent dramatic change, For science, philosophy, religion, and political and social theory, the last century of the Old Regime was a time of transformation from medieval to more modern patterns of thought. In general, a religious conception of man and the universe decayed, being progressively replaced by a secular view. Religion began its long transformation from a common cultural possession shared by everyone to an experience confined to a random few. Political and social theory was equally changed. The medieval ideas of corporate being and a social hierarchy ordained by God gradually gave way to concepts of equalitarianism, and the mutually contracted obligations of feudalism were replaced by differing views on the rights and duties of both the state and individual. Scientific thought, once the adjunct of theology, became the hallmark of Western knowledge theory. During the years from 1680 to 1800, the medieval world view slipped away, and Western man became a stranger to thirty generations of his ancestors.

There was also continuity during the Enlightenment, particularly in the area of high culture. Music, art, architecture, literature, and sculpture remained relatively unchanged, the vagaries of fad and fashion notwithstanding. High culture was essentially aristocratic in nature, designed and executed for the noble patrons who appreciated and paid for it. Indeed, so exclusive was aristocratic possession of high culture that bourgeois families moving upward socially turned automatically to musical or artistic patronage as a major element of their climb. Nothing that occurred between the general crisis of the fourteenth century and the French Revolution disturbed this pattern.

Arts and Letters:
The High Culture during the Enlightenment

The continuity of high culture through the baroque and rococo periods reflected the continuity in the privileges and life style of the

The interior of a church at Wies, Bavaria, designed by Dominikus Zimmermann and built between 1746 and 1754, representative of the baroque style at its most elaborate. *Hirmer Fotoarchiv.*

European aristocracy. Grandeur and ostentation were a part of both aristocratic magnificence and show and baroque art, music, architecture, and sculpture. The gorgeous processions of the doge of Venice, undertaken to celebrate civic and religious occasions, were greatly enhanced by the baroque processionals and brass canzones

Boucher's *Le Dejeuner* **is an example of the charmingly pastel and decorative high rococo style. As a genre scene, it is indicative of the "civilized" tenor of French life in the eighteenth century.** *Photographie Giraudon.*

of Giovanni Gabrieli. The palace ceiling by Tiepolo at Würzburg made the resident bishop a more substantial patronage. When the Barberini family of Rome attained the papacy they built a magnificent palace and commissioned Bernini to design the papal tomb. The presence of George Frederick Handel at the Hanoverian court in London was essential to the prestige of the first two drab Georges. The characteristics of baroque art and music—grandeur, power, exalted themes, richness, ornamentation, sheer size—were essential to the aristocratic dignity and position.

There was another side to aristocratic life and art. Centering around life in the château or town house, there developed an art of interior decor, furniture, portraiture, and chamber music. Grandeur was necessary for public functions, but it could be demanding and uncomfortable. During the eighteenth century, art decor and music accommodated themselves to a more private and intimate life style. Grandeur was sacrificed to elegance and luxury, common traits in both art and life. The development of wallpaper, Aubusson carpets, Louis XV furniture, Mozart and Haydn quartets, Scarlatti sonatas, and Boucher paneling were examples of a consciously limited artistic motif. Scale was reduced and quality often enhanced. The salon was as much a patron of Old Regime art as the court or cathedral.

A major element of aristocratic patronage of high culture was reinforcement of status and prestige. A vast amount of visual propaganda emerged from the buildings, paintings, music, and processions organized by the aristocracy. Everyone could see and marvel; here was a great man indeed! In an age when few could read and the aristocratic life style held unquestioned dominance, the psychological effects of artistic patronage were powerful and enduring. High culture played a political as well as artistic role. As such, its patronage by the aristocracy was assured.

The Crisis of European Thought: 1680–1700

In the generation between 1675 and 1700, the dominant intellectual climate of western Europe underwent a substantial and sudden change. Within a very few years the medieval world view of man, his society and cosmos, began to dissolve, the victim of new knowledge and new questions. A new intellectual climate, called by contemporaries the Enlightenment, took its place. The Enlightenment marked a substantial repudiation of the theologically oriented world view of the medieval period and the rapid dissemination of more modern ideas concerning science, religion, and political theory. In the last three decades of the seventeenth century the ideas of Sir

Isaac Newton, John Locke, and Pierre Bayle mark this abrupt and massive transition.

The implications of Sir Isaac Newton's computations and astronomy collapsed the traditional Christian cosmology, which had survived the onslaughts of Copernicus and Galileo. Early Enlightenment thought also affected the more mundane aspects of religion. Pierre Bayle assaulted the notion of no salvation outside the church, scoffed at much religious belief as superstition, and advocated religious toleration as a clear and obvious duty of Christian man. Secularism made its appearance with the work of Locke and Bayle on toleration and superstition. Political theory also changed. Against the dominant concepts of absolutism, there emerged a new idea of a social contract and the natural liberties of man. The publicist for these opinions was John Locke, who wrote his *Two Treatises on Civil Government* in 1690 to justify the "Glorious Revolution" of the previous year.

The collapse of the Renaissance and Reformation verities that had dominated European thought for the past two centuries was sudden and unexpected. So rapid was the disintegration of the religious, scientific, and political consensus that it may well be called a crisis of European thought. Beginning in France, Holland, and England, the new notions of liberty, toleration, rationalism, and scientific thought spread over the entire Continent. The older explanations of God and man suddenly proved unsatisfactory. The contemporaries of Newton and Locke changed their ideas, while those of Richelieu and Galileo held fast to established doctrine. In a generation, the dominant intellectual themes in European thought had changed from medieval to modern.

The Growth of Scientific Thought

The scientific revolution in Western thought began long before the Enlightenment; indeed, in physics and biology it began with the Renaissance. The astonishing growth of Western scientific thought had four general bases: the precise rational philosophy of the Renaissance; the empirical and experimental work of Italian physicians and professors; the dissemination of ancient Greek mathematics in the sixteenth century; and the invention of printing, which made it easier for one man to know the work of another. In the sixteenth century, almost unnoticed during the disputation and butchery of the Reformation, philosophy, experiment, and mathematics were being melded into a disciplined methodology for scientific thought and research.

In 1500 Nicolaus Copernicus was lecturing on mathematics in Rome and was already working on the development of his theory that the sun was the center of the solar system and the earth was merely a satellite. In 1543, only days before his death, Copernicus saw the first copy of his book, *On the Revolutions of the Celestial Spheres,* which began the destruction of the ancient idea—enshrined in the theology of the Roman Catholic Church—that the earth was the center of the universe. Copernicus arrived at his conclusions from observations and mathematical reasoning, not from experiment, and the evidence he presented was inconclusive. More evidence was eventually provided by the Danish astronomers Tycho Brahe (1541–1601) and Johannes Kepler (1571–1630), who amassed mountainous data demonstrating the essential correctness of Copernicus. The Italian professor and astronomer Galileo Galilei continued the practice of observations, using a much improved telescope of his own invention. In 1632 he published his *Dialogues on the Two Principal World Systems,* a comparison of his own physics and astronomy with that of Aristotle and the Roman Catholic Church. Condemned by the Inquisition, Galileo was arrested and confined for the rest of his life to his house. But his work survived. Despite clerical opposition, his notions spread slowly throughout Europe.

The completion of the revolution in physics, mechanics, and astronomy came with the publication in 1687 of Sir Isaac Newton's *Principia Mathematica.* Newton presented a general theory of motion, for which scientists and philosophers had been searching for as long as there had been scientists and philosophers. Buttressed by mathematics and observation, the Newtonian laws were irresistible. Newtonian physics set the parameters for scientific insight for over a century. Philosophy was equally attracted to Newton. The old Christian view of the heavens did not survive the *Principia Mathematica.* Once the ultimate in mystery, the stars and planets were now seen as a giant clock, fitted together of mutually supporting and interconnected pieces. It was wondrous, it was magnificent—and it was finished. The heavenly clock reflected the greater glory of God and, at the same time, precluded His further intervention in matters physical and astronomical. According to the new cosmology of the Enlightenment, God had completed His work and had retired. With the rapid spread of Newtonian physics during the Enlightenment, the ancient roles of science and philosophy were reversed. Now it was scientific thought that gave form and direction to philosophical speculation. Now, for the first time in Western civilization, philosophy was shaped by scientific experiment and observation.

Other areas of scientific inquiry also prospered during the Enlightenment. In biology, substantial theoretical contributions moved the field from religion and myth toward coherent scientific inquiry. The most influential work was the system of classification for animals and plants postulated by the Swedish biologist Carl Linnaeus. There were many errors in Linnaeus' work. The notion of the fixity of species eliminated any concept of evolution, and a general external description was inadequate to classify species. The system did provide the basis for modern taxonomy, however, and was the first coherent break with the Aristotelian categories. So pervasive was its impact that all other general biology began with Linnaean forms. The French naturalist Georges Buffon added a note of complexity and change to the stable Linnaean system when he postulated that life moved from the simple to the complex, a presupposition necessary to understanding evolution. Most of the laboratory work, however, waited until after the French Revolution, and biology during the Enlightenment occupied the same stage of development that physics and astronomy had known two centuries earlier.

Chemists were also busy during the Enlightenment, particularly in the study of gases. In 1775 Joseph Priestley, an English Unitarian clergyman, published the results of his crucial experiments. Priestly had isolated oxygen in 1774, and thereafter work went rapidly. In 1779 Jan Ingenhousz demonstrated that plants exhale oxygen, and in 1780–1781 Claude Berthollet and Antoine Lavoisier isolated oxygen, carbon, and hydrogen as the elements of organic substances. Three years later Henry Cavendish published his experiments on making water out of hydrogen and oxygen, and in 1789—a notable year in Western civilization—Lavoisier published his *Elementary Treatise of Chemistry*, which summarized the new knowledge and explained his theory of combustion, saying that oxygen was the basic element in both fire and breathing. By the end of the Enlightenment a substantial amount of detailed laboratory work had been done, and chemistry was being rapidly converted into a hard science.

During the Enlightenment the philosophical implications of scientific discovery were slowly accepted into Western culture. Scientific explanations for all phenomena, both natural and human, became almost automatic for Enlightenment philosophes. The eighteenth century was also the time of the first faint connections between science and technology. Science became the intellectual motif of the age.

REASON AND THE ORGANIZATION OF KNOWLEDGE

The Enlightenment has been called .the Age of Reason, largely because of loud contemporary protestations that everything was now being judged by the clear light of reason. These protests, however, covered some serious logical lapses and papered over unprovable assertions that the eighteenth-century philosophes chose to accept as absolute truth. Moreover, reason was not an invention of the eighteenth century, as the philosophes loved to claim. It had been the tool of philosophers from the pre-Socratics onward. Finally, Enlightenment philosophes were not conspicuously better at using reason than their predecessors, whose work they ignored or condemned; indeed, in many cases, eighteenth-century thought rested on flimsier bases and poorer logic than the ideas that were attacked. Nevertheless, the appellation Age of Reason has stuck, and not altogether without justification. For in the Enlightenment, the uses made of reason changed. Previous philosophers and philosophical schools had used reason as a substantive concept. Philosophers as diverse as Plato, Thomas Aquinas, and Descartes thought of reason as the informing principle of the universe, that every human and natural phenomenon was the reflection of divine reason, ideal reason, natural reason, and so on. Great systems of philosophical speculation were built on this basis. There was some of this type of speculative philosophy during the Enlightenment, but not very much. The Enlightenment philosophes used reason as an analytical tool to evaluate the validity and internal consistency of speculative philosophical systems. From Plato to Descartes and Spinoza, older philosophical systems—particularly the dogmas and myths of Christianity—were examined and criticized during the Enlightenment. Empiricism and analytical rationalism were the hallmarks of the knowledge theory of the Enlightenment.

A basic philosophical tool of the Enlightenment, one that was erected into a coherent knowledge theory, was empiricism, the evaluation of sense perceptions, of things seen or touched, and therefore known. Primarily a British philosophical school, empiricism began with John Locke. In his *Essay Concerning Human Understanding* (1690), Locke argues that all knowledge comes, in the first instance, from experience, that is, from sense perceptions. We hear sounds, we see and touch objects, and we learn from this experience. We reflect upon our experience and the experiences of others that we have heard or read about and thus form our ideas. Finally, we constantly test these ideas and impressions against new experiences, new objects seen or touched. There is no innate knowledge, Locke argues, no ideas we are born with. We learn and understand as our experience teaches us. These ideas were wildly popular during the Enlightenment, for they struck at the very roots of Platonism and the Christian theory of the innate idea of God. By the middle of the eighteenth century every philosopher had become an empiricist or its scientific equivalent, an experimentalist.

There were, of course, difficulties in an exclusively empirical or experimental theory of knowledge and understanding, and these were pointed out, *sotto voce*, by some of the best minds of the Enlightenment. For David Hume, the obvious logical conclusion to an empirical knowledge theory was complete skepticism. The descent into skepticism was presented in starkest clarity by Élie Benoist, an exiled Huguenot pastor, in his treatise *Collection of Historical, Philosophical and Theological Remarks* . . . (1712). The main problem with empiricism and philosophical reliance on firsthand knowledge is the lack of proof. How do we know we saw what we thought we saw? Senses are confused and our experience is limited. More especially, because of our limited experience, how do we know that what people tell us is true? People lie, they swear to the lies of others, even when speaking in good faith they are often mistaken. In empiricism, Benoist stated, there is no absolute proof, no certainty, only approximate proof that might well be wrong. Empiricism, therefore, was quite a limited philosophical tool, quite an inadequate knowledge theory. An interesting book, Benoist's treatise was generally ignored during the Enlightenment, but it made a powerful point and advanced a type of criticism that found a later champion in Immanuel Kant. Kant brought together the numerous criticisms that might be made about empiricism and reason and, toward the end of the eighteenth century, embodied them in a series of philosophical treatises that literally killed off the intellectual bases of most Enlightenment thought. But by that time Europe was engulfed in revolution and war, and the Enlightenment was dying of its own accord.

Attempts to create a secular knowledge theory were not the only Enlightenment attempts to systematize man's learning. There was also a consistent effort to organize useful and valuable knowledge for the edification of the enlightened and the reform of the obstinate. The first work in this genre was Pierre Bayle's *Historical and Critical Dictionary* (1699), and it was followed by others, both general and specialized. The most important was the *Encyclopédie,* an immense work undertaken by Denis Diderot and the mathematician Jean d'Alembert. Begun in 1751, it extended to seventeen volumes of text and eleven of plates, and was only finished in 1772. The *Encyclopédie* was a stupendous summary of contemporary knowledge, views, and prejudices, with great emphasis on practical agriculture and handicrafts. Useful knowledge for the philosophe was a positive moral good, more likely to bring happiness and virtue into the world than all the religious dogma ever heard of. Utility was a canon of judgment as important as theoretical truth.

THE ASSAULT ON CHRISTIANITY

Eighteenth-century philosophers saw the church and religion as two of their major enemies, which had to be destroyed to make way for the better world of science and reason. The institutional church was seen as a basic obstacle to the acceptance of religious toleration, the faith itself as a blend of superstition and preposterous myth, which no reasonable man could accept. Enlightenment hostility toward the church was a mixture of anticlericalism and religious skepticism. At the far end of the antireligious spectrum were a few atheists, who denied both the existence and possibility of God. Generally condemned, the atheists were only carrying Enlightenment skepticism to its logical conclusions in demanding that philosophy be based solely on human reason and experiment.

The debate on church and faith began in a singular manner with the appearance of Halley's comet in 1680. The comet inspired more than the astronomer's study; it provoked a large number of dire predictions of future calamities as a result of the comet's flight. This ancient superstition was now to be challenged. In 1682 Pierre Bayle published his *Divers Thoughts on the Comet . . .* and began the Enlightenment assault on superstition and religious belief. It was nonsense, Bayle said, to think that disaster flowed from a comet. Had anyone, of his own knowledge, proved it? Had not good things occurred after a comet's passage? Did not disasters occur every day, without the help of a comet? There was no necessary cause and effect between comets and anything. To believe otherwise meant a mind sunk in rank superstition.

Religion needed a thorough examination by reason and empirical verification. Blatant superstition would no longer do. Accordingly, Bayle set out to examine religious tradition, popular belief, biblical stories, and sectarian dogma, using a rigorous rationalism as his tool. In his *Historical and Critical Dictionary* Bayle subjected religious belief and pious stories to a withering criticism, showing their incompatibility with the tenets of reason, logic, common sense, or morality. For his efforts, he was denounced by kings and prelates everywhere, he was declared a heretic by his own church, and his books were suppressed. To no effect; Bayle's rational criticism of superstition and religious belief became the basis of a major trend of Enlightenment thought.

Bayle also believed in religious toleration as did John Locke, whose *Letters Concerning Toleration* had a substantial impact on contemporary opinion. Both Locke and Bayle tried to show that religious persecution had no Scriptural basis and was morally repugnant and politically malicious. They argued that the mere existence of many Christian sects was itself a manifestation of God's will, and it was presumptuous, perhaps blasphemous, of man to choose one sect as being true and persecute all others as being false and damnable. They also pointed to the immense damage done the realm by the horrors of persecution and religious civil war, the trade and property lost, the taxes unpaid, the lands left barren. There was, of course, much clerical opposition to these opinions, but they prevailed anyway. The heat of Reformation religious conviction was declining, and people were more willing to live and let live. Further, kings and secretaries could sometimes see how sterile and costly religious persecution was, and reasons of state demanded religious toleration.

After 1700 the attack on superstition and persecution broadened into a pervasive anticlericalism, which focused as much on the church as the faith. An entire tribe of philosophers, led by Voltaire, concentrated their venom on the faults of the church. Religious persecution and religious conflicts were insane. They were the fault of the various churches, which had driven men to the hideous brutalities that characterized religious warfare in the West. Not only had churches preached murder and butchery, but they were still doing so. They sanctioned the most ludicrous superstitions, they prevented the progress of enlightened opinion, they grew wealthy while the people starved. Finally, most monstrous of all, churches defended such immoral conduct by declaring it to be the manifest will of God. What could God think of such things? Indeed, what had Christ himself said about the scribes and Pharisees? Did not progress toward a just and equitable society depend on eliminating the power and influence of the church?

The philosophers were unable to deal with genuine religious conviction or explain the mystery and tragedy of the human condition, but they could expose much hypocrisy in church government and inconsistency of proclaimed dogma and could construct a seemingly coherent scientific explanation of the natural world. The immorality of persecution was movingly described, and few churchmen could be found to defend it. To an increasing number of Europeans, progress, peace, liberty, and justice depended on a drastic diminution of the authority of both church and dogma.

The fringe of religious dissent during the Enlightenment was atheism, which claimed a tiny but fanatic band of believers. In spite of the anticlericalism of the age, atheist opinions met with hostility and converted only a few. Everyone thought atheism was destructive of good moral and social order, that people needed to believe in God, that much religious dogma was nonsense but that the existence and benign aspect of God was undeniable. Indeed, so definite was the hostility to atheism that David Hume arranged to have his *Dialogues Concerning Natural Religion* published after his death. Its radical skepticism concerning religious dogma and the existence of God was too strong for the public.

The Search for Virtue and Justice in Society and Government

Assaults on church and faith, while they might clear away much superstition and obscurantism, were not without their defects. Public and private morals and ethics had always been inculcated through religion, the same religion now under such determined assault. No philosophe wished to overthrow ethical conduct and see a society based on blatant selfishness; there was far too much of that already. Moral conduct was as sacred to the Enlightenment as to any age of faith. The philosophical problem was to separate morality and socially ethical conduct from dogma, to find a social basis and guarantor for ethics, to find essence and attributes of morality in the "laws of Nature and Nature's God." From Bayle to the French Revolution, this was the central problem in social philosophy for the Enlightenment philosophe.

"Justice and truth are the common ties of society," wrote John Locke in 1690, and there were few during the Enlightenment who would have denied the ideal. But was this a valid description of eighteenth-century society? If not, and virtually every philosophe doubted it was, then it became the clear duty of the enlightened to show how things might be made right. The philosophe saw himself as the midwife of public ethics, social justice, and political liberty. In this role he tended to lean heavily on two sources of inspiration: the lessons of history and traditions of natural law inherited from the ancient world. From history men sought examples of a better system of government and social organization and searched for the villains that had brought contemporary Europe to such a low estate. In the natural law, Enlightenment thinkers saw the inalienable rights of man, which could never be justly abridged by government and were almost everywhere ignored during the eighteenth century.

The major historians of the Enlightenment, Edward Gibbon and David Hume, regarded history as a branch of moral philosophy. In his *History of England,* David Hume sought to understand how political liberty was established in England, and he looked for his answers in the events of the seventeenth century. Liberty was an absolute political good, fortunately possessed by the English and desired by all others, and the story of its triumph was of the highest importance for the Enlightenment. Hume believed that liberty must be tempered with order. He also remarked that free peoples were the most despotic in dealing with their colonies. For Hume, history offered more than merely an opportunity to draw useful lessons from the past; it gave an occasion to comment on present conditions, manners, and morals.

Gibbon held a similar view of his profession. His *The Decline and Fall of the Roman Empire* was a melancholy saga of the collapse of the greatest, happiest, and most just civilization that the world had seen, and the reasons for this great crash could hardly fail to instruct the enlightened. Gibbon saw Christianity, both as a faith and a church, as the main villain in the collapse of ancient civilization. To inoculate his own time against such a calamitous event, Gibbon advocated a pervasive anticlericalism and a healthy skepticism to the demands of dogma.

The ideals generally praised by the historians of the eighteenth century were political liberty, equality before the law, and public virtue. One of the most important Enlightenment treatises dealing with public policy was *An Essay on Crimes and Punishments* (1764) by Cesare Bonesana, Marchese di Beccaria. Beccaria attacked the practices of torture, of forcing the suspect to incriminate himself, and of exacting barbarous punishments for minor crimes. Let the punishment fit the crime, he said, and let the punishment work toward the rehabilitation of the prisoner. Legal revenge was monstrous. Torture was inhuman. The law had become an accomplice of crime, not a deterrent. The movement to reform the criminal law, which has continued to this day, began with Beccaria.

An even more powerful advocate of liberty and equality was Jean-Jacques Rousseau. A refugee from Calvinist Geneva, Rousseau was a passionate devotee of a peculiarly eighteenth-century form of liberty, the natural rights of man, which ought to be safeguarded under society. "Man was born free; he is everywhere in chains," is the opening sentence of the *Social Contract* (1762), and it expressed Rousseau's indignation at the lack of freedom of contemporary man and his hope that natural rights might be restored. This would be done by a government that rested upon the general will of the people, a nebulous thing more like a Quaker consensus than a majority vote. Through the workings of the general will, a government and society would obtain an unassailable moral legitimacy, would guarantee the freedom of the individual and his equality before the law.

The tocsin for liberty and equality was rung in the documents of revolution as well as moral treatises. The American Declaration of Independence stated the inalienable rights of man to be life, liberty, and the pursuit of happiness and excoriated George III for denying these. Tom Paine's *Common Sense* (1775) also called men to revolt against tyranny for their rights and freedom. And in 1789, the statements of grievance brought to the French Estates General were filled with demands for natural rights, equality before the law, political liberty, and an end to privilege.

Liberty was also to be extended to the economic sphere. Mercantilist regulations came under the hostile glare of the enlightened. In France the physiocrats, who thought all wealth was derived from husbandry, advocated an end to regulations that impeded the flow of agricultural goods. Manorial restrictions ought to go as well, and the regressive French system of taxation must be reformed to reward the industrious peasant. The government could encourage production by establishing a free market, free interchange of goods, low and consistent taxes. In England, Adam Smith concentrated his attention on trade and manufacturing. His *The Wealth of Nations* appeared in 1775 and rapidly became a sacred book for the growing group of British entrepreneurs. Smith claimed that mercantilist regulation of commerce and industry warped the natural paths of trade and production to the detriment of the community, for prices were artificially raised and production levels cut. The intervention of government in the economy could only be harmful. Natural economic forces would provide the greatest economic good for the greatest number of people, checking by themselves rent racking, price gouging, selling shoddy, and the like—all of the familiar and ancient crimes of the business community. In economics as in politics, freedom and the laws of nature would best provide.

It is clear to us today, though it was much less so at the time, that the prevailing ideas of the Enlightenment on political liberty, social justice, equality before the law, and the essential uselessness —indeed, iniquity—of religious dogma were incompatible with the governments and society of Old Regime Europe. Few philosophes were themselves revolutionaries; they thought the necessary changes could be made within the existing framework. But they espoused revolutionary ideas. Political liberty was incompatible with autocratic monarchy, equality before the law could not coexist with social privilege. Assaults on the credibility of doctrine were unacceptable to the established churches of the Continent. The philosophes scoffed at traditional ideas and patterns of thought and created a new climate of opinion, one that was hostile to the existing society. The moral underpinnings of the Old Regime were gradually eroded by Enlightenment thought, and a sense of legitimacy no longer sustained traditional and ancient privileges, now considered iniquitous and inequitable. The Enlightenment worked a revolution in men's minds and thoughts. Toward the end of the century this revolution was transferred to the streets.

SIX

An era of revolution

Wooden shoes going up the stairs of history
pass the velvet slippers coming down.
                                    Anatole France

O Liberty! What crimes are committed in thy
name.
                                    Madame Roland

The age is running mad after innovation. . . .
All the business of the world is to be done a
new way. . . .
                                    Dr. Johnson

INTRODUCTION

In the two generations between 1760 and 1820, the Western world
experienced profound changes that permanently altered the character of modern civilization. Two revolutions took place, one in
politics and government, the other in technology, economic production, and social organization. Toward the end of the eighteenth
century an insistent demand developed for social equality and
increased political participation. At the same time there was a quantum leap in the efficiency of material production and in the sum of
European technical knowledge. Together these two revolutions
brought the Old Regime to an end and tipped Western civilization
toward modernity.

The revolution in politics and government had its greatest
impact in France, the largest, most powerful, and most literate state

in western Europe. After 1750 France began to show serious signs of social strain and political immobility. Although many desirable reforms were announced from time to time by the crown, they all failed for a wide variety of more or less trivial reasons. Existing social and political structures mocked Enlightenment concepts of justice and equality. More and more people saw both government and society as a standing moral outrage, a deliberate affront to common decency and a sense of justice. Privilege no longer commanded respect, but hatred. By the 1780s, therefore, sources for renewal of the Old Regime monarchy and society no longer existed. Conspicuous political failure and the hope for a more just society were able to overthrow in the single summer of 1789 the accumulated traditions, institutions, and attitudes of a millennium.

The revolution of technology and industrial production was altogether different from the dramatic political crisis. After 1760 a cluster of technological innovations in textiles and iron began to change completely the modes of production. Quietly industrialization overturned the traditional economic relationships between people, creating a new class of urban workers and another of business bourgeoisie. Science and technology were linked together, the economic predominance of agriculture was destroyed, and huge new cities were built. The Industrial Revolution changed the way people lived and the way they thought and altered the traditional class and family structures. Finally, the pace of economic and social change accelerated as industrialization fed upon itself, so that the problems and promises of this incredible revolution grew with each decade.

Each of these revolutions was more than merely an event; it was a continuous process. There was no quiet death for the ideas of nationalism, political participation, and social equality that came out of the French Revolution. These spread to all peoples everywhere. It was the same with industrialization. Great Britain continually became more industrialized, and the rest of the European states began to experience the industrial process. Equally important was the interaction between the two revolutions, which provided the impetus for change during the nineteenth and twentieth centuries. In the years between 1760 and 1820 Western civilization passed painfully into the modern era.

THE CRISIS OF THE OLD ORDER

In eighteenth-century Europe, society exhibited remarkable signs of both health and strain. The end of the Old Regime was a period of brilliant prosperity. Population grew everywhere. Advances in agricultural technology increased the food supply, and the beginnings of industrialization started to produce more goods. It was also a time of strident criticism of the prevailing social and political institutions. A series of revolutions broke out in all corners of the European world after 1765. From America to Poland, peoples rose against their rulers, In France the government fell into obvious debility. Furthermore, the intellectual climate of the Enlightenment included a growing concern over the rights of man, as well as over religious persecution, inequality before the law, judicial torture, and the social injustices of privilege. Although great progress had been made in the efficiency and justice with which Europeans were governed, the Old Regime ended in revolution against social, political, and economic conditions that were obviously improving.

It seems clear that by the 1760s the social and political institutions of the Old Regime were losing their moral authority. Ancient forms of privilege, once accepted as valid, were increasingly questioned and pronounced unjust. The traditional society of the Old Regime no longer commanded the respect and allegiance it once had. Torrents of criticism eroded belief in the rightness of contemporary social organization. The moral foundations of society, the general agreement that present conditions were reasonable, just, and good, was slipping away, replaced by loud complaints against the abuses of privilege and demands that these wicked practices end. This loss of moral authority made fundamental social and political changes inevitable.

By the middle years of the eighteenth century several of the European monarchs began to share their subjects' concern over the workings of government and the inequities of society. They saw the legitimacy of their governments being questioned with a dangerous fervor, and they tried to do better. An increase in efficiency might be needed. Some of the most blatant forms of privilege might well be eliminated. Historians have used the term "enlightened despotism" to describe this movement, which included a measure of social justice, an end to religious persecution, some equality before the law, and vastly increased royal efficiency and power.

The program of reform differed in the various European states, but there were common threads. One of these was an assault on the power and privileges of the clergy. In Portugal the prime minister Pombal confiscated church lands and reduced church privileges. In France the persecution of Protestants ended by the 1760s, and limited toleration began in 1787. In Austria the emperor Joseph II closed nearly 700 monasteries between 1780 and 1790 and secularized one-half of the monks of his realm. Toleration was granted to

Austrian Protestants, and secular schools were established to break the clerical control over education. Joseph's attack on church privileges was the most coherent of the Old Regime, and his name became synonymous with anticlericalism. Reduction of church privileges was a triumph of Enlightenment thought and a victory for the secular and bureaucratic state.

A second area of activity for the enlightened despots was administrative and legal reform. In Russia, Catherine the Great reorganized provincial government, increasing the power of the nobility and making it more responsive to central direction. In Austria, Maria Theresa and her son Joseph tried to increase the efficiency and authority of the crown and reduce the power of the nobles. The central administration was reorganized in the 1740s and 1760s, improving fiscal and military efficiency. In Flanders, Lombardy, and Hungary the local gentry resisted these centralizing reforms, and the crown was forced to make concessions. Nonetheless, in 1792 at the death of Leopold II, the Austrian government was considerably stronger and more efficient than it had ever been.

Similar reforms were carried on in several Italian states. In Naples, the justice minister Bernardo Tanucci started the immense project of codifying the laws, introducing concepts of legal equality into his work. Leopold of Tuscany reformed municipal government in the 1770s, giving citizens' councils a large voice in matters relating to local taxes, public works, and welfare. Enlightened despotism in Tuscany, as in Naples, considerably reduced the privileges of the nobility and urban patriciate.

A third area of reform was in economic policy. Economic reform generally followed two lines—encouragement of trade and industry and improvements in the administration of revenues and the collection of taxes. Frederick the Great of Prussia took the lead among his contemporaries in state subvention of industry and agriculture. He supported the textile industry in Silesia, encouraged immigration into Prussia, and gave tax rebates in order to encourage settlement on cleared lands. Joseph II of Austria promoted industrialization and had some success in Milan and Bohemia. Royal land banks in Spain, Prussia, Russia, and Austria were established to provide credit for cultivators attempting to improve their land and farming methods. Several monarchs—among them Charles III of Spain, Frederick the Great, and Joseph II—established model farms and agricultural societies to disseminate the new agricultural technology of the eighteenth century.

Kings also turned their attention to the royal fiscal institutions and practices. Joseph II and Leopold of Tuscany both eased the ruinous policy of allowing royal borrowing to eat up much of the liquid capital of the realm. Frederick the Great ended deficit financing and even accumulated a surplus in his later years. Catherine the Great of Russia provided a stable currency, with great benefit to trade in her vast empire. In Spain, Sweden, Austria, and Tuscany, guild privileges, which stifled commerce and technological innovation, were sharply reduced. Internal tariffs were abolished in virtually all of Spain by Charles III.

Taxes were also subject to the scrutiny of reforming monarchs. Objections were raised to the odious practice of tax farming, whereby the right to collect taxes was sold to a group of financiers, who then squeezed the people dry on the pretext of doing their public duty. Leopold of Tuscany revoked the contract because of corruption. Even in Spain and Naples, the cries of the wretched peasantry reached the crown, and Charles III reduced the scope of the tax farm. Reform was not all one way, however. Frederick the Great actually established a corporation to farm the excise taxes and tolls. But he managed it so strictly that the tax farmers as well as the people complained.

Not all of the pressures created by the decay of moral approval of the political and social order were relieved by enlightened monarchs. Some reform came from the streets. The period from the middle of the eighteenth century to the Congress of Vienna in 1815 was an era of revolutions, both in Europe and America. The uprising least menacing to the social and political structure of the Old Regime was the war in America. Yet, by a curious irony, the American Revolution had a considerable impact on more radical social revolts in Europe. It was the rhetoric of the event—the Declaration of Independence, *Common Sense* by Thomas Paine, and the propaganda of Benjamin Franklin—that made this so. The language of the American Revolution was strong and radical; it denounced monarchs as scoundrels and nobles as jackals and averred that the good, true, and natural order of mankind was one of social equality and political liberty. When the Americans won, it seemed a clear case of virtue triumphant. When European officers such as Lafayette returned home as heroes, they were dramatic proof that a society based on freedom and equality was possible on this earth.

If the American civil insurrection ended gloriously, other attempts at revolution did not. Polish reform attracted the hostility of the eastern powers—Prussia, Russia, and Austria—who did not wish to see a revitalized Polish kingdom. The Polish revolution of 1788–1794, therefore, ended in the partition of the state. In eastern Europe, the forces of conservatism were the same as those of imperial expansion. It was a powerful combination, one that easily overwhelmed Poland and, ultimately, defeated Napoleon.

Revolution also wracked the Austrian Empire. Hungary and Belgium rose up against Joseph II. Nowhere were the limits of enlightened despotism better shown than in Joseph's attempt to modernize the government and society of two provinces where the magnates wished things to remain as they were. The imperial program of religious toleration, administrative reform, abolition of legal inequality, ending serfdom and seigneurial obligations, and establishing a uniform tax structure was met with ferocious and successful revolt. The Belgian and Hungarian revolts were not liberal uprisings; on the contrary, they were another attempt, in a series dating from the sixteenth century, to retain privileges and immunities and oppose the centralizing policies of the emperor. Conservatives as well as radicals found enlightened despotism unsatisfactory.

A last revolution against the inequities of the Old Regime or the inadequate reforms of enlightened despotism occurred in Holland. The crisis in the United Provinces emerged out of the American Revolution. Dutch merchants had seized upon the revolution to strike a commercial blow at their British rivals. Great Britain declared war in 1780 and in three years seized 80 million guilders of Dutch shipping. But the *Stadtholder*, William V, clung fast to his pro-British policy, no matter what the losses. The towns, led by Amsterdam were outraged. Urban merchants made common cause with a growing democratic party, led by a provincial nobleman, Van der Capellen tot der Pol. Van der Capellen and his followers urged the Dutch to overthrow the corrupt and unpatriotic William V. They followed an anti-British line, favored France, and demanded a more representative form of government at home. William V, on his part, allied himself with the hereditary oligarchies in the towns and the highest country nobility, and he leaned heavily on British and Prussian diplomatic and fiscal support. By 1787, the two parties, "patriot" and "Orange," were on the verge of civil war. This was forestalled, however, by British and Prussian military intervention. A Prussian army occupied the country. The "patriots" were dispersed; over 20,000 emigrated, and William V retained his full powers and prerogatives. In the eighteenth century, revolution came from palaces as well as huts.

The pressures that led to revolution and enlightened despotism also existed in France. Both the philosophy of the Enlightenment and the need for efficient government were part of the eighteenth-century political experience in France. But there were differences. No enlightened monarch sat on the French throne. Reforming ministers invariably saw their projects fail. France badly needed constructive and enlightened change but received only condemnations of the old and promises of reform.

As elsewhere in Europe, the desire for change was strongest among government officials. There was a series of reforming ministers, from Machault in 1749 through Necker in 1781, who tried to effect many of the political and social changes that were later made by the Revolution. War first brought home to French ministers the severity of the problems of social privilege and inefficient government. The War of the Austrian Succession (1740–1748) had cost vast amounts of money, which was met by borrowing, not taxation. There was talk of bankruptcy. To avoid both continued loans and bankruptcy, Machault, the comptroller-general of the finances, tried to reform the tax system, making it more equitable and productive. In 1749 he created a new tax, called the twentieth, to be paid by everyone. This destroyed the traditional tax exemption enjoyed by the nobility, clergy, and the more affluent merchants.

The privileged orders were outraged by Machault's new tax. The noble judges of the Parlement of Paris, the greatest law court in the realm, issued loud complaints that taxing the nobility was contrary to the fundamental laws of the kingdom. The estates of the privileged provinces of Languedoc and Brittany made collection of the new tax extremely difficult. The General Assembly of the Clergy met in 1750, denounced the twentieth as heresy, and refused to pay. Machault faced a combination of the privileged elements in Old Regime society, and in December 1751 he gave up. The twentieth was withdrawn and the principle of inequality of taxation was recognized. Privilege had soundly thrashed reform.

In the two decades after Machault it became obvious that the main barriers to reform were the Parlement of Paris and its sister courts in the provinces. The noble and wealthy magistrates would not permit any assault on privilege to go unchallenged, and they had developed such skills in public debate and propaganda that they usually won their point. The chancellor, René de Maupeou, decided to destroy the parlements and replace them with politically reliable courts. On January 19, 1771, he suppressed the Parlement of Paris, and by November he had purged the provincial parlements of their most outspoken judges and intimidated the rest. After twenty years of pathetic failure, here was success. Yet this period of royal supremacy, the last of the Old Regime, was ill used. Maupeou did nothing to reform the French law or judicial procedure. Some tax reforms were attempted, but these were designed simply to increase the revenue, not equalize the burden. Nothing was done about the privileges and exemptions of the clergy, the provinces, the towns, the nobility. The ministers were content to tolerate the grossest inequities if they were borne in silence.

In spite of their manifest virtues, the Maupeou reforms barely survived the death of Louis XV in 1774. The new king, Louis XVI, was incompetent, and his reign began with a fatal blunder. The old parlements were brought back, with their capacity for obstruction intact. Yet Louis XVI was not completely insulated from the political and intellectual currents of the time. He tried to imitate his betters and made a genuine effort to reform. A. R. J. Turgot, a convinced physiocrat and an experienced administrator, became comptroller-general of finances. Turgot thought in terms of profound social and economic reform rather than of changes in the workings of royal institutions. His first project, in 1774, was to free the grain trade from most governmental restrictions. In February 1776, he tried to end forced labor of the peasants on the roads and eliminated the craft and artisan guilds in the towns. Both reforms were salutary. Payment of the peasants for their work was obviously just, and elimination of the guilds opened the way for freer competition, technological innovation, and better municipal government.

These reforms aroused the concerted opposition of many elements of Old Regime privilege. The guilds protested, as did the Parlement of Paris and the queen's coterie in court. The church opposed Turgot as contrary to the best interests of the faith. A bread riot north of Paris in May 1776 finished the minister off. He was removed by Louis XVI with suitable expressions of regret, and his reforms were cancelled.

After Turgot the French government became increasingly concerned with finances in a desperate effort to stave off the bankruptcy that had been brewing for a generation. Beginning with Jacques Necker, who held office from 1776 to 1781, French ministers tried both administrative reforms and massive borrowing but were unable to balance the budget. In August 1786, Calonne, the comptroller-general of finances, placed the truth of the impending bankruptcy before the king. The annual deficit was over 100 million francs, the total debt ran into billions, and debt service took nearly 60 percent of the revenue. Calonne proposed a new land tax called the *subvention nationale*. It was to be a tithe on landowners, collected in kind, with no exemptions for clergy, nobility, or the privileged provinces. To increase prosperity, Calonne proposed abolishing internal customs barriers and establishing a uniform tariff for the whole kingdom. Finally, the peasants' road work was to be commuted into a small tax. The whole package, Calonne thought, would bring enough to balance the current budget, ease the immediate crisis, and avoid bankruptcy.

Calonne's program consisted of reforms that had all been defeated before by the parlements, nobility, clergy, and towns. No one had any reason to assume this opposition had eased. Calonne, therefore, was not eager to send his edicts to the Parlement of Paris. Nor did he wish to convoke an Estates General, for this would be an admission that only the nation, not the king, had the power to make needed reforms. So Calonne induced the confused king to call a special Assembly of Notables and avoid both the Parlement and estates.

On February 22, 1787, the Assembly of Notables met at Versailles and was presented with the Calonne program. The delegates were a massive representation of the privileges and immunities that Calonne was trying to destroy. Of the 144 deputies, seven were princes of the blood royal, fourteen were prelates, thirty-six were high nobles, and thirty-seven were magistrates from the parlements. The opening sessions set the pattern for the meeting. Commutation of the peasants' road work was easily accepted; the main attack was reserved for the *subvention nationale*. The notables maintained the new tax was unnecessary and unconstitutional. It infringed on ancient privileges, both personal and corporate. It was an abomination. The notables would not approve the tax. Calonne was dismissed and the assembly was dissolved. The crown had gained nothing.

Brienne, the new comptroller-general, was now faced with a choice between the seething magistrates of the Parlement of Paris and the unknown factor of an Estates General. He chose the Parlement. But the magistrates refused to register the *subvention nationale* or any other scheme for equalizing the tax burden. In desperation, the Parlement was exiled to Troyes.

Difficulties now seemed to overwhelm the tottering government. Without registration by the Parlement the new taxes were uncollectible. The Dutch revolt went against the French party, with great loss of prestige for France. Belgium was moving steadily toward revolution. The king and his ministers were freely ridiculed. Bankruptcy was just around the corner. All Brienne could think of was negotiations with the Parlement. He brought it back from Troyes, in exchange for a new loan and the promise of the Estates General in 1792.

This move only postponed collapse a few months. The death rattle of the monarchy was clearly audible. The hapless government now turned on the Parlement of Paris as the main obstacle to reform.

On May 4, 1788, two magistrates from the Parlement were arrested, and on May 8 a royal session forced registration of six edicts reforming the judicial system and ending the political powers of the Parlement of Paris. Perhaps this would succeed where everything else was failing.

It soon became clear that this ludicrous hope would be unfulfilled. Resistance to the judicial measures was enormous. They were represented as an attack on the liberty of Frenchmen, a despairing act of a dying despotism. There were public disorders. On June 7, 1788, a riot broke out in Grenoble, followed by trouble in Brittany, Bearn, Franche-Comté, and Provence. Troops were called out, but military loyalties were divided, and the army often refused to shoot the rioters. Moreover, the Paris bankers refused new loans, and the crown was only months from bankruptcy. The General Assembly of the Clergy condemned the judicial reforms, refused to lend the king any money, and called for an Estates General. In August, Louis XVI suspended the stillborn judicial reforms and announced an Estates General would meet in May 1789.

With this decision, inevitable in the circumstances, the monarchy handed in its resignation. After eight centuries, it was finished, and Old Regime society was finished with it. Social reform, so long delayed, was now to be accomplished by representatives of the people. The solutions to social problems instituted by the revolutionaries would not be very different from the ideas proposed by royal ministers from 1749 to 1776. But the Old Regime ministers had only talked of reform, raising hopes they could not satisfy. The privileged aristocracy, whether entrenched in the church, provinces, parlements, or royal court, had been too strong for the monarchy. Enlightened despotism, reform from above, had failed. French government and society stood condemned by contemporaries as morally and politically bankrupt.

The collapse of the French monarchy also brought an end to the Old Regime in most of the rest of Europe. Enlightened despotism had not satisfied demands for social reform, nor had the enlightened despots been able to break the power of the privileged aristocracy. By the 1780s polarization, both intellectual and political, had become virtually complete. The Old Regime was falling apart. Reaction or revolt seemed the only answers. The Old Regime ended in a spate of revolutions and counterrevolutions, of monarchs and peoples arming for social conflict. The privileged and hierarchical society of the Old Regime and the inefficient monarchy of early modern Europe no longer justified their existence.

REVOLUTION IN FRANCE

The decision to call the Estates General was greeted with great public enthusiasm. The Enlightenment had conditioned middle-class Frenchmen to trust the judgment of the representatives of the people. Centuries of misgovernment had ended their confidence in royal officials, and they hoped France was on the edge of the millennium. The evils of the Old Regime would soon end. The perfectability of man and society, so long sought, was now attainable. The eve of the great revolution was a period of tremendous hope and faith that the imperfections of man would be eradicated by a change in the arrangements of society. In 1789 it was easier to believe in such things than it has been since.

The decision to convoke the Estates General concentrated the energies of the government on organizing the meeting and election of deputies. Great differences of opinion on these crucial questions were uncovered. The Parlement of Paris stated that the three orders —clergy, nobility, and commons—would elect the same number of deputies and would debate and vote separately; agreement of all three orders would be needed to pass a proposal. By this constitutional device the aristocracy hoped to keep its privileges intact.

Public opinion, however, was unreceptive to marginal changes that would not touch the substance of privilege. The accumulated hostilities, hopes, frustrations, and enlightened notions of the eighteenth century were too powerful to be denied. Popular orators, songsters, and pamphleteers loosed violent protests. A "patriotic" party of liberals was born, with chapters in salons and coffeehouses. It poured forth torrents of polemics. The most famous, "What Is the Third Estate?" by Abbé Sieyès, stated that all but 500,000 of a nation of 26 million belonged to the third estate and, therefore, noble privileges must be abolished. Liberals also demanded a single assembly with individual voting, half the deputies from the third estate, and only certified liberals elected.

In spite of the uproar, the crown decided on traditional arrangements for the Estates General. Voting for delegates was to be by order. Although the third estate received as many deputies as the two privileged orders, voting in the estates was to be by order. Each deputy was to bring with him a cahier, a statement of his constituents' grievances, to be the basis upon which the Estates General would send proposals to the king. The new estates were to be as much like their predecessors as possible.

The elections, however, amply fulfilled the liberals' hopes. Of the 300 delegates for the first estate, nearly 200 were peasant parish priests and only 46 were noble bishops. Even the nobility included a group of about 50 liberals. Within the third estate there could be no doubt. Virtually all of the 610 delegates were "patriots," determined to win voting by head and to force substantial reforms on the monarchy.

After the opening session of May 5, 1789, the initiative was seized by the "patriots." The crucial question was procedural—vote by head or by order. If the three estates met separately, who could doubt that the privileged orders would reject any real reform? If the vote were by head, would not privilege be swept away in a dangerous tide of bourgeois radicalism? In the ensuing struggle the third estate held all the advantages. The parish priests were numerous enough to prevent the first estate from organizing as a separate chamber, thus isolating the nobility. The king gave no leadership at all. Finally, on June 10, the third estate issued an invitation to the other orders to join them in a National Assembly. After bitter debate the first estate, by one vote, accepted.

Neither the king nor the nobility was prepared to accept this decision. On June 20, therefore, the members of the National Assembly found their meeting hall closed. Indignant, they moved across the street to a tennis court. Here they swore the famous Tennis Court Oath, in which they resolved not to disband without creating a constitution for France. Louis, irresolute as always, gave in after a brief resistance. On July 27 he ordered the remaining members of the nobility and clergy to join the National Assembly. The firmness of the third estate had driven the king to surrender.

The Revolution of the People:
July–October 1789

Although Louis XVI had accepted the National Assembly, he did not wish to keep his word. He ordered troops to converge on Paris and Versailles, hoping such a show of strength would help when he reversed his position. His intentions could not be hidden, of course, and the excitement in Paris grew as the troops came closer. By July 12 Paris was aflame. Mobs roamed the streets, sacking bake shops for bread, looting gun shops, and destroying the municipal customs barriers that surrounded the city. On July 14 the Revolution found the proper object on which to focus popular hatreds and fear. The Bastille, a royal fortress in the city, was assaulted and taken. Flushed with victory, the mob moved on City Hall and threw the municipal government out of office. A new mayor was named, and the National Guard was formed, commanded by Lafayette, with the ranks filled by volunteers from the people. For Paris, thirteen centuries of medieval government had ended.

The repercussions of Bastille Day in the provinces were immediate and dramatic. The provincial towns of France hurried to emulate the capital. Sometimes by riot, more often peacefully, the Old Regime municipal and provincial governments were dismantled and replaced by revolutionary officials drawn from the local leaders of the third estate. In a fortnight the Old Regime government in France was replaced by juntas of bourgeois members of the third estate.

Peasants were also affected by the events of 1789. They remembered their ancient grievances against the lords, the church, and the state. For the peasants, elections to the Estates General were a novel and stimulating experience, which led to the touching belief that old grievances would be quickly redressed. When this did not happen, the peasants revolted. After the Bastille, rural revolution became general. From July 20 to August 6—the period of the so-called Great Fear—there were six great waves of rebellion in the countryside. The pattern was the same everywhere. "Brigands" were supposed to be coming to destroy the crops and rob the people! Excited peasants milled around, armed and waiting for attack. When none came, the peasants marched on the local château and obtained the end of manorial dues and obligations. The Great Fear accomplished what the National Assembly had not—the end of the manorial system in France. This was the great revolutionary demand of the peasants; afterward, they remained largely quiescent and politically conservative.

The last episode of popular violence in the summer of 1789 came with the October Days. Louis XVI and the National Assembly were brought to Paris and thus placed at the mercy of the Paris mob. The way was opened for proletarian as well as bourgeois ideas to be heard. Henceforth government would be conducted in the shadow of the Paris crowd. Questions of prices and bread became as important as great national reforms, and the impact of provincial opinion on the course of revolution diminished. After the October Days, the drama of revolution was to be played between city and assembly.

The avowed purpose of the National Assembly was to give France a constitution that would abolish the iniquities of the Old Regime and safeguard the liberties of the new. But the deputies had no clear idea of what a constitution was or how to go about writing one. The constitutional debates dragged on throughout the summer, making little discernible progress. As a result, reform was made in the streets and village lanes, not in the National Assembly. Increasingly the deputies followed, rather than led, public opinion. They hurried to catch up and began a piecemeal reconstruction of France.

The first response of the National Assembly to outside events was brought on by the Great Fear. As word poured in about peasant uprisings, the deputies realized they would have to do something. On the night of August 4, 1789, the Assembly met to deal with the manorial dues. In an emotional session, deputy after deputy rushed to the rostrum and renounced privileges. Manorial, feudal, and municipal privilege all disappeared.

Equally important was the debate on the Declaration of the Rights of Man. The Declaration was vital to the bourgeois of the towns, who saw in it a statement of their principles and their aims in the Revolution. It combined a statement of rights held to be part of natural law and a prohibition of common abuses of Old Regime government. Thus all men were declared to be "free and equal in rights" (article 1), and such things as arbitrary arrest were prohibited (article 7). Religious freedom was guaranteed, cruel and unusual punishment prohibited, trial by jury upheld, and property considered an inviolable right.

In many ways, this short document was a masterpiece. It stated what eighteenth-century man considered the obvious laws of nature. It provided a standard against which the achievements of the Revolution could be measured. Its most important function was moral. The declaration pointed the way France *ought* to go, embodied the best and most generous impulses of 1789, and reminded men that the good society was not political, but ethical.

An issue of equal importance was the future position of the Roman Catholic Church in France. The richest and most privileged institution in France, the church could hardly remain without change. Moreover, anticlerical bourgeois deputies were determined to make the church conform to the new goals of liberty and equality. In October 1789, Talleyrand proposed that the church lands be nationalized. In return, the state assumed the burden of education, hospitals, welfare and worship, and clerical salaries. This was followed, in July 1790, by the Civil Constitution of the Clergy, a comprehensive reorganization of the French church. The number of bishoprics was reduced from 135 to 83. Both priests and bishops were to be chosen by popular election. Finally, the administrative links to Rome were broken—the bishops were forbidden to accept the institutional supremacy of the papacy. Paid by the state, elected by their flocks, the French clergy were to become a species of civil servant.

Opposition to the civil constitution grew rapidly, and the National Assembly ordered all clergy to swear allegiance to it. All but seven of the bishops and half the priests refused. In April 1791 the pope condemned the civil constitution. This widened the breach with Rome into formal schism, with the huge majority of the clergy siding with the pope. A small rump of "constitutional" clergy remained supporters of the Revolution. State persecution of the orthodox was now inevitable. It was only a question of time. Equally significant, counterrevolution was now possible; the alienation of priests had given it a popular base and cause.

In the midst of urban riot, peasant revolt, the Declaration of Rights, and the increasing bitterness over the Civil Constitution of the Clergy, it was easy to forget that the government of the Revolution was bankrupt. The nationalization of church lands was intended to solve this. Paper called assignats was issued against the value of the lands. At first only 400 million francs was issued. But this was not enough. So pressing were government obligations that an additional 800 million was issued. Having discovered the uses of paper currency, the government could not resist printing more and more. By the winter of 1792–1793, the assignats had fallen below half of their face value, with a resulting inflation in the price of bread. The revolutionary regimes proved no more successful than the old monarchy in living within their means, and the threat of bankruptcy continued to haunt the government until Napoleon.

In spite of having assumed the responsibilities of governing France on a daily basis, the National Assembly did not ignore its prime duty—writing a constitution. On September 3, 1791, the constitution was finished. It provided for a single chamber, the Legislative Assembly; gave the king a suspensive veto only; and restricted the franchise to the middle classes. Moreover, in a burst of disinterestedness, the National Assembly passed a law excluding their members from sitting in the new legislature. The new regime would begin with a clean slate.

From the very beginning, however, the new Legislative Assembly failed to dominate events. Factions within the chamber broke up the unity needed for decisive action. The deputies drifted into destructive bickering. Bread prices rose, the value of the assignats declined, random rural violence was ignored. Emigration from France increased, as the political barometer fell. The king was suspected of maintaining treasonable contacts abroad, while he supported the most conservative faction in the chamber. To all of this, the Legislative Assembly added war. On March 20, 1792, France declared war on Austria, beginning a quarter-century of conflict. Moreover, the war went badly. France was bankrupt, the fortresses were in sad disrepair, and the army was totally unready to take the field. The Austrians and Prussians invaded France. A quick thrust on Paris and the Revolution would be ended. Everyone expected it.

The internal state of France in the fall of 1792 was as troubled as the military. Beginning with the Civil Constitution of the Clergy, political opinion in France had slowly polarized into two large and irrevocably hostile groups, those for and against the Revolution. The provinces moved slowly into the conservative camp, while Paris became increasingly radical. This growing separation between Paris and the rest of France mirrored deep and pervasive fissures in Old Regime society—the persistent hostility between the capital and the provinces, the ancient tensions between town and country. More-over, opinion in Paris was drifting ominously to the left. The artisans and shopkeepers of the city were deeply anticlerical and suspected an aristocratic plot. They called for active persecution of the "refrac-tory" clergy and nobles. Plots to overthrow the government filled the cafes, clubs, and political assemblies of the city. Leaders from the streets demanded death to aristocrats and traitors. Paris was fright-ened, angry, suspicious, baffled. Its citizens prepared for revolution.

The Terror: August 10, 1792–August 1794

From August 9 to 10, 1792, the fears of Parisians about foreign inva-sion and internal subversion burst into revolt. On the evening of August 9, delegates from the sections (electoral wards) of Paris went to City Hall and ousted the municipal government. A new govern-ment, the Commune, was formed from the deputies of the sections— one that would be more responsive to radical opinion in the city. The next day a mob proclaimed the monarchy at an end. Intimidated by the mob and the new city government of Paris, the Legislative Assembly declared the king suspended and issued a call for elections to a National Convention to draw up a republican constitution for France. The constitution promised in those bright and happy days of 1789 had lasted only a year and died in renewed revolt.

The August Days were the work of two groups working together to overthrow the Legislative Assembly. These were the Jacobin and Cordelier clubs, both organizations of radical politicians, and the leaders of the Paris sections, who were more radical yet. The leaders of these sections were alarmed at the activities of the municipal government, which allowed "refractory" priests, nobles, and sub-versives to roam freely through Paris and did nothing about high bread prices. The new Paris Commune took over the functions of police, prisons, the defense and feeding of the city, and safeguarding it from internal subversion. The constant threat of mob violence made it a powerful factor in the calculations of the national government seated in its midst.

The political clubs of Paris were also partly responsible for bringing the monarchy down. Both the Jacobin and Cordelier clubs engaged in constant criticism of the government, calling for stern measures against priests, aristocrats, and traitors. No one could miss the republicanism in the diatribes coming from the clubs, no one could fail to see the call for revolution. Of the two, the Jacobin Club, dominated by Georges Danton and Maximilien Robespierre, was the more influential both in the city and the chamber. Indeed, by August 1792 the debates and speeches in the Jacobin Club were more significant than those of the Legislative Assembly, and it had become clear that the future political leaders were going to be Jacobins.

Although the influence of the Cordelier Club and the Commune was confined to Paris, Jacobin clubs existed all over France. In the provinces the Jacobin clubs had evolved from the "patriot" party of 1789. In the years between 1789 and the fall of 1792 this network of clubs, correspondents, and politicians had developed into the only national political force in France. In the eighteen months of the Reign of Terror, this was to be one of the most crucial political facts of French life.

On September 20 the National Convention, called to give France a republican constitution, met in Paris. Of the 750 deputies, a majority were drawn from local government around France, whereas all but one of those from the capital were Jacobin. The king was at once put on trial. Proof of Louis' treason was clear from his papers. Thus the vote on his guilt was unanimous. But execution was another question. A majority of only seventy was found. This sufficed, however, and Louis XVI was guillotined on January 23, 1793. The First Republic had condemned the legitimate king, the most sacred symbol of the Old Regime, a fact no one could ever forget.

The events in Paris and the conduct of the war between August 1792 and late spring 1793 provoked the most serious divisions within the convention. The two hostile factions in the chamber were the Girondins and the Jacobins. The former included many provincial politicians, their major strength being in the local governments of provincial cities. They were the largest faction in the convention, but their base of power was far from Paris. The Girondins operated in a sort of vacuum; they dominated the convention, but the convention itself was under enormous pressure from Jacobin Paris.

Although outnumbered in the convention, the Jacobins led by

Robespierre and Danton were better equipped for political warfare. They succeeded in blaming on the Girondins the continued defeat in war, the steady decline in the value of the assignat, and the rise in bread prices. The increasing hostility of Paris to the Girondins could have only one conclusion. On May 31 an insurrectionary committee from the radical Paris sections took over control of the Commune and demanded the arrest of prominent Girondin deputies. On June 2 the Paris National Guard surrounded the convention and enforced the purge. The convention fell to the control of the Jacobins, and the Commune fell to street politicians from the most radical Paris sections.

As a result of the purge that lasted from May 30 to June 2, 1793, the government was dominated by the Jacobin Committee of Public Safety, a twelve-man body created by the convention and nominally responsible to it. Provincial administration fell to deputies on mission, nominated by the committee and responsible to it. Judgment of subversives, an important function in a revolution, was entrusted to the Revolutionary Tribunal, which reflected the policy of the Committee of Public Safety. The committee became the mainspring of French government and administration and ultimately assumed dictatorial powers. Driven by the necessities of war, subversion, and famine, the Committee of Public Safety governed France during the Reign of Terror.

The most important immediate problem faced by the Committee of Public Safety after June 1793 was war, both civil and foreign. Foreign war again was going badly. In January 1793 France had added Holland, Spain, and Great Britain to her list of foes. Civil insurrection was equally threatening. In March 1793 a royalist and clerical revolt erupted in the Vendée region of western France. In June and July the Girondin cities of southern France rose against the Jacobin Committee of Public Safety. Lyons, Bordeaux, Marseilles, and Nantes went over to the Girondin side. Throughout the summer and fall of 1793 the committee worked on military affairs. Within the committee this task fell on Lazare Carnot, the "Organizer of Victory." He raised fourteen armies, equipped and supplied them, reestablished discipline, and made and removed generals. Promotions came from the ranks; young Napoleon Bonaparte was a brigadier in 1793, and eight of his marshals were made general officers by Carnot and his colleagues. Soldiers were drafted, given the most rudimentary instruction, and flung into the line. Carnot created an army from an inchoate and defeated mob, an achievement without precedent in Old Regime Europe.

The new armies and untried generals were triumphant. In October 1793 Lyons surrendered to the Jacobin troops. In December, the Vendée rebels were massacred. By the end of the year the Prussians had been driven out of Alsace and Lorraine and the Austrians and British had been defeated in Belgium. The Committee of Public Safety succeeded where previous regimes had failed; it defended France.

At home the committee governed by means of the Reign of Terror. To judge subversives the committee used the Revolutionary Tribunal of Paris. As an instrument of the Terror, it was inordinately successful. Its rules of evidence were elastic, and the judges condemned to the guillotine most of those who came before them. The Reign of Terror was carried into the countryside by deputies on mission. They were given the broadest powers; they directed local administration, helped the local Jacobin Club, drafted men into the army, collected taxes, gathered food for the troops and Paris, and punished traitors and subversives. In this latter capacity the deputies on mission often committed atrocities. At Lyons, Fouché shot more than a thousand people, and at Nantes the deputy on mission, Carrier, drowned nearly 1,200. In the Vendée, the deputies on mission to the revolutionary armies adopted a policy of shooting prisoners and suspects.

In the tense atmosphere of foreign and civil war, the government of the Committee of Public Safety differed markedly from the Old Regime. Jacobins did not attempt to persuade; they gave orders and guillotined those who disobeyed. The deputies on mission found that a few public executions induced a remarkable degree of cooperation among the remaining inhabitants. The Revolutionary Tribunal dispatched its victims with modern efficiency. The compliant National Convention obliged with the most bloodthirsty edicts. The Committee of Public Safety carried these edicts out with a ruthless and savage competence. A sense of desperate urgency pervaded the Jacobin officials and generals. Terror had become the order of the day and the means of government.

Jacobin rule was studded with purges of political enemies. On October 31, 1793, the Girondin deputies were guillotined while their supporters in the provinces were being executed by deputies on mission. On March 24, 1794, Robespierre and the committee executed the radicals of the Paris Commune. Two weeks later, on March 6, Robespierre had Danton and his gang executed for corruption, conspiracy, and general obstructionist tendencies.

The Terror was used by the Committee of Public Safety for more than war and purges. Robespierre and the Jacobins had a vision of a secular paradise. The anticlerical, even anti-Christian, ideals of

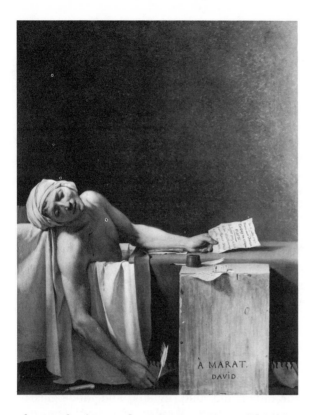

The Death of Marat by **Jacques Louis David is one of the artist's three paintings of "martyrs" of the French Revolution. The neoclassical style, epitomized by David, can be seen here in the simplicity and stylization with which exalted themes are expressed.** *A.C.L.—Royal Museum of Art, Brussels.*

the Enlightenment were a prominent part of the Jacobin philosophy. The Jacobins decreed the abolition of the worship of the Christian God, substituting the cult of the Supreme Being. A revolutionary calendar was adopted, with the year one beginning on September 22, 1792, when the French republic had been proclaimed. Another important element of the Jacobin ideology was the establishment of a Republic of Virtue. Civic virtue, on the Roman model, was commanded. Idleness was condemned. Social equality of all citizens became a major government aim; no one was to act as though he were better than his fellows. A vicious persecution of aristocrats and bourgeoisie, largely through condemnation by the Revolutionary Tribunal, was one result of this view of society. Economic crimes were to be punished by death, as was draft dodging and any refusal to aid the state. Civic virtue would be encouraged by edict and example and enforced by the Terror.

For those of a different church—Christians, Girondins, monarchists, and dissident Jacobins—the Republic of Virtue was a frightening specter. It suppressed dissent, commanded total obedience, and threatened with death all who opposed Robespierre. While those stigmatized as aristocrats or counterrevolutionaries could do nothing, dissident Jacobins who were equally threatened could act against the regime. The fate of Danton was not lost on such men as Fouché, Tallien, and Billaud-Varennes. Although Jacobins in good standing, they were enemies of Robespierre. Although they supported the Committee of Public Safety, they wished an end to indiscriminate terror. Although they agreed with the egalitarian philosophy of the Jacobin Club, they were deeply opposed to the Republic of Virtue. By July 1794, therefore, a serious plot against Robespierre was underway within the convention and the Committee of Public Safety. On July 27 (9 Thermidor, II), Robespierre and his supporters were arrested and executed the next day. Eventually over eighty Robespierrests were executed by the *Thermidoriens*, who brought the Reign of Terror to an end.

Although the Terror faded, the men, events, and ideologies of the Jacobin period were not forgotten. A spirit of nationalism, one of the most powerful forces in modern France, had its real beginning in the Jacobin struggle against foreign enemies. Jacobins created the first modern army. They fed Paris, ruled France, and surmounted the crises of war and subversion. Yet Robespierre and his cohorts were guillotined, and the people approved. Why? One can only say that the Jacobins were victims of their ideology. They promised to end social injustice and lead France to liberty, equality, and fraternity. They could not. Perfect justice is beyond the capacity of man. Robespierre never learned this; he kept preaching the doctrine of civic virtue and trying to build his heaven on the bones and blood of his victims. By the summer of 1794, with France saved from invasion and civil war and the government relatively stable, the moral goals of Jacobinism were as far away as ever. The Terror became an infinite horror, willed by Robespierre to continue forever. No one wanted that. His popular support melted away to nothing, and Robespierre and his cohorts were overthrown with almost contemptuous ease. The Jacobins had outlived their dream.

The Directory: 1795–November 9, 1799:
Epilogue to Revolution

Although the National Convention ruled France through the most tumultuous period of the Revolution, its original purpose had been to provide France with a republican constitution. After the fall of Robespierre and the end of the threat of military defeat, the convention proceeded to draw up a safe, middle-class constitution.

However, the constitution of 1795, which set up a new regime, the Directory, did not bring a stable government to France. In part this was due to inherent defects in the constitution itself. It separated the spheres of legislation and administration so completely that their functionaries could more easily fight than cooperate. There was also a plague of coups and attempted coups. Equally serious were social problems. The most pervasive of these was inflation of the assignats and fluctuating bread prices. The Directory's efforts here only brought a severe depression in 1798–1799. Nor was the Directory able to renounce the anti-Christian heritage of the Jacobins or heal the breach with Rome. The regime conducted a petty, squalid, and ineffective persecution of priests. Most important of all, however, was the pervasive corruption of the Directory government. Political influence was openly peddled; war contracts were the result of bribery; war contractors sold shoddy goods and bought relief from justice. This moral erosion disgusted most Frenchmen and ultimately doomed the Directory.

In only one area was the Directory a marked success—the war. Using the army of Carnot, the Directors won a striking series of military victories. In Italy, Napoleon Bonaparte drove out the Austrians in a series of brilliant campaigns. Client republics were established in Milan and Genoa, and the Austrians were forced into peace. Under terms of the Treaty of Campo Formio in October 1797, Austria ceded Belgium to France, recognized the new French client states in Italy, and agreed that France might annex the left bank of the Rhine down to Mainz. Negotiated by Bonaparte, without the consent of the Directory, the Treaty of Campo Formio was a complete diplomatic triumph and raised hopes for peace.

Victory was not enough, however. Continued coups, inflation, high bread prices, the stench of corruption, the presence of a successful general—all these combined to render the regime helpless against a military putsch. On November 9, 1799 (18 Brumaire, VIII), Napoleon toppled the Directory and replaced it with a dictatorship. With this act the French Revolution ended. France had gone full circle from ineffective to effective autocracy. To an overwhelming majority of Frenchmen the final result of the Revolution was more than satisfactory. Tired of a decade of revolution, inflation, instability, the Terror, religious persecution, and social upheaval, tired of faith and fear, Frenchmen rallied to Napoleon.

NAPOLEON AND THE EUROPEAN REVOLUTION

In 1799 the Directory entered its fifth winter, a tired and stale regime, discredited by monumental corruption and a sharp economic depression. The most successful French general, Napoleon, provided a convenient focus for the contempt Frenchmen felt for their government. The general rapidly gathered a party. Talleyrand, the leading French diplomat, and Fouché, the minister of police, came over to his side. Two of the Directors began to intrigue with Napoleon to overthrow the Directory. Numerous politicians in the legislature were receptive to the idea of one more coup, one last regime that would settle French problems. In this atmosphere, the coup d'etat of November 9, 1799 (18 Brumaire, VIII), succeeded and drew considerable popular applause. Napoleon had conquered France, as others had done before him. Could he hold it, as the others had not?

By December Napoleon's Constitution of the Year VIII had been completed. It provided for three consuls, with only the first consul, Napoleon, having executive power. The consuls were to hold office for ten years, which Napoleon thought would give him ample time to consolidate his power. The electoral process was a miracle of manipulation. All adult males voted, thus conserving one of the important political gains of the Jacobin period. But they voted for only one-tenth of their number, who were called the commune list. Then the commune list voted for a second one-tenth, the department list, who in turn chose one-tenth to be the national list. The legislative branch of the government also was cleverly organized. It had four parts, each with differing functions. The Council of State, whose forty members were chosen by the first consul from the names on the national list, drafted bills but did not discuss or vote on them. The Tribunate, one hundred members chosen by the Senate from the national list, discussed bills but could not vote or initiate legislation. The Legislative Body voted on bills that it could not discuss. Its three hundred members were chosen by the Senate from the national list. Finally, the Senate decided the constitutionality of laws. Its sixty members were also chosen from the national list, thirty-one by the second and third consuls, twenty-nine by co-option. Under this system the legislative function, divided neatly into its constituent elements, was completely powerless. It was merely a republican facade for Napoleon's dictatorship.

Yet this arrangement was not unpopular. The first consul submitted his constitution to a popular vote and promised to abide by its decision. The vote was overwhelming, 3,011,107 in favor of the constitution, 1,567 against. Modern experience has given us a certain cynicism in dealing with such electoral figures; yet in this case there is no doubt that they were substantially accurate. France wanted Napoleon.

Immediately on his seizure of power, Napoleon began to reorganize French administration, incorporating many of the features of the Revolution, returning in some instances to practices of the Old Regime, and giving France a legitimate, stable government. He reformed the tax administration, local government, the relations between church and state, the legal system, the civil service, and the army. Two goals were foremost—efficiency and legitimacy. Napoleon wanted a regime that would command loyalty and would work.

None of Napoleon's achievements was more desperately desired than peace between revolutionary France and the Roman Catholic Church. As soon as he took power Napoleon began serious negotiations for a concordat with the papacy. The provisions of the Concordat of 1801 emphasized government control of the church. The number of bishops was reduced to sixty, archbishops to ten, and parishes to about three thousand. The bishops were to be appointed by the government and confirmed by the pope. Parish priests were appointed by their bishops. Clerical salaries were paid by the state and seminaries were to operate under strict state control. The revolutionary land settlement was accepted and the church was again permitted to receive bequests and gifts. In return, the churchmen, grateful for state recognition and the end of persecution, added their influence to the support of the regime. No institution more assiduously sang the praises and glories of Napoleon than the Roman Catholic Church.

Equally important in liquidating the turmoil of revolution was Napoleon's work on codifying French law. In March 1804 the 2,281 articles of the civil code were approved by the legislature. They were followed in 1806 by a code of civil procedure, a commercial code a year later, then a code of criminal procedure, and finally, in 1810, a penal code. Each was a major legal achievement. Combining both Old Regime experience and revolutionary legislation, the Napoleonic legal codes gave France a unified and coherent law for the first time since Rome. The Napoleonic codes have also remained the basis of French, Italian, and Belgian law until today.

Another phase of Napoleon's legal work was the framework and regulations of French civil administration. Here the basic principle was centralization of power in the national government, a rule followed assiduously by both the Old Regime monarchy and the Jacobins. For the provinces, the government appointed prefects who directed virtually every aspect of local affairs. For tax collection, Napoleon could find no better model than the Old Regime, and he copied the hierarchy of tax receivers that had served Louis XVI.

Napoleon was equally successful in solving the fiscal problems that had plagued France. He established a stable currency by partially repudiating the assignats, and returning to a specie standard. Government credit was restored by the creation of the Bank of France in 1800 and the establishment of a national sinking fund to deal with state obligations. Tax collections were improved, and Napoleon soon collected enough to balance his budget, about 400 million francs a year, close to what Louis XVI had received. The old taxes and state monopolies of the Old Regime were retained—salt, tobacco, playing cards, excises on consumption—with the main direct tax falling on land. Nonetheless, Napoleon's fiscal system was more efficient and honest than any France had known since the Roman Empire. It is not surprising that Frenchmen generally applauded it.

In all of his internal reforms, Napoleon was guided by a very few basic principles. He wanted efficiency, stability, order, and central control. He was eclectic in the means chosen to fulfill these goals. Institutions from the Old Regime, innovations from the Revolution, ideas he had thought of himself were all used. Napoleon cared about results, not ideology; in short, he was an enlightened despot. This emerged also in the men he chose to work with him. Some, like Fouché, were Jacobins; others, like Talleyrand, nobles of the Old Regime who had supported much of the Revolution; still others, such as Marshal Ney, had been enlisted men before 1789. Only the implacably hostile were excluded. Napoleon thought of his regime in terms of permanence. His was to be the last government of the Revolution and would have to represent the whole nation. It is the measure of Napoleon's genius that he succeeded.

However brilliant his domestic accomplishments, Napoleon could hardly hope to retain power unless he won the war. Even the Directory had done that much. While his constitution was being drawn up, Napoleon himself took to the field. After victories over the Austrians in Italy and Germany, the French armies began to advance on Vienna. In 1801 the Austrians gave in and negotiated the Peace of Lunéville, which ratified the abandonment of Italy and the cession of the left bank of the Rhine to France. Lunéville ended the fighting on land and left Great Britain without a Continental ally. British diplomats began to think in terms of peace. After prolonged negotiations, France and Great Britain agreed on the Treaty of Amiens. The treaty was almost a complete British surrender. Except for Ceylon and Trinidad, the British returned all colonial conquests to France and her clients. The major British concession at Amiens was not territory, however, but an end to the crusade against France. Without British subsidies and military support, the Continental powers had no chance against Napoleon. Peace with Great Britain, therefore, was the final seal of European diplomatic acceptance of the supremacy of France.

The brief peace, from 1802 to 1803, was the most crucial period of Napoleon's career. He had gone from triumph to triumph, victorious over his enemies, both foreign and domestic. He had reached the limits of what was reasonable and possible. Amiens was as much as Europe was prepared to concede France. The balance of power was stretched to the limit, and now French victories could only provoke the permanent hostility of the other European states. Napoleon faced his fatal political choice after Amiens. He could accept the peace and the position it gave him. He could continue to expand his power and condemn France and himself to an endless and futile pursuit of dominance that retreated with each victory. Napoleon chose the latter course, abandoning the cold political realism that had so marked his career and surrendering himself to the chimera of world conquest. He was at war again with Great Britain by May 1803.

Within France, Napoleon dramatically increased his stature after the Treaty of Amiens. On May 18, 1804, he was proclaimed emperor of the French by his complaisant legislature and was crowned in Paris by Pope Pius VII on December 2. He immediately created a brilliant court, made princes and princesses of his family, surrounded himself with nobility both old and new, and established an elaborate ceremonial designed to emphasize the position and magnificence of the emperor. Napoleon would not only be greater than his rival monarchs in talent; he would also stand above them in royal rank and title.

By the summer of 1805 the major Continental powers had recovered somewhat from their earlier defeats. Supported by British diplomacy and subsidies, a third coalition was organized against the French. Composed of Great Britain, Austria, Russia, and Sweden, the third coalition aimed at a reduction of French power and a restoration of an effective balance. The results were disappointing.

On December 2 Napoleon won perhaps his greatest victory against a combined Russian and Austrian army at Austerlitz, driving Austria out of the war. Next, the emperor established the Confederation of the Rhine, a diplomatic alliance tying the western German states to France. This wholesale redistribution of German territory outraged Prussia, which promptly joined Russia against France. On October 14, 1806, at the twin battles of Jena and Auerstadt, the Prussian army was routed. In a fortnight Napoleon was in Berlin, and the Prussian state fell apart. Napoleon then pursued the Russians, and at Friedland in June 1807 he won a decisive battle over them. At this point Russia and Prussia decided to ask for peace.

The Treaty of Tilsit of July 1807 reflected the magnitude of Napoleon's victory. Russia recognized the Napoleonic creations of the Grand Duchy of Warsaw and the Confederation of the Rhine, but Prussia paid the real price of peace. She lost forty-three thousand square miles of territory in Poland and western Germany, reducing her size by half. A huge indemnity was assessed, an army of occupation was left in Prussia, Prussian harbors were closed to British trade, and the Prussian army was reduced to forty-two thousand men. Tilsit dropped Prussia from the rank of great powers.

Although the French had done well on land, they were defeated at sea by Great Britain. On October 25, 1805, the British fleet under Admiral Nelson destroyed the combined Franco-Spanish fleet at Trafalgar. The Franco-Spanish ships of the line outnumbered Nelson's fleet thirty-three to twenty-seven, but the British were far better prepared for battle. Their captains were superior officers, and the men were disciplined veterans. British tactics were superior to the French, as were British guns. Finally, Lord Nelson was a superb battle leader, whereas the French commander, Villeneuve, was a nonentity. In the battle itself, both Nelson and his second, Collingswood, cut the Franco-Spanish line and battered the ships into surrender. In three hours, eighteen French ships were struck or sunk, with a loss of over six thousand casualties. No British ship was lost, but Lord Nelson was killed, a victim of a French sniper hidden in the rigging. Like the defeat of the Spanish Armada, Trafalgar was a decisive and final victory. Napoleon acknowledged his defeat and did not again try to contest naval supremacy with Great Britain. He now tried economic warfare. By the Berlin and Milan decrees of 1806–1807, he closed the ports of continental Europe to British trade in an attempt to bankrupt the "nation of shopkeepers." This failed as well. For Napoleon, Trafalgar was the beginning of the end.

In the attempt to seal Europe from the contamination of British goods, Napoleon turned his attention after Tilsit to the Iberian

Peninsula. Portugal was occupied by the French in November 1807 for refusing to ban British trade, and in March 1808 Napoleon invaded Spain and proclaimed Joseph Bonaparte king. However, French attempts to reform the Spanish church in the revolutionary tradition led to a massive popular insurrection. A British army under the duke of Wellington drove the French out of Portugal. In the countryside the Spanish continued to defend church and king. French officials were murdered and small detachments of troops were butchered by the infuriated populace. The French struck back, torturing priests, burning houses and villages, pillaging the land, murdering the men and raping the women. The war became a cancer for Napoleon and an infinite agony for the Spanish.

From 1807 to 1812, in spite of the disasters in Spain, France was acknowledged by all the Continental powers as dominant in Europe. Only the implacable hostility of Great Britain remained. The emperor was at the height of his prestige and power. But Napoleon was not a man of peace. He is said to have thought war was the highest human calling, the only one worthy for himself. Total domination of the European stage was an obsession with him. Only the British Royal Navy and Tsar Alexander I of Russia prevented this. During the spring of 1812, therefore, Napoleon prepared for war against Russia. He pried contingents out of his allies, both major and minor. The Austrians and Prussians supplied men, as did Holland, Italy, Poland, and Germany. Nearly 600,000 men were gathered for this assault. In June 1812 the huge Grand Army crossed the Niemen River into Russia and pushed almost unopposed to Smolensk. At this point the Russian army offered battle at the passage of the Moskova River at Borodino. The battle was a grotesque travesty of Napoleon's maxims and practices. Instead of trying to flank the enemy, the emperor ordered up a massive charge at the center of the Russian line. He did not commit his full force, but held back the Imperial Guard, being so far from home. Instead of avoiding the Russian guns, he charged into them. Yet, the Russians were beaten. In spite of hideous losses, Napoleon pushed on to Moscow, which he occupied on September 14. The Russians did not give up, contrary to all expectations. They burned Moscow and refused to treat with Napoleon. After waiting five weeks in the ruins of Moscow, Napoleon began the terrible winter retreat from Russia. Harried by Cossacks, guerillas, and the Russian army, the French staggered toward Poland. Cold and hungry, the French army disintegrated, and retreat became a rout. Less than 100,000 survived the hideous march; the Grand Army was in complete ruins.

As the news of this catastrophic and unexpected defeat reached

NAPOLEON'S EMPIRE IN 1812

the diplomats, Napoleon's Europe began to come apart. In March 1813 Sweden and Prussia joined Russia and Great Britain. The Austrians sponsored a peace conference, but Napoleon refused the necessary concessions, and Austria joined the allies. The allies concentrated their armies near Leipzig and brought the outnumbered French to battle. In the Battle of the Nations from October 16 to 19, Napoleon was decisively defeated and forced to begin the long retreat toward Paris. Equally bad news came from Spain, where Wellington had driven the French across the Pyrenees by November. Flushed with victory, but wary of the emperor, the allies again offered peace, conceding the Rhine frontier to France. When the emperor failed to agree, allied armies crossed the Rhine. They entered Paris on March 31, 1814. In April, totally beaten, Napoleon abdicated unconditionally. He was exiled to Elba.

Having disposed of Napoleon, the allies replaced him with Louis XVIII. The Bourbons had been out of France since 1793, few remembered them, and almost no one cared about them. But Fouché and Talleyrand, who had taken over the government after the abdication of the emperor, thought a monarchy better suited to the French and the victorious allies than a republic. The allied leaders, particularly Alexander I of Russia, agreed. Louis XVIII returned in May 1814. Except for the episode of the Hundred Days, which ended in the debacle of Waterloo, the Napoleonic drama had been played out.

In many ways the story of Napoleon was one of futile inconsequence. Like Hannibal, he dared great conquests and succeeded for a short time. Ultimately he was defeated, and his empire evaporated. The diplomatic balance that resulted from this twenty years of war remarkably resembled that of 1789. The great victories and campaigns were all wiped out in the final defeat.

Yet the whole episode was not bare of achievements and changes. It was not all a gory and gaudy dream. Napoleon had been the instrument of reorganization of France after an immense revolution. Modern France still has Napoleonic law, civil service, local government, tax structure, and educational system. Outside of France Napoleonic conquests were the greatest single force in ending serfdom in central Europe, breaking up the manor, ending clerical government, and sharply reducing Old Regime privileges in much of Europe. Napoleon extended the Revolution into Europe; indeed, for the Low Countries, Italy, and western Germany, Napoleonic conquest marked the division between the Old Regime and a recognizably modern social and political pattern.

Napoleon's greatest impact, however, was unintentional. His

A drawing by Francisco de Goya, showing in highly stylized fashion the savageries of guerilla warfare during the Peninsular War to liberate Spain from French domination. *Bettmann Archives.*

wars were an immense catalyst of nationalism, which grew to be the greatest political force in modern Europe. The emperor did not wish this; his goal was a universal empire embracing every European people. Yet he provoked a deep national pride in many Europeans— the Spanish, Poles, Germans, Italians—and made this empire impossible. The Peninsular War was fought for a Spanish liberation from the godless French. The campaigns of 1813–1814 were called the War of National Liberation. The Napoleonic era was the dawn of the European peoples. Napoleon found Europe divided into social classes; he left it divided into nations.

THE INDUSTRIAL REVOLUTION

We are separated from the lives of our ancestors by the flow of events as well as years. Nothing has created this sense of separation, this seeming erasure of the relevance of the past, as much as continuing industrialization and technological change. No historical process has so altered the life style of Western man as the Industrial

Revolution. Nor is the change complete. The Industrial Revolution is a process, not an event, and no end is in sight. With the passage of time technological change has affected more and more aspects of people's lives, and new nations have started to industrialize. Once called a revolution because of the comparative suddenness of the change from handicrafts to steam-powered manufacturing, industrialization is now seen as a relentless movement toward more sophisticated technology, more efficient production, and more complex social problems.

The Industrial Revolution involved enormous changes in traditional economic life and social patterns. The application of scientific knowledge to production and manufacturing, rather than to religious insight, was a new and startling element of industrialization. Before 1750 physics had been primarily a discipline to understand cosmology; in the decades afterward it became an instrument to increase mechanical efficiency. A second factor in the Industrial Revolution was economic specialization. Farms, instead of remaining polycultural, were increasingly devoted to a single cash crop. Individual workers moved from the handyman category into a single industry, with skills appropriate to that industry alone. This did not occur immediately or to everyone, but after 1800 it was the pattern of the future.

A new wave of urbanization also resulted from machine industry. Towns grew enormously in size, as the rising population settled increasingly in the cities. In 1800 only London had approached a million people; a century later over a dozen cities did. In preindustrial Europe, a town of 10,000 souls was a large city. By 1850 it was a mere village. Towns also changed character. Many that had not traditionally been centers of industry became known for their factories and mills. The medieval ports, market towns for agricultural goods, or ecclesiastical centers became industrial cities. Domestic crafts gave way to factory production. And the shift involved a quantum increase in the amount of energy applied, the number of people involved, and the goods produced. Urbanization and the factory system were twin products of industrialization.

The transformed towns mirrored new types of social classes and occupations. Karl Marx's industrial proletariat was not created by the Industrial Revolution. But industrialization swelled it in size, while putting it in a stance of powerlessness before the absolute economic superiority of capital. By the end of the nineteenth century it was so unusual for an industrial worker to become an owner in his trade that it was the stuff of Horatio Alger legends. Factory owners, managers, bankers, engineers—Marx's bourgeoisie—constituted another social class transformed by industrialization. From being a small group of merchants, the bourgeoisie rose to a position of political and social dominance in industrialized nations. The growth of industrialization has only increased this dominance.

Industrialization also changed the nature of economic production. In the traditional societies, mass production had centered around primary goods, foodstuffs, wool, lumber, and the like. Manufactured and finished goods occupied a distant second place. The machine turned this around. Agriculture took a second place after the first generation of industrial production, far surpassed by wonders from mill and factory. This new production was not inexpensive, however. Machine industry required much greater accumulations of capital than either commercial or subsistence farming. Factories required heavy initial investment and also substantial capital reserves to absorb temporary losses and longer business depressions. Industry brought men fortunes on a scale unheard of before but demanded reinvestment of such massive sums that public stock sales were needed to subscribe them. Habitual, intensive investment of capital was as much a part of industrialization as the machines themselves.

Industrialization brought two permanent economic and social changes of immense magnitude to the traditional, underdeveloped society of Europe. In the place of a stagnant economy, the machine meant sustained growth. The gross national product increased as did per capita income. Although the new wealth was distributed very unevenly, the general increase was so great that nearly every class benefited. More, the change from a stagnant to a growing economy gave promise that everyone would eventually be enriched, no matter what their class or occupation. Nothing epitomizes the impact of industrialization better than this transformation from general poverty to affluence.

The Origins of Industrial Society

Earlier chapters have stressed the survival of traditional forms of social organization and economic activity over a period linking the Black Death to the European expansion from 1500 to 1650. By 1700, despite the rise of a capitalist agriculture within Europe; the commercial revolution; and the growth of thoroughly bourgeois societies based on industry and commerce in Britain, the Netherlands, and northern Italy, European masses still lived by subsistence farming. Therefore farming technology was primitive, and this inhibited the growth of capital surpluses necessary for industrial production. An economy prevailed that was fundamentally dependent on weather, harvest fluctuations, and natural limits in man's environment. The main outline of social organization remained in 1700 much as it was in 1450.

Nonetheless, there were slow changes in the sixteenth and seventeenth centuries that led toward industrialization. Both cultural and economic factors were involved. The divorce of science from religion can be seen in the difference in the work of Copernicus and the Danish astronomer Tycho Brahe. Copernicus proposed the theory that the earth moved around the sun because the circle was the most perfect form of curve, and planetary motion was most easily explained as a circle around the sun. Thus the planets moved in a perfect manner, the only possible way consistent with God's majesty and being. However, Brahe (1546–1601), a generation later than Copernicus, used totally different methods; he made as exact measurements as possible of planetary and astral movements. The theories of Kepler (1571–1630), who used Brahe's work, were based on the accuracy and completeness of these measurements. No theology, no perfect circles, no estimates of the nature of God's being, just proof derived from experiment and accurate measurement were the methods used by Kepler, Galileo, Harvey, and Newton in their search for scientific law.

An equally important intellectual change was the growing dependence of Europeans on precise statistical information. Mercantilist theories and schemes depended upon exact figures, as did tax collection and modern warfare. The first signs of the usefulness of statistical information can be seen with the explanation by Jean Bodin in 1576 of the phenomenon of inflation, or the reorganization of the French taxation system under Henry IV, or the success of the Dutch East India Company and the Amsterdam Bank. Quite obviously, quantitative knowledge was as important to commerce and industry as to government.

The years of the general crisis also brought economic changes that were a prelude to industrialization. These were most marked in England. The most striking feature of the English economy between 1660 and the American Revolution was rapid and sustained growth, both in overseas trade and industrial production. Growth was accompanied by some significant technological progress in textiles, transportation, and ironmongering. While economic change and technological innovation during the years from 1660 to 1765 was not rapid nor systematic enough to lift England to the takeoff point, when industrial growth became self-sustaining, it did produce noticeable structural alterations in English society. England was more urbanized than any state on the Continent, with a larger industrial base, a more advanced technology, wider literacy, and more social mobility. This combination of industry and commerce made England the richest nation in Europe and provided the necessary base for the economic takeoff, or the Industrial Revolution.

The Process of Industrialization:
Associated Economic and Social Movements

Industrial change did not occur in a vacuum; it was preceded by several important social and economic alterations and produced others that together comprised the process of industrialization. Four main social and economic changes, aside from technological changes in manufacturing itself, were associated with industrialization. They were a tremendous and continuing population rise, a vast improvement in transportation, an equally vast rise in the amount and worth of British trade, and an agricultural revolution, which increased production and dispatched surplus peasants to the city to the soil and soot of the factory. These associated economic and social movements were interdependent, and the technological revolution in the factory owed as much to them as it did to the steam engine. Some of these changes prevailed in most states of western Europe. In England alone they were all present.

During the years from 1750 to 1850 the population of England grew at an astounding rate. The population, which stood at six million in 1740, had risen to near twelve million by the end of the century, and the period of greatest growth was still ahead. Between 1750 and 1780, English population grew by 7 percent a decade, then by 10 percent in the 1780s, 11 percent in the 1790s, and nearly 16 percent in the two decades after Waterloo. Moreover, this huge new mass of people congregated in the cities. The demographic revolution was a twin progress: there were more Englishmen and England became an urban realm.

The late eighteenth century also brought staggering changes in the English transportation system. The need for improved roads was partially answered by the rapid development of the turnpike system, which turned the construction and upkeep of roads over to private companies in return for the right to collect tolls. Canals were a much greater boon to industry, for water transportation was at least ten times less expensive than overland hauling. The first great canal, which was to carry coal from Worsley to Manchester, was built by James Brindley between 1759 and 1761 for the duke of Bridgwater. An immense engineering feat and an astounding financial success, the Worsley canal created great excitement. Other canals followed in quick order: a canal between the Trent and Mersey, connecting the North and Irish seas, also built by Brindley and called the Trunk Canal; a canal between Oxford and Coventry; the Birmingham Canal; and the Grand Junction Canal, all begun in the 1760s. Canals and turnpikes within the seventy years after 1750 remade English transportation along the lines needed by a rapidly expanding heavy industry.

The changes in British trade in the last half of the eighteenth century were equally astonishing. In 1780, British exports in pounds sterling ran at about the rate of 14 million a year; two decades later they had reached the unheard-of figure of 42 million. In just seven years, from 1797 to 1803—and these were war years that included a bankruptcy by the Bank of England—cotton exports alone tripled. The jump in trade figures was so enormous that it obliterated any previous standards of comparison. Moreover, the new trade statistics were reflected in a similar rise in the amount of British shipping. British tonnage had risen steadily from 1700 to 1780, more than doubling to nearly 800,000 tons. Between 1780 and 1800, however, British tonnage jumped to 2 million tons, an incredible figure when one remembers that the size of ships remained almost constant. After 1780 the British were rapidly cornering the world's trade.

The final revolution associated with industrialization occurred in agriculture. Here the process was slower and less dramatic, but nonetheless decisive. In part the agricultural revolution was technological, involving new equipment, new crops, and new methods of farming. In part, building on changes already made in the relations of land and labor by 1650, it was also a social movement, throwing people off the land, enclosing small farms into large estates, and transforming the society of rural England.

The techniques of agricultural production further developed during the eighteenth century included constant tillage, more sophisticated crop rotations, and new machines. The most important mechanical changes were the seed drill of Jethro Tull and the Rotherham triangular plow, patented in 1730. The seed drill inserted seed into the soil at the proper intervals and in rows far enough apart to permit constant tillage between them. The wasteful broadcast method of sowing was eliminated, and weeds were checked. The Rotherham plow permitted an easy turning of the soil by a two-horse team rather than by six or eight oxen and two men. Both inventions made possible an exceptional increase in yield per acre and a similar reduction in animals and plowmen.

New crops and forms of crop management were equally important in the spectacular rise in English agricultural production during the eighteenth century. Fallow fields were slowly abandoned in favor of clover, timothy, and legumes, which permitted constant land use. Turnips and potatoes, the former popularized by the Homeric propaganda of "Turnip" Townshend, also permitted land to be continuously farmed and added to the food supply. As with new implements, the spread of knowledge about new crops was slow, estimated at about a mile a year from the place of origin. But although the agricultural revolution was slow, it was irrevocable.

The social impact of these agricultural changes was staggering despite the earlier precedents. There was a renewal of the movement toward enclosure of remaining scattered strips of arable, fallow fields, large commons, and an invasion of joint rights over the land. The instrument for these changes was enclosure of the land by act of Parliament. Each farmer in the village received his land in one chunk, but most had too little to support a family now that they were deprived of their rights to the common and pasture. These last stages of enclosure thus increased the efficiency of larger farms and drove small farmers to the wall. The number of enclosure acts increased dramatically as the eighteenth century wore on. There was one act a year between 1715 and 1720, but there were 156 between 1750 and 1760 and 642 between 1770 and 1780. Enclosure acts were met with riots, protests, and threats by the angry yeomanry. But the gentry was too strong. Backed by constables and justices of the peace, they forced the enclosures through and drove the surplus labor from the land. They replaced the open fields with new and efficient farms and left behind them Oliver Goldsmith's "Deserted Village." A world had been lost!

The Process of Industrialization:
Technological Change in Industry

Sustained technological change and industrial growth—the economic phenomenon known as takeoff—did not start in eighteenth-century England as a result of one invention alone. What happened was more complex. There occurred in England between 1760 and 1800 a group of innovations affecting all phases of two crucial industries—textiles and iron products. In cotton production, spinning, weaving, power source, and ginning were radically altered by changes between 1760 and 1800. It was the same with iron. Coal mining, coke production, iron puddling, forging and founding, casting and refining were transformed in the direction of efficiency and complexity. The key was a cluster of innovations. Their timing was as important as their substance; the impact on the economy and society would have been far less had these innovations come at widely spaced intervals.

The first industry to experience rapid and continuous change was cotton. In 1733 a weaver named John Kay invented the flying shuttle, one that was driven automatically from one end of the loom to the other, thus increasing the possible width of the cloth and making the weaving process go faster. This invention aggravated the already existing shortage of thread. Before the flying shuttle, it had taken four women to spin enough thread for a single weaver. Now a dozen could not keep up. In due course, a spinning machine appeared—the spinning jenny, invented by the carpenter James Hargreaves and patented in 1770. It contained a number of spindles that were fixed to sliding rails so the spinner could draw and twist the thread at once. Stronger and more uniform thread was the result. The jenny was an overwhelming and instant success (though the poor inventor got nothing for it), and in twenty years it spread all over England.

The next invention was even more significant. In 1769 Richard Arkwright patented the water frame, a machine that spun thread strong enough to be the warp of cloth (whereas the jenny could only produce thread for the weft). Arkwright was not only an inventor, but a man of business as well. Entering into partnerships with two wealthy merchants, he set up his first water frame at Cromford on the Derwent River. Within eight years it contained 3,000 spindles and employed 300 workers. Arkwright expanded into new partnerships, built new and improved water frames, and made a huge fortune. More than that, he built factories. The water frame could not be put in the home; it required a specialized power source and the workers had to come to it. This was reinforced when Samuel Crompton, a small landowner, invented his mule, which combined features of both the jenny and water frame. In 1785 a James Watt steam engine was hooked to the mule, and steam was substituted for water power. Factory organization of labor thus became inevitable. The machine product was cheaper and of better quality, and there was so much more of it.

Factory production of thread and yarn reversed the traditional relationships between spinning and weaving. By the 1780s there was more yarn than the weavers could use. The market in the great boom of the eighties constantly demanded more cloth than the weavers could produce, and men were tinkering with designs and prototypes of a power loom. In 1800 John Monteith established a factory with two hundred looms driven by steam, and in 1803 the first all-metal power looms were produced. During the era of Napoleonic warfare, British manufacturers were setting up a factory industry with steam-powered steel machines and producing goods that were sold everywhere.

These innovations had a revolutionary impact on textile production. In the early 1780s under 10 million pounds of raw cotton a year were imported into England; by the years after Waterloo it had risen to over 100 million pounds. So great was the demand for raw cotton that a new machine—Eli Whitney's cotton gin—was produced to help supply it, and an old institution—slavery—took on new life to grow it. The value of cotton manufacture increased in like manner. Worth no more than a million pounds in 1760, cotton manufacture rose to 5 million pounds at the end of the century. Moreover, the price of an individual piece of cloth dropped precipitously. Since more could be made, it cost less to make each piece. The price of woven muslins in the textile center of Bolton fell from 3s. a yard in 1792 to 1s. 2d. by 1799. Industrialization brought cotton cloth within reach of everyone. It produced an economic phenomenon unknown before—growing production, lower prices, lower costs, and greater profits. To contemporaries it was almost miraculous.

Other major industries transformed by technological innovation were iron, coal, and steel. In these industries technology filled an ancient need, for iron products were high in price, rather scarce, of uncertain quality, and in great demand. Everyone connected with iron knew what technological improvements were needed—a better fuel and improved ways to get the impurities out of the iron ore. Some way had to be found to get the water out of coal mines, and cheap, bulk transportation was needed to get the ore and coal together. Moreover, charcoal, the basic fuel for refining, was in dwindling supply. This scarcity had forced the foundries and forges to migrate across the land, hunting hardwood forests. Also, British iron was brittle and had too many impurities for good steel. Iron differed from cotton in its requirements for industrialization, yet the processes and results of industrialization were to be remarkably similar.

The first element of iron manufacture that changed in the eighteenth century was the fuel. In 1709 coke—cooked coal with the sulphur driven off—was used successfully in casting iron. Abraham Darby, a Quaker millwright and metalwright, found the process while experimenting at his small plant in Coalbrookdale, Shropshire. The first trials were not completely successful, but Darby and his son kept at it, strengthening the bellows to prevent deterioration of the iron and adding limestone to the ore. By the middle of the century coke was nearly as effective a fuel for casting iron as charcoal, and much, much cheaper.

Coke fuel solved the problems of the cast-iron branch of the industry. Production of wrought iron, used for such implements as stirrups and plowshares, still required imported Swedish pig iron and charcoal fuel. Two inventions, less than a decade apart, enabled forges to use coke and British pig iron. In 1775 James Watt perfected an efficient steam engine, which had a number of uses in the iron industry. It could pump water out of mines, thus enabling both iron and coal miners to sink deep shafts and greatly increasing the available supply of raw materials. Steam engines also ran the bellows and supplied mechanical power for the forges. This solved the problem of heat. The impurities still remained, but not for long. In 1784 Henry Cort patented a puddling and rolling process that enabled the British ironmasters to make high-quality bar and wrought with their own ore and coke fuel. Cort, an Admiralty contractor, was so unfortunate as to lose his patent in the bankruptcy of his backer. Thereupon, the English ironmasters, seeing what an admirable and efficient process puddling and rolling was, and seeing it was free, promptly adopted it one and all. Within a decade the puddling and rolling process completed the transformation of British iron.

As with cotton, improvements in iron manufacture resulted in enormous reductions in the cost of the final product and a consequent deepening of the market. Spinning and weaving machines began to be made with iron instead of wood. Iron struts and joists were used in bridges and buildings. By the time of Waterloo, British bar iron was selling at £20 to £28 a ton, half of the Swedish price. Moreover, output rose with spectacular speed. Between 1788 and 1806 the average output per blast furnace rose from 800 to 1,130 tons, exclusively on the basis of more advanced technology.

Science and Technology: A Growing Interrelationship

A continuing characteristic of industrialization has been the close association of science and technology. In the early stages of the Industrial Revolution this association was neither so close nor so important. Scientific thought had traditionally been part of philosophy, allied with religion. Tinkerers and mechanics were seldom philosophers. This was the situation that pertained at the beginning of the Industrial Revolution, and it was a couple of generations before it changed.

The incidence of independent tinkering and empirical invention can be seen in the initial innovations in the English Industrial Revolution. In textiles, John Kay, inventor of the flying shuttle, was a weaver who learned about looms by working them. James Hargreaves, who invented the spinning jenny, was a carpenter. He had been interested in textile inventions by his next-door neighbor. Richard Arkwright, inventor of the water frame, was a barber and wigmaker. James Brindley, builder of the first eighteenth-century canal, was almost illiterate and lacked all scientific information. Abraham Darby was an ironmonger who worked his own mill and arrived at coke through trial and error. Amateurs, tinkerers, self-taught mechanics—these were the men who brought the machines into being. As witness of their lack of sophistication, most of them failed to reap any substantial rewards for their inventions. Their betters beat them out of the money. Richard Arkwright was the notable exception, and to contemporaries he was the wonder of the age.

However, the separation between science and technology in eighteenth-century England was not complete. Part of the gap was closed by the existence of scientific and agricultural societies, which discussed technological achievements, brought scientists and industrialists together, and formed a personal connection between science and business. The most important of these was the Lunar Society, which included Josiah Wedgwood, the pottery manufacturer; James Watt and his partner Matthew Bolton; Joseph Priestley, who discovered oxygen; and the biologist, Erasmus Darwin. The interconnection between science and invention can be seen in numerous industries. In the manufacture of pottery the experiments of Josiah Wedgwood went directly into production. Bleaching and dying were also changed by scientific inquiry. The same was true of soap and glass manufacture. Indeed, in industries where change depended on disciplined scientific inquiry, largely in chemistry, technology and science were simply merged into one single industrial and intellectual process.

The same connection between science and technology can be seen in the premier invention of the age—the steam engine of James Watt—from which, more than any other, the Industrial Revolution emerged. Watt's grandfather had been a teacher of mathematics, his father was an architect, and Watt himself was an educated man, not only in mathematics, physics, and mechanics, but in philosophy, poetry, music, history, and the law. He had superb mathematical and mechanical training and earned his living as a maker of scientific instruments. He obtained a laboratory in the University of Glasgow and attended the lectures in science there. He worked on problems of chemical analysis and tried to improve the barometer. As early as 1761 he began his experiments with steam, to the end of manufacturing an efficient steam engine. He produced his first engine in 1769 and in 1775—when Adam Smith published *The Wealth of Nations* and the American colonies were breaking away—he perfected his engine, based on the use of expanding steam. James Watt further proved the advantages of learning by being sharp enough to go into partnership with Matthew Bolton. Together they manufactured and marketed the Watt engine and made a fortune. But they did more. They industrialized England.

A general separation of science and technology was possible in the earliest phases of the Industrial Revolution primarily because the first machines and processes were relatively simple. No great knowledge of physics was required to increase the size and strength of a smelting bellows and run it by water power. Some patience was required as well as considerable experience with iron founding and an inventive cast of mind. The first inventions could be pieced together from existing materials. Very quickly, however, these conditions evaporated. New machines and processes soon did very complicated things, and a specialized knowledge of science was needed even to know what ought to be done, let alone how to do it. Watt's steam engine was a case in point, and it showed the way of the future. By 1815, science and technology had become irrevocably wedded, and every new scientific discovery led sooner or later to a new machine, process, or medicine.

Brief Conclusion and Divers Views to the Future

The main trends of the first Industrial Revolution, repeated successively in different countries in different times, were quite clear. Factories replaced cottage industry, and technology and science combined to produce a dizzying progress of new inventions and processes. Workers became totally dependent on their skills and jobs, rather than being partly farmers, owning their own tools, and enjoying a precarious, if impoverished, independence. A huge middle class, composed of industrial entrepreneurs, engineers, salesmen, managers, lawyers, and professionals came into being and grew to dominate Western society. The traditional divisions of that society were overthrown by industrialization, and a new society of wealth, mobility, and careers open to talent progressively took its place. This happened first to the British, then to others. Should the world survive, it seems destined to happen to everybody.

SEVEN

The apogee of Europe

He who has not lived in the years before 1789 does not know how pleasant life can be.
Charles-Maurice, Prince de Talleyrand

Right forever on the Scaffold; Wrong forever on the Throne.
Revolutionary epigram

Italy . . . rises with one spontaneous impulse, in the name of the Right and Duty inherent in a people, to constitute itself a Nation. . . .
Guiseppe Mazzini, To the Italians

INTRODUCTION

With Napoleon safely exiled to St. Helena, the European ministers and monarchs believed that an era of revolutionary turmoil had ended. Revolutionary fanaticism had surely burned out in a quarter-century of world war, and even the embers of ideological devotion ought to die in a new era of peace, balance, and moderation. Wealth, not liberty, would become the goal of Europe's middle classes. Land, not equality, would satisfy peasants. Moderation instead of adventure would characterize the new diplomacy. Men hoped that the conservative values of tradition would replace the dogmas of liberty, equality, and nationalism. Europe in 1815 was going to be a world restored to peace and stability.

Only one of these hopes came true. The Congress of Vienna was a stupendous diplomatic achievement: it produced a balance of power that lasted until World War I began in 1914. Time devoured the other dreams. The ideologies of liberalism, socialism, and nationalism grew mightily, completely overshadowing tradition and stability. The Industrial Revolution dramatically changed European economics and society. A new colonialism fashioned empires far larger than Napoleon's. Popular participation and interest in government increased steadily. The peace settlements of 1815 began a century of change.

The basic cause of nineteenth-century change was the Industrial Revolution. In the years after the peace, industrialization changed methods of transportation, communications, agriculture, and every type of manufacturing. The social impact of this industrial growth was stupendous. A new class of industrial workers developed, and the bourgeoisie grew so rapidly that they dominated society, both by skills and numbers. The industrial and technological revolution, as it spread throughout Europe, became the most important factor in Western history.

With the nineteenth century also came a vast popular cultural change. There was an enormous increase in literacy, a product of the new public schools and newspapers. Both enabled people to take a more effective interest in their governments and made public opinion an awesome political and social force. Popular ideologies—notably liberalism, socialism, and nationalism—enjoyed a luxuriant growth. Nationalism was particularly powerful, striking a deep and responsive chord among Europe's masses. The growth of ideology accompanied a profound decline in religious belief. European culture became increasingly secular and democratic.

The techniques of government also underwent profound alteration during the nineteenth century. European governments embraced democratic forms and, often reluctantly, established parliaments, extended the suffrage, introduced a secret ballot, extended freedom of the press, and enlarged civil liberties. In spite of reservations, democracy increased in form and spirit.

The years between 1814 and 1914 were the apogee of European power and influence. The arts of peace flourished. There was general economic prosperity increasingly shared by all classes. Currencies were sound, and the social order seemed secure. Western industrial civilization dominated the world, and its ideals, values, achievements, and authority were supreme everywhere.

REACTION AND REVOLUTION: 1815–1852

Even before their armies had disposed of Napoleon, the leaders of the allied powers were gathering in Vienna to discuss peace and the new world that had emerged from the era of revolution. Ineradicable changes had altered many of the old ways. Revolution, industrialization, or the silent passage of men from one opinion to another had buried much of the Old Regime. But the ideals of obedience, hierarchy, legitimacy, and faith lived vividly in the minds of the statesmen at Vienna, and they had won an unparalleled opportunity to reorder the European world. The Congress of Vienna was, therefore, more than the end of a war. It was also to be a partial restoration of the ordered and comprehensible world of the Old Regime.

The Vienna Settlement

The work of the Congress of Vienna followed traditional patterns of diplomacy. Diplomats from the great powers—Austria, France, Great Britain, Russia, and Prussia—settled everything. Prince Metternich, Prince Talleyrand, and Viscount Castlereagh, representing Austria, France, and Great Britain, were all astute and experienced men, who shared a belief in the need for peace, a balance of power, and a generally conservative diplomatic settlement. The Russian delegation was a galaxy of wondrous personalities. Headed by Alexander I, who had messianic delusions, it included a Corsican adventurer, Pozzo di Borgo; a Polish nationalist, Prince Czartoryski; and a Greek revolutionary, Capodistrias. Nonetheless, they were no match for their western colleagues.

The congress was conducted amidst a lavish round of parties, dinners, and balls. It was a time for celebration as well as negotiation. A French supernumerary, Prince de Ligne, who was nearly eighty, waited on a rainy street corner for a prostitute, caught pneumonia, and died. He was given a magnificent funeral. The emperor of Austria organized a secret police service that rifled wastebaskets and corrupted maids. There was an immense assortment of illicit rendezvous, lovers' spats, and secret drinking. Except for the nervous interlude of Napoleon's Hundred Days, everyone enjoyed the congress immensely.

In spite of the diversions, diplomats from the great powers worked steadily. In matters such as the Bourbon restoration in France, Spain, and Naples, or the reestablishment of petty states in Italy and Germany, there was easy agreement. The diplomats split over eastern Europe. Alexander I was determined to make Poland a Russian client state. He was supported by Prussia, which was anxious to trade Polish lands for Saxony. The western powers opposed this, fearing the positioning of Russian troops so far west and wishing to preserve a balance of power in the east. At the threat of war, Alexander I and the Prussians drew back. Russia received two-thirds of Poland, and Prussia got two-fifths of Saxony. After this crisis, the congress moved quietly to a conclusion.

The basic diplomatic principle used at Vienna was balance of power. Everyone agreed that there could be no peace unless each great power was satisfied that its interests and security were protected. There would have to be an approximate equality of power and an absence of aggressive alliances. There was considerable wisdom in this view of diplomacy. The Vienna settlement prevented general war for 100 years, the longest period of peace in the west since the Pax Romana.

A second characteristic of the Vienna settlement was the search for legitimacy. Future revolutions might be avoided by a general return to legitimate and customary forms of government. Traditional royal houses were restored all over Europe, and the returned monarchs were urged to govern as autocratically as possible. In every case they eagerly complied.

Not everything could be restored, however. The Old Regime political ideas of absolutism and enlightened despotism had been largely discredited in the era of revolution. Their places had been taken by liberalism and nationalism, ideas that had come out of the revolutionary experience. The new ideas were only slightly checked by a conservative political and diplomatic settlement.

To the restored monarchs, liberalism appeared to be the most serious problem. Its doctrines contained audacious heresies. Basic to the liberal faith was the Enlightenment notion that sovereign power resided in the people, who should be represented by a parliament. Elected parliaments ought to control the ministers and policies of the state, with the monarch and nobility reduced to a largely honorific position. Liberalism meant freedom of the press and religion and support of the civil liberties enunciated in the Declaration of the Rights of Man. Liberals were anticlerical, hostile to the traditional alliance of throne and altar. Finally, liberals were usually nationalists, and thus enemies of peace abroad as well as at home.

Nationalism, a simple ideology that aroused a religious frenzy in those it infected, was also dangerous. It was the sense of community felt by those who spoke the same language or had a common history or culture. Language most frequently determined the national group. Thus those who spoke German were coming to think of themselves as Germans, wherever they lived. To them it seemed they ought to be part of one state from which other linguistic groups were excluded. Italians, Poles, Serbs, Hungarians, Rumanians, and others held the same views on the linguistic basis of national unity. There was also an appeal to history, to the past glories of the community when it was larger, more powerful, and more inspiring than in the modest present. Historical nationalism sometimes transcended language. The inhabitants of Alsace-Lorraine spoke a German dialect, but they had experienced the agonies and triumphs of the French Revolution and felt themselves to be Frenchmen. Polish nationalists appealed for a restoration of the medieval Polish Empire, which extended far beyond Polish linguistic boundaries.

A sense of community could also exist within the culture of a people. There were peoples who had never been united into a historical state and whose language was a dialect or local anomaly. Yet they retained a strong sense of community, expressed in dialect, folklore, costumes, dancing, games, or locally venerated saints and religious observances. The Basques and Bretons fell into this category, as did the Corsicans. Cultural nationalism also extended to much larger groups, such as the French, but in these cases it was often an element of government policy through education and patriotism, rather than the basic nationalist tie.

The belief in national superiority was not a strict logical necessity in theories of nationalism; indeed, the first major philosopher of nationalism, Johann Herder (1744–1803), explicitly denied it. But it was a popular necessity. Nationalism was preeminently a movement of the people, the first since the Reformation. Logic and reason were irrelevant. Tolerance was anathema. An emotional appeal was the essence of the thing. Nationalism aroused the satisfying feeling of belonging to the best ethnic group on earth. It had a strong moralistic cast, giving the activities of the national group an aura of righteousness. Nationalism, not religion, was the true opiate of the masses.

In deciding the territorial changes needed for an effective balance of power, the diplomats at Vienna gave scant consideration to questions of national unity. The idea of a united Germany frightened all the great powers; a united Italy would reduce intolerably Austrian power; an independent Poland would destroy the delicate balance in eastern Europe. At Vienna, the diplomats cut across national lines with Old Regime insouciance in their search for peace and a balance of power. This decision, inevitable in the circumstances, was to prove the great element of failure in a brilliantly successful diplomatic reconstruction.

Liberalism in Great Britain: 1815–1850

In 1815 Britain was governed by a parliamentary system that had matured since the Glorious Revolution. Based on late medieval precedents dating from Edward I, the House of Commons contained two representatives from each shire and two from selected towns. The franchise was quite restricted; even in London there were less than seven thousand voters. There were no uniform voting qualifications; each town had its own, passed down for many generations. There had been no change in apportionment since Elizabeth I, in spite of substantial population shifts. Some areas were overrepresented. Old Sarum and Dunwich-by-the-Sea no longer had any population at all, but still sent two members each to Commons. There were several of these pocket boroughs, so called because the owner of the land held the election in his pocket. Equally unfair were the rotten boroughs, where the number of voters was so small—a dozen or two—that the local lord could corrupt each one and appoint the members of Parliament. Since elections were infrequent, the House of Commons was dominated by a few dozen rich magnates.

Within the Parliament as well as without, the British system had worked to centralize power in a very few hands. The cabinet ministers during the course of the eighteenth century had effectively reduced the power of both the king and the ordinary members. Large, semipermanent parliamentary factions had been formed, usually by wealthy lords, and these blocks were combined to sustain a ministry. Members voted as their faction demanded and enjoyed the patronage and perquisites of power. Issues were generally unimportant; rewards, pressure, and family connections kept the members in line. In 1815 the government factions were run by Lord Liverpool, Viscount Castlereagh, and the duke of Wellington, who dominated the ministry and ran the country.

Although the political system had endured for more than a century, the economic condition of England had changed greatly. Enclosures had increased the size and efficiency of farms, factories were rapidly replacing hand production, new mines had been sunk, and new towns had grown up. Urban problems, such as slums, crime, unemployment, and disease, were on the march. The prevailing social legislation was insufficient to deal with these new problems. By 1815 there was a new England with an old system of government.

Immediately upon the negotiation of peace, the appalling disparity between new problems and old systems struck England full on. Peace was followed by a savage depression, which included the new phenomenon of large-scale industrial unemployment. Currency deflation added to the general distress. The rise of bread prices caused widespread hunger. The depression was also accompanied by considerable public disorder. Demands for reform of Parliament expanded into riot, which the government answered by seriously curtailing civil liberties.

After 1820, however, the economy improved, popular agitation died down, and the Liverpool ministry began to make reforms. The legal system was overhauled by Robert Peel, secretary of the home office, and the criminal code was made more rational and humanitarian. Tariffs were reduced. Laws were repealed prohibiting Protestant nonconformists and Roman Catholics from holding public office.

These reforms were insufficient, however. The death of Lord Liverpool in 1827 greatly weakened the government, and Wellington, the new prime minister, could not deflect growing demands for parliamentary reform. When George IV died in 1830, forcing a general election, it was obvious that Wellington and his Tory factions could not win. The opposition Whig factions, led by Earl Grey, campaigned on the single issue of parliamentary reform and won a majority in the House.

The new king, William IV, called upon Earl Grey to form a cabinet, perhaps the first real party government in British history, one that rested on the twin supports of a majority in the House of Commons and a popular mandate. After a great deal of parliamentary maneuvering and a second general election to reinforce his mandate, Lord Grey and his Whig ministry brought in the Reform Bill of 1832. The bill eliminated 56 pocket and rotten boroughs, which returned 111 members and deprived 32 small towns of one member each. These seats were redistributed. Shire members were increased from 94 to 159, 13 members went to Scotland and Ireland, and the rest went to the larger towns of the realm. The franchise extension was equally important. Urban householders paying £10 annual rent got the vote, and a reduced property qualification in the countryside enfranchised virtually all landowners.

The fight over the Reform Bill of 1832 marked the beginning of a real party system in Great Britain. It polarized the voters and members into two camps and forced the ministry to enact the program of the majority. Parties and party discipline did not develop at once, but the era of cozy faction management was coming to an end. The sociology of British politics was not greatly changed, however. The nobility and landed gentry retained power. Indeed, the Reform Bill may well have helped them, for it deflected popular agitation from the iniquities of noble rule to the iniquities of factories and mines. Nonetheless, the Reform Bill marked the beginning of the general democraticization of nineteenth-century British politics and society, and it established a pattern of liberal reform that the British have since retained.

Following the Reform Bill, the Whig cabinet introduced a series of important social measures. Slavery was abolished in the British Empire in 1833, the culmination of a long campaign that grew out of the humanitarian movement of the Enlightenment. This was followed by the Factory Act of 1833, designed to correct the worst of the hideous working conditions in British industry. The act forbade employment of children under nine, established a forty-eight-hour week for those between nine and thirteen, and a modest sixty-nine-hour week for children between thirteen and eighteen. Those older could work continuously. The Factory Act also provided for a system of paid inspectors to enforce the law. It was the first piece of labor legislation that was even marginally effective.

By mid-century, however, there was a definite pause in reform legislation. The men of 1832 were gone, and the issues they fought for would not be raised again until after 1865. In the interim, other things seemed more important. The revolutions of 1848, the Crimean War, Italian unification, the American Civil War, imperialism, the reorganization of India—these claimed the center of the political stage. The first era of liberal reform in Great Britain had ended; the second was not yet begun.

Revolutionary Crises: 1820–1831

The legitimate monarchs restored at Vienna returned to their thrones seething with hatred for the French Revolution and all its works. The new governments were frequently reactionary, dismantling with mindless hostility the improvements introduced by Napoleon. The new Italian rulers quickly restored a corrupt and vicious despotism, while Austrians were ruled by a sort of amiable incompetence. In Spain, Ferdinand VII restored the Inquisition, persecuted suspected liberals, and governed in an incompetent and capricious manner. The Ottoman Turks misgoverned in the traditional manner, and even in France and Holland the restored kings were far more conservative than most of their subjects wished. Restoration governments proved to be worse than Napoleon.

Between 1820 and 1822—only a few years after the Congress of Vienna—serious revolts began. These were followed by another wave of revolt from 1830 to 1831. The last and greatest spasm of revolution came in 1848. Primarily liberal and national in origin, the revolts of the first half of the nineteenth century arose from the huge contrast between the wretched government they received and the glowing promises of the new ideologies. Thus they threatened basic premises of the Vienna settlement.

The first wave of revolution, from 1820 to 1822, was replete with failure. Occurring so close to the end of the French Revolution, renewed uprising could not fail to frighten the Continental powers. A series of great-power congresses met to deal with the hydra of liberal revolution. Over the strenuous objection of the British, the congresses agreed on the principle of collective security against revolution. The Austrians were dispatched to Naples, where they easily restored the abominable despotism of Ferdinand I. The liberal regime in Sardinia was also crushed. In Spain, a French army won the Battle of Trocadero in August 1823 and restored Ferdinand VII to his full powers. Ferdinand at once abandoned himself to a savage clerical repression. There were limits to military intervention, however. No troops were sent to help the Ottoman Empire in its unsuccessful struggle against the Greek revolt.

As the revolutions of 1820–1821 were repressed, the restored monarchs considered the ease with which the revolutionaries had been routed, rather than the manifest feebleness of their own rule. Thus they fell back into the old patterns of misrule and corruption. Renewed revolution seemed inevitable, for the middle classes of western Europe were increasingly converting to liberal and nationalist notions. The new revolutionary crisis came in 1830. Between July 28 and 30 the clerical and autocratic government of Charles X of France was overthrown by a Paris mob. The new king, Louis-Philippe, was considerably more liberal than his predecessor, and he extended the franchise, eased press censorship, and formed a ministry responsible to the majority in the Chamber of Deputies.

Repercussions of the successful French revolution were felt immediately in the Low Countries. Since 1815 Belgium had been unhappily united to Holland to form a barrier against future French aggression. The Catholic Belgians did not like the Dutch Calvinist religion, the Dutch language, the Dutch tax and customs system, the Dutch officials, or the Dutch king. When the news of the July Revolution reached Brussels, the Belgians revolted. They declared independence, framed a liberal constitution, and elected Leopold of Saxe-Coburg as king. A second liberal revolt had succeeded.

Two other revolutions between 1830 and 1831 failed, suppressed by Austria and Russia. In 1831 Austria sent in her army to repress liberal and national revolts in the Papal States, Parma, and Modena. The uprising in Poland was more serious. Revolutionaries expelled the Russian garrison from Warsaw and declared a provisional government. Russia invaded Poland in the spring of 1831, defeated the rebels, and disbanded the revolutionary government. Poland lost most of her internal autonomy and became, in effect, a huge military district garrisoned and governed by the Russian army. In Italy and the east, liberal and national revolts were too great a threat to the internal security and vital diplomatic interests of the great powers to be allowed to succeed.

The Uprisings of 1848

In 1848 the numerous revolutions appeared as a sudden and terrifying storm, surprising and overwhelming the most stable European thrones. Revolution spread like influenza. The news of each revolt inspired an uprising elsewhere. In the spring of 1848 liberal and national ideologies seemed irresistible. It appeared that the people themselves would remake the map and character of Europe, discarding the autocratic governments and nonnational boundaries and creating a Europe of democratic and national states. It was the "springtime of the people."

As in 1830, France gave the signal for a general European uprising. On February 22, 1848, rioting began in Paris. The July monarchy collapsed, and a republic took its place. The Second Republic, however, was unstable from the start. Urban unemployment was high, thousands of people faced starvation, and workers were in a rebellious mood. Socialist thought made great progress in workers' districts, and in June 1848 workers in Paris rose in revolt to establish a socialist republic. The terrified government called in the army, and the June Days were filled with the slaughter of Paris workers. The bourgeoisie of France were much relieved, convinced that property had been saved, but workers saw the massacre as proof that the government and middle classes were their permanent enemies. The June Days marked the beginning of the profound class consciousness so characteristic of French workers and paved the way for the conservative regime of Napoleon III.

The Italian peninsula was also the scene of revolution. In January 1848 a liberal revolt broke out in Naples, similar to the uprising of 1820. News of events in Naples and Paris stimulated revolt in Turin, where King Charles Albert granted a liberal constitution, the *Statuto*. It was revolution in the Austrian provinces of Lombardy and Venetia, however, that thrust Italy onto the stage of great-power politics. Encouraged by the Milanese revolution, the kingdom of Sardinia declared war on Austria in the hope of forming a united kingdom of Italy. It was a futile gesture. The Austrian commander,

Marshal Radetsky, was an old and able soldier, and on July 24 he decisively defeated the Sardinians at Custozza and reconquered Austrian Italy.

While Austria was reestablishing its hegemony over northern Italy, an important drama was taking place in Rome. In February 1849 Pope Pius IX was chased from Rome, and the leading Italian nationalist of the age, Giuseppe Mazzini, established a republic. Although the republic had considerable popular support in Rome, it had none abroad. Pope Pius IX appealed for help, and France sent an army to restore him. A three-month siege ended with the return of the pope in the baggage train of a French army. The brief Roman republic died, a victim of international Roman Catholic pressure.

The Italian experience with liberal and national revolution in 1848 and 1849 decisively changed the course of Italian nationalist agitation. The republican ideal so eloquently espoused by Giuseppe Mazzini was thoroughly discredited. The romantic conceptions of revolution—as a spontaneous rising of the people against hideous oppressors, which would succeed by sheer righteousness of cause—simply collapsed. Nationalist and liberal hopes henceforth focused on Sardinia, which alone kept a liberal constitution after 1849 and showed promise of actually being able to drive out the Austrians.

The third arena of revolution between 1848 and 1849 was in Prussia, Germany, and the Austrian Empire. The Prussian revolution was much the smallest but in many ways the most important. From March 15 to March 21 there was sporadic rioting in Berlin, but it was nothing that the police and some military detachments could not have handled easily. However, King Frederick William IV became frightened and gave way to the liberals, although the crown and the army still retained all real power in the country. Thus the king was able to change his mind, cancel the liberal reforms, and issue a constitution that retained autocracy intact. Revolution barely touched Russia.

While Prussian liberals were debating in Berlin, another assembly representing all Germany was meeting in Frankfurt to draw up a constitution for a united national and liberal German state. The Frankfurt Assembly met first on May 18 and plunged immediately into the creation of Germany. The assembly represented no existing state and had no army, bureaucracy, king, or boundaries. It did have the support of thousands of German liberals and nationalists. During the glorious months of revolutionary success in the spring of 1848, this was enough.

The Frankfurt Assembly, however, quickly ran into an intractable problem. It was the question of the relationship of Austria to the new national Germany. In the spring of 1848, when Austria was falling apart into its national constituent units, it was easy for Frankfurt deputies to envision the incorporation of Austrian Germans into a greater Germany. As Austria began to put her empire back together again, however, it was difficult to see how a German national state could incorporate the millions of Italians, Poles, Czechs, Hungarians, and Croats who were Austrian subjects. It was equally hard to imagine Austrian Germans giving up their empire to be merged into Germany. The ideal of greater Germany, a state including all Germans, rapidly became a distant dream in the summer and fall of 1848.

Lesser Germany was still possible. Perhaps all the non-Austrian Germans could be united. After October 1848 the liberals at the Frankfurt Assembly devoted themselves to this task. On May 27, 1849, they brought forth a constitution for a liberal lesser Germany. Including all German states except Austria, ruled by the king of Prussia, and governed by a parliament and responsible ministry, the new national Germany seemed all that liberals and nationalists could reasonably expect. In fact, it was too much. May 1849 was a year too late to reorganize Germany. Austria opposed it, the king of Prussia refused to "pick up a crown from the gutter," and liberal and nationalist sentiment had waned. The project collapsed and the Frankfurt delegates went home. Germany remained a loose confederation containing two jealous great powers, Austria and Prussia.

The most astonishing of the revolutions of 1848 was the precipitate collapse of Austria. On March 12, 1848, a student riot in Vienna led to revolt over the entire realm. In March, also, the Italian provinces broke away from Vienna; on March 31 Hungary declared a modified independence; on April 8 the Czechs received a promise of a constituent assembly from the frightened monarchy. Metternich, long the arbiter of Europe, was toppled from power; he left Vienna disguised as a traveling violinist.

The Hapsburg empire, even in this condition, was stronger than it seemed. The emperors still possessed an army, a bureaucracy, and the loyalty of the German-speaking people. By the middle of June the crown was beginning to put the country back together again. Field Marshal Windisch-Graetz bombarded Prague into submission. Radetsky defeated the Italians, rewinning Lombardy and Venetia. On October 31, 1848, Windisch-Graetz bombarded Vienna, and the Hapsburgs reentered their ancient capital. In December 1848 the government was reorganized. The moronic Ferdinand was forced to abdicate in favor of the young Franz Josef. A new and vigorous ministry was formed under Prince Schwarzenberg, who was dedicated to reviving the old monarchy. War was pushed with Hungary.

Russian aid helped considerably, and by August 1849 the Hungarians had been completely defeated. The Hapsburgs had triumphed over their peoples. After the first shock of revolt, they had done so without any particular difficulty.

The revolutions in central Europe all ended in failure. The liberal aims of the Prussian middle classes fell before the army, nobility, and bureaucracy of a modern state. Within a wider Germany, revolution also failed. Because of the inherent contradictions between greater Germany and lesser Germany, Germans came to feel that liberal methods would never unite the nation. In Austria the Hapsburg emperor emerged from the fighting with a stronger government than before, and a new policy of ruthless administrative centralization. For the time being, national and liberal ideals were less powerful than armies.

The years between 1815 and mid-century saw a constant struggle between the revolutionary demands of liberalism and nationalism and the Vienna settlement. Stability and order conflicted with the increasingly popular liberal and national ideologies. Only in Great Britain were these two conflicting social needs compromised; elsewhere in Europe there was revolution. Although the partisans of order and stability won most of the battles, they lost the war. Public opinion swung inexorably toward liberalism and nationalism. After 1850 it was only a question of time before nationalism won its victories and every European state obtained a parliament. The revolutions of 1848 were not the last despairing spasm of a dying revolutionary faith. They were the proclamation of the Europe of the next half-century, a time of growing democracy and rising national consciousness.

THE POLITICS OF NATIONALISM

The first care of kings and ministers after the terrifying events of 1848 was to put everything back as it had been before the year of revolution. In purely formal terms, that was done. The rather ramshackle Austrian Empire was stuck together again and given a new administrative lease on life. The dreams of an Italian nation died in the trenches before Rome and the fields of Custozza. The Frankfurt Assembly drifted into oblivion. Napoleon III was elected prince-president of France. The Vienna settlement seemed safe once more.

However, the issues raised by the revolutions of 1848–1849 could not be so simply dismissed. Liberalism, socialism, and nationalism were not eliminated because their adherents had lacked sufficient military force to defend the revolution. They remained to disturb the diplomacy and administration of European states. The most powerful and immediately threatening of the ideologies thrust into the middle of European politics by the revolutions was nationalism. It was the common thread linking revolutions as different as those in Rome and Hungary. Nationalism had been a factor in revolutionary upheavals since the Greek revolt in 1822. By the 1850s it was a vast and frightening idea.

The diplomatic implications of national ambitions were genuinely stupendous. Great states such as Prussia, Austria, and Russia would have to be torn apart to satisfy the national aspirations of Poles, Hungarians, or Rumanians. The Ottoman Empire might be broken into its national fragments, creating Greece, Bulgaria, Serbia, or Syria. Nations such as Italy or Germany might spring out of the fragments. But such wholesale changes in the map of Europe were unimportant to the sectarians of the new faith, who regarded national self-determination as divinely ordained and morally right. Thus nationalism justified in advance any adventure a government might care to consider. Astute and cynical men, such as Napoleon III, Bismarck, or Cavour, understood this and schemed to use the force of nationalism in their diplomatic and military calculations.

The first European statesman to try to harness the nationalistic torrent was Napoleon III, emperor of France. Having come to power in a revolutionary situation, he did not fear the voice of the people as did many of his contemporaries. Revolutionary mass movements were to be used, not avoided. Popular support could add an element of strength to a man or regime that no army could match. He would use that strength in his diplomatic calculations.

"The Empire means peace," Napoleon III had said to European governments that were fearful of the militaristic connotation of his name and that were accustomed to regarding France as the strongest of the Continental powers. In one sense, Napoleon III meant what he said: He had no intention of beginning a general European war and uniting the powers against him as his uncle had. Yet, he wanted to play a great role. He did not abandon the thought of expanding the borders of France, but he would do it piecemeal, through limited adventures. He began in Italy.

The Creation of an Italian National State

The French emperor was enticed into Italian waters by the astute diplomacy of Camillo Cavour, the premier of Sardinia. Cavour had decisively changed the visible patterns and tactics of Italian nationalism. He avoided any mention of a republic and maintained a strictly respectable allegiance to his king. He eschewed conspiracy. He looked instead for military allies against Austria. They were hard to find. Russian would not help, and Prussia was too weak. Great Britain was sympathetic to Cavour's plans, but the British army had performed so poorly in the Crimea that no one trembled at the thought of meeting it. Only France, headed by the enigmatic Napoleon III, was a possible ally.

The agreement to intervene in Italy was concluded between Napoleon III and Cavour at the resort of Plombières in July 1858. The basic outline was clear. The French army was to fight if Austria attacked Sardinia. Austria would be driven out of Italy, Sardinia would annex Venetia and Lombardy, and France would get Nice and Savoy. As for the rest of Italy, nothing was clearly decided.

Cavour had elicited a firm commitment from Napoleon III at Plombières, so the emperor began to prepare his people for an Italian war. He unleashed a vast propaganda campaign justifying French interest in Italy, dwelling on Austrian misgovernment there, and reassuring everyone that no harm to the pope was intended. He also proposed an international congress of the great powers, which would settle the Italian question once and for all. The congress idea fell through, but the propaganda campaign continued..

Both Austria and Sardinia were also preparing for war, but Austrian efforts were increasingly disconnected from reality. Austria did not surmise from the press campaign that France would join the war. Nor did she search for allies or put her army in readiness. Finally Austria succumbed to Sardinian hectoring and declared war on the small Italian kingdom in April 1859. Napoleon III promptly honored his word. The war for Italian unification had begun.

For a while all went well for France and Sardina. Aided by France's railroad network, the French army moved rapidly to the front. At Magenta the Austrians were driven back on Milan, which could not be held. French and Italian troops occupied the city and advanced toward Venetia. They caught up with the Austrian army at Solferino, where the climactic battle of the war was fought. The Austrians were entrenched on a series of hills, strongly supported by artillery. On a blazing hot day the French and Italian armies charged up the hills into the teeth of the Austrian positions. Austrian gunners cut the assault to pieces. The allies regrouped and charged again. Then they charged a third time. A French attempt to turn the flank failed to dislodge the Austrian army. A last frontal assault by the French troops finally carried the hill, and the Austrians were bayoneted in their trenches. The allies had won another victory, but the cost was appalling. The battle was an orgy of blood and death. Thousands were butchered by the Austrian artillery. The scrub on the hillside caught fire, and the wounded were burned to death. The agony and slaughter sickened the emperor, who had never quite realized the horror of battle. And a Swiss named Henri Dunant, overwhelmed by the suffering, organized the local peasants into a hospital to care for the wounded. Dunant's hospital was the beginning of the Red Cross.

After Solferino, the Austrians fell back into Venetia, where they were strongly supported by fortresses and reinforcements. The allied advance halted, but the victories were sufficient to stimulate revolt in the duchies of Parma, Modena, Tuscany, and in the Papal States, where the revolutionaries were clamoring to join the new kingdom of Italy. Napoleon III had not planned on the creation of a large Italian state. The revolutions embarrassed him, particularly the revolt against papal misrule. In July 1859 he concluded an armistice with Austria, which ceded Lombardy to Sardinia.

For France and Austria the war was over. But for Italy, unification was just beginning. Tuscany, Parma, Modena, and the northern section of the Papal States voted themselves into the new kingdom of Italy. This was only the beginning. The hero of 1849, Garibaldi, landed in Sicily with about 1,500 men and announced his intention of freeing the rest of Italy from princes and pope. With tremendous courage and considerable tactical skill, Garibaldi outfought the Neapolitan

THE UNIFICATION OF ITALY

troops and marched on Palermo. He then crossed the Strait of Messina and marched on Naples itself. Resistance collapsed, and by September 1860, five months after landing in Sicily, Garibaldi was master of Naples. He announced plans to march on Rome. This threw everyone into panic, particularly Napoleon III. French troops were in Rome guarding the pope, and the emperor faced the appalling possibility of fighting his Italian allies in a war to thwart the national unity that he himself had done so much to bring about. Cavour was also disturbed. In the event of war with France, Austria could reenter Italy, and the new Italian kingdom would be dismantled. Cavour proposed to the French that the Sardinian king and army march south, intercept Garibaldi short of Rome, and accept Naples and Sicily into the new Italy. The distraught emperor could only mutter, "Do it, but do it fast." The Italians did. King Victor Emmanuel reached Garibaldi before the march on Rome was really begun. Garibaldi and the king rode through Naples in triumph. Naples and Sicily were added to the growing Italian state. And, on the march south, the papal provinces of Ancona and Umbria also were absorbed by the kingdom of Italy. By March 1861 an Italian national state existed. It still lacked Rome and Venice, but it was no longer merely the small kingdom of Sardinia.

Bismarck and the German Empire

The events of these two years made a considerable impression on Europe, but nowhere more than in Prussia. The focus of German nationalism had been swinging toward Prussia since 1849, as everyone realized that the Austrian Empire could not lead a united Germany without itself breaking apart. Prussia was not considered as powerful as Austria; certainly it lacked Austria's prestige, and was an absolutist, illiberal state, governed by a reactionary landed gentry. But, in spite of these deficiencies, Prussia was the only power capable of uniting those Germans not under Austrian sovereignty. So the liberal German nationalists were forced to look to Prussia, whether they wanted to or not.

In Prussia, the army was more important than anything else, and the process whereby Prussia became the paladin of German nationalism demonstrated that clearly. In 1859 the activities of Napoleon III had aroused great anxiety across the Rhine, and the Prussian government decided to expand and modernize the army. That required money, and the king and his ministers asked parliament for increased funds. Parliament was controlled by rich liberals, who were antimilitaristic and opposed to new taxes. The credits were refused. For three years the crisis dragged on, while the generals fumed and King William I contemplated abdiction. As a last resort he called upon Otto von Bismarck to be his prime minister. Bismarck saw the impasse in clear terms. If the king wanted money for the army—the basic institution of the Prussian state—then the opposition was unimportant and irrelevant. He collected the necessary taxes, modernized the army, and increased its size. Parliament protested. Bismarck ignored it. Parliament voted no confidence in the government. Bismarck remained.

The Prussian prime minister soon was able to turn his attention to foreign matters and to find a chance to use his new improved army. The opportunity came with the Schleswig-Holstein affair. The king of Denmark was also duke of Schleswig and Holstein, although these duchies were not part of Denmark. In 1862 the Danes adopted a new constitution, which made the union between Denmark and the duchies much tighter. Bismarck professed to be outraged by this insult to the sacred honor of the German people and maintained that the new constitution was only a prelude to outright annexation of the German-speaking duchies by Denmark. His stand was very popular throughout all Germany. The Austrian government, quite sensitive to nationalist agitation, was bullied by Bismarck into joining Prussia in armed intervention in the duchies. To no one's suprise Prussia and Austria were able to defeat Denmark and jointly agreed to rule the duchies. Prussia administered Schleswig, Austria, Holstein. This arrangement was quite satisfactory for Prussia. Schleswig was close to Prussian territory and was virtually incorporated into the Prussian state; but for Austria it was a disaster. Holstein was far away, surrounded by Prussian territory, and at Bismarck's mercy. From the end of the Danish war in June 1864, Bismarck harassed the Austrians. His tactics worked, and by June 1866 Austria, supported by most of the smaller German states, had stumbled into war with Prussia. With its new army and an alliance with Italy, Prussia was ready. Austria was not.

The war lived up to Bismarck's most sanguine expectations. The new Prussian army, moved rapidly into Bohemia by railroad, was aligned for battle long before the Austrians were ready. At Sadowa the Prussians won a major victory, driving the Austrian army completely out of Bohemia and throwing it into defensive positions along

EUROPE IN 1870 ▶

the Danube. By this time, the Austrian emperor, Franz Josef, had had enough, and he asked Bismarck for an armistice. The war had lasted seven weeks.

Bismarck moved as rapidly in peace as he had in war. He wished to forestall a possible French effort to mediate, as well as any Russian alarm at the sudden growth of Prussian power. Bismarck imposed a harsh peace on Austria and her German allies. Four north German states were annexed by Prussia, and Austria was excluded from the German Confederation. Venetia was ceded by Austria to Italy, in spite of the fact that Austria had defeated the Italian army in battle. A North German Confederation was created out of the lands north of the Main River, so even those states not annexed by Prussia fell completely into the Prussian orbit. Had the terms been any more severe, had Prussia annexed some Austrian territory, the Austrian Empire might well have come apart. Bismarck knew this, but it was no part of his plans to dismember Austria, a move none of the great powers would have permitted. Bismarck was no nationalist; his great objective was not the unification of Germany but the aggrandizement of Prussia. The terms of the Peace of Prague, which ended the war with Austria, were perfectly calculated to serve that goal.

However, the domination of Germany by Prussia was not completed in 1866. The south German kingdoms, led by Bavaria and supported by French and Austrian diplomacy, had stayed aloof from the North German Confederation. The Catholic states of the south were fearful of Prussian dominance and clung to their separate identity. Only the threat of French aggression in Germany could drive them into a united Germany dominated by Prussia, and Bismarck set about creating the conditions of that aggression. He frightened the south German states with disclosures of French attempts to annex Belgium or Luxembourg. However, the main weapon against France was the Hohenzollern candidacy for the throne of Spain.

After the Spanish revolution of 1868, the provisional government of Spain approached the Catholic relatives of William I of Prussia and asked one of them to take the vacant Spanish throne. Bismarck pressed for acceptance, and in July 1870 the secret of the negotiations leaked out. French consternation was great, and French demands for a withdrawal of the Hohenzollern candidacy were insistent and vigorous. Indeed, they were too vigorous. The French ambassador to Prussia, an incompetent named Benedetti, insisted that William I renounce the Spanish offer in the name of his family. William was insulted and telegraphed his indignation from the resort of

Ems to Bismarck in Berlin. Bismarck seized upon the Ems telegram and published an edited version that made it appear that Benedetti had grossly insulted King William I. If the wording was altered, the substance and tone of the Ems telegram nevertheless represented the feelings of Benedetti and his government. France intended to use the incident to crush the pretensions of Prussia once and for all.

Instead, it was France that was crushed. The French were out-fought; their military leadership was atrocious; the Prussian army moved easily through France and surrounded Paris. Two large French field armies surrendered at Metz and Sedan, and the emperor himself was captured. Napoleon III was deposed and a provisional republic was established. The provisional government tried to hold out in Paris but failed. After a lengthy siege, the city fell. The war was over, and treaty negotiations were started.

The Franco-Prussian War was a momentous event. Out of it emerged the German Empire, by far the strongest power in Europe. The south German states succumbed to national feeling and joined the new German state. France was reduced to a state of the second rank for the first time since the sixteenth-century wars of religion. Italy took advantage of the French defeat to annex Rome. The German Empire annexed Alsace-Lorraine, two provinces in eastern France. Thus the end of one national problem was the beginning of another. Frenchmen never accepted the loss of the two provinces, and France and Germany became permanent enemies. Napoleon's attempt to harness the demons of nationalism had ended in disaster, and two abler men—Cavour and Bismarck—had succeeded in using nationalist emotions in the service of their diplomacy.

The Germans and Italians were not the only European nations that wanted unification or independence. The Hungarians wanted a separate state, as did the Poles, the Rumanians, the Serbs, and all the rest of the Balkan peoples. Nationalist agitation continued and even rose in intensity, but the Franco-Prussian War was the last major conflict of national unification in Europe before World War I. The territory of Europe had become too valuable to be left to the mercy of national passions. European diplomacy had had enough of great national adventures.

THE DEVELOPMENT OF AN INDUSTRIAL SOCIETY

Industrialization is an expanding process. During the nineteenth century it spread inexorably over most of Europe, and this geo-graphical expansion was matched by a continuous increase in the pace of invention. The new machines were more complex, more productive, and much more expensive than those they replaced. Scientific knowledge gradually became the basis for invention. Moreover, as new machines and industrial processes multiplied they produced a vast amount of wealth, which was most unevenly distributed. Finally change became a way of life. The search for social stability proved an inadequate response to industrialization. In the nineteenth century continuing industrialization became the informing principle of Western civilization.

The Spread of Industrialization:
1815–1914

Until 1815 the Napoleonic wars confined industrialization to Great Britain. Demands for war materiel kept British factories awash with orders, while war diverted Continental capital from investment. After Vienna this all changed. The need for British iron and textiles made mechanization attractive. Continental industrialization began in Belgium, where manufacturers imported British steam engines and textile machinery. As in Great Britain, industrialization in Belgium was based primarily on an abundance of coal—the basic raw material—and on the manufacture of iron and cloth; the transition to machine industry was fairly rapid. By 1860 Belgium was already a predominantly urban and industrial state.

Industrial growth in France was much slower than in Belgium. In 1840 France was still a traditional society with almost no modern industry. Extensive French industrialization came only when Napoleon III made the modernization of French industry his main domestic concern. The French railway system was completed, the textile industry adopted the most modern British machinery, French iron manufacture finally abandoned charcoal for coke, and French shipbuilding turned from sail to steam. The Second Empire also witnessed the modernization of Paris, and the City of Light received its boulevards, parks, water supply, opera house, and sewers. The economic dynamism of the Second Empire did not survive the end of the regime, however, and it was not until 1900 that France once again enjoyed sustained economic growth. On the eve of the Great War France still remained the least urbanized, least industrialized of the western European states.

The German industrial revolution began in the decade after 1850, a period of roaring prosperity everywhere. The Zollverein, or customs union, and railway construction helped tie Germany together economically. After 1870 Germany industrialized at an incredible pace, matched only by the United States. The addition of Alsace-Lorraine, the most heavily industrialized French provinces, greatly stimulated the German economy. The Ruhr valley became the largest center of heavy industry in Europe. Equally important was the development of a huge chemical industry, based originally on potash mining. By 1914 German coal production, steel tonnage, and electric power exceeded that of the British. Imperial Germany entered World War I with the strongest economy in Europe.

Industrialization in southern and eastern Europe began much later and was far less complete than in the west. Russia, Austria, Italy, and the Balkan states remained primarily traditional societies where small islands of intense industrialization were spotted in a great peasant sea. There was considerable industrial development in the Donbas region of Russia, in central Bohemia, and around Vienna in Austria, in Milan and Turin in Italy, and in the Ploesti oil fields in Rumania. Moreover, a rather extensive rail network linked Russia and eastern Europe into a single market. But beyond this, industrialization had not yet transformed society as in England or Germany.

There were therefore several patterns of industrialization in nineteenth-century Europe. Germany, Great Britain, and Belgium industrialized rapidly and completely. France differed widely from this model, retaining a thriving peasant culture and numerous luxury industries, such as the manufacture of tapestry, china, perfume, lace, and women's clothes. These were extremely profitable, labor-intensive, and hardly mechanized at all. A third pattern existed in eastern Europe. Here, modern industrial enterprise made only a modest impression on traditional peasant and mercantile customs. Peasant and factory remained two widely separate worlds. Industrialization was frequently the result of state sponsorship, and the government was industry's largest customer. The most modern and efficient plants invariably manufactured guns. Nonetheless, European states by the time of the Great War were all committed to the urbanization and factory production embodied in the German experience.

Effects of Industrialization: Capital and Labor

Industrialization was a quantum leap away from the traditional forms of production, and it substantially altered the old methods of investment and organization of labor. The change to industrial patterns was too rapid for society and government to react properly. Thus industry was afflicted with incurable and savage business cycles, in which deep depression alternated with a roaring boom. Many laborers experienced an agonizing decline in status, independence, and living standard, which governments seemed powerless to correct. Finally, a salient feature of an industrializing economy was the development of new patterns of work, profit, and investment.

The new machines cost gigantic sums of money, and the cost rose as the machines became more efficient. Huge amounts of investment capital were needed to build the factory, buy the machines, and sustain the company through business cycles. While industrialization produced colossal wealth, it also demanded that this wealth be reinvested constantly in newer, more sophisticated, and more expensive machinery. The process seemed endless, as science and technology fed upon itself and investors poured forth a constant stream of new devices. Telephones, typewriters, electric lights—all increased the productivity and profits of doing business. For the inefficient, however, they increased the costs even more.

By mid-century the costs of industrial investment were so heavy that they could no longer be carried by the profits of an individual company. Therefore, manufacturers approached banks for substantial loans, mortgaging their businesses in the process. In France, Napoleon III, the first European ruler to realize the importance of industrial credit, established national banks to increase industrial investment. The largest of these, the Crédit Mobilier, financed French railroads, the rebuilding of Paris, the Suez Canal, and the conversion of the French steel mills from charcoal to coke. Although few banks lent as much speculative capital as the Crédit Mobilier, they were all finding the most profitable investments to be in industry.

Soon it was beyond the ability of banks to meet demands for money and credit. In the years after the Franco-Prussian War, industry began to "go public" by selling bonds and stocks to anyone who would buy. Industry issued huge blocks of stock, which tapped an unlimited source of funds, the general public. This diversified ownership, but left management virtually untouched. The stock owner received his dividends and capital gains, if any, but unless he owned a large amount of stock indeed, he had no voice in the company's management. Gradually industrial investment replaced government bonds as the standard method of utilizing liquid capital. For corporations, as for kings, the public became the ultimate reservoir of new money.

Stocks and loans were not the only means used by big business to expand or protect their solvency. Corporations turned to internal consolidation as well. Market agreements, interlocking directories, patent pools, cartels, and trusts were all instruments of industrial concentration. Although different in detail, they all had the same purpose: to reduce competition, cut costs, increase profits, retain management control, and dominate the market. These monopolistic practices existed everywhere. In 1900 the American Sugar Refining Company controlled 98 percent of American processed sugar. German finance was dominated by four great banks, chemical production was controlled by I.G. Farben. A.G., and coal mining by the Kohlen syndicate. Royal Dutch Shell combined the huge British and Dutch petroleum interests. Monopoly was the inevitable result of increased efficiency in capital formation.

These concentrations of economic power and industrial capital did not go unnoticed by governments or the public. Corporate leaders pleaded that monopolistic practices were necessary for industrial efficiency and protested that mere size was not in itself dangerous to the public good. These arguments were not well received. Labor unions suspected, not without cause, that large trusts were better able to hold down wages than reduce prices. Bourgeois reformers lamented that large corporations were against public schools, municipal sewerage systems, and adequate housing because of the taxes involved. A few government officials regarded such mammoth concentrations of private power with suspicion and in any case were sensitive to voters who disliked and feared the trusts. Therefore the years just before World War I saw the beginning of governmental control over big business.

Labor also felt the continuous impact of industrialization. In many ways workers had been better off before the machine. The rhythms of rural life were kinder than those of the factory. Ownership of even a tiny plot of land conferred a sense of self-respect that an urban laborer seldom achieved. The customary charity of church or neighbors helped one through crises. None of these things existed in the industrial city. Moreover, the quality of life declined as well. Brick and soot replaced the open country. The worker was crowded in dismal slums. His church lost track of him. He was oppressed by the discipline of the time clock. Seen from below, industrialization was a curse.

Descriptions of labor exploitation can also be supported by hard evidence. As prices rose in the first half of the nineteenth century, workers' real wages dropped. In England and France in the 1840s, a worker's wages fell about one-third short of mere subsistence. Parliamentary commissions in Great Britain uncovered appalling conditions in industry. A sixteen-hour day was customary. Orphans were rented to mill owners, who worked them from dawn to dark for a few pennies. Miners preferred to sell their daughters into white slavery than to see them in the mines. Factory inspection acts were passed, but these made little dent in the exploitation of factory labor. In short, much of the investment capital plowed into industrial development was accumulated by exploiting labor.

The brutalities of the police were added to those of the boss. Authorities everywhere viewed the urban poor as criminals or revolutionaries. Municipal magistrates feared riot above all else and viewed workers as the basic source of trouble. No one made a distinction among strikes, bread riots, or revolution. Strikes were uniformly prohibited, and when they occurred anyway, the government took the management side. Unions were not legalized anywhere before 1850. Finally, a steady increase in the numbers and efficiency of the police enabled the authorities to oppress the poor even more closely.

Labor found three responses to conditions of poverty and oppression. The first and most important was unions. Second, union leaders were able to organize their members into political parties and fight for their interests at the polls. Finally, workers turned to revolution, both in its standard Marxian formula and in numerous heretical ideologies. While all varieties of labor action existed in the early nineteenth century, none showed the slightest success until after 1850. Only when industrialization had proceeded so far that workers were too numerous to be ignored did European governments admit them to political power and a larger share of the national wealth.

After 1850 unionization and labor parties were increasingly common, although successful attempts to overthrow the private-sector economy would await the colossal destruction of World War I. The first successful union, the Amalgamated Society of Engineers, was formed in 1852. In the next three decades, numerous craft unions were organized in Great Britain, and in the 1880s, unionization began to spread to the less skilled industrial workers. The great London dock strike of 1889 showed the direction British unionization was taking. In 1900 British labor entered politics, and in 1905 the Labour party became part of the government coalition. German unions were equally well organized, and they officially espoused a revolutionary Marxist theology rather than the pragmatic economic demands of the British. The German labor party, the SPD, was organized long

One of Vincent Van Gogh's lesser-known works, portraying the bleakness of nineteenth-century prison life. *Courtesy Novosti Press Agency from the Pushkin Museum of Fine Arts, Moscow.* ▶

before the British, indeed, German unions were considerably more political in their aims than the British. By 1882 the SPD had already so alarmed the government that laws were passed against it; but it was the largest party in Germany when war came. In Scandinavia unions followed the German pattern, forming disciplined political parties.

Elsewhere in Europe labor was less successful in organizing powerful unions or mass political parties. In both France and Italy workers were beguiled by the chimera of general strikes, which would paralyze everything and allow unions to take over the country. Somehow it never worked out that way, with the police and army breaking the general strike in both countries. In France the notion of random violence entranced the more romantic believers in the labor millennium. The epidemic of assassination and industrial bombings attracted the attention of the police, however. Such activities proved incompatible with effective use of union power, either at the bargaining table or in parliament. Unions therefore became markedly hostile to anarchism.

When the Great War came, labor was not yet as powerful as capital. Wages, though they had risen considerably, were still low. Hours still averaged at least ten a day. Working conditions could not yet be described as luxurious. Little attention was given to factory safety, and industrial accidents were common. Often as not, strikes were broken. In politics, however, labor had done much better. Universal suffrage and a bloc vote had forced numerous reforms through the various legislatures. Public education, so necessary to workers, had become general in 1914. Public sanitation had made great progress. Accident, sickness, and unemployment insurance had been enacted almost everywhere. Some governments had old age pensions and minimum wage laws. Reluctant legislators were beginning to enact laws regulating the conduct of business. New taxes, such as those in the Lloyd George budget of 1909, were beginning to hit accumulated wealth. By 1914 labor had been a growing political force for half a century, and the dream of transforming society through the ballot box did not seem so distant.

Effects of Industrialization:
A New Social Mobility

Industrialization had an awesome effect on the traditional society of the Old Regime. The machine gave two kinds of movement to an essentially static society—social mobility, in which a man might move up or down the economic ladder, and geographical mobility, in which people migrated from country to the cities.

Industrialization progressively dissolved the Old Regime ladder of society, which had persisted for nearly a millennium. In an industrial city the traditional hierarchy lost its meaning. By mid-century the old ways were visibly dissolving. Now, as Giuseppe di Lampedusa's aristocratic *Leopard*, Don Fabrizio, knew, compromises and adjustments had to be made quickly. Society changed so fast. Wealth and position were gathered and lost so quickly. Industry rewarded capital investment and managerial talent, not inherited status or birth. Quite obscure men, through education, luck, and business skill, rose to positions of great wealth and power in a few years. After 1860 it became commonplace for men to move rapidly up and down the social ladder, to do in years what had previously taken generations.

People were also geographically mobile. Industrial migrations of the nineteenth century were the largest sustained folk movement in Western civilization. Industrialization forced people into the cities. In the century between Waterloo and the Marne, nearly 35 million Europeans migrated to the New World, mostly to American cities. Within Europe itself, Vienna expanded from 250,000 to 1.5 million between 1800 and 1900, London from 1 to 6.5 million, and Berlin from 172,000 to over 2.5 million, while Essen, an industrial town in the Ruhr, grew from 5,000 to 216,000. Urban growth rates of less than 500 percent for industrial cities in the nineteenth century were unusual, and growth of over 1,000 percent was frequent. The great migration from country to city could hardly have been less than 100 million and it changed Europe into a predominantly urban society.

It was more the rapid concentration of population than the mere increase that was responsible for many of Europe's most intractable social problems. Slums resulted from the need to build great quantities of housing rapidly as much as from the poverty of industrial workers. The new inhabitants' acute need for social services always outran the imagination and resources of both municipal and private agencies. Moreover, for the rural migrant the city itself was a continual experience in pain, loneliness, and anxiety. Being uprooted from familiar surroundings often produced lifelong cultural shock. The noise, the crowding, the dirt, the chicanery, the complications of a money economy, and the overwhelming need for education were parts of a new life that many industrial recruits never understood or mastered. They became urban casualties, demonstrating

NINETEENTH-CENTURY EUROPEAN EMIGRATION TO THE NEW WORLD

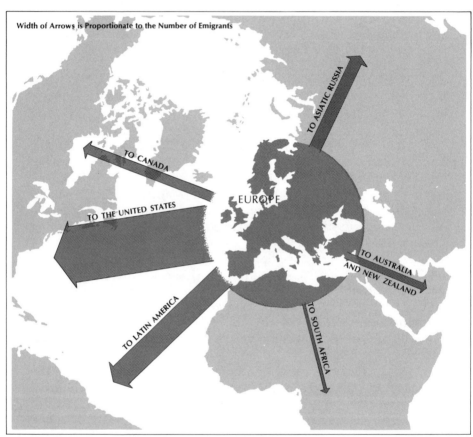

Width of Arrows is Proportionate to the Number of Emigrants

TO ASIATIC RUSSIA
TO CANADA
TO THE UNITED STATES
EUROPE
TO AUSTRALIA AND NEW ZEALAND
TO LATIN AMERICA
TO SOUTH AFRICA

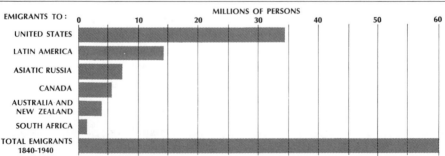

MILLIONS OF PERSONS

EMIGRANTS TO:						
	0	10	20	30	40	50	60
UNITED STATES						
LATIN AMERICA						
ASIATIC RUSSIA						
CANADA						
AUSTRALIA AND NEW ZEALAND						
SOUTH AFRICA						
TOTAL EMIGRANTS 1840-1940						

their illnesses in apathy, drunkenness, crime, insanity, suicide, or drugs.

European governments and cities never solved these problems or even understood them. The authorities passed laws, of course. There were laws regulating hours in factories, elaborating building codes, providing sewers and street lighting, and fighting crime and pollution. Most were poorly enforced, since they ran counter to the general climate of social and industrial exploitation. Moreover, cities did not have the tax resources to provide basic social services to the new migrants. Government bureaucracies were not organized to deal with permanent urban growth. Kings and ministers found it hard to preside over the democratization of the social order and impossible to help the urban casualties. Mobility and the freedom it brought were harsher masters than the ancient nobility. This was the overwhelming social fact of the nineteenth century.

Effects of Industrialization:
Social and Economic Thought

The ideologies men live by and die for did not escape the pervasive influence of industrialization. Once it became clear that the new means of production had powerful effects on how men lived, philosophers, theologians, historians, economists, and even politicians began to write and sometimes think about it. They divided themselves into two general schools, socialism and laissez-faire liberalism, each with innumerable subdivisions and interminable theological bickering, and each presenting to an eager public claims to most, if not all, of the truth.

The first into the field were the liberals, who preached a doctrine of minimal government intervention into economic matters. This view took the general name of laissez faire and was to appeal primarily to industrialists and other beneficiaries of the new wealth. Laissez-faire economic thought antedated the Industrial Revolution and began as a reaction to the stringent and complex regulations of mercantilism. As the Industrial Revolution progressively altered the forms of production, the theories of the liberal economists changed also. After 1815 liberal economists argued that government ought not to interfere in labor contracts; employer and employee should negotiate wages and hours themselves, as individuals. Unions, then, were as harmful to the economic laws of nature as government. This individual negotiation between owner and worker, the liberal economist admitted, was hard on labor, but it was part of the natural and free play of the labor market, and noninterference in the workings of the market for services was as much an icon to laissez-faire economists as free play in the market for goods.

After mid-century, mere repetition of the dogmas of laissez-faire economics was no longer sufficient to win uncritical public acceptance. The manifest misery and torment of the urban masses was too obvious to go utterly unnoticed. Victorian humanitarianism and the urge for social uplift demanded considerable government action. To humanitarian impulses must be added the growth of unions, which was fairly rapid after 1870. Therefore laissez-faire economics needed new intellectual defenses. These were provided by the notions of "social Darwinism," which were taken from the work of the great biologist. Social Darwinism held that the idea of "survival of the fittest" could be applied to the social sphere as well as nature. Ill-adapted or inferior species in nature died out; by analogy therefore ill-equipped, stupid, and ignorant individuals sank to the bottom of the social order—and belonged there. At the same time, the strongest and most intelligent rose to the top. Wealth, power, and position were only the natural reward for a natural superiority. Governments and unions should not put artificial supports under those too weak and helpless to stand on their own, nor should they interfere with the designs of the able. Doing so would only impoverish society as a whole by demoralizing the best without being able to help the worst. Supported by a sort of "social Calvinism," which held that the godly made money, social Darwinism became the basic economic philosophy of the rising bourgeoisie in the last decades before the Great War.

Not all the social and economic thought of industrializing Europe came from the rich. There was a second general stream, called socialism, which saw industrialization in terms of the exploitation of labor. Socialism had three basic strains: the first, utopian socialism; the second, orthodox Marxism; and the third, heresies and variations on a Marxist theme.

The years between 1815 and 1848 were the heyday of utopian socialism, a loose group of social and economic theorists whose penchant was creating ideal communities where their ideas could be tested. In spite of wide differences in detail, the utopian socialists did have certain general ideas in common. One was an abhorrence of violence; the socialist millennium would be brought about by persuasion. A second was great social compassion; the utopians were genuinely outraged at the conditions in which workers lived and labored, and they wished to change this. A third was a sort of missionary compulsion; the utopians believed in educating and converting the public. As a group, the utopian socialists were quite attractive, possessed of a great deal of common decency and real concern for the malfunctions of industrialization.

Marxian socialism, however, was much sterner stuff. Developed between 1848 and 1880 by Karl Marx and Friedrich Engels, Marxism was grounded in German dialectic philosophy and was touted as being completely "scientific." Dialectic philosophers maintained that change was the result of the conflict between two antagonistic forces, which resulted in compromise. Thus the thesis and its direct opposite, the antithesis, ultimately formed a new entity, the synthesis. In diagram:

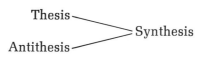

which itself becomes the new thesis. Marx translated this into social history. In looking at Europe since the Middle Ages, he found two of these dialectic cycles. In the first, the feudal nobility (thesis) and mercantile bourgeoisie (antithesis) had formed the synthesis, capitalism, which was the prevailing economic system. In the second, the industrial bourgeois (thesis) and the proletarian (antithesis) would form socialism as a synthesis. It had not yet happened, but it would. One of the great comforts of the Marxist dispensation to true believers was the assurance of inevitability.

Marx and his followers presented a number of reasons for this inevitable collapse of capitalism. There were many more workers than owners, and the number of workers was growing geometrically. The thesis, the industrial bourgeois, was becoming a smaller segment of society. Moreover, Marx argued that as businesses became larger, competition would become more savage and business cycles more ruinous. He also believed that as the number of workers grew and their oppression became harsher, their sense of grievance and class consciousness would grow, thus producing a true revolutionary element. The bourgeoisie held the reigns of governmental power, of course, and with it the police and army. These would be used to aid industry in its role of oppression. But it would not work; the enraged proletariat would rise up in a cataclysmic revolution, sweep the bourgeois capitalists into "the dustbin of history," and establish the classless, stateless socialist society.

There were weaknesses aplenty in this view of things. Absolutes were a dangerous form of historical analysis, and Marx's claims of inevitability fell into this category. There was no discernible reason why things must inevitably happen as Marx said they would, and in fact, they have not. "In politics," as Napoleon III remarked, "we never use the word 'never.'" Marx also thought the industrial system would produce poverty and increasing class separation. After the initial dislocations of urban and industrial growth, it did exactly the opposite. Industrialization was coining money and providing an unprecedented social mobility. Marx thought the bourgeoisie would grow smaller; in his lifetime it became enormous. Marx thought the worker would overthrow the bourgeoisie; he ended by joining him, a process discernible at mid-century by such observers as Napoleon III. Finally, Marx believed that man was primarily a social and economic being. As an explanation for human behavior this was all too simple; the existence of numerous bourgeois Marxists demonstrated that social class was not the mainspring of human motivation.

These weaknesses were more than overcome by some awesome strengths. More clearly than anyone else, Marx saw the impact of technology on production. He understood the differences between factory and shop and saw the growing economic helplessness of the worker and the clerk, who were utterly dependent on their wages. And he saw that political democracy, the vote alone, was insufficient to overcome the inherent power of accumulated capital in a private-sector economy.

The greatest strength of Marxism, however, was not Marx's analysis, but his uncanny knowledge of the moral weakness of capitalism. Capitalism was overwhelmingly selfish, admitting no higher value than profits for the owners. There were no canons of social utility, no strictures against polluting the environment, no obligations to protect the health and safety of workers on the job, no requirement that men must be paid a decent wage. Any scheme or practice that made money was good, anything that made more money was better. Capitalism did not recognize any such thing as the public interest. Marx claimed that businessmen would sell poisoned meat, shoddy shoes, and inflammable baby blankets without compunction. Most Europeans agreed with him. Events proved him a prophet. The critical weakness of capitalism was moral and Marx was like an Old Testament prophet denouncing sin and corruption and crying for justice. He was heard and believed, and he was right.

The power of Marx's vision soon made Marxism the standard brand of socialist thought. Utopian socialism was simply blotted out. Alternative dispensations, such as anarchism or the syndicalist calls for general strikes and random industrial violence, sadly lacked Marxism's moral grandeur. Like all religions, however, Marxism did not escape the siren song of heresy. Many of the faithful abandoned the Marxist prophecy of a violent social revolution in which the workers would butcher the bourgeoisie. Particularly within the trade-union movement, new leaders became disenchanted with the Marxist emphasis on revolution. Wage increases, social legislation, collective bargaining, and reduction of working hours seemed more important and immediate than the barricades. By 1890 the workers' share of the national wealth was rising, socialist parties were growing rapidly, and revolution seemed less necessary or desirable. These ideas were given organized form by the German socialist Eduard Bernstein, who called his theories revisionism.

As workers' incomes grew and as socialist parties became more powerful and respectable, revisionism grew with it. It became the prevailing philosophy of socialist parties in all industrialized states by the Great War, while there was a sharp decline in revolutions both attempted and successful. But the call for revolution was never louder. Orthodox Marxist stump preachers sweated and bellowed in thousands of dirty halls, exhorting the proletariat to throw off their chains and take over everything. They never did. Workers confined their revolutionary impulses to the murderous Marxist litany, which they did not really believe. Under cover of repeated calls for a bloody apocalypse, there began a great *embourgeoisement* of workers. Like everyone else, they simply wanted to get rich.

VICTORIAN EUROPE

European society was not static during the long years of the Victorian peace. Europeans enjoyed a vast and delightful increase in wealth. There was much hustle and movement as millions left the farm for cities and other millions went to America. It was a time of new and strange notions—Darwinism, antislavery, ideas of social responsibility, democracy, secularism, and perhaps strangest of all, the view that women should have the same rights and privileges as men. At the beginning of the Victorian era, revolutionary creeds frightened people; at the end, Freudian concepts of sexuality revolted them. European society was expanding in imperial adventures, which invariably succeeded. There was optimism and enthusiasm and a vast assumption that the world was progressing, a vigorous belief that the future was going to be better than the past. It flourished and grew until 1914, when the hopes, ideals, treasures, and freedoms of Victorian Europe dissolved in a nightmare of blood and iron. But the memory has lingered, and in many ways the Victorian era has come to be remembered as the "good years."

During the revolutionary years of 1848 and 1849, European monarchs and ministers had fought hard against the demon of democracy and had won a temporary triumph. They shot or exiled their foes, shut up their newspapers, turned off democratic orations, and reestablished a seemly autocracy in the world. But democracy was a hydra that could not be cut down, and new recruits rose to fill the places of the martyrs of 1848. Within a decade, democratic fervor was clearly on the rise, and those same kings and ministers who had cried repression were now seeking to accommodate themselves to a new age of democratic government. Political liberty and equality before the law were two ideas whose time had come.

Reform in Great Britain

In Great Britain the reform and democratization of government and society in the years after 1848 proceeded much as they had before. Measures were proposed, discussed, and finally passed by Parliament. The process sometimes took years, occasionally decades, but the ground rules for change and inevitability of reform were understood by nearly everyone, and there was a minimum of revolutionary agitation, confined mostly to Ireland.

An old issue, electoral reform, regained the center stage in the aftermath of the depression brought on by the American Civil War. In 1867 the Conservative prime minister, Benjamin Disraeli, brought in the second Reform Bill. It extended the suffrage in towns to all householders paying the poor rate and all renters paying £10 a year. In the countryside, landowners who held property worth £5 a year and tenants paying £12 a year rent could vote. The districts were also reapportioned. All boroughs of less than ten thousand lost a member. Manchester, Leeds, Liverpool, and Birmingham were each given a third member, and twenty-five members were scattered among the counties. Disraeli's bill doubled the electorate from one to two million and altered the balance of power to favor the industrial cities. As a reward, he was soundly defeated in the November 1868 elections by the Liberal party led by William Gladstone.

The election of 1868 was strictly a party contest—Liberals against Conservatives, each with a recognized party leader in Parliament, with established positions on the salient issues of the times, with the power and willingness to maintain party discipline among the members, and a recognized internal ladder of ascent from backbencher to ministry. With the struggles between Gladstone and Disraeli, two leaders of the first rank who dominated the electorate as they did their parties, the trends toward party government in Great Britain emerged in their modern form. After 1868 elections would be party affairs.

In the years between the Reform Bill of 1867 and World War I, British politics was dominated by the Irish question and social problems incident to industrialization. The Irish question had two facets —the issue of independence for Ireland and the problems of British landlords and Irish tenant farmers. Home rule was strongly advocated by William Gladstone, leader of the Liberal party, but he was not able to carry his members with him, and Liberal ministries in 1886 and 1894 fell on the issue. After the failure of home rule, both parties turned to problems of land and tenancy. Between 1885 and 1903 five bills passed, establishing funds for Irish tenants to purchase their land. This policy proved fairly successful. Rural violence in Ireland declined after 1895, and there was a steady transfer of land to the Irish peasantry, who wanted land more than independence. An economic policy replaced a political one.

In dealing with the problems of industrialization, British governments also followed the traditional methods of reform. There was no wholesale reorganization of British institutions and laws, but rather a steady flow of individual reforms. Parliament passed bills establishing a system of public education, introducing the secret ballot, reforming the court system, and extending sanitary and building codes. Most social legislation, however, waited until British unions were sufficiently organized to exert political power. Not until the election of 1905, when the Labour party returned twenty-nine members, did the pace of social legislation accelerate. Parliament passed a pension law (1909), a workmen's compensation act (1906), a national health insurance system (1911), a minimum wage law (1912), and a trade disputes bill (1906), which freed unions from lawsuits resulting from the acts of their members. The Lloyd George budget of 1909 was equally important. It attempted to shift the burden of taxation to the wealthy, and it was the beginning of the effort to redistribute British income.

When the Great War came, in 1914, it cut like a guillotine through the fabric of debate and decision, ending reforms and replacing them with the incredible problems of modern conflict. Moreover, the war upset the delicate balance between cabinet and Parliament, tipping the scales heavily in favor of the cabinet. Thus the war not only ended debate on Victorian issues, but also quietly swallowed the Victorian parliamentary system.

French Democracy Under the Third Republic

In France, the other great nineteenth-century European democracy, the process of liberalization was far more traumatic than in Great Britain. The Third Republic was established only after defeat in the Franco-Prussian War, and it had to overcome strong monarchist opposition to survive. A sizable antidemocratic opposition existed throughout the entire Victorian era and was actively engaged in trying to subvert the government by propaganda, through elections, and occasionally by attempted coups. Antidemocratic groups included the monarchists on the right and various gangs of Marxists on the left. Their presence plagued the government, and ministers in France ruled with one eye on their programs and the other closely fixed on the antics of the ideological opposition.

Since France lacked a stable consensus on the proper methods of government, democracy came to be associated with a fairly precise set of political goals instead of becoming a political form. The democratic parties of the political center were generally anticlerical, opposed to direct taxation, in favor of a high tariff, and generally hostile to unions and strikes but solicitous of the welfare of peasants and small shopkeepers. French democrats were clearly in favor of a free press, reluctantly in support of personal and civil liberties, and enthusiastically addicted to private vice and license. The deputies to the National Assembly during the Third Republic were from the small towns and villages of the countryside, and they were solidly and respectably middle class. Their political system tolerated a huge dose of wire pulling, logrolling, and outright graft, corruption, and favoritism. Deputies grew unaccountably rich from a tour in the Chamber of Deputies, and graft was a constant and demeaning companion of French government. But the system worked; it beat back political and ideological challenges from both right and left, it brought prosperity to France, it nurtured a superb culture, and it fulfilled the economic and social wishes of the large majority of Frenchmen.

The French National Assembly did not have the solemn dignity of the British Parliament, nor did the deputies exhibit the sober dedication to good government, social reform, economic progress, and fair play that so characterized the Victorian Members. The National Assembly, with its multiplicity of parties, was less well organized. Every government was a coalition, subject to instant oblivion by minor parties and factions, and the average life span of a ministry was only a few months. The proceedings were often chaotic, and personal jealousies were as important as issues. Speeches took the place of debate, and genuine reform was hard to get.

Change was needed, of course, and the succession of ministries sometimes faced up to it. The continuing issues were social reform, ensuring the workers a just share of the national wealth, the relationship of church and state, antidemocratic opposition, and constant political corruption. In dealing with the Roman Catholic Church, French cabinets swung slowly toward an anticlerical position. The church's preference for a monarchy was a major factor in this political evolution. The deputies were more reluctant to deal with social issues, however. Unions were not legalized until 1884, and the government was unwilling to pass accident, sickness, or unemployment insurance. Unlike Great Britain, the election of Socialist deputies did not increase social legislation, for doctrinal disagreements on the left and the chimera of the general strike prevented the effective use of labor's growing political power.

Corruption and scandal were also difficult burdens for the cabinets of the Third Republic. In the Dreyfus affair, which rocked the political, military, and judicial system of the republic to its core, France endured the most stupendous scandal of the Victorian era. It began with an indebted officer and rampant anti-Semitism within the French general staff. Eighteen-ninety-four was a depression year, and Major Walsin-Esterhazy, a roué and a crook whose main investments were in a London brothel, was feeling the pinch. Needing money, he became a spy for the Germans. In due course the treason was discovered and blamed by the general staff on its Jewish officer, Captain Alfred Dreyfus. Tried in secret, he was sent to Devils Island. In 1897 his brother, Mathieu, found information exonerating Dreyfus, made it public, demanded explanations, found supporters in the National Assembly, and created a gorgeous scandal. The novelist Émile Zola interested himself in the Dreyfus case and published an open letter accusing the president of France and officers of the general staff of deliberately framing Dreyfus. Amidst immense furor and publicity, Zola was tried in the winter of 1898, and he swung public opinion to his side. The general staff grew panicky, forged some new evidence against Dreyfus, and then presented it in a second trial of the Jewish captain. The evidence was so patently fraudulent that the ministry collapsed. A pro-Dreyfus government replaced it, pardoned, promoted, and decorated Dreyfus, cashiered the officers involved, and moved against Dreyfus' most vocal enemies. Among these were monarchists, ultraconservatives, and the Roman Catholic Church. It had taken ten years, but the French government had finally done the honorable thing. The Dreyfus affair, which so characterized the sordid side of the Third Republic, ended by ennobling it.

The Drift Toward Democracy in Central Europe

In central Europe, democracy also made gains during the Victorian period, although appearances in Germany and Italy often outran the democratic reality. In Germany, Prince Bismarck, after victory in the Franco-Prussian War, had carefully written the constitution for the new German Empire to provide the trappings of liberal democracy while denying the substance. The Reichstag, lower house of the German legislature, was elected by universal suffrage, but the upper house was appointed by the princes of the German states. Legislation required assent of both houses. The executive was even less amenable to public opinion. The emperor was also king of Prussia, and the chancellor was responsible to him alone, not the legislature. No matter what happened in the Reichstag, the chancellor remained as long as he had the confidence of the emperor. The Reichstag's only real power was in deciding the budget and voting taxes, but the experience of the 1860s had shown that the government would not hesitate to set taxes on its own if the deputies proved balky. Imperial Germany was to be an extension of autocratic Prussia.

In spite of Bismarck's constitution, however, Germany evolved steadily toward political democracy, although it never achieved the genuine democratic spirit of France or Great Britain. Certainly no one in power, either in 1871 or 1914, wanted a democratic state. The political system was supposed to stay firmly in the emperor's grasp. But even Bismarck was careful to win major votes in the Reichstag and propose popular legislation. His successors, lacking his prestige, were more dependent on a Reichstag majority, and the election of 1907 was held because the chancellor, Prince Bülow, lost a major Reichstag vote. In an effort to win a Reichstag majority, various governments passed a comprehensive system of pension, insurance, and unemployment laws, beginning as early as 1883. The liberal government denied by the constitution was slowly emerging through the force of public opinion.

In spite of the progress of democracy, there were many elements of autocracy left in imperial Germany. The ministry never became formally responsible to the Reichstag, nor did the emperor relinquish his constitutional authority. The armed forces remained more responsive to the crown than to the people. The bureaucracy remained a pillar of imperial authority. Nationalism remained a far more powerful ideology than liberalism, reflecting the events of 1848 and 1849. Democratic realities in Germany fell short of appearances.

Italy had been unified during the same period as Germany, but under somewhat different circumstances. Count Cavour was a convinced liberal, who once remarked that the dullest chamber was superior to the most brilliant antechamber. Italy inherited the liberal constitution of Sardinia and the multiparty system with it.

Coalition government and the temptations of power and office were two continuing problems for Italy during the Victorian era. Multiparty cabinets were at the mercy of petty jealousy and intrigue, and governments found it almost impossible to adhere to a definite program of action. The deputies themselves were generally corrupt and vulnerable to ministerial pressures, much like their colleagues in France. Party discipline was loose, and the art of government was primarily one of manipulation.

Beyond the purely political problems of corruption and factionalism, Italy faced two huge issues: the relations between church and state and the problem of dealing with social change. As in France, continuing papal hostility forced the government into an anticlerical posture, and the papal residence in Rome made conditions that much more delicate. Social problems were even more serious, and neither deputies nor ministers were particularly anxious to face them. Southern Italy, the *mezzogiorno*, was incredibly poor and backward, while in the north, urbanization and industrialization were proceeding at a fairly rapid pace. The government did nothing for the southern peasants, who remained virtual serfs, nor did it deal effectively with the *Mafiosi*, who formed a shadow government in the *mezzogiorno*. Nor did the various cabinets face the issues of industrialization. Parliament passed no insurance, pension, or unemployment laws, and the deputies persisted in considering unions as revolutionary societies and strikes as insurrections to be met by the army. This political *immobilismo* was a bad preparation for the future.

In eastern Europe, democratization lagged behind even Italy and Germany. In part this lag was due to nationalism, which dominated eastern politics and made the numerous ethnic minorities potential foci for revolutions. A second factor impeding democratization was the slow progress of industrialization and the absence of its accompanying social mobility. The traditional class structure of the Old Regime persisted until the Great War.

The substance of oligarchy or autocracy was retained east of Venice, but the forms of democracy proved irresistible. In Austria the parliament reflected national conflicts between Poles, Germans, and Czechs. A stable majority was impossible, and after 1897 ministries governed by decree. Things were much the same in Hungary, where political leaders worked to turn the new generation of all nationalities into Hungarians. As in Austria, social reform was

THE BALKANS, 1878–1914

nearly nonexistent. In the dual monarchy parliamentary life was only a facade. The empire was held together by the army, the civil service, and the Emperor Franz Josef. The smaller states of the east—Greece, Serbia, Rumania, and Bulgaria—were basically autocracies. Murders, banditry, coups d'etat, insurrections, and overwhelming corruption punctuated the lives of the people. Democratic forms were simply eyewash for absolutism.

By the Great War, democracy had become the accepted and legitimate way to govern—or appear to govern. Monarchs everywhere had extended at least a formal acceptance of parliaments, and socialist parties were rapidly succumbing to rampant revisionism. Europe's rapidly expanding middle classes found liberal parliamentary democracy exactly suited to their political and economic needs. Cabinet ministers discovered that laws passed by parliament had greater moral authority than mere decrees. In the century after Waterloo, democracy and industrialization seemed to march together. They have not always done so since.

The Modernization of Russia: 1855–1914

Russia did not suffer unrest during the revolutions of 1848, and Tsar Nicolas I and his ministers congratulated themselves. They had insulated Russia against the pernicious doctrines of the West, which had lately brought so many proud monarchies into disrepair. Isolation had its drawbacks, however, for while the West was industrializing, Russia was not. Yet Russia needed the new technology of war and industry, and the cost would be a disruption of the prevailing Russian social patterns. Serfdom, social privilege, and local governments would have to be reformed in the light of a modern industrial society.

Reform came with Alexander II, who assumed the throne in 1855. He knew that there must be change if Russia were to remain a great power and avoid a revolution. Therefore he proposed emancipation of the serfs and on March 3, 1861, issued the emancipation edict. It gave personal freedom to all serfs, and the lord lost his judicial authority over them. The peasants also received about half the arable land, though the lords retained most of the pasture and woods. The lords were paid for this land by state treasury bonds, which the peasants were to refund in redemption payments lasting for forty-nine years. The land did not go directly to individual peasants, however. It was given to the mir, or village commune, which then divided it up among the peasants according to size of families. The mir was to redivide the land every decade or so. Finally, the mir was collectively responsible for the peasants' redemption payments. While the peasant was no longer a serf, he was not yet free.

The emancipation of the serfs was a huge change in Russian rural life, and local government had to change with it. In 1864 the old system of class courts was abolished, and a judicial ladder based on the French model was put in its place. The tsar also began limited local self-government. Boards, or zemstvos, were established with the bourgeoisie, nobility, and peasants represented. Zemstvos were given responsibility for roads, bridges, schools, hospitals, and the like and were allowed to levy taxes to support them. Both of these reforms proved a huge success and did a good deal to ease the severe transition from serfdom to limited independence.

Emancipation had not solved all problems. It left enough land to the lord so that most peasants did not have enough to support their families. Those who could not farm well enough to add to their plots were slowly squeezed into the class of landless laborers or forced to emigrate to cities. Thus great class differences grew among peasants, based on the social and economic power of landowning. The able peasants, known as kulaks, grew to dominate rural society. They obviously did not want the mir redividing the land every decade and were frequently powerful enough to prevent it. Hated by lord and peasant alike, the kulaks prospered, favored by the government's need to export grain for foreign exchange. Emancipation exposed Russia's chronic rural overpopulation. Thus the emancipation brought change, technological progress, and increased production to the Russian countryside. But the price was high, and the process was incomplete when the Great War came.

Russian ministers were also concerned with industrialization. Under the direction of the finance minister, Count Sergei Witte, the government began to foster the growth of industry. A high protective tariff was passed, and heavy investments were made in opening the Donets iron and coal fields. An immense railroad system was constructed, tying the country together economically for the first time. Heavy borrowing abroad provided most of the capital for these initial capital investments.

Tsar Alexander intended his reforms to modernize Russian society, but he did not want any Western notions of democracy, civil liberties, equality before the law, or socialism. The autocratic political system had to remain more or less intact. Repression, however, could not keep these subversive ideas out of Russia. The liberals wanted a Western constitution, and the radicals, who quickly became terrorists and revolutionaries, wanted a reorganization of the fabric of society. On March 13, 1881, terrorists killed the tsar. Alexander III, the new tsar, immediately began a regime of severe police repression, but revolutionary agitation spread. In 1898 the Social Democratic Party, the Russian affiliate of the Marxist Second International, was founded. In 1903 the Union of Liberation organized and became the focal point of liberal opposition to tsarist autocracy. When the government faltered in 1904, the opposition was ready.

On February 8, 1904, hostilities broke out in Manchuria between Russia and Japan. The Japanese won a stunning series of decisive victories. So great was the loss of prestige that the government began to stumble. A zemstvo congress in St. Petersburg demanded a constitution, and on January 22, 1905, a procession of peaceful factory workers led by Father Gapon was massacred outside the winter palace. Bloody Sunday was the signal for a series of riots and strikes. Tsar Nicolas II announced hasty concessions. He intended to convoke a "consultative assembly," he was decreeing religious toleration, and he would cancel part of the peasants' redemption payments. These measures did not work. In October there was a general strike, which paralyzed the country. The tsar then agreed to a constitution in the October Manifesto, and this concession split the united opposition of moderates and radicals. Russia had avoided, though barely, a real revolution.

After the events of 1905 the government began to face its problems. The tsar restricted the suffrage so that the Duma, or parliament, would not be too critical of royal policies. An able man, Peter Stolypin, was appointed prime minister. He was anxious to retain the parliamentary system and hoped to use it for needed reforms that would gradually undermine the revolutionary movement. Stolypin saw the main problem as the peasants. He abolished the *mir*, allowing peasants to hold their land as private property. This was a clear victory for the kulaks. But Stolypin had not forgotten the landless peasant. He opened up territory in Siberia and moved more than a million peasants to virgin land. He established banks to help peasants buy land, canceled the remaining redemption payments, and allowed peasants to consolidate scattered strips into coherent farms. Stolypin felt that the government should base itself less on the nobility and more on the support of an independent peasantry.

On the eve of the Great War, Russia was a land struggling toward Westernization and plagued by deep social fissures. The Stolypin plan and Witte's program of industrialization represented attempts to accomplish in Russia what had already taken place in England, Germany, and America. But these efforts only masked underlying problems in Russian society. The landless peasants were a constant rural problem, and the factories could not absorb them. Workers were inadequately paid, and the crown regarded their unions as subversive. The terrorist organizations had not been destroyed after 1905, but had merely been driven further underground. The tsar's bureaucracy was one of the most inefficient in Europe and was incurably hostile to the Duma. The tsar was weak and stupid. Neither the government nor society was prepared for the pressures of the Great War, to say nothing of those of defeat.

Organized Religion and the Secular World: 1850–1914

The ideology and legislation of the French Revolution had not settled the difficult issues of the proper place of religion in the world or of how a peaceful relationship between church and state might come to be. Nor had the apostles of reaction done so after 1815. Before 1789 questions of belief, skepticism, or dissent, when referred to public authorities, had always been settled on the side of belief. There were laws against atheism or recusancy. Kings regarded religious devotion as a good thing. The church was a state church, and its chief clerics were appointed by the monarch. The era of revolutions threw the relations of church and state into turmoil. In the nineteenth century, then, churches faced the delicate task of redefining their relationships with the state, while the faith itself labored against socialism, secularism, and Darwin. The Victorian era was a time of groping and stumbling toward a new way, which the Italian prime minister, Count Cavour, called a "free church in a free state."

During the revolutions of 1848 European governments had been toppled so easily that their successors sought ways to strengthen the ties between king and subject. Many turned to the church for support. The old alliance between throne and altar was renewed after the gigantic red scare of 1848 to 1849. Monarchs who had forgotten now remembered how conservative priests could be. Governments that had gently scoffed at the multinational Roman Catholic Church veered completely about in these dangerous days of nationalism. Education, which had been slipping increasingly into the hands of village Voltaires, now would be returned to the clergy, who would preach the refurbished virtues of discipline, order, obedience, and piety. Political currents after 1848 favored an increase in authority and esteem given the Roman Catholic Church.

The new attitudes were quickly apparent. In the France of the Second Republic, conservatives who dominated the National Assembly passed the Falloux Law, which greatly increased Catholic control over French education. In Austria the new emperor, Franz Josef, signed a concordat with the papacy, giving the Austrian church extensive powers in education. In Spain, too, fear of the radical masses led to a new concordat wtih Rome; the Catholic religion was recognized as the only acceptable faith, and the Spanish church gained great powers in education and censorship.

Not only did the state move toward partnership with Rome after 1848, but the church itself began to strengthen its doctrine against the modern enemies of liberalism, nationalism, and social change. The main papal blast against the Victorian world came in 1864, when Piux IX issued the "Syllabus of Errors." In it he condemned most of the main currents of Enlightenment and nineteenth-century thought. Article 15 stated that it was false to believe that "every man is free to embrace and profess the religion he shall believe true"; article 42 said that the canon law was superior to the civil law; article 45 claimed for the Roman church "the entire direction of public schools"; article 55 denied that the church and state should be separated; article 79 denied "civil liberty of every mode of worship"; and the last article, 80, denied that the pope ought "to reconcile himself to, and agree with, progress, liberalism, and civilization as lately introduced." Finally, the "Syllabus of Errors" repeated previous denunciations of "Socialism, Communism, Secret Societies, and Biblical Societies."

The culmination of Pius IX's efforts to strengthen his church and define its dogma came at the Vatican Council of 1870. Here Pius proclaimed the dogma of papal infallibility, which stated that the pope, when speaking *ex cathedra,* was infallible in matters of faith and morals by reason of his apostolic position. This dogma completed the creation of a papal monarchy, freeing the pope from any dependence on councils and reaffirming his tremendous power over the hierarchy. Infallibility of the pope effectively equated the papal opinion with the Catholic opinion.

In the years after Vatican I and the Franco-Prussian War, European governments gradually hardened their attitude toward the Roman Catholic Church. There was a marked recrudescence of the old suspicion and anticlericalism of the Enlightenment. Problems began immediately in the kingdom of Italy, which annexed the last remnants of the Papal States in 1870. Rome became the new Italian capital, and the government moved to define its relations with the papacy. The Law of Papal Guarantees declared the person of the pope inviolable, guaranteed his royal prerogatives and full freedom in the exercise of his office, granted full diplomatic status to ambassadors at the Vatican, and recognized the Vatican City as a state. Pius IX would not accept this; he declared himself the "prisoner of the Vatican," refused to recognize the kingdom of Italy, and ordered all Catholics to boycott Italian political life. Consequently, in the years between 1870 and 1914 the government usually had an anticlerical tinge.

The French reaction to the "Syllabus of Errors" and papal infallibility was also severe, though delayed by the need to recover from defeat in the Franco-Prussian War. In 1880 nonauthorized Roman Catholic religious orders were given three months to apply for governmental authorization and the Jesuits were expelled outright. Almost 9,000 men and over 100,000 nuns were affected by the law. The nuns were not expelled, but the men were, and over 250 religious houses were closed down. Although the law was not completely enforced, it remained on the books ready for future use.

The associations law was followed by one on education. The primary education law of 1882 established free, compulsory public schools for children from six to thirteen years of age. Religious instruction was permitted only under restricted circumstances, and the schoolbooks were changed to eliminate the Catholic catechism. Again, the law was not enforced with all possible rigor, and the secularization of French primary schools was the work of a generation, not a year. But the trend was clear. The state was increasingly suspicious of the church.

The great assault on institutional Catholicism came after the Dreyfus affair, with the 1901 law of religious associations. This repeated earlier legislation forbidding religious orders that did not have government approval. In 1904 religious orders were flatly forbidden to teach, French diplomatic relations with the Vatican were broken, and, a year later, the Napoleonic concordat of 1802 was denounced, thus separating church and state. Freedom of conscience and worship was guaranteed, and the church no longer had any claim on state support. The results of this drastic law were not surprising to shrewd observers. The church used separation to begin a massive campaign for support, both moral and financial, from French Catholics. The genuinely religious rallied to their church, but they proved to be a smaller minority than the bishops had expected. Most Frenchmen remained indifferent and tended to view their church more as a political institution than as a part of their faith.

Positive Catholic attempts to deal with nineteenth-century secular society and the growing hostility of national states came only with the papal encyclical *Rerum novarum* in 1891. In it Leo XIII tried to apply traditional Christian principles to the problems of an industrial society. The pope declared workers to have natural rights and employers to have a moral obligation toward their employees. The welfare of the workers was not to be left solely to the market-place or to the struggles of union bargaining; it was a primary duty of both state and church to improve the lot of workers and modify the rigors of capitalism. Leo XIII coupled this declaration with a denunciation of socialism and a strong defense of private property, but he reiterated that property carried heavy moral and economic obligations. Thus, where Pius had breathed total defiance of Victorian civilization, Leo brought a spirit of collaboration, emphasizing those areas of life where the church had a special message. Moreover, Leo abandoned the doctrinal political conversatism of his predecessor, stating that the form of government was less important than its actions in caring for its citizens. *Rerum novarum* was a beginning.

The Roman Catholic Church in the Victorian era suffered from two interconnected ailments—the ineffective political policies of the papacy and the growth of secularism and religious indifference. About religious indifference the church could do little. Politics was another matter. By the 1860s the Old Regime alliance between throne and altar was definitely dead, though the reigning pope did not see it. Thus the papacy became involved in political issues it was ill-prepared to handle. The twists of daily politics obscured and compromised the spiritual mission of the Roman Catholic Church. No matter who carried the political debates, the church lost. Cavour's hope for a "free church in a free state" was buried under the hostilities of national and political rivalries.

Protestant churches suffered from a different group of problems, but they were no less severe or debilitating. Protestant churches fell victim to the intellectual currents of the Victorian age. Evolution brought the major Protestant crisis, dividing Calvinist churches into two warring halves—those who believed literally in the garden of Eden and those who put greater faith in the testimony of scientists. A second, and related, issue involved what might be called modernism—whether the church should concern itself only with the salvation of its faithful members or be a witness for social justice in the world.

There had been intimations about evolution before 1859—when Charles Darwin published *The Origin of Species*—but these had not reached the general public. When the general public *did* hear that man had evolved from apes and that, indeed, every present species had evolved from a previous one, such untoward notions were shocking and revolting to pious Victorian citizens and were declared by Protestant pastors to be in contradiction to the revealed word of God as contained in the Book of Genesis. But Protestants were trapped by their doctrine of belief based solely on Scripture. They now had to abandon a literal interpretation of the Bible or fight the hideous Darwinist heresy. Most churches split over the issue. Fundamentalism became a name for a literal belief in the Garden of Eden. Socially, the fundamentalist sects and congregations were concentrated in rural areas, among the less educated, and among folk who were hostile to industrial civilization. The fundamentalists held their faith with a savage intensity, and the taunts of their liberal brethren only strengthened them in it. There was nothing vague or indecisive about fundamentalism; it was a powerful and colorful religion, and no one held it lightly or with indifference.

Liberal Protestants, those who came to terms with Darwin and his data, were a different breed. Having enough education to recognize the futility of denying scientific fact, liberal Protestants abandoned literal belief in the Bible as a necessary part of their faith. The Scriptures might be viewed symbolically or historically and might be considered an allegory or a poem as well as divine revelation. Such latitude in interpreting the Scriptures was in accord with the advancing pace of scientific discovery, but it weakened the faith. Various forms of deism, or pantheism, or "Christian humanism" afflicted liberal Protestant churches, which were unable to distinguish those who believed the traditional doctrine from those who viewed it symbolically. Liberal Protestant congregations became fashionable among the industrial bourgeoisie, who built imposing edifices in the cities, but their faith seemed pale and withered beside that of their fundamentalist brethren. All too often, liberal Protestantism was a guise for religious indifference.

Liberal Protestant churches were also riddled by disagreement over social issues. Lacking the fervor of the fundamentalists, liberal Protestants frequently turned to social witness and action. They tried to succor the poor, ameliorate the lot of industrial workers, and eradicate the worst effects of slums. They pushed for public education; improved sanitation, penal reform, and humane treatment for the mentally ill; and advocated family planning and the like. While the fundamentalists concentrated their ire on "demon rum" and whooped for temperance, liberal Protestants covered a much wider range of social uplift. Involvement in such projects, however, meant taking part in the savage political struggles over what was then called "the social question." It meant asking for taxes on property and industry to pay for social improvements; it meant calling for laws to restrict the powers of factory owners and managers. And it meant assaults on slum lords, corrupt urban politicians, and complacent bourgeoisie. Many of these were members of fashionable liberal Protestant congregations, and they vigorously opposed the social gospel, claiming that the church should stick to saving the souls of such as wished it and not meddle in economic or political issues. Such quarrels split churches as effectively as did the demon Darwin, for the industrial bourgeoisie, although they might be indifferent to the faith, were mightily concerned with profits. Many liberal churches found industrialization as hard to deal with as the fundamentalists did.

In retrospect we can look back on the Victorian era as a time uncongenial to churches or religious doctrine. Scientific and historical inquiry played havoc with established dogma and habits of religious thought. Unqualified resistance to modernity made churches appear to be the sworn enemies of progress and enlightenment. Appalling political blunders made the religious establishment seem the enemy of most organized governments and many schemes for national salvation. Socialists were convinced that organized religion was opposed to workers' rights and were quite successful in convincing their constituents of this. Moreover, churches ignored the great challenges of industrialism to religion. No real effort was made to recast theological systems in the light of industrial and scientific civilization. Little energy went into ameliorating or dramatizing the appalling social changes that industrialization involved. The church did not take the side of the poor, exploited, and unprotected. Rather, church leaders engaged in various evasions. Protestants tore themselves apart over Darwin, Roman Catholics fought meaningless, degrading, and petty political battles, and the Anglican Church retreated into a wistful and romantic veneration of medieval England called the Gothic Revival. If Victorian civilization was hard on organized religion, the main responsibility fell on the churches themselves, which either evaded or ignored the real issues of the times.

Conclusions

Victorian society, from Great Britain to Russia, was the first to regard change as a permanent condition. Previously, men had envisioned society as static, with the ways of the fathers appropriate for the sons. In the Victorian era such attitudes began to disappear. Industrial change, intellectual movements, political reforms, social mobility, all combined to erode the notion of stasis. "Everything," as a Briton smugly remarked, "now . . . wore the face of speed and dispatch."

Moreover, contemporaries believed these changes were definitely good. Things were getting better all the time. Industrialization was making Victorian society more affluent. Society was becoming more open and free. Upward mobility was becoming the rule rather than the exception. Men lived longer, and doctors were at last curing more patients than they killed. In the years before the Great War the benefits of progress were reaching workers and peasants, who were the last in line.

There were defects, of course. Secularism had not led to universal religious tolerance. During the nineteenth century, European attitudes toward the Jews invariably justified the cynical aphorism that anti-Semitism "consists of hating the Jews more than is necessary." Nor had society outgrown deep social hatreds. Terrorism and anarchist bombs were a constant feature of Victorian politics. Nationalism deeply divided the peoples of Europe. Militarism and the threat of war hung over Victorian Europe like the shroud it proved to be. Even so, Victorians looking at their society thought it was good and, looking ahead, thought the future would be even better.

EUROPEAN IMPERIALISM

The first wave of European imperialism, which had begun in the fifteenth century, fell victim to the era of revolution between 1760 and 1830. First in the thirteen colonies, then in Haiti, and finally in Latin America, colonials threw off their dependent status, defeating the mother country in pitched battle. European statesmen learned the disconcerting truth that colonial peoples, even former slaves, could beat the mightiest European military forces, including the British navy and Napoleonic army. Colonial domination, a subject of bitter and prolonged European warfare from 1550 to 1763, no longer seemed so desirable. Interest waned as expenses and colonial insubordination grew. Between 1820 and 1850 European concern over colonial adventure reached its nadir.

Remission of European interest in dominating the rest of the world was short-lived, however. Demands for expansion began again after the revolutions of 1848. The new wave of imperialism started in Russia and France, with Great Britain joining and quickly dominating the colonial race. In the 1880s Italy and Germany became colonial powers, followed by Japan, the United States, and Belgium, while Portugal, Spain, and the Netherlands tried to hold what colonies they already had. By World War I all the Western powers except Austria-Hungary had embarked on an imperialist course, and only China and Latin America had escaped division into colonies. In 1914 the West owned most of the world and dominated all of it.

This second wave of European expansion differed somewhat from the first. The empires formed between 1450 and 1763 were largely in America; Africa, India, and Indonesia were secondary spheres of activity. Europeans emigrated to the colonies in vast numbers in the early modern period and undertook a systematic extermination or enslavement of the natives. The original cultures in America, southern Africa, and the West Indies were destroyed to make room for European colonists, and vast numbers of blacks were imported from Africa as slave labor to support a European civilization. In the nineteenth century this pattern was not followed. Europeans enlarged their military superiority over the traditional cultures in Asia and Africa and were able to subdue them almost at will; but no mass extermination or enslavement followed. Nineteenth-century colonialists established small industrial or commercial stations to exploit the colony and military garrisons to hold it down. Both imperial eras, however, were part of the same immense expansion of European civilization.

There were several general causes for nineteenth-century im-

EUROPEAN COLONIZATION OF AFRICA, 1914

perialism. The first of these was the general love of exploration and adventure. The nineteenth century was a great age of travel literature and adventure stories. Charles Darwin and Rudyard Kipling, as well as adventurers and explorers, found a huge audience for their books, stories, and lectures. Livingstone became a European hero, as did Stanley when he found him. General Charles George Gordon, who led the "Ever-Victorious Army" against the T'ai P'ing rebels and was slaughtered by the Mahdi in 1885, became a contemporary legend, and his death was a factor in the fall of the Gladstone government. Romantic and dangerous exploits thrilled the industrial bourgeoisie of Europe, and the many additions to geographical knowledge seemed a desirable thing. Where the explorers and adventurers went, the flag was sure to follow. It might take a generation, but the engineers everywhere received government support for their demands to organize and profit from the newly explored lands.

Also figuring in the imperial expansion were the activities of Christian missionaries. Both Catholic and Protestant faiths engaged in immense efforts to convert the pagan, infidel, or Oriental to what they conceived to be the true faith. These missions, posted in dangerous and remote places, were often accompanied by schools or hospitals. Most of the missionaries were deeply religious men, but they were also often smug and officious, totally committed to Western culture and their particular faith. They frequently offended the natives mightily, undermined their customs and often their state. When resisted in these good works, as in the T'ai P'ing (1850–1864) or Boxer (1899–1901) rebellions, the missionaries and their principals at home howled for help. They got it. Victorian public opinion everywhere was not prepared for the slaughter of its holy men. Troops were sent in, the natives were put down, colonies or protectorates were established, and the pious work of conversion went forward. And where perchance the colony came first, missionaries were urged in by governments as a civilizing and pacifying force necessary to bring the benighted natives to a closer understanding of what the Europeans wanted of them.

Less powerful an emotion than Christian evangelism, but one still capable of stirring men, was the "white man's burden." The natives' souls were still to be saved, not for God but for the benefits of modern industrial civilization. No matter how ancient or magnificent the culture of the traditional societies, it was deemed inferior to that of the West. The duty of the colonial magistrate or merchant was, therefore, to lead the native out of darkness into the polluted sunlight of Western technological civilization. Concepts of the superiority of Western civilization coincided nicely with the view that non-Western peoples were naturally and properly subjects of colonial powers. And it was comforting to think that the white man was noble enough to do his duty, to shoulder his burden.

A secular emotion of much greater strength, impelling Western nations on an imperialist course, was nationalism. It was impossible for the French or Germans to sit quietly and watch Great Britain gobble up the whole world. National emotions ran too high for that. All of the Western peoples felt colonies enhanced their national prestige. Within the context of nationalism it hardly mattered whether the new colony had any value or not, or whether the Europeans had any business taking it in the first place. Viewed in this light, the Italian defeat at Aduwa by Ethiopia was the greatest disaster possible, and this was exactly how Italians in 1896 viewed it. Appeal to national pride, therefore, was the basic propaganda technique used by imperialists, business promoters, missionary societies, and others to gain wide support for imperial expansion and force governments into action.

Yet another motive for imperial expansion was the hope of economic gain. Although this expectation was frequently disappointed, promoters, engineers, and investors never gave up hope. Occasionally, as the career of Cecil Rhodes demonstrated, men might make vast fortunes in imperial ventures, and overseas investment frequently paid a modest but steady income.

Sometimes a bonanza was discovered in areas not colonized, and industrialists called for the troops. Although the troops were not always sent, they often were, as the Boer War (1899–1901), waged by the British against Dutch South Africans, indicated. Industry also invested in areas already colonized and asked for subsidies, guaranteed loans, semislave labor, guaranteed markets, and other kinds of preferential treatment. American railroad grants in the trans-Mississippi West followed this pattern. Gain was a powerful persuader. Even where other reasons were officially advanced for expansion, economic motives often existed.

Another reason for imperial adventure was simply inertia. Expansion had been set as a desirable policy and it continued on its own momentum. The British expanded from the Cape Colony into Natal, Basutoland, Bechuanaland, Swaziland, Southwest Africa, and, ultimately, the Boer states; from Kenya they pushed into Uganda; from India into Burma. When pressed for explanation of this constant expansion, ministers at home and officials on the spot mumbled about defense of the colony, or rounding out boundaries, or dealing with hostile natives, or the Cape-to-Cairo railroad chimera, or something. When asked to explain Captain Marchands' epic march from the Congo to the Nile, French imperialists retorted that expansion of the French Empire was a good thing. Such reasoning was not closely examined at home. Expansion was its own justification. It would be hard to say exactly how many colonies were the result of this sort of automatic expansion for its own sake, but the number was high. We should not assume that things happened as a result of a coherent and consistent policy. Often enough, they just happened.

In spite of the sustained imperialist effort during the nineteenth century, convinced colonialists—even in Great Britain—were always a minority of the nation. In France the chambers of commerce that supported imperialism in the hope of markets were a tiny fraction of the business community. No German industrialist was very enthusiastic over the activities of small traders in the Cameroons. Established French banks vigorously opposed the Suez and Panama canal schemes on the ground they would lose money. Imperialism was the profit and policy of a small group, even in business, in nineteenth-century Europe. Laborers, peasants, nobles, clerks, and bureaucrats did not care about it at all unless convinced that national interests and pride were at stake. And even then the concern of the nation was short-lived, for the duration of the crisis only. As far as most Europeans were concerned, empire was unimportant. Governments, however, were above this apathy. While their peoples were occupied elsewhere, they took over the world.

When the imperialist fever began to rise at mid-century, Russia and Great Britain already possessed immense advantages in the renewed race for colonies. The Russians were well established in Siberia, and they met only weak Chinese opposition as they pushed steadily eastward after the Crimean War. Not until Russian interests clashed with those of Japan did Russian expansion stop. The British were equally well prepared, having conquered India from the French and native rulers in the eighteenth century. In Africa the British alone possessed a colony with a large European population— the Cape Colony at the southern tip of the continent. In addition, commercial, naval, and industrial superiority in Europe gave Great Britain a decided economic and military advantage over her weaker rivals. Although France, Italy, and Germany entered the colonial race and obtained sizable empires, they never were able to overcome the British and Russian lead.

Imperialism, which lasted from 1450 until World War II, had stupendous impact on both European and non-Western societies. For non-Western cultures, contact with European imperialism was the crucial event in their history, for the Europeans brought with them technology and industrial political administration, neither of which could be ignored or culturally absorbed. Imperialism over its four centuries was the beginning of the ties that now have irretrievably bound together Europe and the traditional societies of the non-Western world.

For Europeans, the major impact of imperialism, particularly in the first phase before the eighteenth-century revolution, was its hastening of the development of industrialization. Both the markets that the American colonies provided for European goods and European imports of colonial plantation produce were major factors in the growth of industry. Great Britain, with the largest colonial trade and empire, developed machine industry first, largely in response to colonial demands. Handicrafts could supply local needs, but could not fill a world market. During the nineteenth century, industrialists and governments made valiant attempts to continue the symbiotic relationship between colonialism and economic development at home. Railroads were built all over the world, plantations set up in tropical provinces, natives pressed into labor gangs, and oil and mining concessions obtained and exploited. Although much of this activity made money—and a lot of money in certain cases—colonial trade and investment played an increasingly smaller part in strictly European economic development. The reasons for this trend, so disturbing to contemporary promoters, were not hard to discern. The cost differential between raw materials and manufactured products steadily increased, and the colonies did not produce enough to take a large percentage of Europe's manufactured goods. It took too many bananas to pay for a railroad system; thus European states traded with each other. As industrialization in Europe progressed, the importance of colonies to the European economy declined, and the gap between European and non-Western standards of living widened. The intimate economic connection between colony and mother country was a product of the Old Regime.

War was a second area of colonial impact on Europe. Beginning in the sixteenth century and culminating in the great war for empire was a vicious series of colonial conflicts between European states, replete with massacres, acts of piracy and pillage, and an occasional battle. Colonies and overseas trade were regarded as subjects well worth any amount of blood and butchery, and after 1575 colonial warfare was almost continuous. The development of European gunnery and naval architecture was almost exclusively a product of the imperatives of this continuous war. In the nineteenth century, however, the equation between war and imperialism changed radically. No longer did European powers find colonies worth fighting over. Excepting the Russo-Japanese War (1904–1905), there were no great-power conflicts fought over colonial affairs. Negotiation was the accepted method of dealing with imperial difficulties. Such a method did not, of course, extend to the natives who were given the benefits of the most advanced Western firepower by generals eager to shoot. But in dealing with each other the European powers kept the peace. It seems clear that colonies once so vital a part of

EUROPEAN COLONIZATION OF ASIA, 1914 ▶

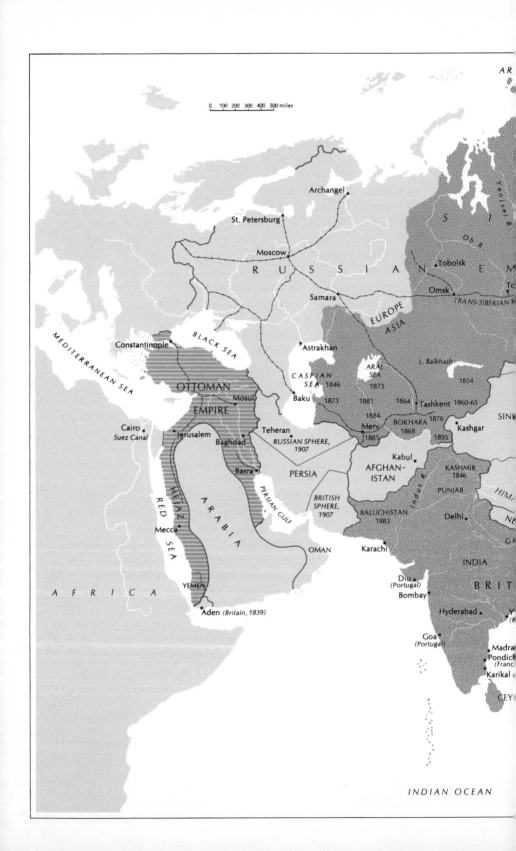

AR

0 100 200 300 400 500 miles

Archangel

St. Petersburg

Moscow

R U S S I A N   S I   E M

Tobolsk

Samara

TRANS-SIBERIAN   Tc

Omsk

EUROPE

ASIA

MEDITERRANEAN SEA

Constantinople

BLACK SEA

OTTOMAN

Astrakhan

CASPIAN
SEA   1846

ARAL
SEA   1873

L. Balkhash

1854

EMPIRE

Mosul

Baku

1873

1881

1864   Tashkent   1860-65

1884

Cairo

Suez Canal

Jerusalem

Baghdad

Teheran

RUSSIAN SPHERE,
1907

Merv   BOKHARA   1876

1885   1868   Kashgar

SIN

Basra

PERSIA

Kabul

AFGHAN-
ISTAN

KASHMIR
1846

HIM

BRITISH
SPHERE,
1907

PUNJAB

Delhi

NE

Mecca

HEJAZ

A R A B I A

RED
SEA

PERSIAN GULF

BALUCHISTAN
1883

OMAN

Karachi

INDIA

BRIT

AFRICA

YEMEN

Diu
(Portugal)

Bombay

Aden   (Britain, 1839)

Hyderabad

Y
(

Goa
(Portugal)

Madra

Pondic
(Franc

Karikal

CEY

INDIAN OCEAN

the European economy were now of relatively minor importance, and that contemporaries, for all of their rhetoric, recognized this fact.

Of all the European powers, only Great Britain and Russia made imperialism pay. For the Russians the annexation of Siberia—an apparently permanent acquisition—made the difference between great- and small-power status. The natural resources of Siberia were —and still are—enormous. For the British, from the time of Elizabeth I, empire meant greatness. The British turned their first colonial empire into an industrial revolution and great-power status. During the nineteenth century, Great Britain was the only colonial power to show a clear economic profit from the efforts of imperialism. Gold and diamonds from South Africa, tin and rubber from Malaya, cotton and tea from India, railroad investments in South America—all made money. French, German, Italian, Spanish, Belgian, and Portuguese colonies satisfied national ambitions, pleased chauvinist politicians and editors, and tantalized promoters, but they swam in red ink.

Important as was imperialism in the history of the developing West, its effect on non-Western societies was infinitely greater. European conquest had a traumatic effect on the traditional societies of America, Africa, and Asia. Most of those societies were technologically primitive by European standards. During the nineteenth century, the technological gap between Europe and the non-Western world grew enormously, increasing already existing differences in production, business management, the organization of labor, and political administration. European determination to develop or colonize Asian, African, or American lands, therefore, meant the destruction of native societies. Old social structures, clan relationships, and political institutions were unable to withstand European pressures. In some places the non-Western culture was simply obliterated—and often the people with it. Elsewhere, as in India, China, and Indonesia, the traditional civilization was much stronger and able to survive intact for several hundred years. But this was due as much to a lack of European colonists as it was to the magnificent Oriental culture. In the end, however, Western industrial patterns have begun to change even Oriental civilizations.

An obvious concomitant of the economic, political, and technological inferiority of many non-Western cultures was a casual brutality in the European treatment of the brown, black, and red peoples. European colonials and officials were interested in native culture only insofar as it contributed to the prosperity of the colony. They were not generally interested in substituting European customs for the native ones they were demolishing. No efforts were made before

World War I to prepare the colonial peoples for self-government or for them to take over the mines, factories, plantations, and railroads of the Europeans. White men provided native education that was rudimentary at best. A model of this system of colonialism existed in Egypt during the rule of Lord Cromer from 1883 to 1907. Lord Cromer was an honest man; he did not steal from the Egyptians, and he made great efforts to prevent Egyptian officials from doing so. He built roads, railroads, the first Aswan Dam, drained swamps, supported vast archaeological efforts, and ran an efficient and inexpensive government. But he did nothing for education, he failed to train Egyptian officials, and he excluded Egyptians from positions of real responsibility. For Lord Cromer the Egyptians' natural position in the world was as laborers, peasants, and servants because they were inferior. Yet, compared to many of his contemporaries, and from a Western viewpoint, Lord Cromer governed well and honorably, and modern Egypt dates from his reign.

A final element in the European mistreatment of non-Western peoples was the deep racism and cultural nationalism of European society. Only the Portuguese were able to establish a successful multiracial society in Europe; it was composed of Europeans, Moors, and blacks. In their colonies, however, the Portuguese maintained the barriers between Europeans of whatever color and "natives," whose culture was African. For the English, Dutch, and Spanish, the natives were both culturally and racially inferior. Whether in Carolina, Mexico, South Africa, or Java, caste lines were drawn on the basis of race. Indians and blacks were subpeople to the Spanish rulers of Mexico, and if they were enslaved, brutalized, or killed, this was only a natural and normal state of affairs. In North America the British colonists had the same opinions about Indians and butchered them with light conscience. The Belgian treatment of Congo tribesmen and the Dutch attitude toward South African blacks was part of this larger contempt. Black and slave, Arab and peasant, became synonymous terms to Europeans. White men mostly thought of native culture as beneath notice and the non-Western peoples themselves as units of labor, or children, or untamed savages, or souls lost to God, or subpeople, racially inferior and unable to learn.

A balance sheet for imperialism is hard to draw. Western conquests and exploitation brought modern dentistry, radio, inoculation, miracle rice, machine guns, typewriters, electricity, insecticides, nationalistic aspirations, notions of socialism and equality, pollution, and Coca-Cola to non-Western peoples and cultures. Are these benefits? Some of them surely must be. Certainly the non-Western peoples and states want these things desperately. Have the real and imagined benefits been worth the price, which is the irreversible destruction of tradition, cultures, arts, crafts, family ties, life styles, religious beliefs, and social customs? Are the gains brought by Western technology and life styles worth obliteration of the past and the anxiety and rootlessness that follow? It is difficult to judge. We can only say that the process of change, once having begun, runs inexorably to ends not yet seen or known.

EIGHT

The twentieth century: theater of the absurd

> The lamps are going out all over Europe; we shall not see them lit again in our lifetime.
> Viscount Grey, *Twenty-Five Years (1914)*

> Every revolution by force only puts more violent means of enslavement into the hands of the persons in power.
> Lev Tolstoy, *The Kingdom of God Is Within You (1883)*

> You know—it's a great mistake to imagine that it's great victories that win wars. On the contrary—it's great blunders. We ought to put up a statue in Trafalgar Square to Hitler for having been such a fool as to attack Russia.
> Marshal Jan Christian Smuts

INTRODUCTION

The history of our own time began on August 1, 1914, with the sounds of guns and death. The pitiful lines of refugees who fled the German invasion of Belgium and France were the first of a continuous caravan that has since covered the world. The fabric of Victorian political stability, painfully woven over four generations, began to unravel that August day, and we have not been able to repair it. A mighty increase in government power began with wartime controls and has continued in an era of permanent war. Monstrous secular ideologies variously called communism, fascism, Nazism, or Maoism have harried us with all the fury medieval man ascribed to demons. It has become a major theme of Western thought that man has lost control over his society; he is adrift and abandoned in contradiction and absurdity. Since July 1914, the last month of peace and security, the modern world has seemed a confused and fearsome place.

Warfare in our time has become permanent. Peace in the nineteenth century, like the Roman peace, is now seen as an aberration, a pause in the constant noise of war. Since 1914 there have been only ten years, from 1921 to 1931, with one or all of the great powers not fighting. Two types of conflict have dominated modern history: the confrontation between great powers and the largely successful struggle of colonial peoples for independence. Twentieth-century man has found no peaceful solution for either.

Conflict has found a focus in the divergent ideologies that gained a mass following after the Great War. Modern ideologies have managed to develop a frightening exclusivity and intensity unmatched since the Reign of Terror. Each has claimed a monopoly on truth, enlightenment, and wisdom and has freely called on men everywhere to abandon former loyalties for a total commitment to the new dispensation. Such a closed cast of mind has provided much of the fuel for modern war and revolution.

A universal result of constant war, revolution, and ideological commitment has been the steady growth of governmental power. Theoretically absolute since the days of the Renaissance debate on sovereignty, government since the Great War has come close to realizing this in practice. Growth of government has meant a colossal increase in the number, size, and complexity of bureaus and agencies, which administer an endless variety of hospitals, industries, welfare schemes, unions, educational institutions, police forces, and programs. Beyond this, government agencies have steadily amassed an overwhelming amount of information about the private citizen—his income, his fingerprints, his employment record, his credit rating, his political reliability, the esteem of his neighbors, his misdemeanors. The growth of the state has been accompanied by a decline in the autonomy of the citizen.

Our time, therefore, is an age of immense cultural paradox. There has been more talk of liberty and more searching for personal freedom than ever before, yet governments are stronger, ideologies demand total personal surrender, and revolutions seem only to strengthen the forces of coercion, rather than those of freedom. Governments struggle valiantly to fight inflation, provide for the welfare of the citizens, and control social change, yet stability is a distant dream. We live crowded into megalopolises and cozily aware of other men's doings through radio and television, yet anxiety, aimlessness, and dehumanization are major social problems everywhere. We are bound together in great fraternities by nationalism and ideologies, yet alienation is a common psychic disorder. We long for peace, yet we fight constant wars. We suffer from a surfeit of social change, yet enormous technological and scientific progress has been made. Modern history, therefore, is a tale of contradictions, of immense problems, enormous obstacles, unlimited possibilties— and hope.

THE GREAT WAR

June 28, 1914, was a hot and drowsy summer Sunday. Most Europeans were thinking about vacations during the annual August holidays. In the major European capitals the governments of the great powers were in a state of repose. Parliaments were in recess. Diplomatic business was slack. The English cabinet was dispersed in the country for a long weekend. The German foreign minister, von Jagow, was in Switzerland on his honeymoon. The French premier and foreign minister, preparing to go to Russia, were involved in the details of a state visit. The German chief of staff, von Moltke, was in Karlsbad, taking the waters. Nothing seemed to be happening.

One major European figure was about, however. Archduke Franz Ferdinand, heir to the throne of Austria-Hungary, was viewing the annual summer maneuvers of the army, which was struggling and straggling over the barren hills of central Bosnia. The archduke arrived in Sarajevo, the ancient capital of Bosnia, at about ten o'clock Sunday morning to review the troops and attend a reception in his honor. He brought his wife, Sophie. But Franz Ferdinand and Sophie were not the only people in Sarajevo for the review. Three Serbian youths had arrived, supplied with guns and bombs from Serbian army arsenals and filled with Serbian nationalist propaganda from Belgrade coffeehouses. They were in town to kill the archduke.

The first attempt at assassination took place on the drive to city hall. One of the youths threw a bomb onto the folded hood of the archduke's landau. Franz Ferdinand reached up and pitched it out the back of the car onto the pavement, where it exploded, almost destroying the following vehicle. The archduke escaped without injury. Following the reception at city hall, Franz Ferdinand and his staff discussed plans for the rest of the visit. Because of the bomb incident, they decided not to drive through the narrow streets of the old town, but continue along the boulevard on which they had

Les Demoiselles d'Avignon **(1907, oil on canvas) by Picasso initiated the Cubist movement in painting and sculpture. Picasso's use of schematization, and the reduction to essential forms, foreshadow the abstract movement of the twentieth century.** *Collection, Museum of Modern Art, New York.*

entered. The archduke's chauffeur did not fully grasp this change. On the return trip he started to turn into the old town as originally planned. One of the archduke's staff shouted the new directions to the confused driver, who stopped to put the car in reverse. The chauffeur's mistake gave the assassin his chance. Gavrilo Princip fired two shots, one hitting the archduke's neck, the other hitting his wife. Desperately wounded, Franz Ferdinand called to his wife, "Sophie, Sophie, do not die. Live for our children." They both died within an hour.

Alliances and Crises: The Background of the War

The assassination of Archduke Franz Ferdinand led inexorably to world war, an event long dreaded in the streets and chancelleries of Europe. But, despite the best efforts of statesmen and diplomats, the European nations had long moved toward this eventuality. The great powers lurched from crisis to crisis, struggling to preserve peace in an atmosphere of deepening suspicion, rising armaments, and the dangerous rhetoric of nationalist propaganda. When the fatal crisis came the diplomats were caught in the web of their making—the alliances, hostilities, and ambitions of their nations. All viewed a general war as an immeasurable disaster that would ruin their world. The diplomats tried to save the peace. They failed, and the nineteenth century ended with the guns of August.

The diplomatic antecedents of World War I dated from 1870, when Germany annexed Alsace-Lorraine, one of the colossal blunders of European diplomatic history. French nationalism and pride never accepted the loss of the two provinces. No French government could survive without maintaining an attitude of hostility toward Germany. Alsace-Lorraine added a new factor to the diplomacy of the nineteenth century—the permanent enmity between two great powers. Thus were created two stable diplomatic poles, around which formed alliances, combinations, ententes, imperial adventures, and ultimately war. European diplomacy managed every alignment of great powers except one—an alliance between France and Germany.

The German pole first attracted foreign powers. The German chancellor Bismarck, aware of French hostility, began to construct alliances tying the great powers to the German Empire and isolating France. The first of these combinations was the League of Three Emperors, established in 1872 by Germany, Austria, and Russia. The three conservative eastern empires were united in their distrust of liberal and republican France, and Bismarck played on that sentiment. The league was the major diplomatic force in Europe until 1876, when the progressive deterioration of the Ottoman Empire drove Serbian and Bulgarian peasants to revolt. This suited the Russians, who wished to annex Constantinople and control the straits. They aided the rebels, declared war on Turkey, and pushed to the gates of Constantinople itself. This disturbed nearly everybody. In order to restore the diplomatic situation, Bismarck called the great powers to the Congress of Berlin in 1878. There the Russian gains were considerably reduced. Austria received the right to occupy Bosnia and Herzegovina, and Bulgaria, a Russian satellite, lost most of her gains. Britain took Cyprus as a naval base to counter Russian pressure on Turkey. The Congress of Berlin was a serious diplomatic defeat for Russia, and the League of Three Emperors dissolved.

Bismarck began to rebuild at once. In 1879 Austria and Germany signed the Dual Alliance, providing for mutual aid in case Germany was attacked by France or Austria by Russia. In 1881 Italy joined, and the treaty became the Triple Alliance, still defensive in nature, with its primary aim to preserve German diplomatic supremacy and keep peace.

Bismarck was not yet satisfied. Not only did he want to avoid war with France, he wanted to avoid war anywhere. He continued to work for the renewal of the agreements between the eastern courts as a form of insurance against renewed Balkan problems. In 1887 Bismarck's diplomacy reached its zenith. He renewed the Triple Alliance, which had become his basic diplomatic tie. He also signed the Reinsurance Treaty with Russia, providing for consultations between the two powers on international problems and mutual assistance against aggression. Finally Bismarck encouraged the Mediterranean Accord of Italy, Spain, and Britain, which was designed to check French and Russian expansion. Bismarck had isolated France and had made Germany the diplomatic arbiter of Europe.

The Bismarck system of alliances and understanding was one of the great creations of European diplomacy. This was partly attributable to the personality of the old chancellor. By 1887 everyone, even the French, firmly believed that Bismarck's diplomatic combinations were designed to preserve peace. His word was trusted, his ability to see the other point of view respected and appreciated. In part, also, Bismarck's success was a reflection of German power. The German Empire was the strongest single state in Europe, the greatest industrial power, with the best army and a stable government. A German chancellor of the ability and character of Bismarck automatically dominated Europe.

Within a month of Bismarck's fall in 1890, however, his system began to come apart. The Mediterranean Accord dissolved. The Reinsurance Treaty with Russia was allowed to lapse. By 1892 only the Triple Alliance was left. The work of twenty years, the constant effort to isolate France and restrain Russia and Austria, was lost.

After the fall of Bismarck diplomats were no longer certain that Germany would retain a diplomacy of peace. Both France and Russia began edging toward alliance, which was concluded in 1894. It was supplemented by military staff discussions, a step Bismarck had never thought necessary. The balance of power was beginning to swing against Germany.

Construction of a solid diplomatic system against the Triple Alliance was mainly the work of the French foreign minister Théophile Delcassé. In 1900 he began to woo Italy away from the Triple Alliance, promising support for Italian pretensions to Tripoli. In 1904 Delcassé concluded an entente with Great Britain and added to the diplomatic agreements the military and naval staff consultations that were a standard feature of French diplomacy.

The Triple Entente of France, Russia, and Great Britain provided the Allies with protection against certain threats to vital interests. British governments after 1900 found German naval construction an increasingly serious threat to British trade and security. The Russian foreign office saw the entente as an end to the interminable colonial quarrels with Britain and hoped it would provide diplomatic support for adventures in the Balkans. France viewed the entente system as protection against Germany and hoped it would help France regain Alsace-Lorraine. Mutual interests held the Triple Entente together.

Serious diplomatic crises from 1904 to 1914 solidified both alliance systems and placed ever increasing importance on the military and naval aspects of collective security. The first Moroccan crisis from 1905 to 1906 set the pattern for most of the immediate prewar diplomacy. Franco-German differences over economic investment and political control of Morocco pushed the two powers to the point of war. The Algeciras Conference of 1906, called to mediate the dispute, ended in a great victory for the Triple Entente. France was confirmed in her control over Morocco, and Italy supported the entente powers. German diplomacy was weak and futile. The entente powers viewed the first Moroccan crisis as the end of

German diplomatic dominance in Europe. Germany, however, saw the Algeciras Conference as confirmation of a dangerous encirclement by hostile powers and consequently drew even closer to her one dependable ally, Austria.

Following the Moroccan affair, peace became more fragile. Austrian annexation of Bosnia in 1908 nearly provoked war, so great was Russian outrage over this insult to the little Slav brothers. In 1911 a second Moroccan crisis was settled by international conference, though with a notable lack of good will on both sides. Italy conquered Tripoli in 1911, supported diplomatically by Russia, France, and Great Britain. Germany tended to sympathize with Turkey. In 1912 and 1913 the two Balkan wars provided the last international crisis to be settled by a great-power conference before the Great War. During the prolonged Balkan crisis the ambassadors of the great powers negotiated continuously in London. The London conference was instrumental in settling the Balkan boundaries, but the ominous split between entente powers and Austria and Germany plagued the deliberations. The next international crisis was the murder of Franz Ferdinand. One by one the great powers honored their treaties and went to war.

Stalemate and Disaster:
The War from 1914 to 1917

When war came in August 1914 nearly everyone thought it would be short and glorious. As the German troops marched down Unter den Linden boulevard in Berlin, the kaiser predicted they would be home by Christmas. The French and Russian mobilization plans, both drawn up by the French general staff, envisioned a Russian march through East Prussia to Berlin and a French thrust over the Rhine. The German mobilization scheme, the Schlieffen Plan, outlined a great drive through Belgium, entry into Paris in forty days, and victory in the war. The Austrians expected to crush Serbia before Russia could effectively intervene. No nation had stockpiled more than a six-month supply of materiel.

None of these sanguine expectations was fulfilled. Such expectations never are, of course, but this time the staff officers were even more wrong than usual. The war immediately turned into a gigantic holocaust—unmanageable, hideous, and frightening—that devoured men and machines. Casualty figures were unbelievable. Armies shot off in one month more shells than staff planners had thought necessary for a year. Nations had to be mobilized to meet the demands of total war. Huge battles were fought that no one understood and no staff was able to control. The chimera of rapid military victory dissolved into the nightmare of the Great War.

The war was not only enormously bigger than anyone had imagined, it was also a technological war. Men were killed by an awesome array of new weapons. Fragmentation mines bounced into the air and exploded with a killing radius of fifty feet. Light field artillery brought rapid and accurate cannon fire into support of forward positions. A remarkable variety of machine guns chopped apart the most determined infantry assault. Poison gas, tanks, submarines, airplanes were all added to national arsenals in the Great War. Men were simply overwhelmed by their technology. Firepower became more important than manpower, supply replaced tactics, and perseverance was the only strategy.

The whole course of the war was determined in the opening months. In the west, Germany employed a modification of the Schlieffen Plan. Two huge field armies cut through Belgium and fell upon the lightly defended frontier of northern France. The German objective was to capture Paris and end the war. But the French held. At the first battle of the Marne, the German drive turned into rapid retreat. When the Germans stiffened and held, fifty miles behind their furthest advance, both armies dug into defensive positions. By December 1914 a line of trenches from the North Sea to Switzerland was being furiously constructed. The war of movement in the west had ended. The war of trenches and defense and position had begun. Opportunity for quick victory had passed, and the war in the west assumed its characteristic form of stalemate, which lasted until German collapse in 1918.

War was fought differently in eastern Europe. Distances were so great that trench warfare could never snuff out mobility. Armies kept moving. The initial advances in the east were Russian, in accordance with the mobilization plan provided by France. Two Russian armies lurched into East Prussia and a smaller Russian advance was made into Austria. Russian command and coordination in East Prussia was wretched, however, and after initial successes the two Russian armies were destroyed at Tannenberg and Masurian lakes. This stupendous Russian defeat set the tone for the entire eastern war. Russian command and equipment could not stand up against the Germans.

In the spring of 1915 the Allies unveiled a new strategy, the only sensible military plan either side had in the entire fifty-two months of war. Having gained a stalemate in the west, the Allied planners tried to strike at Germany and her allies from the south and to reach Russia, which was clearly in need of help. This southern strategy had three main elements. The first was to lure Italy into the war, which succeeded. On May 23, 1915, Italy declared war on Austria and Germany and began an invasion of Austria toward Trieste along the Isonzo River. The second Allied effort, in the Balkans, was quite unsuccessful. An Austro-German-Bulgarian offensive against Serbia in October 1915 completely overran the Balkans. The third Allied southern offensive, against Turkey, was an attempt to conquer Constantinople and open the straits to Russia. The idea belonged to Winston Churchill, who was probably the ablest Allied war leader. Certainly the Turkish campaign was the best single strategic idea of the war. British field command, however, was atrocious, exceeding even the level of incompetence displayed on the western front. In April 1915 British troops landed at Gallipoli, trying to capture the heights that dominated the Dardanelles. Turkish resistance, combined with British timidity and blunders, sealed the failure of the assault. Finally, in December, the British forces were withdrawn, and all realistic hope of reaching Russia abandoned. It was a sad end to an intelligent strategy and was clearly the last hope for an early end to the war.

The failure of the Allied southern strategy meant that the war would drag on in the old patterns until one side collapsed from exhaustion. In the east the Russians were continuously forced back by the German armies, precisely as they had been in the battles of 1914. In the west the trenches were supreme, and any attempt to break through was repulsed, with terrible casualties resulting. Nonetheless, attempts were made by generals who could think of no better way to use their men than to send them out against enemy positions in wave after wave of fruitless assaults that ended in blood and death. At Verdun the Germans tried to break the French lines from February to December 1916, gaining only two miles. The losses ran to nearly 700,000 men. That same summer the British tried a great offensive along the Somme River. They gained about seven miles in five months, and the casualties were about 1,100,000 men. In the next year this insane tactic was repeated by the Allies in the battles of Arras, Aisne, and Champagne. Nothing was gained. There were nearly a million casualties. Mud, disease, filth, snipers, boredom, punctuated by occasional suicidal offensives—frontal assaults against machine guns and artillery—were the elements of life on the western front until the spring of 1918. It was a hideous existence, purposeless and brutal. Breakthrough and victory were impossible. Men served only to die.

The Allied Victory

By 1917 political events began to dominate the war. The Russian Revolution of February 1917 was the beginning of Russian withdrawal from the war. The resistance of Russia, already weakened by three years of steady defeat, was increasingly feeble. The Allied failure to open a supply route to Russia in the Gallipoli campaign had doomed the Russians to defeat. In January 1918 the Soviet government of Lenin began peace negotiations with Germany and Austria. The country was dissolving under the pressures of war. Finland, the Baltic states, the Ukraine, and Poland had proclaimed independence from the new Red government. In these circumstances peace was inevitable on Germany's terms. The Germans based their demands on the current political and military situation in eastern Europe. Finland, Poland, the Baltic states, and the Ukraine were recognized as sovereign states in the Treaty of Brest-Litovsk, as the Russians gave way on every issue.

An equally important political decision was reached concerning warfare at sea. Unrestricted submarine warfare had long been urged by the German high command as the only way of breaking the American supply line to the Allies. On January 8, 1917, the military won reluctant agreement to begin unrestricted submarine warfare on February 1. Everyone recognized that this would bring America into the war, but the general staff took an optimistic line and assured people that Germany would win the war before American aid could make any real difference. The United States made strong protest, broke diplomatic relations with Germany on February 3, and declared war on April 6.

In the spring of 1918 the Germans tried to take advantage of victory in the east and force a decision in France before the Americans could intervene. The great German offensive began on March 21, the first day of spring, and ended in defeat on the Marne in July. After holding on the Marne, the Allies gained the initiative and began to drive the Germans back. The success of the offensives unnerved General Ludendorff, the German commander. In a panic he informed the kaiser and the ministry that the war was lost and it was time to ask for terms. Bewildered but obedient to the military, the German government began conversations with Washington about an armistice. Conversations dragged on during October, while the German army crumbled in the field. At home, the government disintegrated. On November 3 the sailors of the High Seas Fleet mutinied at Kiel and formed a sailors' soviet in imitation of the Russians. The revolution spread and within a week all of Germany was in revolt. The abdication of the kaiser was announced in Berlin, and a republic was proclaimed. When the armistice was finally signed on November 11, 1918, German government, society—even the army—had begun to fall apart.

The Allies were also victorious in the east. With the collapse of the Austrian army, various national groups seized their independence. On October 29, 1918, the Yugoslav National Council at Zagreb proclaimed the independence of Yugoslavia. On October 21 the Czechs declared their independence. Transylvania joined Rumania on December 1. The Austrian Empire had broken into its constituent national elements. Political reorganization in eastern Europe did not await the peace conference. As in Russia, military defeat had brought total political collapse.

In November 1918, the war had lasted fifty-two months. It had cost an estimated $330 billion, the savings and investments of a century of industrialization. There had been 30 million military casualties and perhaps half again as many civilians. In France, one-half of the men between eighteen and thirty-five had been war casualties. Everything had been sacrificed. A stable currency, a stable government, an entire generation, a world of security and hope for the future; all quite gone. All Europe had kept the appointment that Alan Seeger had written about:

> I have a rendezvous with Death
> At some disputed barricade . . .

This had not been like other, lesser wars. This time there were no winners, no losers. Everything had been consumed in the destruction. This was not immediately apparent. Some men talked about having fought a "war to end all wars" and "making the world safe for democracy." Some men still babbled about the "victory" and rejoiced in it. In the next two decades, however, the meaning of the war would gradually be revealed to all. The poets had been right. The meaning of World War I was death.

The Versailles Peace Conference

Peacemaking, 1919: It would be an awesome task. The poisonous hatreds of war impeded all rational consideration of problems of reconstruction and diplomacy. The peace conference was also hampered by the numerous secret treaties between the European powers dividing up the spoils of war before they had been won. In reviewing this mass of treaties and promises, the delegates to the peace conference found their freedom of action severely limited. Not less serious, they also found these treaties and promises provided enormous opportunities for severe, perhaps nonnegotiable, disagreements between the Europeans and Woodrow Wilson, the American president, whose peace proposals, the famous Fourteen Points, had been outlined in a speech on January 8, 1918. The Fourteen Points included proposals for "open covenants, openly arrived at," freedom of the seas, restoration of Belgium, an independent Poland, independent states for the various nationalities of Austria-Hungary, disarmament, impartial adjustment of colonial claims, and a League of Nations to guarantee peace and political independence for all. The Allies had accepted the Fourteen Points as the basis for peace in November, but they had numerous doubts. Out of deference to the prestige and power of Woodrow Wilson, however, these doubts were not communicated to the Americans. Rather, they emerged during the course of the negotiations.

European peace objectives emerged from the realities of war. The French, who had suffered horribly during the war, were overwhelmingly concerned with security against another German attack. In her present condition, France could never defeat Germany. All French diplomacy revolved around that fact. Thus the French wanted huge reparations, an independent Rhineland state, as much German territory as possible given to Poland, total German disarmament, and French annexation of the Saar valley and its coal mines. The British were less vulnerable militarily; their deepest need was for economic recovery. They needed a settlement that would restore prosperity. Italian demands were different still. The Italian government was under heavy pressure at home from both fascist and communist groups. Only full implementation of the secret treaties with the Allies might strengthen the government enough to avoid collapse. These peace aims were mutually exclusive and in every case contrary to the spirit and letter of the Fourteen Points.

The delegates to the peace conference were as much at odds as their policies. The French delegate, Clemenceau, was particularly contemptuous of Wilson, whom he considered a fool. He commented that "Wilson bores me with his fourteen points. God Almighty had only ten," and observed that Wilson thought he was Jesus Christ. David Lloyd George, the British prime minister, understood the overriding need for economic recovery, but he lacked the strength of character to fight for a peace that could bring prosperity. Like Clemenceau, he held Wilson in contempt; unlike Clemenceau, he was afraid of Wilson and the power America represented. Woodrow Wilson was unquestionably the tragic figure of the conference. A rigid Calvinist, he viewed the world in simple terms: his views were right and those who agreed with him were godly; his opponents were wrong, both morally and in fact, and their honor was suspect. He was thus totally unable to negotiate, as he felt that disagreement with his own position was immoral. This was not suitable intellectual equipment to bring to the problems of peacemaking in 1919. Wilson's intervention in the peace talks was catastrophic. Ultimately, his efforts only served to make the treaties worse than they had to be. No American president since Lincoln had faced so important a duty, and no American president ever failed so utterly to rise to the challenges of that duty.

The actual negotiations reflected the divisions of men and policies. The League of Nations, which the Europeans generally considered a bit of naive Wilsonian folly, was disposed of quickly. On January 25 a resolution setting up the league was passed unanimously, and a committee organized to write the charter. Peace terms with Germany aroused severe conflicts. French desire for the Saar, an independent Rhineland, and Polish annexation of large chunks of Silesia were summarily rejected by Wilson. Wilson also opposed the British proposal that Germany ought to pay for war destruction. Nor was Wilson prepared to recognize the Italian territorial claims, which seemed large even to the French and the British. These disagreements produced furious wrangling. Although the conference never quite broke up, personal negotiations between the heads of government had to be suspended on several occasions. Nonetheless, in spite of trying moments and monumental personal hatreds, the Allied leaders hammered out a set of peace treaties to be imposed on Germany, Austria, Hungary, Bulgaria, and Turkey.

The subsidiary treaties for the minor defeated powers came easily. Bulgaria lost her Aegean coast to Greece and paid small reparations. Austria and Hungary signed treaties that ratified the nationalist revolts of the last year of the war. Poland, Yugoslavia, Czechoslovakia, Rumania, and Italy all took parts of the old Austro-Hungarian monarchy which had collapsed in 1918. Turkey lost her Syrian and Mesopotamian provinces, which the British had conquered during the war. However, the Turkish nationalist movement, under Kemal Atatürk, was able to repel Allied attempts to carve up Anatolia, and the spheres of influence the Allies had promised themselves never materialized. Alone of the smaller defeated powers, Turkey made a striking national recovery after the war.

The Treaty of Versailles with Germany better reflected the disagreements among the Allies than any coherent view of what the peace terms ought to be. Germany lost almost 10 percent of its territory. Alsace-Lorraine went to France; parts of West Prussia, most of Poznan, and much of upper Silesia went to Poland. The French also occupied the Saar bases for fifteen years. The lost territory was rich in mineral resources and heavy industry and contained about 12 percent of Germany's prewar population. The German army was to remain under 100,000 men and to have no tanks, large guns, or military aircraft. The navy was forbidden to have submarines. Western Germany was to be demilitarized, and the Rhineland was to be under Allied military occupation for fifteen years. The total German reparations bill was not set; Allied disagreements had prevented that, but the figure was going to be a large one, for a $5 billion preliminary bill was included in the treaty. On June 28, 1919, Germany signed the Treaty of Versailles.

The Versailles Treaty:
A Disastrous Truce

Even at the time, many suspected that the Versailles treaty was not a very good one. A British delegate, the economist John Maynard Keynes, claimed that the reparations were so high they made economic recovery impossible, and in any case Germany could not pay them. His book *The Economic Consequences of the Peace* (1921) made a powerful impression on everyone, and the sad history of reparations collections made it seem prophetic. The United States Senate rejected the Treaty of Versailles outright. Marshal Foch, when shown the treaty, commented that it was no peace, only a twenty-year truce. The German delegation protested that the harsh treaty would undermine democracy in Germany. Everyone pointed out that the treaty made no provision for Russia, whose borders and form of government were being decided in open war throughout 1919. Opinion was divided on whether the League of Nations was a foolish farce or the hope of the world.

The sad truth is that all the foregoing opinions were true. The Treaty of Versailles did not provide France with security. Reparations did prevent rapid postwar recovery, and the Germans could not pay. The criticisms by American senators were frequently accurate. The German contention that the harshness of the treaty would undermine democracy was unquestionably correct. The league was both a farce and the hope of a badly wounded world. The treaty failed to solve the diplomatic problems that started the Great War, and it also failed to deal with the problems created by the war. Moreover, it commanded the moral support and allegiance of almost no one. Only a very few of the European diplomats were prepared to try enforcing the provisions of the Treaty of Versailles, even the few that happened to be beneficial, such as German disarmament. From the beginning, the Treaty of Versailles was a moral and psychological dead letter. It existed only to be changed or ignored. It was a monument of folly.

The signing of the Treaty of Versailles on June 28, 1919 brought the Great War formally to an end. But the fighting did not end. Rumania invaded Hungary in the summer of 1919. Poland fought through 1920 to capture the Lithuanian city of Vilna and went to war with Czechoslovakia over the city of Teschen, and with Russia over their common boundary. In 1919 Greece invaded Turkish Anatolia. An Italian filibustering expedition led by Gabriele D'Annunzio occupied the Yugoslav town of Fiume in 1919. American, French, and British troops intervened in 1919 to aid the Whites in the Russian civil war. German *Freikorps,* remnants of the imperial army, continued to occupy territory in the Baltic states until 1920. According to the many treaties signed, 1919 was a year of peace and reconciliation. In fact, the intensity of fighting was only a little less than the year before.

The problems of transition to peace were also felt on the home front. Huge inflations wiped out the currencies of virtually every state east of the Rhine. Unemployment mounted as armies were demobilized and war industries stopped work. The succession states of the Austrian and Russian empires struggled to establish their authority against the prevailing anarchy in the east. Trade collapsed, and in many smaller cities the economy reverted to barter. Virulent national and religious hatreds erupted into riot and persecution. "In some countries the spirit of revolution was abroad, while in others the curious belief prevailed that the vast damage wrought by war would somehow make it easier to maintain a higher standard of life than had ever existed in the past" (D. H. Robertson, *Money* [Cambridge Economic Handbooks, London, 1948], pp. 109–110). The transition from war to peace was difficult, much too complicated to be accomplished by signing treaties. The return to normalcy, to the life of 1914, would be impossible.

AN AGE OF IDEOLOGY AND REVOLUTION

After the Great War, ideology came into its own. In a world shorn of security, where the future seemed bleaker than the past, ideology provided a form of stability, an anchor for belief. The utopia promised by the ideological revolutionaries seemed better than the halted economic progress and apparent disorder of democracy. The years after Versailles, therefore, became an era of conspiracy and revolution. Ideology and revolution came to characterize the politics of the postwar West. They have proved to be uncomfortable companions.

The Russian Revolution

In spite of confident assertions of readiness, the Russian government was not prepared for the Great War. No one was, but the strains of total war showed more rapidly and completely in Russia than elsewhere. The initial problem was military defeat. After the spring of 1915 Russian armies were in retreat everywhere. Shortages of equipment and ammunition hampered them, and casualties rose to incredible figures. The home front also showed signs of disintegration. Wartime pressures threw the railroad system into confusion, and supplies of food to cities and raw materials lagged badly. Food prices rose to famine levels in the major Russian cities by the winter of 1916. The Russian bureaucracy collapsed under the strain. Direction from the tsar and his cabinet failed. By the beginning of 1917 both the government and the army had almost broken down.

On March 8, 1917, strikes and riots broke out in St. Petersburg, followed by a mutiny of the city garrison two days later. A new provisional government took over from the tsar. Russia became a democratic republic, with guaranteed civil liberties, a ministry responsible to the Duma, and plans for a constituent assembly. Promises of reform notwithstanding, the March revolution meant very little. Conditions did not change simply because the men did. Russia was still losing, the workers were still rebellious and hungry, and the peasants still wanted land. Kerensky, who emerged as the strongest personality of the provisional government, was too weak to build up an armed force loyal to the government and make peace with Germany. Instead, he kept on with the old policies, hoping that an Allied victory and the downfall of the tsar would pull him through. During the summer and fall of 1917 Kerensky faced increasing threats of revolution, both from the army on the right and the workers on the left. By winter it was clear that the provisional government was doomed.

The most powerful of the enemies facing Kerensky and the provisional government were the Bolsheviks, the Leninist faction of the Marxist Social Democrats. Tightly organized in workers' and

EUROPE IN 1921 ▶

ARCTIC OCEAN

Reykjavik
ICELAND
(Denmark)

Narvik

Areas Lost by Germany
Areas Lost by Russia
Areas Lost by Ottoman Empire
Austria-Hungary 1914

0   100   200   300 MILES

NORWAY

SWEDE

FAEROE I.
(Denmark)

Oslo

Stockho

ORKNEY I.
SCAPA FLOW

Edinburgh

NORTH SEA

DENMARK

Copenhagen

BALT

ULSER

GREAT BRITAIN

Da

IRISH
FREE STATE
Dublin

Liverpool

Hamburg

POLIS
CORRIDO

ATLANTIC OCEAN

London

NETHERLANDS
Amsterdam

Rhine

Bremen

GERMANY

Berlin

WEIMAR REPUBLIC
RUHR Weimar

Brussels
BELGIUM
Cologne

Paris
Versailles

LUX

Frankfurt

Prague

CZECHO

Metz
ALSACE-
LORRAINE

SAAR

Stuttgart

Strasbourg
Munich

Vienna

FRANCE

SWITZERLAND
Geneva Locarno

AUSTRIA

Bordeaux

Trent

Trieste
Fiume

YU

Bilbao

Marseilles

ADRIATIC

Zara
(Italy)

Florence

PORTUGAL

Lisbon

Madrid

SPAIN

Barcelona

CORSICA
(France)

ITALY

Rome

Seville

SARDINIA

Naples

Cadiz
Tangier

Gibraltar (Britain)

BALEARIC I.
(Spain)

SPANISH
MOROCCO

Algiers

SICILY

MOROCCO
(France)

ALGERIA
(France)

TUNISIA
(France)

MEDITERRANE

MALTA

NORTH CAPE

Murmansk

Archangel

Sverdlovsk

FINLAND

L. Onega

L. Ladoga

Helsinki

Leningrad

val

ESTONIA

Volgoda

SOVIET UNION

Orenburg

Moscow

Samara

Riga

LATVIA

Volga R.

THUANIA

emel

Kaunas

Vilna

Saratov

KAZAK S.S.R.

WHITE
RUSSIAN
S.S.R.

OLAND

Brest-
saw Litovsk

Kiev

Tsaritsyn

Astrakhan

GALICIA

UKRAINIAN S.S.R.

Dniester R.

CASPIAN SEA

BUKO-
VINA

BESSARABIA

CAUCASIA

CRIMEA

TRANSYLVANIA

Sevastopol

GEORGIAN S.S.R.

RUMANIA

Tiflis

Baku

grade

Bucharest

DOBRUJA

BLACK SEA

Batum

AZERBAIJAN
S.S.R.

Danube R.

ARMENIAN S.S.R.

Sofia

BULGARIA

Istanbul

Tabriz

Ankara

TURKEY

IRAN

AEGEAN SEA

Smyrna

Mosul

Athens

Tigris R.

GREECE

Baghdad

SYRIA

CYPRUS

DODECANESE I. (Britain)

Euphrates R.

(Italy)

IRAQ

CRETE

LEBANON

TRANS-
JORDAN

A

PALESTINE

SAUDI ARABIA

soldiers' soviets, the Bolsheviks possessed substantial military power. On November 6, 1917, they struck down the decaying provisional government. Units of the St. Petersburg garrison, sailors from the fleet of Kronstadt, and workers' Red guards captured the offices of government, the banks, the telephone exchanges, and the rail yards and arrested most members of the provisional government. The new Bolshevik government organized itself under the name Council of People's Commissars; its leading personalities were Lenin, Trotsky —who was to organize the army—and Joseph Stalin. A secret police was established to round up "counterrevolutionaries" and went at its task with brisk energy and obvious enjoyment.

The Soviet government began at once to deal with the problems of war. On March 3, 1918, the Treaty of Brest-Litovsk ended the war in the east. Although Russia gave away a huge amount of territory, Lenin thought the peace was well worth the sacrifices. The treaty would hold only if Germany won, and peace gave the Soviets a chance to consolidate their position. The growing Red Army and secret police could turn full attention to domestic enemies, the most important being the Whites, who were supporters of the old provisional government. The White armies under General Deniken were driven from the Ukraine in the fall of 1919, and the Reds managed to hold the province against a Polish invasion in 1920. In the Baltic the Reds were not so successful. A combination of the Whites, Finns, Poles, and remnants of the German armies kept Finland, Latvia, Estonia, and Lithuania from falling to the Soviets. In southern Russia and the Caucasus the Red Army did better. In spite of considerable local support for the Whites, the Soviet government was ultimately victorious. By the end of 1920 the Whites were driven from the Crimea, their last stronghold in the south. The Soviets were similarly victorious in Siberia, driving the Whites into China in 1920.

In addition to the Whites, the new Soviet government faced the united hostility of all of the Western states. British troops were landed at Archangelsk and Murmansk and were reinforced by the French and Americans. The Allies supported the Whites and became the main prop under anti-Soviet forces in the north. The French also occupied Odessa on the Black Sea, and the Japanese took Vladivostok. The French strongly supported Poland in its efforts to conquer White Russia and the western Ukraine. The Western powers were not willing to undertake extensive campaigning in Russia, however. The war had taken too much out of them. The main battles would have to be fought by the Whites. Had the Whites done well, limited Allied intervention might have tipped the scales their way. With the Whites being beaten everywhere, Allied intervention was rapidly withdrawn. Two years of fighting had made certain facts quite clear. The Soviets had far greater popular support in Russia than the Whites, and it was going to take a major war by the great powers to dislodge them.

In addition to fighting foreign and civil wars, the Soviet government began Marxist social reconstruction. The land was nationalized, and the peasants were to work it, not own it. Workers were ordered to join government labor unions and were forbidden to strike, and the government gradually introduced a system of compulsory labor. Problems of feeding the cities and the Red Army led to a food levy, in which the peasants were systematically stripped of their entire surplus. "War communism," as Lenin called his repressive measures in 1919 and 1920, was designed to strengthen the government, increase the powers of the central administration, and help the Soviet regime survive.

War communism was too harsh to be endured permanently. This became clear when the sailors at Kronstadt revolted in February 1921. Lenin was not Kerensky, and he repressed the mutiny with great severity. Nonetheless, the time had come for moderation. Therefore, Lenin announced the New Economic Policy (NEP) in March. The NEP was designed to placate major segments of the Russian population. The food levy was abolished and replaced by a limited grain tax, which left the peasants with part of their harvest. A new land law in 1922 allowed small private peasant plots. Freedom of trade was restored, allowing the peasant to dispose of his harvest. Private commercial establishments were permitted in the cities, and individuals were again allowed to go into business and small manufacturing. The NEP was clearly a step in the direction of re-creating a private sector in the Russian economy, and it worked nicely. The Russian economy, on the verge of collapse in 1921 after seven years of war and revolution, began to grow steadily after the introduction of the NEP.

Economic development was not Lenin's only concern. He also built the basic apparatus of an autocratic, communist state. In these matters the scripture of Marx gave little guidance, but Lenin had been a revolutionary politician all of his life, and he had learned from the experience. The Communist party grew up in a huge bureaucracy beside that of the state. Individual cells functioned as the basic blocks of the party apparatus. Above the cells were town committees, then district committees, then regional executives. Each of the Soviet Socialist Republics had a Communist party headquarters, along with ordinary civil administration. The party also had specialized cells. Each labor-union local had a party cell, and there was the party youth group, Komsomol. Party political officers were attached to army units and headquarters. The major ministries and bureaus of the state were staffed with Communist party members. Of course, Communists controlled the secret police and the courts. Thus the party and state constituted a dual hierarchy of officialdom, with the party being the more important. Not all state officials were party members, but the important ones were, and all were watched by party spies and police.

Beyond this, the Communist party was committed to extensive central economic planning through its adherence to Marxist orthodoxy. The central planning agency, Gosplan, was as much a part of the party as the state hierarchy. From Gosplan came the complex directives on factory quotas, the type of goods to be produced at each plant, and the goals to be attained by each sector of the economy—agriculture as well as industry. Gosplan's activities grew more numerous and difficult after Russia embarked on five-year plans in 1928, for this added the dimension of priority to that of simple growth. In spite of the obvious bureaucratic inefficiency and self-serving built into the system, neither Gosplan nor the party hierarchy was changed. Whatever their drawbacks, Gosplan, the party hierarchy, and the secret police made superb instruments of social control, which is the essential requirement of a totalitarian regime.

The growing strength of the Communist party and the economic recovery provided by the NEP was matched by the increasing physical debility of Lenin, who died on January 21, 1924, leaving a major void in the Soviet leadership. Two factions emerged at once. One, led by Stalin, sought a concentration of Russian problems and a continuation of the NEP. The other, led by Trotsky, fought for increased emphasis on world communist revolution and an early end to the NEP, leading to a resumption of more orthodox Marxist economics. From 1924 until the Fifteenth Party Congress in December 1927, the two factions struggled for Lenin's inheritance. Stalin, who had better support within the Communist party, triumphed at the congress. The Trotskyites were expelled from Soviet leadership positions, and the Stalinists took over.

Abruptly, Stalin repudiated his previous positions and opened a "New Socialist Offensive," which meant the end of the NEP and the beginning of forced industrialization through the First-Year Plan. The Five-Year Plan placed considerable stress on the development of heavy industry. In agriculture the Stalinists returned to the ideas of war communism. The land was again nationalized, and the kulaks driven off. The farms were organized into collectives, *kolkhoz,* or state farms, *sovkhoz*. The peasants again worked for the state, which set production goals and controlled the entire harvest. Only the tiniest plots were left for individual peasants to cultivate. Collectivization was carried out with great violence, and millions of former kulaks starved in the famine of 1932–1933. In spite of the brutality and the serious economic dislocations, Stalin continued his collectivization program.

Stalin's attention was not exclusively riveted on farms and factories. His career as a bank robber, convict, professional revolutionary, competitor in the deadly struggle for power, and finally dictator had marked his soul. He was pathologically suspicious, and he saw traitors and enemies everywhere. In 1933 he began to purge the Communist party. About a million members were expelled. This was followed by purge trials with most of the old Bolshevik leaders being condemned as Trotskyites. The public trials were only the tip of a huge iceberg of extermination. Thousands of smaller officials and army officers were summarily arrested and dispatched to slave labor camps in Siberia. By a strange irony, it was now safer to be a Communist in the United States than in Russia.

Stalin also kept a weather eye on the slow drift toward World War II. The Russo-German nonaggression pact of August 1939 was designed to protect Russia from Nazi invasion. It bought only about twenty months of peace, which were not well used. When war came, in June 1941, with sickening surprise, Russia was totally unprepared. Most of European Russia was ravaged, and casualties ran well over 20 million. Most of the economic progress of twenty years of communism was destroyed, but the system itself survived. The conclusions from this were inescapable. The Communist army and bureaucracy were able to survive great adversity. Moreover, victory in war gave the Soviet regime a national legitimacy that it had previously lacked. The war raised Russia to the rank of a great power once more and added significantly to the prestige of communism as an ideology.

Postwar Russia, therefore, confronted the new problems of reconstruction and great-power status, as well as the old questions of industrial development, peasant agriculture, internal repression, ferocious power struggles, and the old Stalin/Trotsky dilemma of world revolution versus Russian national interests. Past experience gave solid direction in dealing with industry. New five-year plans were drawn up and all of the prestige of the victorious party was thrown into their fulfillment. Heavy industry and armaments were given considerable priority in an effort to make Russia the strongest military and industrial power in the world. Russian industry, however, did not attain the growth goals set in the latter five-year plans. The built-in inefficiencies of bureaucratic management limited industrial production and increased waste and costs. Factories were prone to produce goods that no one wanted to buy. In order to fulfill quotas, shabby products were manufactured. Quantity vastly overshadowed quality. The inflexibility of bureaucratic management and fixed goals made adaptation to technological change much more difficult than it had to be. The modern Soviet experience has shown that total centralized planning works better in theory than practice.

Central planning also included agriculture, of course. Again, the example of Stalin set the patterns. In spite of overwhelming evidence that the peasants worked better on their own land, the system of collective farms was rigidly maintained. The collective farms were generally inefficiently managed and badly farmed. They absorbed a huge percentage of the labor force. Well into the postwar period over half of Russia lived on the land. Efforts by Khrushchev to increase the harvest by extending the collectives eastward into the virgin lands beyond the Volga also met with very limited success. The Khrushchev experiment worked well for a couple of years, but the environment struck back. Plowed prairies turned to huge dust bowls. A major problem of the postwar Russian economy has been inefficient and unwieldy agriculture, and the problem seems no nearer solution now than it was in 1880.

A third persistent postwar problem was the relationship of the Communist bureaucracy to the intelligentsia. Alterations in the system of government and economic management meant serious threats to the power and prestige of the Communist bureaucrats. The bureaucrat, or "apparatchik," who had been the main beneficiary of the revolution and was the main support of the regime, would suffer. Such alterations, however, were exactly what the intellectuals wanted. They demanded more freedom of thought and expression— freedom to say and publish what they wanted. After the death of Stalin in 1953, some intellectual freedom was granted, but in 1968 the party leaders grew nervous and began a new repression.

Equally threatening to the party bureaucrat were the theories of the Russian economist Lieberman. Lieberman's theories demanded a considerable loosening of the ties of total central economic planning. In an attempt to break through the appalling inefficiency of bureaucratic management, Lieberman proposed that factories abandon their quotas and produce for the open market. They would be forced to sell what they made, produce goods of adequate quality, and only those goods actually wanted. The Russian economy would reach new levels of growth, inefficiency and waste would diminish, there could at last be enough consumer goods for all, and worker absenteeism, drunkenness, and sabotage would decline. This was truly a golden vision. But what of the consequences of such radical steps? What would happen to the doctrines of Marx, which expressly condemned an open-market economy? What would happen to the government if it relinquished its tight social control? After a brief flirtation with Liebermanism in the late 1960s, the Russian leaders decided the vision was not worth the risks. The orthodoxy of centralized planning was retained.

Postwar Russia also saw a renewal of the power struggles among the Communist elite, reminiscent of the Stalin-Trotsky duel for leadership after Lenin's death. The death of Stalin in 1953 led to a struggle among Nikita Khrushchev, Georgi Malenkov, Lavrenti Beria (who headed the secret police), and the foreign minister V. M. Molotov. Molotov, who was old and tired, soon dropped out, and Beria was arrested in July 1953 as an "enemy of the people"—which, considering his position, was not unreasonable. Between 1954 and 1956 Khrushchev slowly gained control of the party machine, and won support in the ruling Politburo, which was the governing council of the party, and thus the country as well. After 1956 Khrushchev seemed supreme. Supremacy, however, was not infallibility, and Khrushchev had to admit failure in his agriculture program and shoulder the responsibility for the quarrel with Communist China. In October 1964 Khrushchev was toppled. His place was taken by Alexei Kosygin and Leonid Brezhnev.

Postwar Russia had to face an acceleration of the splintering of communist ideology and the resultant fracturing of the political and diplomatic unity of the communist nations. The first heresy occurred in Yugoslavia, which was led by President Tito to an independent position in 1948. In 1956 Russian troops were needed to repress a revolt in Hungary, which showed all the signs of going Titoist. During the years after Stalin's death, relations between Russia and Communist China slowly cooled until, by 1966, the two nations were close to war. In 1968 Russian troops were sent into Czechoslovakia, which was going Titoist and experimenting with Liebermanism. Even the subservient western communist parties took to criticizing Moscow. These alarming "deviationist tendencies" did not seem to be diminishing; indeed, they seemed to be growing in number and strength. Unquestioned Russian leadership of world communism was becoming a memory of Stalin's times.

In looking back over the Russian Revolution and the years of communism, what may we say about it? Certainly the major impact has been in diplomacy. Ideological differences have been added to the normal tensions of great-power diplomacy. Inside Russia, however, it is difficult to see what significant differences the Russian Revolution and communism have made. Russian government was autocratic before and after the revolution, and the secret police simply became larger, more powerful, and more efficient after 1917. Russian agriculture has been in a state of constant crisis since the 1850s. Low production, technological backwardness, and gross inefficiency have been continuing problems. In opening the virgin lands, Khrushchev was only following what Stolypin did from 1907 to 1912, and not doing it nearly as well. The policies of Stalin in dealing with industrial development were essentially the same as those used by Count Sergei Witte from 1893 to 1905. Russian economic growth was not appreciably greater after the revolution than before it; indeed the revolution had only a marginal effect on the Russian economy. It is ironic that the greatest revolution of our times has brought more continuity than change to the land of its birth.

The Nazi Revolution in Germany

Before he would consent to discuss an armistice in 1918, Woodrow Wilson demanded that Germany institute a democratic government. The Germans made a few changes in their regime, including establishing a republic and promising to draw up a new constitution, and Wilson, who did not really know what democracy was, pronounced himself satisfied. Thus, while the Allies were wrangling over the Treaty of Versailles in Paris, Germans were drawing up a constitution in the Thuringian town of Weimar. Weimar gave its name to a tragic republic, which staggered fitfully from crisis to crisis until its demise in January 1933 at the hands of Hitler.

The Weimar Republic suffered through distinct periods. The first, from 1919 to 1924, was a time of severe economic dislocation, when political extremism flourished and attempts to overthrow the government were commonplace. The second period, from 1924 to 1929, was one of brief and ephemeral prosperity; and the third, from 1929 to 1933, was the Great Depression, when the Nazis grew strong enough to take over the state. The essential continuing characteristic of Weimar, however, was political weakness. The government was not able to bring the economy under control, except for a brief period, and then with foreign help. Nor was the government able to prevent the growth of extremist political movements. The party squabbles in parliament had no real relation to the mammoth problems of the German people. Weimar politicians lived in a "house without windows," and their efforts were insignificant against the background of economic disaster and the disintegration of traditional German society.

After imperial Germany had lost the war, she immediately faced a stupendous economic crisis. The currency collapsed, demobilized veterans could not find work, and German industry and trade were at a standstill. The reparations burden was also added to Germany in 1921. Tariffs in eastern Europe deprived Germany of traditional markets. By September 1923 the German economy had collapsed altogether, and the government was on the verge of disintegration.

Accompanying economic catastrophe was an alarming resort to political violence. Revolution began as soon as it was clear that the war was lost. In November 1918, riots began in the port of Kiel that soon spread throughout the country. They precipitated the overthrow of the monarchy but stopped short of serious social reconstruction—an alliance between the army and the trade-union leaders then ruling Germany prevented that. The modest revolution of November 1918 did not satisfy everyone, however. On the left, the Spartacists, a communist faction in Berlin, tried to emulate the Soviet success in St. Petersburg. The army was ready for this and the Spartacists were defeated. This was the last gasp of the divided and unpopular German left. Thereafter, revolutionary agitation—and there was a great deal of it—came from old-fashioned Prussian militarists or new-style fascists and Nazis.

The assault from the right took several forms. In 1920 the Socialist premier of Bavaria, Kurt Eisner, was assassinated, and the province was taken over by a conservative bureaucrat, von Kahr. The same year there was an attempted revolution in Berlin, the Kapp *Putsch*, which was supported by veterans of the war, big industrialists, and royalists who wanted the kaiser back. The army would not shoot its former comrades in arms, and the Kapp *Putsch* was only broken by a general strike of workers in Berlin. In these years, also, Germany swarmed with veterans' groups similar to the Luttwitz Brigade, which was the armed force of the Kapp *Putsch*. These were the *Freikorps*, basically units of the imperial army that had not demobilized in 1919. They retained their arms and engaged in street battles with Socialists, supported conservative politicians, and posed a constant threat to the government. Beyond this, there was a rash of political assassinations of democratic politicians, the *Feme* murders. Between 1919 and 1924 more than three hundred liberal political leaders were killed, including Walther Rathenau and Matthias Erzberger. Finally, in September 1923, came the beer hall *Putsch* in Munich, the first attempt of Adolf Hitler and his Nazis to seize power. It was not yet time; the army put the revolt down.

By the fall of 1923 the Weimar Republic was near death. American intervention, which had created a republic in 1918, saved it in 1924. An American banker, Charles Dawes, headed an international commission that reduced reparations, provided foreign loans to support the German economy, and reorganized German international payments. The Dawes Plan and the loans that followed it were astonishingly successful in reviving the German economy. Economic reconstruction was accompanied by growing international acceptance of Germany, as the war hatreds in the West diminished. In 1925 Germany signed the Locarno Treaty, accepting her western boundaries as permanent. The next year she was admitted to the League of Nations, and in 1929 the Young Plan reduced reparations still further. Prosperity was also reflected in a sharp reduction of extremist politics within Germany. Social tensions were also less severe, and the German middle class began a halting recovery from the blows of war, depression, and inflation. For a brief time it looked as if the Weimar experiment might work.

The Great Depression ended these fragile hopes. Foreign loans ceased, trade declined, factories closed, and unemployment rose spectacularly toward its 1932 high of 6 million. In this crisis the German state and society began to come apart. Extremist politics again became attractive, with the Nazis and Communists growing at a phenomenal rate. In the 1930 elections the Nazis increased their representation from 12 to 107 seats. Two years later they occupied 230 seats. By 1932 the votes for totalitarianism, whether Communist or Nazi, were a substantial majority of the electorate, demonstrating that faith in the democratic Weimar Republic was dead. In January 1933 Adolf Hitler, as leader of the largest party, was made chancellor of Germany. Depression, unemployment, fear, social and religious hatreds, nationalism, and a deep disgust with the Weimar Republic had carried the Nazis to power.

Like the Soviets they so hated and emulated, the Nazis set about creating a totalitarian society and state. The state itself was purged of all possible opponents of the Nazis. The legal system was drastically changed. The established rights of defendants were discarded, and the needs of the state became the determining element in most trials. In 1934 new peoples' courts were established, with wide powers over political activities. Their proceedings were secret, with execution the usual sentence. The National Socialist Party (Nazi) became the only legal political organization. Universities were purged of their most distinguished professors. After 1933 German public institutions became increasingly a branch of the Nazi movement.

In addition to putting Nazis in state positions, Hitler and his cohorts built a huge party. The earliest party organization was the S.A. (*Sturmabteilung*), or storm troopers, which ultimately grew to over 3 million members. Organized in a paramilitary manner, the storm troopers wore a brown uniform, hence the nickname, Brownshirts. They were used to beat up Jews and Socialists, hold election rallies, march in parades, sell party newspapers, and, in general, show the Nazi flag. After 1933 the Brownshirts became essentially superfluous, even embarrassing, for they had nothing to do. In a massacre in 1934 their leadership was butchered, and the organization declined in importance, being dissolved in all but name in October 1941.

A mass institution, the S.A. was insufficiently elitist to remain in the center of the Nazi movement. In 1928 it fathered a new group, which grew steadily in importance during the Nazi era. The S.S. (*Schutzstaffel*) found much to do in the Nazi paradise. They took over the concentration camps, showing a far greater aptitude for brutality and sadism than the poor Brownshirts. They became elite troops in the war, a sort of private Nazi army of several divisions, the *Waffen-S.S.* They specialized in murdering Jews, Poles, Russians, and other occupied peoples. The S.S. also produced their own secret police, the S.D. (*Sicherheitsdienst*), which spied on Nazi and civilian alike.

Next to the S.S., the most loathsome and feared Nazi organization was the Gestapo (*Geheime Staatspolizei*). Originally designed for harrying the ordinary German, the Gestapo expanded as war came. They followed the army into defeated countries and assumed much of the task of destroying the local underground. In Germany itself, the Gestapo undertook suppression of defeatism and war weariness among civilians. Not a pleasant task, perhaps, but the Gestapo approached it with the dedication of their calling.

Not all Nazi institutions involved police; there were youth, labor, and propaganda organizations as well. Like both the Communists and Fascists, the Nazis paid great attention to the indoctrination of young people, making sure they acquired the proper Nazi values. The *Hitler Jugend* was for young men, and its training emphasized Nazi propaganda, physical fitness, and weapons training. The proper party member was, after all, a warrior. The BDM (*Bund deutscher Maedel*) was for girls, and it heeded Hitler's admonition that women ought to stay in the kitchen, nursery, church, and bedroom. Training was concentrated on such domestic virtues as sewing and child care, along with a huge dollop of propaganda.

Propaganda was a major concern for all authoritarian regimes after World War I, but few gave it such loving attention or showed such technical skill at concentrated lying as the Nazis. By films, radio, newspapers, cartoons, speeches, broadsides, advertisements, parades, processions, and rallies the Nazis pushed their message on the German people, who were generally receptive to it. Nazi propaganda operated on the simple premise that people will believe anything that they have heard again and again. The content of the message is less important that its utter simplicity and repetition. The Nazi technique was constant reiteration of simple slogans, such as the "sacred German soil and blood," the German need for "living space," the perfidy of Western democracies who imposed the "*Diktat* of Versailles" on the unsuspecting Germans, and the historic wickedness of the Jews who were both cunning and subhuman.

This multi-institutional party was directed by Hitler toward several purposes, all of them evil. The first, and most disturbing to the rest of the world, was German rearmament and the drift toward war. Hitler proclaimed in 1935 that Germany would rearm, and by 1936 it was clear that Germany wanted war. Western and Soviet leaders twisted and delayed, but Hitler, who frequently got what he wanted, got war also.

Hitler's program also included religious and ethnic hatred. Hatred of Jews was the essential core and one of the most popular elements of the Nazi ideology. Rooted in the traditional culture of German peasants and petty bourgeoisie, anti-Semitism was brought to new depths by the Nazis. In April 1933, they organized a national boycott of Jewish business and professionals. The Civil Service Law retired all Jewish officials, notaries, and teachers, envisioning their replacement by Nazis. This was followed by a concerted government and party effort to drive Jewish businessmen, doctors, and lawyers out of practice. In 1935 the Nuremberg Laws deprived Jews of their citizenship and forbade them to marry other Germans. Party persecution also grew in intensity, with mobs of Germans, led by S.A. goons, beating up men, raping young women, and burning and robbing stores. Organized public persecution reached its disgusting climax with Crystal Night in November 1938, when gangs of Nazis roamed the streets, destroying Jewish property and murdering any Jews they found. Synagogues were particular targets, and almost all were destroyed.

At this point the Nazis were still intent on driving the Jews out of the country. The refugees were of all types, some famous, most obscure. Professor Albert Einstein left Germany, and philosopher Paul Schrecker was physically kicked down the stairs of the University of Leipzig as a prelude to his flight from the "Aryan paradise." Others attracted less notice. On Crystal Night fourteen-year-old Hans Kaufmann, who spoke no English, was deposited on the New York docks, another stop on his flight from Hanover to Baton Rouge, La., where he was being sent by his family to escape the Nazi terror. But the line of refugees was too small. Too many stayed. The Nazis would not allow emigrants to take any property, and aid from abroad was too little to get many of the Jews out. Moreover, as war approached, the Nazi leaders began to change their minds about the Jews. They thought less of emigration and more of the "final solution"—sending the Jews to concentration camps, there to murder them.

Concentration camps were the quintessential Nazi institution. In them the Nazis excelled. While German government was falling apart in 1943 and 1944, the concentration camps were being run with even higher efficiency. When supplies could not get to the front, train after train packed with Jews, Poles, Russians, and Czechs arrived at the concentration camps. Nothing demonstrated so clearly the essential sadism and psychopathology of Nazism.

In the camps the prisoners were starved, brutalized, degraded, tortured, and beaten. However, this was all preliminary. It was done to amuse sadistic guards and officers. It was done because Nazis did not consider Jews and Slavs as people. It was done to keep the inmates busy. The real purpose of the concentration camps was death. The inmates were there to be killed, as quickly and efficiently as possible. Initially, firing squads were used, but these proved too slow and too public. They were replaced by poison gas and huge ovens in which the bodies were cremated. This quickened the pace, and the Nazis ultimately murdered 6 million Jews and several million Russians and Poles as well. This hideous slaughter was the logical fulfillment of Nazi ideas about race, culture, and nationhood.

A further element of Nazi ideology and purpose—indeed, the foundation of Nazi religious and ethnic hatreds—was the ludicrous notion that the Germans were an "Aryan master race." Hitler and his cohorts were fond of telling the Germans that they were a race of blond, Nordic supermen who were brighter, more honorable, decent, and cultured, and stronger than the decadent nationalities around them. As the master race, surely all Germans were entitled to live in Hitler's Aryan paradise. Hence the rationale for absorbing Austria and annexing most of Czechoslovakia. Moreover, as the master race, the strong, decent, bright, and honorable Germans were certainly entitled to take anything they wanted from despised sub-humans such as Jews, Poles, and Russians. Within the Nazi ideology, it was all so clear.

The element of Nazism that tied together the ideology, the institutional party, the captive state, and the concentration camps was the leadership principle. According to this principle, which was taken very seriously in the Third Reich, Adolf Hitler was the supreme master of the master race. His word was law, and his immediate subordinates in the Nazi leadership corps carried out his word and were more important than all but the *Führer* himself. The principle applied all down the line in the paramilitary institutions of the Nazi party. Unquestioning obedience to one's superior was the first rule for a good party member. The leadership principle, almost a necessity for a totalitarian party, had an untoward result with the Nazis. Because of the peculiar nature of the Nazi ideology, it was more compelling to the sick and insane, to sociopaths and psychopaths, than to other people. The impact of inflation and depression could drive one to fascism, but to be a Nazi leader one had to believe, or come close to believing, the ideology. Thus Nazi leaders were strange people. S.S. chief Himmler, for example, was an emotional cripple who could not see others as people, and his deputy Heydrich was a sadist. The German diplomat Franz von Papen was reputed to have said that Nazi Germany was run by a collection of overgrown juvenile delinquents. He was too mild. In Nazi Germany the inmates ran the asylum, and their regime was a monument to all the types of evil in Western society.

The Drift Toward Dictatorship: 1919–1939

Communist Russia and Nazi Germany were the only thoroughly totalitarian societies in postwar Europe, but not the only ideologically antiliberal and antidemocratic governments. The immense costs of war and the unsatisfactory peace treaties that followed placed huge strains on the governments of the smaller states of Europe. The people of southern and eastern Europe, already poor, were utterly impoverished by the postwar depression. The succession states of the Austrian and Russian empires inherited corrosive nationalist hatreds and ambitions and were frequently on the verge of war. In none of these states had the ideals of democracy ever received more than casual adherence, and now how could democracy with its demands for tolerance, trust, compromise, and freedom meet the awesome postwar problem? Fewer and fewer thought it could. Losing faith in freedom, men turned to authority. In over a dozen countries, an authoritiarian revolution overthrew the feeble and demoralized defenders of democratic practice. Dictatorship became the political panacea of Europe in the wake of the Great War.

The most admired and imitated dictatorial regime in postwar Europe was established in Italy, called, by courtesy at least, one of the great powers. The Great War had badly battered Italy, and the immediate postwar period was no better. There had been enormous casualties in the war, and Italian industry was run-down and worn-out. The costs of war prevented the investment of the necessary social capital to restore it. Demobilization left millions unemployed, and rapid inflation cut deeply into real wages. The result was a rash of strikes, riots, and uprisings, both in town and country. In 1919 and 1920 sit-down strikes frightened industrialists, who thought nationalization was coming next. Riots tore Milan and Turin. In the country, peasants refused to pay taxes and rents and burned estate buildings. In September 1920 a lockout in the metallurgical factories in northern Italy led to paralyzing urban disorder and increased demands for a "strong hand." The palsied liberal governments did nothing. Ministerial instability and a genuine bewilderment about what to do frustrated what feeble will they had.

Amidst such social confusion a renegade socialist, Benito Mussolini, formed his Fascist party. Mussolini had literary and oratorical ability and had served in the war. Vastly dissatisfied with the official timidity of democratic government, he formulated a political program based on the qualities of courage, movement, and vitality. Fascism had no intellectual base at all. It stood for nothing except adventure and the advancement of its adherents. Mussolini appealed to veterans, who missed the excitement and camaraderie of war. He was supported by industrialists and landowners, who feared the workers and peasants. He appealed to the urban middle class, which was suffering acutely from inflation and was also terrified of social unrest. In the spring and summer of 1922 the Fascists acted out their fantasies of action and adventure and seized the government of Fiume, then Bologna, then Milan. The national government was helpless. In October, Mussolini demanded a cabinet seat. When the premier refused him, he ordered his Fascists to march on Rome. The march on Rome on October 27, 1922, brought the government down, and Mussolini assumed power.

The immediate result of Fascist assumption of power was a startling reduction in overt social disorder. Strikes ended, peasants went back to work, and tension eased. Economic recovery and a sharp decline in inflation accompanied these heartening developments. Moreover, Yugoslavia ceded the city of Fiume to Italy, a great boost to Italian national pride. Because of these successes, Mussolini and the Fascists received 65 percent of the vote in the 1924 elections, which provided for a continuation of his dictatorial powers. Although the elections were marked with considerable fraud and violence, there can be no doubt that Mussolini, so far, had governed better than his predecessors and was genuinely popular.

The Fascist government fashioned by Mussolini differed in many important ways from the totalitarian regimes in Germany and Russia. In Italy the party never achieved unquestioned predominance over the state nor attained the high degree of organization seen in Germany or Russia. There was a Fascist militia, but it posed no real threat to the army and in 1928 was merged into the army. The armed services had considerable autonomy, and the traditional aristocratic officer class retained command. Labor unions, though forbidden to strike, were not under total party domination. The *Ballilla*, a Fascist youth organization, was diffuse and incoherent compared to the Russian Komsomol or the *Hitler Jugend*. The court system generally retained its autonomy, and the Roman Catholic Church was publicly recognized in the Lateran treaties of 1929 to be a privileged corporation within the state. Also, Fascism lacked a clear ideology that would give order and purpose to the government and party.

Mussolini's authoritarian regime did not exist without substantial reductions in the civil liberties and personal dignity of most Italians. The sludge of fascism was never far from view. Fascist officials, who had no real program to follow, engaged in an enormous amount of plain bullying. They shook down shopkeepers, threatened citizens who did not show proper deference, beat and jailed vocal opponents, and in general swaggered about the country with adolescent arrogance. In 1924 Fascist goons murdered the Socialist deputy Giacomo Matteotti, who had written a book exposing Fascist violence. Murder, however, remained exceptional. The Italians were not Nazis. Bullying, graft, and bombast were the Fascist style.

Dictatorships had become fashionable after the Great War, and Italy was not the only victim. In 1921, Admiral Horthy established a "strong" government in Hungary, which repressed dissent, persecuted Jews, allied itself with fascist governments, and dreamed of the day when Hungary would reconquer what had been lost in the war. Democracy of a sort lasted in Yugoslavia until 1929, when King Alexander, tired of continual bickering between Serbs and Croats, proclaimed a dictatorship. Greece became a military dictatorship in

1922. In Poland, Marshal Josef Pilsudski became dictator in 1926, and Portugal came under military rule the same year, though Antonio de Oliveira Salazar did not become the dictator until 1932. In Spain a military coup in 1923 placed General Miguel Primo de Rivera in power. The bitter disputes in Spain between left and right did not end, however, and in 1936 the existence of a popular-front government with Communist participation brought the revolt of General Francisco Franco and the beginning of the Spanish Civil War. Franco was successful. He set up the Falange, a party on the Italian model. The fascist Falange established a corporate state and quickly came to terms with the Roman Catholic Church. Largely because of the superior political abilities of General Franco, the Falange enjoyed more success than similar parties in other European states.

By the time of the Munich crisis in 1938 only in Scandinavia, Czechoslovakia, and along the Atlantic Coast did democracy still survive in Europe. The taste for freedom, so strong in the nineteenth century, had given way to a longing for strength, action, sacred national hatreds, and vicious minority persecution. These dubious political values were well thought of, and it was the remaining democratic regimes that were menaced by revolution and subversion. Moreover, the partisans of fascist and totalitarian governments had taken to calling the democracies decadent and believing it. In the years before World War II the defense of democracy and civil liberties was a lonely and difficult task. No one seemed to believe in them any more.

Conclusions: The Nature of Totalitarian Democracy

During the nineteenth century many thought that an increase in mass participation in government could lead only to more freedom and democracy. Liberals pleaded and sometimes revolted for the vote, convinced they were protecting civil liberties and the civilized conduct of public affairs in general. Such faith in popular virtue had been appropriate for Victorian security and stability, but it often proved false in the chaotic politics of our times. Since the Great War, mass political movements have not usually demanded more freedom and greater civil liberties, but rather the end of these things. Since the Great War, mass politics has forsaken the tolerance and has become a refuge for the true believers in a secular religious vision. In the nineteenth century large political parties tried to democratize society, to open it up to participation by all. Since the Great War, such mass movements have advocated various types of closed societies.

The large parties of the nineteenth century thrived in a time of peace, but mass movements since 1919 have grown great on war and threats of war.

Totalitarian democracy after the Great War differed markedly from military dictatorships, which have existed at all times and everywhere. Totalitarianism has not been an elite autocracy, a sort of modern type of enlightened despotism. It has been a mass movement with a large political party drawn from all social classes. Totalitarian regimes have provided the occasion for considerable immediate social mobility. Every totalitarian movement overtly aimed to overthrow a "corrupt and decadent" social structure that "oppresses the people." The religious appeal of totalitarianism has enabled it to cut across class lines, which are the sharpest divisions in any society. Successful totalitarian movements, therefore, brought in new men, often from the very dregs of society. There is no better example than the social scum and gallows birds surrounding Hitler. Military dictatorships, on the other hand, such as those in Poland, Brazil, Japan, or Italy, invariably operated to keep the traditional ruling classes intact, preserving their privileges and reinforcing the accepted social structures.

As totalitarian regimes destroyed the existing authorities, they also created a new ruling class of immense power, brutality, clannishness, and suspiciousness. The new men came to power largely through their predecessors' mistakes and incompetence, and this could not be permitted to recur. Therefore totalitarian governments created vast secret police networks to watch the people who had been "liberated from their oppressors." They organized their mass followings into a rigid, multi-institutional party hierarchy that paralleled that of the state. In very short order the party hierarchy became a tight, closed society whose only function was the maintenance and extension of power. This two-tracked hierarchy proved to be a superior method of maintaining social control, repressing dissent, extinguishing personal dignity and freedom, and ensuring loyalty. It also provided status, jobs, and functions for the faithful.

Totalitarian movements differ from traditional political forms by raising the intensity of political life to a religious experience. Totalitarian ideology promises something like a New Jerusalem here on earth, a society freed from unhappiness, injustice, inequality, and compulsion. The New Dispensation awaits only the destruction of the present corrupt rulers. Then will come the reign of the Saints, who Know the Truth and have been saved. Totalitarianism is essentially a millenarian or messianic movement, little different from the radical Reformation of the sixteenth century, save that then God would save us and now it is a social system.

This kind of millenarian and absolutist psychology is impervious to rational persuasion or analysis. The true believer in a totalitarian mythology is supremely intolerant of dissent, or even discussion, and contemptuous of opposition. Politics is raised to the level of worship or ecstasy, and, not infrequently, martyrdom. An act of terrorism becomes an act of faith, a type of sacrament. Propaganda becomes a form of liturgy. The true believer has escaped from freedom, from reason, from the necessity for hard personal choices. He has abandoned the fatiguing problems of moral and ethical judgment. He has fled from uncertainty to commitment. He has embraced Truth, he has been absolved from sin, and his hideous and nagging personal inadequacies are forgiven. He has, in his own estimation, been Born Again.

For most men of critical intelligence, such idolatry eventually breeds disillusionment. The Yugoslav heretic Milovan Djilas was excommunicated and imprisoned for his critique of communism, *The New Class*. In his book Djilas pointed out that a Communist elite had replaced the old feudal elite, and that the new masters were more brutal, more repressive, more rapacious, and more arrogant than their predecessors. In 1944, German army officers who had embraced Hitler tried to assassinate him, without success. In the book *The God That Failed*, six ex-Communists explained their conversion to the cause and their disillusionment. Successful totalitarian movements and parties have been afflicted with another type of heretic—the cynic, the careerist, the man who does not believe the gospels when he hears them but who gets along by going along—in short, the "apparatchik." He is not disloyal to the party or the regime; indeed, he is a pillar of them both. He simply does not believe the myth, the ideology. An effort to eliminate such cynics and "apparatchiks" stimulated the Great Cultural Revolution of 1966 in China, but to no avail; organized religion has always been afflicted with the Sunday Christian or the cell-meeting communist, as well as the disillusioned intellectual.

Although totalitarian democracy shows striking structural differences from other participatory regimes and military dictatorships, these are not the whole story, or even the most important part of it. The basic difference is ideology, or religious belief, the desperate personal need for millenarian deliverance. This gives totalitarianism its mass touch, its participatory element, and also its brutal autocratic and dictatorial form.

Since the Enlightenment, Western man has congratulated himself on his rationality and progress. He no longer believes in God. Instead, he believes in idols.

THE ECONOMIC IMPERATIVES

In 1914 ministers and deputies thought that their most important decisions concerned diplomacy, arms, and nationalism. Who in Great Britain thought the budget more important than Ireland? Few indeed, and those were liable to be radicals and thus ineligible for public trust. Most politicians viewed strikes less as an economic issue than as a threat to public order or an attempt at revolution. Monetary policy was confined to joining the gold standard or issuing government bonds. Taxes were to support armies, not to redistribute national income or finance welfare legislation. Tariff adjustments or subsidies to business were the standard items of Victorian economic legislation.

The Great War swept away these comfortable habits. The war was so costly, the economic disruption so general, currencies so disturbed, physical destruction so great, that economic decisions suddenly became the most important ones ministers could make. Economic necessity eroded the barriers between government and business and drove governments toward responsibility for the whole spectrum of economic activity. Obvious economic and social need overcame antique notions of private property. General economic policy became a fundamental public responsibility.

The social structure of industrialized nations also experienced vast upheavals after the Great War. Society had become dangerously mobile, and it was possible to go down as well as up. Savage economic tides destroyed entire classes, and the increasing affluence of the years after 1950 irresistibly turned workers into a species of bourgeoisie and shifted unions from a liberal to a reactionary political posture. Class structure in the West came to depend more on money and less on inheritance than at any time previously, while education became a stronger dike against disaster than a good name or notable ancestors. These changes were not always well understood, nor were people prepared to deal with rapid and constant social change. All too often, social *déclassement* and economic adversity left people in a revolutionary mood, as the growth of totalitarianism indicated. Western governments since the Great War have had to cushion social change as often as they have dealt with economic issues.

Attempts at Recovery: 1919–1929

The "dismal" science of economics had progressed far enough by 1919 for everyone to know that the war had squandered an immense treasure and destroyed the prewar patterns of trade and finance. The victors were as impoverished as the vanquished; the passions of war and the need for political and military security worked against attempts to mold the peace treaties toward economic reality and recovery. As the military action died out, a vastly more complicated war began—against inflation, loans and debts, sluggish international trade, unemployment, reduced economic growth rates, and industrial obsolescence—and none of the Western governments was prepared to fight it.

An immediate economic result of the war was progressive devaluation of the currencies of Europe. War had been financed mainly by loans, both domestic and foreign. When peace came, governments were left with huge debts and few assets to back them. Pressure on currencies became unbearable, and they began to slip in value. The French franc, worth 20 cents in gold in 1914, was stabilized only in 1927 at 4 cents. The German gold mark, worth 25 cents in 1914, had fallen to 6,000 to the dollar in December 1922. By July 1923 a dollar bought a million marks, and by November 1923 the mark stood at one trillion to the dollar. Only in Great Britain did money ever reach its prewar value even temporarily. Valued at $4.86 in 1914, the pound dropped to $3.40 before regaining its prewar value in the spring of 1925 when Great Britain went back on the gold standard.

A companion to currency devaluation was a massive price inflation, a certain indication of crippled economies. In Austria prices rose to 14,000 percent of their prewar level. In Hungary the ratio was 23,000 percent. Polish prices rose to nearly 2.5 million times their 1914 level. In France prices in 1919 reached three and a half times their prewar level and moved irregularly up to 700 percent in 1926. In Germany, during the 1923 inflation, the price structure collapsed completely, with people bartering goods and services. British inflation was more modest. Prices climbed to three times the 1914 level in 1920 but then subsided to about half that and drifted irregularly downward.

The monetary crisis in postwar Europe was reinforced by war debts, loans, and reparations. These were all connected economically, though they differed politically. Inter-Allied war debts totaled about $20 billion, of which half had come from the United States. In view of the diminished economic strength of all European states, these debts were extremely onerous and a standing menace to regular international payments. Without German reparations they were totally uncollectable, a fact so elementary that it should have been obvious even to politicians. The United States, however, refused to admit any connection between reparations and insisted that war debts be payed regardless of reparation receipts or European postwar economic problems. Calvin Coolidge's remark, "They hired the money, didn't they?" epitomized the American position.

Reparations were at the heart of the international payments problem. The victorious Allies knew they could not recover from the war without help, and they believed Germany ought to provide it. The final reparations figure was set, in 1921, at $33 billion. When asked by an astonished banker how he had come up with such an astronomical sum, the governor of the Bank of England, Lord Cunliffe, replied, "It came to me in church."

It soon became clear that Germany could not pay. In August 1922 the British tried to obtain a general cancellation of war debts and reparations in order to bring international payments under control. American and French opposition doomed the British efforts, the first sensible economic proposal since the war. In January 1923 Germany was declared in default, and France occupied the Rhineland and Ruhr valley to collect her own reparations. German workers declared a general strike, and the mark collapsed under this pressure. The franc and the pound sterling fell also. In September the British prime minister, Stanley Baldwin, obtained a promise of American economic aid, thereby averting the complete collapse of the international payments system. Thus, in just two years, war debts and reparations had bankrupted everybody except the United States.

To bring some stability out of the international monetary chaos, a commission under banker Charles Dawes was formed to reorganize reparations and payments. The Dawes Plan, unveiled in April 1924, was accepted by everyone, for there was nothing else to do. Reparations were scaled down to $9 billion, and Germany was to receive huge foreign loans, principally from America. Thus began the huge merry-go-round, which alone kept order in international payments during the brief prosperity of the 1920s. German loans were floated in New York and London. Some were invested in German industry, and some went into reparation payments. Then the Allies were able to meet the installments on their war debts. Money thus returned to America was sent back to Germany in the form of new loans, and the process began again for another year. It was a fragile base of liquidity, however, and when the American stock market between

1928 and 1929 began to offer better investments than foreign loans, the golden flow dried up. Europe, and then America as well, slid into bankruptcy.

Monetary problems were not the only issues facing governments after the Great War. On the Continent there was the problem of rebuilding towns, farms, and factories destroyed by the fighting. In France alone 200 coal mines, 34 iron mines, 9,300 factories, 900,000 houses, and 1,500 miles of railroads had been destroyed. The damage in Belgium was substantial, while the destruction in eastern Europe was beyond measurement. The French began reconstruction immediately after the war. Extreme energy and heavy expenses characterized the French program. By the beginning of 1927, when the job was almost complete, the cost had run to more than $5 billion. Indeed, so heavy was the burden of reconstruction that it could only be paid by inflation. The franc circulation went from 32 billion to 52 billion between 1919 and 1926, while the government borrowed heavily from the Bank of France. As a result, of course, the value of the franc fell, and the price index rose rapidly. But there was no other way.

The real economy of goods and services also required great attention. In the period between the end of the war and the Depression, the economies of Western nations went through three separate phases. The initial reaction to the armistice was a huge buying spree, as the pent-up consumer demand from the war years sought satisfaction. By the third quarter of 1920 the boom was over, and Europe and America slid into a depression. The third phase, from 1925 to 1929, was a brief and gaudy prosperity, fueled by American loans, capital investments, and tourists. By the fall of 1929, however, everyone was tumbling rapidly into economic chaos.

In some ways the prosperity of the late twenties was quite genuine, representing a clear growth over the prewar levels of production and income, particularly in France. Foreign trade and national income levels grew also, though much more slowly than they had before the war. Manufacturing output gained as well, though only a fraction as rapidly as American industry grew. In spite of European recovery, American economic preponderance grew in the decade after the war.

European recovery was not without problems, however. Unemployment was one of the worst. From 1921 to 1940 Great Britain never had less than one million men unemployed, and the unemployment percentage was usually around eleven to twelve. In Germany unemployment was usually around 12 percent, which meant almost 2 million were without jobs. Moreover, these figures refer almost exclusively to male industrial workers, so the real unemployment, including women and farm workers, was much higher, averaging for western Europe as a whole perhaps 18 or 20 percent. Prosperity was further threatened by a relative decline in the traditional industries in most European states. European textiles were badly hurt by Japanese, American, and Chinese competition after 1919, and shipbuilding, iron and steel, coal, and pottery also were depressed. Finally, the decade after the war saw an extremely slow growth of international trade and foreign investment. Every European state continued some of the wartime controls and quotas, and attempts to lower tariffs and reestablish full currency convertibility were repeated failures.

The economic whiplash of war, inflation, and depression created immense social problems for the middle classes as well as workers. The astronomical postwar inflations virtually wiped out the Continental Victorian middle classes. Everything that the middle class owned went. Bank accounts lost all value. Stocks, bonds, all negotiable and commercial paper fell to nothing. Pensions, the result of a life of labor, vanished, and those retired from business or the professions literally begged or starved. Salaries became worthless. In Germany in 1923 men were paid twice a day, in billions of marks, so they might eat. This mass destruction of the middle class, so extensive as to be a form of social genocide, took place everywhere east of the Rhine. The brief boomlet from 1925 to 1929 was not long enough to reestablish the middle classes after the catastrophe of postwar inflation and depression, so when the Great Depression hit, the business and professional families were ruined all over again. In desperation, they turned to fascism.

Recovery from the war was therefore only a partial success. Economic growth accompanied a dangerously unbalanced international payments system. Unemployment was a persistent problem. Agricultural prices were extremely low, and farming was chronically depressed. Nor could the Western states cooperate on war debts, reparations, tariffs, balance of payments, quotas, or currency convertibility. In such conditions, depression only awaited a faltering of the American economy.

The Great Depression: 1929–1939

In the spring of 1928 American prosperity had never seemed more glittering. New products such as radios and automobiles added to the impression of limitless wealth. Depressed farmers were tucked back into the hills or out on the prairies, comfortably out of sight.

Low wages in industry were offset by relatively full employment. Taxes were low, income was up, new houses went up everywhere, and stocks had started into the great bull market. America seemed to have discovered the secret of endless prosperity, and the Republican party was not bashful about claiming credit for it. Elect Hoover, went the campaign rhetoric of 1928, and America will enjoy good times forever. Almost everyone believed it.

On Labor Day 1929 the American bull market reached its peak. Radio Corporation of America, which had never paid a dividend, stood at 505, General Electric at 396, American Telephone and Telegraph at 304. During the rest of September and early October, the market drifted irregularly downward. Slowly, invisibly, inaudibly, confidence in the great bull market oozed away. Thursday, October 24, was the beginning of doom. Almost 13 million shares were traded, the ticker tape fell hours behind, prices collapsed, wild rumors circulated, and huge stabs of panic paralyzed the brokers. Only the organized support of the major New York banks stopped the panic. This was all prelude, however. Tuesday, October 29, 1929, brought total catastrophe. Volume was over 16 million shares, the ticker broke down, and the lack of knowledge made the disaster seem even worse. The *New York Times'* industrial averages dropped 43 points in one day, wiping out the gains of the whole year. Industrial stocks plummeted and whole investment trusts simply disappeared. The incredible thing is that American brokers, mired in the pathological grip of panic, found buyers for all of those 16 million shares of stock. The rest of the event had an almost mechanistic simplicity. Overpriced stocks, crooked manipulations, too much buying on margin, a declining economy, and the mystical evaporation of confidence—all made a brutal deflation inevitable. After October 29 the market careened downward as Americans woke up to a most alarming fact—in the land of endless prosperity, it was still possible to lose money.

European economies moved with America into catastrophe. Great Britain, always sensitive to the vagaries of international trade and exchange, was immediately affected. Unemployment vaulted from 9.7 percent in 1929 to 16 percent in 1930 and 22 percent in 1931 and 1932. In human terms, this meant 2.25 million unemployed, particularly in mining, shipbuilding, textiles, and steel. The British gross national product remained frozen from 1928 through 1932. Depression in the real economy was accompanied by financial disaster. The pitifully inadequate gold reserves of 1928 were instantly swept away. By 1931 His Majesty's government was bankrupt, and in September Great Britain went off the gold standard. In this appalling crisis the government could think of no better solution than sharp deflation. The price index fell by almost one-third from 1929 to 1933, relief was cut, and the pay of civil servants and the armed forces was cut as well. Bereft of ideas, the ministers simply waited for the inexplicable economic storm to pass.

Things were worse on the Continent. Germany followed the same deflationary policy as the British, with the same alarming results. The price index dropped one-third, along with industrial production. Foreign trade collapsed, and unemployment mounted to nearly 6 million in the last quarter of 1932. In eastern Europe the chaos was limitless. In May 1931 the Kreditanstalt bank of Vienna collapsed, pulling down the entire financial structure of central Europe. With soft currencies and little industry, eastern Europeans fell back on barter, both for personal accounting and in bilateral international trade agreements. Agricultural exports to the west fell off alarmingly, which only exacerbated savage class hatreds in the countryside. Governments replied to this by sliding into various forms of dictatorship and preparing for war.

The Depression went somewhat differently in France. The French economy attained a greater degree of real health in the 1920s, partly through reconstruction, which kept unemployment extremely low, partly through tourism, and partly through a fairly even balance of trade. The initial collapse in 1929 did not really affect France, which had a huge gold reserve and could back her currency. Industrial production did not fall sharply until 1932. It was the same with foreign trade, which declined sharply and fell badly out of balance only in 1932. Unemployment also rose in 1932, reaching the huge figure (for France) of 300,000. Tourism collapsed, and so did French luxury exports. Industrial production dipped about a third and stayed there. Because France still possessed a large peasant class, there was a perceptible movement from the cities back to the farms, as unemployed workers sought refuge with their peasant relatives. The government, riven by savage ideological disputes, did nothing. In 1936 a popular front government composed of all the parties of the left, including Communists, took office promising a new deal, American style. It could not deliver. By 1939 America and Great Britain had begun to recover, but France, even under the stimulus of rearmament, remained depressed.

There had been depressions before, of course, but not like this. Previous downward curves of the business cycle had taken place in an expanding economy with basic fiscal and industrial institutions in good working order. Previous depressions had occurred in times of peace and substantial governmental stability. Before World War I, depressions had been fairly short, reasonably predictable, and rather mild. Not this time. The Great Depression came on the heels of the narrow prosperity of the twenties, when the industrial economy of the West had rested on American industry, tourism, and loans. The Depression came after the most destructive war of modern times, when the fiscal and economic institutions of the industrial nations were out of joint, and the Depression stayed. It went on and on, finally disappearing only with a new world war. It was inordinately severe. Around 30 million people were unemployed in the industrial nations. Factories did not merely lay men off; they did not even shut down for a time—they went out of business. This depression was completely unpredictable and apparently insoluble. Governments did not know what to do, and, by and large, what they did was wrong. Men could not solve a phenomenon they did not understand. In human affairs, however, almost nothing is completely hopeless. Just when it seemed that the Depression would go on forever, World War II came and dissolved the unemployment in a clash of arms.

When the fighting began in 1939, Europeans could look back on a quarter-century of economic disaster. Since the murder of Archduke Franz Ferdinand there had been no net economic growth in Europe at all. Moreover, America and Japan had adopted technological improvements that made their industries more efficient. America dominated the industries that had developed after 1914, such as automobiles, airplanes, radios, oil, and nylon. But European industries were not only depressed; they were outmoded, uncompetitive, and underproductive. European economic institutions themselves were defective. The banking structure was inflexible; it could support neither currency nor credit. European stock markets did not direct a steady flow of private capital into industrial investment. European businesses were generally too small to compete with the American and Japanese giants. Moreover, with a few exceptions such as the German chemical cartel I.G. Farben A.G., European industry was loath to invest money in research and development. Finally, the European states themselves stood in the way of real growth. Their national economic policies were too divergent, and their mutual hostilities were too sharp. If Europe was to enjoy any sustained economic growth, then institutions as well as policies would have to change. Even the politicians and businessmen could see that.

The Prosperity of War and Cold War:
1940–1973

During World War II those countries not being invaded or bombarded experienced a gratifying wartime boom. The unemployed went back to work or into the army, and the underdeveloped nations enjoyed rising prices and a limitless market for their primary products. The war boom, however, was largely one of wasted consumption. The products of war industry were shipped to the front, where they were expended on destruction. Investment in new plant and social capital lagged. The new technology was not applied to civilian uses. The wartime boom added no basic strength to the battered European industrial economies, nor did it provide more than temporary profit to the underdeveloped nations. It simply increased America's industrial and economic dominance.

To combat the postwar economic dislocations that had been so crippling in 1919, Allied diplomats negotiated several economic accords. At the Bretton Woods Conference in 1944 the delegates tackled the problems of international payments, fluctuating currencies, and postwar industrial development. The dollar emerged as a world reserve currency, with a status similar to gold. The International Monetary Fund was organized, with a capital of $8.8 billion, to bolster sagging currencies and stabilize international exchange rates. The International Bank for Reconstruction and Development was also founded to help recovery from the war and provide funds for investment in social capital in underdeveloped countries. Later, a third agreement—the General Agreement on Tariffs and Trade (GATT)—followed American trade policy of the New Deal, constantly lowering tariff barriers in a general movement toward free trade.

These international accords, useful as they were, proved insufficient to meet postwar economic problems. There were two deficiencies. The first was that the GATT and the Bretton Woods agreement were too limited. The $10 billion allocated to the International Bank for Reconstruction and Development everywhere barely met the needs of Europe and only for one year. The GATT functioned best when everyone had something to trade, not just the United States. The second weakness of these agreements was their wide, international character. The most diverse economies were represented— the industrialized West and the impoverished societies of Asia and Latin America. This was simply too disparate a group to be well served by the GATT and the Bretton Woods agreement. Recovery after the war would be in blocs of similar economies, and the job would be far larger than anyone had imagined.

The most successful of the postwar economic blocs was formed in western Europe. So great was the need for development and rebuilding funds, and so serious was the communist threat, that the United States in 1947 offered massive economic aid to the European states that wanted it. Those not under Soviet control accepted. In the four years between 1948 and 1952, $11 billion in Marshall Plan aid was sent to Europe. Used to modernize industry and agriculture, finance trade, and support new industry, the Marshall Plan provided the base of postwar European prosperity.

In western Europe the success of the Marshall Plan stimulated efforts to integrate the various national economies. In 1951 the French foreign minister, Robert Schuman, proposed the European Coal and Steel Community (ECSC), which would create an international high authority to control these basic industries. France, Germany, Italy, Belgium, Luxembourg, and the Netherlands accepted the ECSC, while the British stayed out. The European Coal and Steel Community was the nucleus for further economic integration of western Europe. In 1957 the ECSC nations met in Rome and formed the European Economic Community, or Common Market. Again the British refused to join. The Common Market was designed to eliminate internal tariffs among the members, to create a common external tariff, to coordinate policy on agriculture, transportation, and social welfare, and to permit a free flow of persons and capital within the community.

From the first, it was a huge success. Roaring prosperity in the Common Market made the six members eager to fulfill the treaty. By 1968, several years ahead of schedule, all internal tariffs were abolished, and a common external tariff followed quickly. After considerable wrangling the member nations agreed on a common agricultural policy. The Common Market also acquired great international prestige. Its immense prosperity attracted requests to join, and Greece and Turkey became associate members. Even the British, who had held aloof from institutional ties with the Continent, tried to join. Twice rebuffed by French President Charles de Gaulle, they were not admitted until 1971 along with Ireland and Denmark. The prosperity of western Europe since the Marshall Plan has been spectacular, an astounding contrast to the harsh stagnation of the previous thirty-five years.

Sustained prosperity brought many social changes in its wake. Rapid growth in both industrial productivity and profits reduced management opposition to wage increases, and wages in western Europe rose rapidly after 1950. Equally important were impressive social welfare programs, health insurance, improved pensions, family allowances, and the like, which added to the workers' income. Industrial workers were therefore able to move into the economic middle class, though they maintained a working-class identification through unions and persisted in voting Socialist or Communist. Peasants, clerks, and the poorly organized, casual or nonindustrial workers did not enjoy such rapid prosperity, but even for them, the general economic growth was proving beneficial. Moreover, for the less skilled and lower-paid workers, free movement of labor within the Common Market, particularly to France and West Germany, provided quick entry to good jobs.

Business also underwent a substantial change in the postwar prosperity. Corporations became larger, requiring much more capital investment and demanding constant adaptation of the most efficient technology. As a result, the old entrepreneurs, who both owned and managed their concerns, began to disappear. The entrepreneur system retreated to smaller businesses and to industries where the technology was more stable and less expensive. Elsewhere, companies were taken over by salaried professional managers. Ownership became diversified through the sale of stock and further diluted by a form of government partnership, in which the appropriate ministry set basic industrial goals and approved major contracts.

Although in western Europe the managerial revolution is not so far advanced as in the United States, the American managerial system has caught on rapidly, and the managerial elite is replacing the old industriel. Beyond any efficiencies the managerial revolution might bring, it has provided a considerable element of western Europe's postwar expanded social mobility and may well be the base for eventual European political unity.

In eastern Europe, however, the economic history of the postwar era has been considerably different. The east was badly torn up by the war, and there was no immediate postwar recovery. The Russians tried to emulate the Marshall Plan in 1949 with the Council for Mutual Economic Assistance (COMECON), an economic recovery program for eastern Europe. It did not work very well. The Russians were unwilling to commit very much money to it; indeed, they saw it as a method of forcing the eastern European states to help them. Bureaucratic management of the economy proved hideously inefficient. Moreover, eastern Europe, except for Bohemia and Germany, was extremely backward and could not be transformed from want to wealth in a few years. Thus, except for East Germany, the eastern European states lagged far behind the 300 percent increase in general industrial production that the Common Market enjoyed.

The economic difficulties of eastern Europe reflected those of the underdeveloped nations in general. In the postwar world only those states that already had an industrial base have really been prosperous. A very few others—Mexico, Venezuela, Taiwan, perhaps Turkey and Spain—have shown enough economic growth to begin sustained industrialization. The rest have struggled along in varying degrees of poverty. From all reports it appears that they will continue to do so.

Conclusions

The events after 1914 were sufficient to convince public officials that decisions concerning the economy were among the most important they could make. But that realization did not tell anyone what to do. The industrial economies after the Great War proved to be enormously complex and enormously difficult to understand. In an effort to elucidate the mysteries of industrialism, economists elaborated increasingly complex theories. They relied heavily on a close examination of masses of statistical data and built complicated mathematical models of growth and inflation. They analyzed the money supply and growth curves for industrial production, invented such things as index figures and the gross national product. As a result, modern politicians came to know much more about the technical behavior of modern industry, although prescriptions for controlling and directing it remained curiously imprecise.

Other economists moved away from technical analysis, looking at the economy in its social matrix. The Austrian economist Joseph Schumpeter dealt with the comparative performances of public-sector and private-sector economies. The private-sector economies, or capitalism, sustained general economic growth for more than a century. Yet at the same time private-sector economics were morally grotesque. The highest value was to make money at any cost, which represented utterly selfish egotism. Socialism, a public-sector economy, had the opposite problems. In theory, at least, the public interest was paramount in socialism. In practice, however, socialist enterprises were so weighted down with bureaucratic delays and inefficiencies that sustained growth was almost impossible. Public-sector economies might make people feel virtuous, but they also made them poor. As a sort of corollary to Schumpeter's insight, the mixed economies that have evolved in the West since the Great War have found it extremely difficult to find the proper mixture between efficiency and the public good.

That should cause us no surprise. No matter how subtle the theory, reality has always outreached it. All industrial states have high councils composed of the most brilliant economists the government can persuade to advise it. But inflation, depression, unemployment, imbalances of international payments, pollution, price fixing, and incredible bureacratic bungles persist. Meanwhile, the economists push on with their researches and analyses, knowing they cannot repair the economy if they cannot understand it. The grail of this search is the most ardently desired goal of public policy everywhere—the correct formulae for controlling the economy. This search has much in common with the medieval attempts to find an all-embracing theology that would enable man to understand God and attain salvation. Perhaps the economists will succeed. If not, their discipline will remain aptly named—the dismal science.

AN AGE OF PERMANENT WAR

On September 18, 1931, the long truce that followed the Great War came to an end. A military incident was used by the Japanese as an excuse for seizing the Chinese province of Manchuria. Thereafter a series of military and diplomatic confrontations among the great powers—in Ethiopia, Spain, Austria, Czechoslovakia, and finally Poland—marked the passage from limited conflict to World War II. With the defeat of Germany and Japan in 1945 the fighting did not end; it simply decreased in intensity. The cold war between Russia and the United States was carried on below the level of nuclear confrontations, but conflicts such as Korea, Indochina, Algeria, and Malaysia continuously engaged at least one of the great powers. After 1914 came only a single decade when a great power was not at war. Since 1931 the fighting was continuous, a sad confirmation of the vision of George Orwell in 1984.

The Futile Search for Peace

In the decade after the Treaty of Versailles the great powers suffered from exhaustion, war weariness, and the manpower losses of the Great War. Many of them had been struck by revolution; all of them needed time to regroup politically, time to assess the damages of total war and survey the prospects of peace. Rebuilding and internal political and social problems took temporary precedence over diplomatic adventure. In the 1920s, then, there could be naval disarmament conferences (1922), France and Germany could sign the Locarno Peace Pact (1925), Germany could enter the League of Nations (1926), the reparations question could be settled peacefully (1924 and 1928). People turned first attention to recovery, toward a longed-for resumption of normalcy.

But the hostilities had not vanished. Disarmament conferences and treaties renouncing the use of war or the lengthy deliberations of the League of Nations only disguised very real and powerful enmities. France and Germany were not reconciled. The Germans remained hostile and angry, the French nervous and fearful. Germany was absolutely determined to regain lands lost to Poland in 1919. Hungary had substantial territorial designs on Rumania, Czechoslovakia, and Yugoslavia. Russia had a huge catalogue of eastern provinces she intended to regain and added these ambitions to confessional hatreds between communism and other ideologies. Japan coveted huge tracts of northern China, and the Chinese wanted Japan out of the smaller bases she already had. Many of these problems dated from 1919, for the Treaty of Versailles had increased the number of potential dangers in international affairs. Thus the "war to end wars," as Woodrow Wilson so piously termed it, was simply the opening phase of a permanent war.

When war came, it began in the Orient. During the tenuous years of peace after 1919, relations between China and Japan had frequently come very close to war. In the summer of 1931 an explosion on the Mukden railroad during Japanese army maneuvers led to the rapid occupation of all of Manchuria, where Japanese military and economic penetration had been most pronounced. Manchuria was the province with the greatest natural resources, and Japan reorganized it and set it up as the independent state of Manchukuo under Japanese protection. This time there would be no compromise; Japan, driven by the depression and a xenophobic nationalism, was going to keep what it had taken.

Reaction abroad was generally hostile to Japan. The American secretary of state, Henry Stimson, circulated a note among the great powers stating that the United States would not recognize any conquest by force. The League of Nations sent a commission of inquiry under the earl of Lytton to the Far East to examine the situation. Lytton turned in a balanced document. He found that the Japanese conquest of Manchuria was an act of aggression, but he also called for an autonomous provincial government, under clear Chinese sovereignty, with due protection for Japanese economic interests. The league approved the Lytton report and accepted the Stimson formula of nonrecognition of Manchukuo. But the Japanese were outraged at the rebuke and walked out of the league. Unless the Western great powers were prepared to go to war as China's allies, Manchukuo would stand.

The Western great powers were not ready for war. Manchuria was far away, the Chinese government was weak, and no one would negotiate with the Soviet Union, the only great power capable of immediate action. Intervention seemed an impossibly romantic and quixotic adventure. The realists in foreign offices everywhere were against it. Nor would the Western powers apply any real economic sanctions in the middle of the Great Depression. Nothing was done. It was not the end of Sino-Japanese war, however. Skirmishes, incidents, steady Japanese penetration south of the Great Wall, all continued with deadening regularity, punctuated by an occasional, ineffective protest. The Asian war was well under way.

The Western great powers were also opposed to intervention three years later in another remote spot, the highlands of Ethiopia in East Africa. The Ethiopian crisis began in December 1934, with a dispute over the isolated oasis of Ualual in the border regions between Italian Somaliland and Ethiopia. It was a totally artificial crisis, concocted by Mussolini for the purpose of aggression. Mussolini claimed the oasis, and demanded an apology and reparations from Ethiopia for allowing tribesmen to drink there. Haile Selassie, the emperor of Ethiopia, appealed to the League of Nations. The league equivocated abominably, saying that neither side was at fault, the oasis being in disputed territory. The British and French, on their own, tried to appease Italy, offering Mussolini wide economic privileges in Ethiopia, which he refused. He had taken the measure of the French and British people and politicians, and he knew he could get away with conquering the whole country. The invasion of Ethiopia began in October 1935. The capital, Addis Ababa, was occupied by May 1936. Italy annexed the country and began pacification and occupation. Britain and France, meanwhile, were in a difficult and false position. The league had declared Italy the aggressor and had called for sanctions. Britain and France were the leading supporters of the league, but they were loath to offend Italy. Thus the British and French exempted oil from the sanction list, which permitted Italy to complete the conquest. After it was all over, France and Great Britain reluctantly followed Germany's lead in recognizing the Ethiopian conquest. Emperor Haile Selassie made a speech before the league, condemning Italian aggression, asking for league support, and warning the Western democracies that dictators could not be appeased. No one listened to him. He made everyone uncomfortable.

Italian intimidation of France, Great Britain, and the league did not go unnoticed. Adolf Hitler understood weakness, irresolution, and fear well; these qualities in his opponents had made his fortune. If the Western powers could do no better in Europe than they had done in Ethiopia and Manchuria, they were decadent and rotten, suffering from irremedial moral and political decay. An alert dictator would take advantage of such things. On March 16, 1935, Germany denounced the disarmament clauses of the Treaty of Versailles and began open and massive rearmament. A year later, on March 7, 1936, Hitler abrogated the Locarno Pact and sent his troops into the demilitarized Rhineland. The French, who were shocked and frightened, hesitated, asked the British for advice, and then caved in, accepting the German move. The remilitarization of the Rhineland was not a minor matter. Both Hitler and the French understood what was at stake. The coming war between France and Germany would now be won by the Germans.

In the summer of 1936 another severe crisis broke out in Europe —the Spanish Civil War. On July 18 the revolt against the republic began with the army in Spanish Morocco and spread rapidly to Andalusia and Castile. Led by General Francisco Franco and supported by most of the armed forces, the revolt made rapid initial progress. By November the fascists had taken Badajoz and Toledo and begun to besiege Madrid itself. It looked as if the Loyalist government would collapse. But Madrid held out in spite of tremendous shelling and bombing. Retention of Madrid, combined with Loyalist strength in Valencia, Catalonia, and the Basque provinces, ended Franco's hopes for a short campaign and quick victory and ensured a long and brutal civil war with the ultimate victor in considerable doubt.

Both Hitler and Mussolini hastened to aid a fellow Fascist. Germany and Italy recognized the Franco government in November 1936 and began to send supplies, arms, and men to Spain to aid his cause. This aid presented Great Britain and France with an acute diplomatic dilemma. They wished to avoid intervention and still see the Loyalist government win. Moreover, they did not want to cooperate with Russia in aiding the Loyalists for fear that the Communists would dominate the Madrid government. The aims were incompatible, and Franco-British diplomacy soon collapsed into confused and pitiful indecision. Russia gave limited aid to the Loyalists, which greatly bucked up the Communist faction. Italy poured materiel and men into Spain, while piously proclaiming at international conferences that the latter were all volunteers who did not have the support of their government. Nazi Germany sent elite units to Spain —mostly armor and air support—and tested their new tanks and planes. The Germans also formally adhered to the principle of nonintervention. The British and French did almost nothing but complain.

The war rapidly developed into a series of hideous atrocities.

The Loyalists, who were fanatically anticlerical, shot priests and nuns with gusto. Both sides murdered prisoners and civilians, and the fascists bombed and shelled towns and villages indiscriminately. Spanish society broke open along its traditional divisions, clerical against anticlerical, worker against the bourgeoisie, lord against peasant, city against countryside, and the Basque and Catalan separatists against Madrid and the Castilians. New chasms were created by the ideologies of war, fascism against communism and anarchists against everyone. This guaranteed that the war would be fought with extra savagery, that the sieges and guerilla operations would be conducted against civilians as much as armies, and that the prime object of tactics would be to break the enemy's will to fight. Franco, with his German and Italian aid, inevitably triumphed though the process was slow and agonizing. During the summer of 1937 Franco's troops subdued the Basque provinces, and in the winter of 1938 they began driving the Loyalists out of their major bastion, Catalonia. The Catalan nationalists fought to the last ditch, but German armor and Franco's manpower were too much for them. On January 26, 1939, Barcelona was taken, and the Loyalists were finished. The Spanish Civil War had ended in a fascist victory.

By 1938 Europe was slipping rapidly down the last diplomatic slopes toward total war. Anglo-French weaknesses in Manchuria, China, Ethiopia, Spain, the Rhineland, and the League of Nations had convinced the three salient European dictators, Hitler, Stalin, and Mussolini, that the Western democracies could be bullied into accepting anything. Hitler moved against the ripest target, Austria. On February 12, 1938, he summoned the Austrian chancellor, Kurt Schuschnigg, to Germany to discuss the status of the Austrian Nazi party. Using generous threats of force, Hitler obliged Schuschnigg to give amnesty to all imprisoned Nazis and to put the Austrian Nazi leader Arthur Seyss-Inquart in the cabinet as minister of interior, with full powers over the police. This was really the death knell of independent Austria, but Schuschnigg played a desperate card. In spite of numerous Nazi disorders and riots, he called a plebiscite to ask the Austrians if they wished to remain independent or become part of Nazi Germany. At this there were still more riots and a German ultimatum that Schuschnigg resign. The Austrian chancellor had no choice but to comply, and on March 12 German troops crossed the border. Austria had ceased to exist, and Hitler had liquidated the 1848 dilemma of excluding Austrians from the national German state.

France and Great Britain protested, of course, but they felt themselves too deeply involved elsewhere to do more. If the Western powers thought the annexation of Austria was the end of Hitler's ambitions, they were soon undeceived. A single day after the annexation of Austria, Hitler began his diplomatic offensive against Czechoslovakia, the only democracy remaining in eastern Europe, and one allied to France and Russia by solemn treaties and obvious self-interest. As in Austria, native Nazis were Hitler's allies and cat's-paw. Konrad Henlein, leader of the Sudeten Nazis, became the focal point of Nazi agitation against the Czech government. Late in March 1938 the German parties withdrew from the Czech cabinet, forcing a prolonged crisis. Hitler supported the demands of the Germans, which were formulated by Henlein on direction from Berlin, and made discreet threats of force if the Czechs were so foolish as to rely on their friends the British and French and disregard Germany. The Henlein demands included equality of status between Czechs and Germans, full automony for the German areas, reparations for Germans, freedom for the local Nazis, and a reversal of Czech foreign policy toward a German alliance. If met, these conditions would have destroyed the integrity of Czechoslovakia, which is why they were made. Negotiations between the Czech government, Henlein's Nazis, Germany, France, Russia, and Great Britain continued all spring and into the summer. France and Great Britain devoted their efforts to searching for a peaceful solution to an issue that could be settled only by war or surrender.

In September 1938 the crisis finally broke open. The Sudeten Nazis broke off negotiations with the Czech government, and Germany began to mobilize along the Czech border. On September 15 the British prime minister, Neville Chamberlain, met with Hitler in Germany and decided to urge Prague to accept Hitler's terms. After immense agony, the Czechs conceded, having been left in the lurch by all their friends. Victorious, Hitler suddenly demanded more—the annexation to Germany of the German territories in Czechoslovakia. Chamberlain flew at once to Germany to try to dissuade Hitler and failed. Would Great Britain and France now fight? The answer was no. At Munich on September 29, Chamberlain, Mussolini, Hitler, and the French premier, Édouard Daladier, signed the hideous fate of their only dependable eastern European ally, Czechoslovakia. They gave Hitler everything he wanted. Was this awful appeasement the result of cowardice, or stupidity, or a bit of both? It is hard to say, and perhaps it no longer matters. What can be said, however, is that the Munich appeasement was more than a blunder; it was a crime.

Following Munich, everyone, even the appeasers, could see that war between Germany and France and Great Britain was just a question of time. A sort of international anarchy resulted, with every dictator trying to get as much as he could before the storm broke. In March 1939 Hitler took the remainder of Czechoslovakia, except for a small chunk he gave to Hungary. The same month he stole the city of Memel from Lithuania and submitted a list of demands to Poland about Danzig and the Polish corridor. In April Italy grabbed Albania. Italy demanded, but did not get, Tunisia and Corsica. Turkey got the sanjak of Alexandretta (Iskunderun) from France in exchange for a mutual assistance pact. Other mutual assistance pacts were signed as states prepared for war. A Franco-British pledge was given to Rumania and Greece and to Poland.

It was Poland that Hitler selected for his next victim, in spite of her pact with France and Great Britain. The two Western powers had made so many such pacts in the past, and what had they been worth? By August 1939 it was time to push the Polish demands. Hitler wanted to incorporate Danzig into Germany and obtain numerous concessions from Poland. Poland refused these demands, supported by France and Great Britain. Hitler had surprises of his own. On August 23, 1939, the Russo-German nonagression pact was signed, bringing Russia into the German orbit, sealing Poland's fate, isolating France and Great Britain, and astounding the world. The Russo-German pact annihilated the Anglo-French peace moves and made war a question of days. It came on September 1, 1939.

The Ordeal of Total War: 1939–1945

War in 1939 marked a continuation and intensification of the issues and conflicts of the previous years. Years of derision and provocation from totalitarian leaders had convinced the British and French of the basic dishonesty of dictators and had worn their patience raw. But everyone was fighting for the same reasons in 1939 that he might have fought for so much more cheaply in 1931. The power alignment had been set as early as 1935. Nothing had changed in the interval; Poland had simply raised the level of confrontation between two well-defined groups of great powers from diplomatic war to total war. But there was this difference: France and Great Britain could no longer win.

World War II divided itself into two distinct periods. The first— from 1939 to 1941—saw the decisive victory of Germany over France and Great Britain. The two strongest great powers, Russia and the United States, did not enter the war until 1941, when they came in as a result of sudden attack. The German invasion of Russia on June

22, 1941, and the Japanese attack on the United States at Pearl Harbor on December 7, 1941, decisively changed the balance of power. After Pearl Harbor it was only a question of time until Germany, Italy, and Japan were destroyed. Thus the folly of their enemies rescued the French and British from total disaster. Seldom has the impact of blunder and stupidity been so great.

In many respects, World War II continued the trends established in 1914. The conflict was one of technology and industrial might that mobilized entire populations and industries and put a premium on efficient planning and organization. British possession of radar in 1940 played as large a part in the Battle of Britain as the planes and pilots themselves. American sonar defeated the submarine, which was the sole effective German sea weapon. The atomic bomb ended the war—and also opened a new era in history. The importance of new inventions was matched by the mass production of the old. By the end of the war, Soviet Russia, although brutally battered, was producing two thousand tanks a month. American production figures were simply incredible. By 1942 the United States was producing as much war materiel as were Japan, Germany, and Italy combined. Transport ships were being completed in two weeks, aircraft carriers in less than a year. President Roosevelt called America the "arsenal of democracy," a nation that could turn out more planes and tanks in a single month in 1945 than Germany began the war with.

Technological innovation and mass production did not occur on their own. The war brought an immense increase in government planning and with this a great gaggle of new bureaus and organizations. Every belligerent had its war production board, along with specialized agencies to supervise the flow of strategic raw materials into the proper hands. Such agencies as the American Office of Price Administration were part of the mobilization of the home front, while the American Pentagon, with its interminable bureaus, offices, files, and functionaries, was essential to the mobilization of the war front. The growth of supporting troops went far beyond anything seen or imagined in World War I. The supporting services outnumbered the warriors by six to one. Total war in the twentieth century had become a conflict of organization, planning, transportation, supply, invention, while the actual fighting played a secondary role.

At dawn on September 1, 1939, 1,700,000 Germans invaded Poland. Strongly supported by armored units and by tactical air strikes, the German army broke Polish resistance within two weeks. So powerful were the German blows that Russia became alarmed. Russian troops invaded Poland from the east, securing the booty promised in the secret articles of the nonaggression treaty. On September 29 Russia and Germany divided Poland between them. Russia then absorbed Latvia, Estonia, and Lithuania, and next declared war on Finland, which capitulated in March 1940, ceding over 16,000 square miles to Russia. By the spring of 1940 Russia and Germany had conquered eastern Europe.

Great Britain and France had honored their commitment to Poland and declared war on Germany on September 3, 1939, but had done nothing beyond that. When war finally came to the west, it fell upon Scandinavia first. On April 9, German troops conquered Denmark and landed in Norway. Hitler then turned to France and the Low Countries. On May 10, German panzer divisions broke through the French army. Within a month the French were beaten. Hopeless and defeated generals faced the Germans without planes, tanks, or reserves. Most of the French troops, sensing the magnitude of the catastrophe, gave up. The government collapsed. Marshal Philippe Pétain, a defeatist World War I hero, became premier and on June 22 signed an armistice with Germany at Compiègne. France had fallen. The French people themselves, never believing in the possibility of victory, were defeatist to the core, and rallied to Pétain and his Fascist goons. The fall of France was more than the military defeat. It was the destruction of a nation.

The British troops trapped at Dunkerque between Germans and the sea fought on. The British army held together under terrible bombing and strafing, and the Royal Navy began to lift them off the beach. The soldiers waded out in the sea in long lines, waiting for rescue. Submarines, destroyers, troop ships, freighters—all were used in the evacuation. Dunkerque involved the nation as well as the navy. In the cool spring evenings a thousand private boats set course for France. By June 4, 215,000 British and 120,000 French had been evacuated from the beaches of France. The army had been saved and the British, rallied by the miracle and heroism of Dunkerque, were at last ready to fight.

In the days after the fall of France, Winston Churchill, the British prime minister, became the voice of defiance and freedom. Speaking to the House of Commons on June 4, he said: "We will fight . . . if necessary, forever, if necessary, alone. . . ."

> We shall not flag or fail. We shall go on to the end, we shall fight in France, we shall fight on the seas and oceans, we shall fight with growing confidence and growing strength in the air, we shall defend our island, whatever the cost may be, we shall fight on the beaches, we shall fight on the landing grounds, we shall fight in the fields and in the streets, we shall fight in the hills; we shall never surrender. . . .

A fortnight later Churchill spoke of the war to come: "I expect that the Battle of Britain is about to begin. Upon this battle depends the survival of Christian civilization. . . . The whole fury and might of the enemy must very soon be turned on us. . . . Let us therefore brace ourselves to our duties, and so bear ourselves that, if the British Empire and its Commonwealth last for a thousand years, men will still say, 'This was their finest hour.'" With biblical oratory, Churchill called his people to war and to victory.

These words of defiance would soon be tested. In July, German commanders began to prepare the invasion of England, for which the Germans needed complete air superiority. On August 8 the battle with the Royal Air Force began. Between August 24 and September 6, the Germans were winning. German numerical superiority and the drain of British pilots was beginning to tell. But the German losses were staggering—over 1,100 planes. On September 7 the Luftwaffe attacked London, a change of strategy that cost the Germans all chance of victory. Goering's new idea was to break British morale, not to fight British planes. The Royal Air Force had won the Battle of Britain; Germany had suffered a major strategic defeat. France was the last major Allied country to be knocked out of the war.

For the campaign of 1941, Hitler turned east. On June 22, 1941, after a month spent in conquest of the Balkans, Germany attacked Russia. German initial success was overwhelming. The Russian air force was destroyed, and huge chunks of the Russian army collapsed under German blows. By October the Germans were nearing Moscow. The advent of winter caught the Germans unprepared, however, and a Russian counterattack saved Moscow. Germany had won a tremendous victory in Russia, but Russia was still in the war.

In the summer of 1941 only a single great power, the United States, was not at war. Nevertheless, America had drawn closer to war throughout 1941. Congress had passed the Lend-Lease Act, which put American war production at the service of the British. Also, America was drifting toward war with Japan. Scrap iron and steel and oil were placed on an embargo list by the American government in an effort to force the Japanese to end the war in Asia. The Japanese spent November 1941 preparing an attack on the American fleet at Pearl Harbor and in conducting negotiations to hide this intention.

At seven o'clock on Sunday morning, December 7, 1941, Japanese bombers hit the American fleet at Pearl Harbor. Planned by Admiral Yamamoto, the assault was a masterpiece of precision and timing. Yamamoto achieved perfect surprise. His planes virtually wiped out battleship row, sinking five battleships and three cruisers. The Japanese destroyed 177 planes and inflicted 4,000 casualties. In one blow Japan had cripped the American Pacific fleet. Yet, in spite of the success, Admiral Yamamoto had a somber reaction. When he heard the battle reports, he only replied, "I fear that all we have done is to arouse a sleeping giant and to fill him with a terrible resolve."

American entry into the war meant that the strategic preponderance was overwhelmingly in favor of the Allies. So great was the Allied strength, even in unreadiness, that they began to win the war within months of Pearl Harbor. On May 7, 1942, the American navy won the crucial Battle of the Coral Sea, preventing an invasion of Australia. A month later at Midway Island the American navy sank four Japanese carriers, thus destroying the offensive edge of Japanese naval power. In August American marines landed at Guadalcanal Island in the Solomons, beginning the strategy of "island hopping" toward Japan; the idea, devised by General Douglas MacArthur, was to capture a chain of nonconsecutive islands for use as base and supply stations. In October the British under General Bernard Montgomery defeated the Germans at El Alamein in Egypt and began a long pursuit that ended in Tunisia. On November 8, 1942, American and British forces landed in French North Africa and occupied Morocco and Algeria. And on November 19, the Russians began their counterattack at Stalingrad, which was to end in February 1943 with the German loss of an entire field army. These Allied victories were only the beginning. After El Alamein the Allies never suffered defeat. They had won the tactical initiative as well as having strategic preponderance. In the autumn of 1942 the end of the war might be years away, but the outcome was no longer in any doubt.

Between 1944 and 1945 the Allies closed in on their enemies and destroyed them. On the morning of June 6, 1944, the Anglo-American army landed in five places on the Norman coast of France. Paris was liberated on August 24, and by September the Allies were in Belgium and on the German border. A gigantic Russian offensive in 1944 on a thousand-mile front destroyed the German forces in the east, and on May 7, 1945, the Germans surrendered. The Third Reich, which was supposed to last a thousand years, fell 988 years short of that goal.

The final act of the war came in the Pacific. Although Japan had been beaten, she had not surrendered. American generals and politicians were convinced that an invasion of the home islands would be needed for that. There was no doubt how the invasion would end, but in view of heroic Japanese resistance on Okinawa and Iwo Jima, everyone assumed that the invasion would be frightfully costly. Half a million, perhaps a million, casualties were the figures the planning staffs considered. All of this carnage might not be necessary, however. Science and technology presented the American government with an alternative—the atomic bomb. After considerable discussion, President Harry Truman decided to use the new weapon. On August 6, 1945, an atomic bomb was dropped on Hiroshima, Japan, obliterating the city. Several days later a second bomb was dropped on Nagasaki. That did it. On September 2 the Japanese signed formal surrender terms aboard the battleship Missouri. World War II was over.

Political Reconstruction and the
Hopes for Peace: 1945–1946

The shape of peace had concerned many Allied statesmen from the earliest days of the war. Winston Churchill, remembering the fiasco of Versailles, was particularly sensitive to the problems of winning the peace. In August 1941, when the British were not doing well at all, Churchill and Roosevelt issued the Atlantic Charter, a definition of Anglo-American war aims. The charter declared that neither state sought territorial aggrandizement, that both wanted to see the sovereign rights of conquered peoples restored, and recognized the need for postwar economic recovery. Within one month fifteen nations had endorsed the Atlantic Charter, including Russia and the British dominions. Churchill hoped that the general aims of the charter would be a better framework for peace than the secret treaties and Wilson's Fourteen Points a quarter of a century earlier.

In 1945, when the Allies were on the edge of total military victory, the general statements of the Atlantic Charter needed sharpening. This began at the Yalta Conference in February 1945. Roosevelt, Stalin, and Churchill agreed to divide Germany after the war, to assist liberated countries, and to support a United Nations. These decisions were amplified even further at the Potsdam Conference, held in July after the defeat of Germany. There the occupation zones of Germany were hammered out. German territory east of the Oder and Neisse rivers went to Poland, and the rest of Germany was divided among the four Allies—Great Britain, Russia, France, and the United States. Germany was to be disarmed, National Socialism rooted out, war criminals tried, reparations collected, and democratic institutions encouraged. This last meant different things to the different victors. Although the division of Germany was to be a temporary measure only, the hostilities of the cold war hardened it into permanence. Without intending to, the diplomats at Potsdam fixed the contours of postwar Europe.

A major decision of the Yalta Conference was to establish a United Nations of some sort, preferably one superior to the old League of Nations. Accordingly, a conference began in San Francisco in April 1945 to draw up a charter for the United Nations. The delegates rapidly produced a charter. It provided for a Security Council, representing mainly the great powers, where each would have a veto to protect their vital interests. A General Assembly representing all states equally was also created, to be a forum for world opinion. The International Court of Justice was carried over from the league, and an Economic and Social Council was created. To these were added specialized agencies, such as the World Health Organization, and a Secretariat, presided over by a secretary-general, to provide a permanent supporting staff for the whole organization. In 1945 no one knew whether it would work, but hopes were high. Certainly the past fifteen years had shown the need for effective international organization.

With the surrender of Japan, peace negotiations among the great powers included Asia. Japan itself was occupied by the United States, and Korea was made into a United Nations trusteeship territory. American troops occupied the southern half of the peninsula, and the Russians controlled the north. Manchuria, Inner Mongolia, and Formosa were returned to China, although no headway was made in ending the civil war between the Communists and Nationalists. Outer Mongolia was to become a Russian dependency. Because of the opposition of France, no action at all was taken on the future of Indochina. As in Europe, these arrangements were designed to be temporary, but great-power hostility froze them into permanence.

The wartime summit conferences were supposed to establish the general outlines of peace. At some time in the future a general peace conference would be held and definitive treaties signed. No such general peace conference was held. The great powers—Russia, the United States, China, and Great Britain—could not agree on what ought to be done; more, they were frequently on the verge of war. Therefore the states liberated by each of the great powers began to assume the political and social complexion of their liberators. In eastern Europe, Rumania, Poland, Bulgaria, Czechoslovakia, Albania, Hungary, Yugoslavia, and East Germany became communist countries with autocratic governments and strong, perhaps permanent, ties to Russia. The western European states emerged as representative democracies with mixed economies, civil liberties, and equally strong ties with the United States and Great Britain. The same thing happened in Asia. China went communist, and Japan, occupied by the United States, emerged as a representative democracy on the European model. Korea, cut in half, suffered from two governments, a communist regime in the north under Russian aegis and a democratic state in the south with American support. It was Winston Churchill who described the phenomenon in a speech delivered at Westminster College, Fulton, Missouri, on March 5, 1946: "From Stettin in the Baltic, to Trieste in the Adriatic, an iron curtain has descended across the Continent. Behind that line lie all the capitals of the ancient States of Central and Eastern Europe . . . and all are subject . . . to a very high and increasing measure of control from Moscow."

By 1947 the great powers, instead of conducting negotiations for a final peace, were breaking the world into competing diplomatic, economic, and military blocs.

Continuing Conflicts:
The World Between War and Peace: 1946–1974

After World War II the end of total war simply meant the beginning of several forms of confrontation. The basic division after 1945 was the great-power conflict between Russia and the United States. Confrontation between the great powers remained at the level of cold war, a stalemate in which the great powers competed through propaganda, foreign aid, subversion, and manipulation of client or allied states. Occasionally, however, the cold war became uncomfortably hot, as in Korea (1950–1953) and Vietnam (1964–1973), when the United States was actively fighting, and the Cuban missile crisis (1963), when Russia and the United States seemed close to war. Colonial struggles for independence represented another aspect of continuing war. Almost all of these struggles were successful. The fighting involved in them was usually limited—though Indochina and Algeria were exceptions. The conflict between Israel and the Arabs, which began after World War II and dragged on steadily, was still another element of continuing hostility that would not yield to diplomacy. Finally, the world after 1945 was plagued by an endless series of political revolutions, most of which were connected with the great-power conflict, the colonial drive for independence, or the

EUROPE IN 1946 ▶

Arab–Israeli conflict. Varied forms of conflict replaced total war, but, for the great powers at least, the stakes were what they had always been—world domination.

By 1947 Europe was breaking into two competing blocs, each sponsored by one of the great powers. The formation of the Western bloc began with the Truman Doctrine of 1947, which guaranteed American aid to any state menaced by communist subversion. Greece and Turkey were the immediate recipients of guns, money, and advice. In 1949 the North Atlantic Treaty Organization (NATO) was formed, a military alliance of the Western bloc designed to prevent Russian expansion in Europe. Associated with military defense were plans for economic recovery. The Marshall Plan of 1947 provided American economic aid to western European states. This was followed by moves to integrate the economies of those states.

In the years since 1947 the Western bloc has drawn quite close —so much so that divergent political positions have not affected its basic unity. The military character of the Western bloc has diminished, but the economic power has vastly increased.

The Soviet bloc in Europe resembled the NATO powers and their allies. In February 1948 the Communist party executed a coup d'état in Prague to prevent Czechoslovakia from accepting Marshall Plan aid and drifting toward the Western bloc. The enormous initial success of the Marshall Plan soon forced the Soviet Union to draw its bloc of states into a tighter economic unit to facilitate recovery from the war. In January 1949 the Council for Mutual Economic Assistance (COMECON) was organized, and in 1955 the Warsaw Pact was signed, providing eastern Europe with a military counterpart to NATO. The Berlin Wall, built by the Soviets in 1961 to divide East from West Berlin, was a final measure in the formation of a cohesive Eastern bloc.

The Soviet nations have not enjoyed the same continuous economic growth and increasing social unity shown in the West. Poverty has been a consistent problem, and bureaucratic mismanagement of the economy by communist ideologues and "apparatchiki" has only made things worse. Nationalism, always very strong in eastern Europe, has run directly against the Russian insistence on cooperation. The Soviet bloc has not been diplomatically stable; Yugoslavia broke off in 1948 to become an independent communist state, and Albania has followed the Chinese rather than the Russian brand of communist orthodoxy. The governments of the eastern European states have experienced frequent revolution. In 1953 a major revolt in East Germany had to be put down with Russian troops. In 1956,

riots in Poland forced a change in government, an experience repeated in 1970. Russian troops put down a revolt in Hungary in 1956
and in 1968 intervened in Czechoslovakia. Unlike the Western bloc,
which has had considerable internal cohesion, the Soviet bloc in
Europe has been held together largely by force.

The great-power struggle did not consist solely of building up
economic and political power blocs. Occasionally the cold war
became hot. The first such instance was in Korea. In June 1950 the
North Korean army launched a sudden attack on South Korea, an
American client state. The United States, under the aegis of the
United Nations, rushed to the rescue. Two years of fighting, in
which the Chinese Communists intervened for the North in November 1950, restored the boundary between North and South to about
what it had been before the war. Long and painful negotiations in
1953 produced a sort of truce, in which the front lines were turned
into an international border and the fighting was scaled down to
small raids. Asia was also the scene of the next war involving the
three biggest great powers. By 1965 Communist gains in Indochina
had become more than the United States government thought it
could permit, and large-scale American intervention in Vietnam was
the result. Heavy American commitment brought substantial Russian and Chinese aid to North Vietnam. In spite of the American
intervention, which reached nearly 550,000 men and an incredible
array of machines and weaponry, the South Vietnamese government
was not able to win a military decision. Negotiation between the
United States and North Vietnam in 1972 laid the groundwork for a
cease-fire in 1973. Between 1969 and 1973 the Americans slowly
withdrew, attempting to leave behind a government and an army in
South Vietnam that could continue the fight. If the American aim suc-
ceeds, the war will go on indefinitely and will also change character.
It will gradually lose its standing as a great-power conflict and
resume the status of a local civil war.

Great-power hostilities have also superimposed themselves on the
lasting conflict between Israel and much of the Arab world. In 1948
the British pulled out of Palestine, abandoning the task of keeping
peace between the Arabs and the Jews who had been coming in large
numbers since 1900. War between Jew and Arab broke immediately.
Israel has been continually victorious, but the Arab nations have
been unable to admit defeat. There are accusations and recrimina-
tions by both sides. Propaganda feeds on itself, hate and hostility
grow. In the intervals between wars, indiscriminate terrorism both
feeds and assuages the hate.

Since Israel enjoyed the support of the United States, the Arabs turned to Russia. Russia poured military aid into Egypt, Syria, and Iraq, though without noticeable effect on their military abilities or performance. Nonetheless, the level of confrontation was raised. Western oil interests were threatened, and the southern flank of NATO might be turned. When the Arabs proved unable to use effectively the modern weapons being supplied them, Russian technicians and advisers were added to the aid package. Still the threat of atomic confrontation grew as Russian and American interests remained starkly contradictory in the Near East.

The second great threat of continuous war since 1945 was the successful struggle of European colonies for independence. In most cases the surrender of colonial empires was accomplished without war. There were many reasons for this. Colonialism had become frightfully expensive, far too great a luxury for the war-torn states of Europe to support. Nationalism had also become a major force in the various colonies. Colonial peoples put considerable pressure on the European states for independence, pressure which the home governments were unable and unwilling to resist. Moreover, European governments after the war drew considerable support from organized labor and liberals, who had traditionally opposed imperialism. Finally, colonialism had gone out of style. Condemned in the United Nations, assaulted by most of the world's press, attacked in universities, denounced as uneconomic and immoral, colonialism no longer found any influential defenders. It was not the power of the colonial peoples that drove the Europeans out; the example of Portugal demonstrated that even the weakest European state could hold its colonies if it wished to. In most cases colonial demands for independence met a growing European desire to be rid of the burden and costs of colonies.

Sometimes, however, the imperial nation tried to hold on. The state most prone to this response was France, which looked on its colonial empire as essential to French recovery. In 1945 the French tried to regain control over Syria and Lebanon, only to meet armed resistance from the Arabs. In this instance, opposition from the United States and Great Britain forced the French to back down. There was no such international pressure a year later in Vietnam. The French colonists there refused to deal with the Vietminh, Communist forces led by Ho Chi Minh, and the result was a protracted guerilla war that ended in 1954 with the defeat of the French at Dien Bien Phu and their expulsion from the country. After Indochina, France was involved in a second colonial war, which was even more costly in treasure and prestige. On November 1, 1954, a revolt began in Algeria. The French were determined to hold on. About a million

Frenchmen lived in Algeria, the French had been there over a century, and there was oil. The Algerian war was fought with savage brutality, and atrocities became commonplace. After six years the French army and Foreign Legion restored a considerable measure of peace to Algeria, reducing the rebels to isolated acts of terrorism. At home, however, the French political structure was not able to stand the strain. The army, defeated by Germany in 1940 and by the Vietnamese in 1954, vowed to make its stand in Algeria. It would save its honor in the desert. The politicians were under no such commitment and by 1957 were looking for a way to negotiate. An army revolt in Algeria in May 1958 toppled the Fourth Republic and replaced it with the authoritarian Fifth Republic under General Charles de Gaulle, leader of the French resistance in World War II. De Gaulle also favored negotiations, and in 1962 Algeria gained independence.

Whether independence was easily gained or the product of long wars, the former colonial states faced huge problems. They were desperately poor and lacked capital, educated manpower, and industrial infrastructure. Societies of the new nations were usually badly fragmented. The rich and those with European educations were a stark contrast to the peasant. Tribalism rent most new states. Population growth was frequently so great that it offset the modest economic growth that was attained. Moreover, the gap between the industrial nations and the former colonial states grew, with the rich getting richer and the poor poorer. The new nations also tried desperately to remain unaligned, outside the great-power conflicts, and were only marginally successful. The pull of great-power politics and the need for economic and military aid proved too strong. The underdeveloped nations were unable to resist asking the great powers for military assistance against their enemies. They also showed an unhappy weakness for coups and dictatorships. In addition, the discovery that independence solved none of these problems—in fact, it made them all worse—was quite unnerving and had a disastrous effect on the political stability of the new nations.

Conclusions

War is the dominant motif of our times. Since 1914 our divisions have been so deep and deeply felt that they were not amenable to diplomatic solution. Thus the colonial wars have ended only with independence for the colonies or total victory for the former colonial peoples. The Arab-Israeli conflict drags on, although neither side has anything to gain by continued war. Russo-American hostility continues, in spite of the recognized threat of the People's Republic of China to both. Diplomacy, trade, economic policies, cultural missions, the space program—all have become a form of war. People have become accustomed to war. Although everyone says he wants peace, any relaxing of tensions anywhere draws loud complaints and solemn warnings about the utter duplicity of the other side, about "not letting our guard down," or about the dangers of appeasement. Huge domestic establishments support permanent war; the "military-industrial complex" exists in every major power. In our time, we have at last achieved the Clausewitz condition that all international affairs are only war by another name.

CIVILIZATION AND CHANGE

The Great War, which was a watershed for Western civilization in politics, society, economics, and war, brought substantial changes in the way Europeans thought and the things they thought about. Most dramatic of all was the utter collapse of the popular notion of progress, the notion that things were getting better all the time. Allied with this change was a reconsideration of morality and reason. Victorian certainty about sin was replaced with moral relativism, and Freudian introspection about man's irrational nature sapped a confidence in rationalism that had begun with the Enlightenment. Dissonant music and nonrepresentational art forms reflected the growing pessimism and the sense of cultural fragmentation. Academic philosophy spawned existentialism, which denied all forms of knowing and certainty. Frustration and fear drove men to the idolatrous certainty of communist or fascist ideologies. The Victorian mind, three generations in the making, was almost blotted out.

But not entirely. One line of intellectual endeavor remained unchanged. Scientific investigation continued as before. The flow of scientific discovery and technological innovation was unimpeded. The method was the same—systematic, patient, rational inquiry; constant checking; continuous additions of small bits of knowledge; endless refinements of techniques. Such things as these are not disturbed by mere war.

Progress and Disillusionment

In 1914 life for most Europeans had been steadily improving for as long as they could remember. Industrial society had grown richer, and even the workers were less miserable than previously. Governments were secure, currency stable, prices low, justice and education more attainable, and wine cheap. Upon occasion, art imitates nature, and Victorians elaborated a theory of progress to explain and celebrate the general improvement in life. The nineteenth-century bourgeoisie defined progress as pertaining to increasing wealth, expanding industry, and technological innovation, of course, but it meant more than that to all but the crassest Babbitts. To many Victorians the idea of progress meant the steady democratization of society, the growth of social opportunity. It also implied moral progress. Men were now better than they had been; surely the absence of war and an increasingly egalitarian society proved that.

Then war came, the worst in modern history. All of the easy Victorian assumptions about moral and economic progress collapsed. Within a decade of Sarajevo, notions of progress had vanished everywhere except America. In Europe everything was obviously much worse than it had been. The world had turned sour, there was nothing anyone could do about it, and man had totally lost his sense of control over his life and destiny. The present was bleak, and the future looked bleaker. The wave of disillusionment was general and profound.

Popular disillusionment found expression in the literature of the period. The historian Oswald Spengler based his massive *The Decline of the West* (1918) on the assumption that Western civilization was on the verge of internal collapse. By 1925 many believed it. The poet T. S. Eliot ended his great work "The Hollow Men" (1925) with these lines:

> This is the way the world ends
> This is the way the world ends
> This is the way the world ends
> Not with a bang but a whimper.

In 1925 the whimper at least was within earshot. Perhaps the most sensitive representative of the new mood of despair, frustration, and disillusionment was the novelist Franz Kafka. In *The Trial* (1925) he described a man charged with a nameless crime, investigated capriciously, jailed, and broken—all without reason. The more he searched for reason, the less he understood. The world was absurd and it led only to destruction. Indeed, did the world lead anywhere at all? Consider the novels of Alain Robbe-Grillet. Why are things happening? No one knows. What is happening? No one knows this either. In fact, is anything happening at all, or is it all just shadow?

The theme of absurdity was reemphasized in the French theater of the absurd after World War II. Plays by Jean-Paul Sartre, Eugene Ionesco, and Samuel Beckett elaborated on the futility of everything.

The title of Sartre's play *No Exit* gave the theme: Man is locked in his own individual prison; he cannot escape to his neighbor, nor can he even really communicate with him. He is trapped in his own private journey, his own meaningless ritual of "becoming." In Samuel Beckett's play *Waiting for Godot* the characters wait in utter futility for Godot, who does not exist. Eugene Ionesco was reduced to turning his characters into rhinoceroses in his 1960 play *The Rhinoceros* in order to show the bleakness, inhumanity, and despair of the modern world.

Philosophy followed an equally bleak path. The developments of modern science and psychology deleted two traditional themes of philosophical speculation and analysis—the nature of matter and the universe and discussions of knowledge theory. Flung back from these traditional themes, philosophers turned to the philosophy of science, an attempt to explain how scientists investigated and what their discoveries meant. These investigations were not very fruitful. Whatever the theoretical merits of inductive investigation were, simple observation showed that scientists thought, argued, experimented, and made mistakes like anyone else. It was simply that they measured things more exactly, kept better records, went over the same ground again and again, and worked on a definable project. Allied to the philosophy of science was modern logical positivism, a product of the thought of the British mathematician Bertrand Russell. Logical positivists attempted to bring the rigor of mathematics into philosophical analysis and hence were forced to abandon the human and philosophical questions of ethics, morality, and conduct.

Moral philosophers were not in much better condition. Attacks by philosophers of science and logical positivists and the postwar climate of futility and despair forced moral philosophers to abandon any objective, empirical, absolute standard for moral conduct. Instead, moral philosophy turned to relativism. It is apposite that one of the main texts—by Sartre—of this existentialist school should be called *Being and Nothingness*. For the existentialists man was alone, utterly cut off from the judgments, even the communication, of his fellows. Thus the overriding facts of modern life were anxiety, fear, frustration, boredom, and random action. Man never "is"; he is always changing, but he is going nowhere; always "becoming." This was the perfect philosophy to express the sense of futility and disillusionment that spawned it; however, existentialism was useless, indeed destructive, for it offered no hope nor help in dealing with the complexities of conduct in the postwar world.

What did it mean, man being helpless to alter his own destiny? As Franz Kafka pointed out: "In a quarrel between you and the

A 1964 work by Robert Rauschenberg, entitled *Tracer,* in which can be seen the freer association of forms and ideas that came to distinguish Western art of the twentieth century from that of previous eras. *Leo Castelli Gallery, New York.*

world, back the world." The author of *The Trial* should know. But despair is hard to live with, and men began shortly to flee from futility. Some swallowed the organized and systematic nonsense of ideology. They became Communists, Nazis, Fascists. Others gave up, falling into an astonishing lassitude. When questioned about the

German remilitarization of the Rhineland in 1936, the French foreign minister Georges Bonnet replied that he realized that it meant that France would now lose the war. But, he said, it would not happen for a few years. In the meantime, let us enjoy things, and perhaps something will turn up.

The Interior Life:
God, Freud, and Reason

From the beginnings of Greek philosophy, men have attempted to penetrate the mysteries of human thought and motivation. Various knowledge theories about how and what we thought, and why we did it, were accumulated over the millennia and deposited in the industrial society of the nineteenth century. There they reposed, a form of intellectual terminal moraine. Philosophers in an industrial world were less and less willing to believe the tenets of Platonic idealism, or Lockian empiricism, or notions about the soul. Instead they turned to psychology.

The most important of the nineteenth-century psychological schools was Freudianism. It was based on the observations and insights of Sigmund Freud. Freud was born in Vienna in 1856, and he participated in his first psychological experiments in the 1880s while a medical student. He was fascinated by the calm exhibited by hysterical patients after they had relived certain painful and repressed moments of their life. Originally, this "cure" had been effected by hypnosis. Freud was hopeful it could be accomplished through a dialogue between patient and doctor that would result in the patient understanding his entire psychic history and not merely the single incident that had caused hysteria.

Freud's theories on the topography of the mind and the nature of mental illness first appeared in 1899 in his book *The Interpretation of Dreams*. Freud regarded the conscious mind as only the tip of the iceberg, far less important than the subconscious. Emotions were thus more important to mental health than reason. The subconscious "id" was the seat of primitive emotions that were constantly boiling up to frustrate the demands of both reason and society. The "ego" was the seat of reason, and the "superego" fulfilled the function of conscience. Both the ego and superego reflected the demands of society and education and thus repressed, both in action and consciousness, the lusts of the id. But not altogether. Rigid social repression only hid the id, it did not destroy it. The emotions of the id had their revenge. They surfaced in dreams, which were a form of symbolic emotional language. They appeared in nervousness, in a sense of dissociation, in sudden assaults of violence and lust, crime, hysteria, and even madness. Within the individual, therefore, raged a ceaseless war between reason and conscience and emotion. In *Civilization and Its Discontents* (1930) Freud limned the conflict between civilization and the natural, emotional man, which ended in the psychological crippling of so many people.

The most powerful of the emotional drives of the id was sexual. According to Freud, this drive overcame all else, both in its intrinsic pleasure and in its relation to the biological demands for survival of the species. Within Victorian society sexual urges were the most harshly repressed, and many emotional disorders stemmed from that fact. Freud catalogued a gaudy array of sexual catastrophes: girls suffered from feelings of sexual inferiority, and boys fell prey to the universal Oedipus complex, which was the desire to kill the father and possess the mother. Children could not escape these loathsome horrors, so commanding was the human sexual urge. It dominated life and reason.

Freudian analysis of the human condition proved extraordinarily persuasive. Within a decade of *The Interpretation of Dreams* an entire school of Freudians had developed and was already on the verge of schism. In 1913 the master's most original disciple, Carl Jung, broke away, having disagreed with the cardinal theory that sexual drives were the ultimate master of man. Freud's dialogue system of cure, called psychoanalysis, also gained immense popularity. An entire medical establishment, psychiatry, developed around Freudian psychoanalysis. The basic technique of Freudian analysis was the patient's recitation of his life history, prompted by the psychiatrist. Having heard the tale of personal travail, the psychiatrist evaluated the patient's problems according to the prevailing Freudian school. Like all faith healing, psychoanalysis rested on two struts—the ancient truth that confession was good for the soul and the patient's belief in the validity of the Freudian assumptions. The latter was not too hard to find, for the Freudian claimed their master's insight consisted of eternal laws, like gravity, good in all times and everywhere. Moreover, Freudian psychology was composed of esoteric complexes articulated in language complex enough to impress the most hardened cynic. Indeed, the very priests themselves became believers in the new faith healing, and many abandoned the traditional solace of the confessional.

While some of the traditional functions of religion were being swallowed up in the dubious fads of psychology, the churches themselves and the faith they upheld survived. Neither prospered, in the main, but both survived. Both Protestant and Catholic churches found in the twentieth century an intensification of the religious problems of Victorian Europe. Secularism and divisiveness remained basic Protestant issues, in spite of great emphasis on the ecumenical movement, "witness," and "involvement" in the 1960s. The rather weak attempts to create an existentialist theory or to dilute the natural law with situation-oriented ethics further divided the Protestants. For the Roman Catholic Church, politics remained the basic issue. There were long and complicated negotiations between Rome and various dictatorial regimes, which were quite hostile to an international church that claimed an independent authority of its own. Within Roman Catholicism, the strict papal control over theology and the hierarchy has begun to break down. A general council, Vatican II, met in Rome from 1962 until 1966 and revealed the presence of a strong liberal minority within the church that wanted reform in liturgy, theology, and church government. The council itself tended to take positions that diluted papal power in fact while leaving it theoretically untouched. Papal authority was further challenged in the struggle over birth control. Pope Paul VI's condemnation of the birth-control pill in 1968 ran counter to the ideas and practice of millions of Catholics and was only indifferently received. Strong pressure to end clerical celibacy followed Vatican II, but the papacy resisted such a change. A wide variety of new liturgies in the vernacular also emerged in the post-Vatican II period, some with papal approval, but most without. In addition, there was pressure from several national hierarchies for a collegial form of church government to replace the papal monarchy that had been a millennium in the making. Within the Roman Catholic Church there have been increasing freedom of thought and growing institutional fragmentation in the years since World War I. And in all churches, both Protestant and Catholic, there was a marked decline in the obedience given the clergy by their flocks.

Widespread belief in the idols of psychology and ideology, while damaging to transcendental religious faith, has not been able to take its place. The comforts and consolations of religion are not to be found in Freud and Marx—at least, not for long. Compared to religion, psychology and ideology are inherently trivial. The result of such substitutes has been the growing sense of aimlessness, anxiety, purposelessness, and rootlessness that characterizes so much of Western civilization. These spiritual disorders have been much less severe among workers and peasants, whose lives are much more highly structured, whose religious faith tends to be stronger, whose economic needs have transcended other considerations, and whose standard of living, while not lavish, has been steadily rising since

World War II. Those classes and occupational groups where mobility and freedom of choice have been most limited have been least affected by the aimless anxiety that drives their social and economic betters to their wits' end. Business and professional persons, and intellectuals in general, have been most profoundly afflicted by an agonizing sense of the purposelessness of life. A heroic consumption of material goods and services has not satisfied their sense of social duty. Various "causes" have generated great initial enthusiasm but have ultimately proved boring. Expensive psychiatric cures have not brought peace of mind, nor has satisfied ambition done so. This malaise has radically affected the most privileged class—the university students—in Europe, Great Britain, Japan, and the United States. Students have been in conscious revolt against the dehumanization and purposelessness of industrial society. To sense the fragmentation of industrial society, however, is not to end it. Almost everyone knows that something is wrong with a civilization that has seen its technology run beyond social control and witnessed its diplomats unable to win the peace. Anxiety, then, has become a constant element in the interior life of industrialized Western man, a situation strikingly like that of fifteenth-century northern Europe. Today, as then, man views the world and the future with a profound pessimism. Like men of half a millennium ago, men today are neither satisfied nor reassured by the standard cultural disciplines, from philosophy to art, from literature to social doctrine.

The Scientific Society

Many of the greatest scientific discoveries were made in the seventeenth century, and there were some before that, but in those days science was called natural philosophy and had not gained full independence from theology. Scientific discoveries enhanced man's understanding of nature and assisted his philosophical speculations. Scientific knowledge did little to change the way men lived and worked. Not until 1850 did scientific discovery become the essential, informing principle of Western civilization, around which all else moved. In the last century this is precisely what has happened. The technical, industrial civilization of the West finds its basic cultural unity and resource in scientific knowledge. Religion, art, philosophy, and social doctrine no longer bind us together. The West is now different from the rest of the world. We have become the scientific society.

Scientific investigation in the West today is no longer a haphazard affair. It is too important. Great laboratories are supported by universities, governments, and industries. Thousands of men work in them, and well-endowed graduate degree programs in major universities send annual hordes of new recruits into scientific research. Thousands of journals report the results of research and computer memory banks keep track of the immense technical bibliography. The popular media covers fully such spectacular events as disease cures, moon shots, and progress toward effective birth control and test-tube babies. Knowledge, therefore, seldom lies dormant for years, but enters into other men's research rather quickly. Work in one laboratory aids work in another to such an extent that few major discoveries these days are made by one man alone. Scientific discovery thus feeds upon itself, and successful experiments enhance the possibility that other programs will be successful also.

During most of the nineteenth century, scientific investigation tended to confirm the mechanistic and positivist theories inherited from Newton and the Enlightenment. The natural world was composed of firm components, such as matter and energy, and held together by inexorable laws, such as those of gravity and magnetism. Scientists agreed that the atom was the irreducible building block of all matter and that the periodic table was composed of ninety-two different elements, each composed of different atoms. Moreover, mechanistic physics postulated the existence of "ether," a static substance that was weightless and motionless, which filled the universe. It was also assumed that a single, objective concept of time and space existed. Thus the physical world was understandable and did not depart too radically from notions of common sense.

Toward the end of the nineteenth century these comfortable notions began to come apart. The immediate effect of new research was to show that many of the things "known" to be so were not so. In 1895 the German physicist Wilhelm Roentgen discovered mysterious penetrating rays that he could not explain. He called them X-rays. Two years later the English scientist Joseph Thompson solved the X-ray mystery. He identified them as given off by electrons, particles much smaller than atoms, previously accepted as the immutable minimum of mass. Thompson showed that electrons held a negative charge and moved with enormous speed.

Thompson's discoveries were enormously widened by the work of Pierre and Marie Curie. Between 1898 and 1904, they separated radium from pitchblende. The new element contained many unusual properties. The Curies found that it was radioactive—that is, it spontaneously discharged electrons and rays. Radioactivity possessed considerable energy. It could damage human tissue and penetrate metals. The Curie experiments also upset some cherished laws of physics. They narrowed the distinction between energy and matter. They destroyed the immutability of the elements of the periodic table, for the disintegration of radioactive elements changed their composition and moved them down the periodic table. The notions of conservation of matter were disturbed by the spontaneous discharge of subatomic particles.

The lines of investigation opened by Thompson, Roentgen, and the Curies were quickly followed up. In 1900 the German physicist Max Planck presented his quantum theory. Planck noticed a curious absence of high-frequency light waves emitted in the radiation from hot bodies and argued that the energy flow from a radiating body is not continuous, as had been thought, but consists of irregular and discrete bits, or quanta, of energy. The energy exchange was in discontinuity. Thus it was not possible to determine an electron's exact position in time and space, but only to certain limits of probability. The old and happy notion that ultimately everything could be known died with a thump.

Between 1911 and 1913 Ernest Rutherford and Niels Bohr combined the work of the Curies and Planck into a model of an atom. They envisioned the atom as having a positively charged nucleus, which contained most of the mass, surrounded by negatively charged electrons. This notion, which conformed to the spectrum of hydrogen, was modified and refined by further research. Louis-Victor de Broglie determined that electrons, which had been considered exclusively as particles, would under certain circumstances behave like a wave. In 1931 Ernest Lawrence invented the cyclotron, which became the basic tool of atomic research. After this, research went rapidly. In 1932 the neutron, a subatomic particle that held no charge, was discovered. In 1938 and 1939 Otto Hahn and Otto Strassmann bombarded uranium with neutrons and produced atomic fission. In the process they released millions of volts of electricity.

By 1939 research into something as powerful as the atom had become at least theoretically a political and military problem. As war approached, the great mathematician Albert Einstein wrote a letter to President Roosevelt. He explained that Hahn's recent experiments indicated the possibility of making an atomic bomb, which would have an incredible destructive force. After some deliberation the American government began to support the necessary experiments under the name Manhattan Project. The project had its first spectacular success in 1942. In a laboratory under the grandstand at the University of Chicago's Stagg Field, a group of scientists under the direction of Enrico Fermi set off the first sustaining, controlled laboratory nuclear chain reaction. Three years later the atomic bomb was built and dropped. Since 1945 the United States and all other world powers have established atomic energy commissions, thus making much research into the possibilities and nature of the atom a state secret. Military and industrial goals have replaced free and open research.

No scientific advance of the twentieth century was so spectacular or so destructive of traditional notions as was the theory of relativity developed by Albert Einstein. In 1905, Einstein published his special theory in a thirty-page article, "On the Electrodynamics of Moving Bodies." Einstein abandoned the notion of a single framework of space and time and argued that these were relative for each physical system. He broke down the immutability of mass, showing that the mass of an object depended on its velocity. Greater speed would mean a larger mass. Thus mass was latent energy. The relationship between the two Einstein expressed in the formula $E = mc^2$. Energy (E) was the mass (m) times the square of the speed of light (c^2). In 1916 Einstein added his general theory of relativity, which stated that light was bent by the force of gravity. As soon as World War I ended, Ernest Rutherford traveled to Brazil and during an eclipse made the measurements that confirmed Einstein's theory.

These discoveries had tremendous impact on the structure of scientific disciplines. A new understanding of the universe emerged, one that was considerably more complicated and sophisticated than the Newtonian synthesis it replaced. New lines of research were opened up. An enormous technology developed, which, although partly centered around the development and improvement of weapons, had large applications in medicine, electronics, and agriculture. A civilian application of the new technology began, and it would be strange if a basic characteristic of Western society—the progressive translation of scientific insight into technology—would not apply in this case.

The new insight did not completely obliterate the old, however. The newly discovered laws of relativity, radioactivity, and quantum mechanics did not mean that the familiar laws of mechanics and optics were useless. These still applied to bodies on earth with small mass and limited velocity. Moreover, as nearly all of Western technology dealt with such conditions, methodical investigation along traditional lines continued without any interruption at all. In the realm of popular thought the new discoveries had only a modest impact. While almost everyone ultimately heard of relativity and quantum physics, few people understood it. When a few philosophers tried to incorporate the collapse of absolute physical laws into their philosophy, no one understood that either. Casual observation

and common sense reinforced the inherited world view of most educated Westerners, and the new scientific insights seemed remote
from existence, as indeed they were. Thus the cultural experience of
the Enlightenment, when most educated men radically changed their
opinions on the nature of the physical world, was not repeated. The
inability to close the gap between scientific theory and the general
world view was simply one more instance of the cultural fragmentation of modern Western civilization.

The Fight Against Disease

In 1850 Europeans had an average life span of less than fifty years,
and they were as vulnerable to major disease as they had been at the
time of Christ. Doctors knew a little more than Hippocrates had
known, but not very much. It was still thought that the damp night
air killed and that bleeding would assist recovery. No surgeon
scrubbed up before operating, and the Austrian who began the practice, Semmelweis, was dismissed from his position. Hospitals were
invariably filthy; people went there to die, not recover. Priests still
effected as many cures as doctors, and nature accomplished more
than both.

After the middle of the nineteenth century these conditions
began to change. Medical research and practice moved toward the
conquest of disease. In part this move involved a general application
of things already known. Few doctors after 1850 could be found to
argue that medieval sanitation was a benefit to health, though there
were some who thought it caused no real harm. Nonetheless, both
deputies and doctors began to agitate for sanitary codes—for sewers
and toilets, clean drinking water, and paved streets. There was persistent propaganda against the public drinking cup. Constant demands
were made for food and drug inspection. Slowly, business and government gave way to the weight of medical and public opinion, and
the necessary laws were passed and even enforced. It was the same
with personal cleanliness and hygiene, which expanded steadily in
the years after 1850, both in terms of technology and propaganda.
Indoor bathrooms became more elaborate and more widely dissemi-
nated among all levels of society. Both doctors and schools preached
increasingly rigorous standards of personal hygiene. By the twentieth
century, diligent attention to personal cleanliness had become a
standard element in treating almost every known disease.

For the most part, increased longevity and reduced vulnerability
to disease came from new discoveries. The major theoretical advance
came between 1862 and 1877, when the French scientist Louis Pas-

teur developed his germ theory of disease. Pasteur speculated that microorganisms of various types caused diseases. The way to cure illness was to identify the responsible microbe, develop a method of killing it, and then find a vaccine that would work in man. Pasteur himself proved his thesis through his work on rabies and the pasteurization of milk.

Pasteur's theory had much to recommend it, and it caught on quickly. Robert Koch isolated the bacilli of tuberculosis, anthrax, and cholera. In 1911, Paul Ehrlich found a cure for syphilis. It took him several years, and 606 experiments. There was also work on Pasteur's theory itself. Theobald Smith demonstrated that parasites often acted as vectors for disease that killed people but left the parasites themselves undisturbed. This insight opened the way for the assault on malaria, yellow fever, encephalitis, and dysentery. More recently, sophisticated applications of the basic germ theory, coupled with vastly improved medical research equipment, led to the discovery of the viruses, along with ways to kill a few of them.

Medicine also progressed in terms of surgery and drugs. In 1850 surgery was a heroic remedy. The patient was numbed with whiskey, and the doctor operated with fire axe and handsaw. These techniques, which at least had the merit of speed, were gradually refined. Anesthesia became quite widespread by the last quarter of the nineteenth century and was used even by country doctors in the remote wilds of Galicia or America. In 1865 Joseph Lister perfected antiseptic surgery using a sterile operating room and sterile instruments, thus permitting the patient to die from his original complaint rather than operating-room infections. By 1900 techniques of bloodless surgery were in common usage, and it had become safer to have the operation than do without it.

It was the same with chemotherapy. Medication steadily improved over the dismal standards of calomel, Peruna, and Lydia Pinkham. Aspirin, which appeared in the first decade of this century, became a powerful comforter of human woes. So did penicillin, discovered in 1929 by Sir Alexander Fleming. Properly applied, penicillin would rout streptococcus, most varieties of venereal disease, and pneumonia, a great killer of children and the elderly. In 1935 Gerhard Domagk discovered sulfa drugs, just in time for battlefield use during the carnage. Since 1950 scientists have introduced antibiotics that slaughter a wide variety of microorganisms, though these appear feeble at best against the elusive viruses. And chemical therapy seems to be making progress against some severe mental disorders, many of which apparently have a biochemical base.

Beyond these accomplishments, physicians slowly evolved the

techniques of vaccination. This work began with the discovery by Edward Jenner in the eighteenth century of a way to prevent small-pox by injecting the patient with a lesser disease, cowpox. From his success came a long line of inoculations, steadily expanded in the twentieth century. The diseases one can be inoculated against now include tetanus, typhoid, diphtheria, measles, polio, and some strains of influenza. Inoculation has become one of the major factors in the steady increase of longevity by preventing diseases that doctors had found difficult to cure.

Solving the Mystery of Life

The growth of medical knowledge has been part of the general expansion of information and understanding of the life sciences. It is certainly in this area that science has raised the greatest havoc with traditional notions about God and man. This has not been confined to Darwin and his exegetes, but has extended into such areas as birth control and the possibilities (now clearly inevitable) of creating and transforming life. For modern man, the most serious scientific challenge to his limited capacity for reasoned action has come in the twin fields of genetics and molecular biology, which have seemed to lead to the test-tube baby.

Intensive work in genetics began with the Austrian monk Gregor Mendel, who experimented with sweet-pea plants in the monastery garden. In 1865 he published a paper outlining the principles of dominant and recessive inheritance. Mendel's work went largely unnoticed at the time, though it became the basis for the next generation of experiments in genetics. In 1883 Édouard Beneden described the equal division of chromosomes in the conjugation of microorganisms, giving new support to Mendel's theories. A decade later August Weismann elaborated the theory of continuity of germ plasm to account for the mysteries of inheritance. In 1911 Thomas Morgan made the most important contribution to genetics since Mendel. He demonstrated that certain inherited characteristics were genetically linked on chromosomes, which opened the possibility of genetic maps and models. This line of research reached fulfillment in 1953 with the publication of the work of Francis H. C. Crick and James Watson. The two announced that they had discovered the secret of life. They had made a model of DNA, the nucleic acid which accounted for gene replication, and thus had broken the biochemical code of genetic information. Crick and Watson and their successors opened extraordinary possibilities of human engineering. Man can now tamper with genetic information, and soon he will be able to create human characteristics on demand. There seems little reason to doubt that when the techniques become available, this will be done.

The Domination of Science

Wealth, comfort, and power are not the only differences between underdeveloped and scientific societies. These are the most readily perceived, of course, and they excite the envy and hostility of traditional societies everywhere. But the impact of science and technology on the West goes beyond the construction of bathrooms, vaccines, automobiles, and bombs. Scientific knowledge dominates the way we think. Mythic, poetic, or philosophical explanations for natural or human phenomena are no longer acceptable; we demand data, experiments, statistics, and "laws," in short, all the impediments, language, and methodology of science. Science and technology also direct the lines of social change. Pollution cannot be eliminated by a retreat from technology. If industrial and clerical workers find their jobs dehumanizing, they cannot return to the handicraft production of the Old Regime. The increase of scientific knowledge is an endless path that we cannot abandon.

Science also provides a measure of intellectual and physical unity in a fragmented culture. Scientists maintain a common methodology and language, and their work informs our entire society. The rest of us lack such unifying bonds. Freudians cure Freudians; existentialists write for each other; and ideological journalists, such as communists, fascists, Maoists, and liberals, endlessly convince the already converted.

Science and technology have raised ethical and religious questions we cannot answer. As science has relentlessly reduced the role of God to the point where some think Him dead, it has become quite clear that almost everyone needs some coherent view of the universe to avoid aimlessness, dehumanization, and despair.

Ethical and social problems are equally perplexing. Should scientists manufacture test-tube babies as soon as they are able and eliminate such human characteristics as irascibility, drive, aggressiveness, and independence, which give the race its vanity, truculence, and savor? What are the ethics of the atom bomb? A totally destructive weapon poses a staggering problem in a society of nationalism and state sovereignty. What are the moral issues involved in civil disobedience and sabotage, which can so easily paralyze the interdependent industrial society? How will a meritocracy work, when it is clear that such a system will condemn the incompetent and stupid, which are a large percentage of us, to remain in a perpetual lower class? Does this mean we must abandon careers open to talent and return to a system of careers open to privilege? The increasingly effective attempts to measure ability also open another difficult question. What if they show that racial differences are genetically inherited? What will happen to traditional social structures when it is demonstrated, as is almost certain, that women are in most ways superior to men? Ethical and social issues in an industrial and scientific society far transcend the simple canons of a more primitive world. For us, moral decision making, which is necessary for sheer survival, has become fuzzy and confused. We face too many situations in which the decision is between two good goals rather than between good and evil. For Western man it is no longer sufficient that he love, honor, and care, that he hunger and thirst after righteousness. He must also know, as science has given him the means of knowing. This is our hope and our curse.

Bibliography

CHAPTER FIVE

There are several multivolume narrative histories that the student might consult for further information about the Old Regime. The best-known and most easily available are the volumes in the * Rise of Modern Europe series. These begin with Carl J. Friedrich, *The Age of the Baroque* (New York, 1952), and include Frederich L. Nussbaum, *The Triumph of Science and Reason: 1660–1685* (New York, 1953); John B. Wolf, *The Emergence of the Great Powers: 1685–1715* (New York, 1951); Penfield Roberts, *The Quest for Security: 1715–1740* (New York, 1947); Walter Dorn, *Competition for Empire: 1740–1763* (New York, 1940); and Leo Gershoy, *From Despotism to Revolution: 1763–1789* (New York, 1944). The series is quite uneven; the books by Dorn, Friedrich, and Wolf are very good, the others much less so, and Roberts' volume is not useful. A second series is now under way, and some of the volumes have been completed. It is edited by J. H. Plumb and entitled * History of Europe. The relevant volumes are John Stoye, *Europe: 1648–1688* (New York, 1970), and David Ogg, *Europe of the Ancient Regime: 1715–1783* (New York, 1966). Both these books are good.

There are also more-specialized volumes that would benefit the beginning student. * John B. Wolf, *Louis XIV* (New York, 1968), is a long and rather detailed biography of the Sun King, but it gives a clear picture of life in the French court and the upper reaches of the French government during the process of state-building. * B. H. Sumner, *Peter the Great and the Emergence of Russia* (New York, 1951), is an excellent and short account of the beginnings of Russian Westernization. H. Rosenberg, *Bureaucracy, Aristocracy and Autocracy* (Cambridge, Mass., 1958), is an excellent, though difficult study of the growth of the Prussian government and its impact on Prussian society. For Germany, the student should begin with Hajo Holborn, *The Age of Absolutism* (New York, 1930), the second volume of a large study of German history. This is a difficult book, in part because Holborn writes in a confusing manner, but it is still the

*Available in paperback editions.

best general survey and will repay the careful reader. For England, there are numerous works. Three books on the English revolution are particularly recommended. They are * *The King's Peace: 1637–1641* (New York, 1959), **The King's War: 1641–1647* (New York, 1959), and **A Coffin for King Charles* (New York, 1964), all by C. V. Wedgwood, and all beautifully written. For an excellent study of English colonial policy, see *C. M. Andrews, *The Colonial Period of American History* (4 vols., New Haven, 1934–1938), all exceptionally good. Volume IV deals with English commercial policy and the Navigations Acts, and is especially important.

On war and diplomacy during the Old Regime two books are recommended. *Albert Sorel, *Europe Under the Old Regime* (New York, 1968), is the best single, short analysis of the conventions, assumptions, and aims of prerevolutionary diplomacy. * C. V. Wedgwood, *The Thirty Years' War* (New York, 1962), is a superb book on war and diplomacy, and covers that confused conflict better than any other work. On the seventeenth-century depression, there is a paucity of literature, especially in English. The best book for the beginning student is a collection of essays edited by *Trevor Aston, *Crisis in Europe: 1560–1600* (New York, 1965). Some of these articles are difficult, particularly the one by Hobsbawn, but they are all excellent. On European social history, see *Albert Goodwin, *The European Nobility in the Eighteenth Century* (Gloucester, Mass., 1967), another collection of essays, and quite an uneven one.

CHAPTER SIX

The most important work for the student to read in order to understand the events and trends of the era of revolution is Robert R. Palmer, *The Age of the Democratic Revolution* (2 vols., Princeton, N.J., 1969, 1970). In these volumes, Palmer presents the thesis that there was a general current of democratic ideas circulating in Europe during the second half of the eighteenth century, and that this current was matched by an increasing determination on the part of the privileged to hold on to their privileges. Such a trend could have only one result, a prolonged and multinational revolution. Except for the unexpected American victory in the civil war against the British, all the revolutions before 1789 ended in defeat for the revolutionaries—the "democrats" or "liberals." The French Revolution of 1789, however, changed all that and threw final victory to the revolutionaries and their "democratic" ideas.

In addition to the volumes by Palmer, there are other books that will help the student understand the era of revolution. *John G. Gagliardo's *Enlightened Despotism* (2nd ed., New York, 1967), is an excellent and short introduction to that complicated topic. *L. H. Gipson, *The Coming of the Revolution: 1763–1775* (New York, 1954), is an excellent short volume on the breakup of the old British Empire. In dealing with England, the student should read two rather difficult, but very rewarding books. They are both by *Sir Lewis Namier: *England in the Age of the American Revolution* (2nd ed., New York, 1961), and *The Structure of Politics at the Accession of*

George the Third (2nd ed., New York, 1957). These books provide a superb analysis of the complicated structures and patterns of eighteenth-century English politics. They play down the importance of party and ideology and emphasize family, patronage, and common interests.

There are numerous books on the French Revolution and Napoleon. *Albert Goodwin, The French Revolution (New York, 1966), is a short narrative, ending with the death of Robespierre in 1794. *James M. Thompson, The French Revolution (2nd ed., New York, 1966), is also a narrative. It is much longer than Goodwin, contains considerably more analysis and opinion, and is quite good. *Georges Lefebvre, The Coming of the French Revolution (New York, 1957), is a short, brilliant book dealing with the events from 1787 to 1789. It is indispensable for the interested student. *Robert R. Palmer, Twelve Who Ruled (New York, 1965), is a superb study on the Committee of Public Safety. George Rude, The Crowd in the French Revolution (New York, 1959), is an interesting and somewhat difficult book on the sociology of crowds during the various Paris riots of the Revolution. *Alfred Cobban, The Social Interpretation of the French Revolution (Cambridge, Eng., 1968), is a provocative series of comments on various aspects of social change and participation in the Revolution. It is a superb book. On Napoleon, one book ought to be mentioned. It is *Robert Holtman, The Napoleonic Revolution (New York, 1967), which presents the thesis that the lasting effects of the Revolution were the work of Napoleon.

On the subject of industrialization, two books stand out. The first is *Paul Mantoux, The Industrial Revolution in the Eighteenth Century: The Beginnings of the Modern Factory System in England (New York, 1962), which examines the social, economic, and technological conditions during the early Industrial Revolution. It contains an immense amount of detail, but it is quite readable and a superb book. A somewhat shorter and less detailed work covering the same ground is *Phyllis Deane, The First Industrial Revolution (Cambridge, Eng., 1966), which examines the process of industrialization in the light of Rostow's theory of "economic take-off." The great and overriding merit of this book is its crystal clarity.

CHAPTER SEVEN

Basic, narrative texts relevant to Chapter Seven can again be found in the *Rise of Modern Europe series. The pertinent volumes are: Frederick B. Artz, Reaction and Revolution: 1814–1832 (New York, 1968); W. L. Langer, Political and Social Upheaval: 1832–1852 (New York, 1969); Robert C. Binkley, Realism and Nationalism: 1852–1871 (New York, 1935); and Carlton J. Hayes, A Generation of Materialism: 1871–1900 (rev. ed., New York, 1958). All are fairly good books, which contain a vast amount of detailed information—much more than can be given in any single-volume text.

There are also numerous good national studies for the nineteenth century. One of the best for the beginning student is *Werner E. Mosse,

Alexander II and the Modernization of Russia (rev. ed., New York, 1966), a short volume on a crucial period in the Westernization of Russia. For Italy, there is *Arthur J. Whyte, *The Evolution of Modern Italy* (New York, 1965), which is particularly strong on the *risorgimento* and unification. For Germany, see *A. J. P. Taylor, *The Course of German History* (New York, 1962), a short and hostile survey of modern Germany. There are several excellent books on Victorian England. *Lytton Strachey, *Eminent Victorians* (New York, 1918), is a smooth, clever, and beautifully written biographical study of four Victorian eccentrics. *George Dangerfield, *The Strange Death of Liberal England* (New York, 1961), deals with the failures of the Liberal party and British society and politics on the eve of the Great War. See also *David Thomson, *England in the Nineteenth Century: 1815–1914* (Gloucester, Mass., 1950), which is a general survey, and George M. Young, *Victorian England: Portrait of an Age* (2nd ed., New York, 1964), a difficult but rewarding synthesis. For France, see *Roger L. Williams, *The World of Napoleon III* (New York, 1965), a witty series of biographical studies of the major figures of the Second Empire. For an unusual treatment of Paris during the *Belle Époque* see Cornelia Otis Skinner, *Elegant Wits and Grand Horizontals* (New York, 1962), which gives a view of aristocratic Paris around the turn of the century.

For the revolutions of 1848, there are three very fine books. *Priscilla Robertson, *The Revolutions of 1848* (Princeton, N.J., 1952), is a fairly detailed narrative study of the various upheavals and is clear and well written. *Lewis B. Namier, *The Revolution of the Intellectuals* (New York, 1964), is an important but complicated book that deals with the abortive German attempt at unification. And Donald C. McKay, *The National Workshops: A Study of the French Revolution of 1848* (Cambridge, Mass., 1933), examines the Paris revolution, with its socialist and liberal issues.

On intellectual and social history, see *James Joll, *The Second International 1899–1914* (New York, 1966), a study of the futile dream of uniting all workers into a gigantic, multinational unit that would bring Europe to socialism. See also *Joseph Schumpeter, *Capitalism, Socialism and Democracy* (3rd ed., New York, 1950), an extremely important, though somewhat difficult book dealing with the relationships of politics and economics, which is unequivocally capitalistic and democratic, an unusual position for Western intellectuals. See also *Edmund Wilson, *To the Finland Station* (New York, 1972), a superb study of European radical thought, leading to the philosophy of Lenin, and H. Stuart Hughes, *Consciousness and Society* (New York, 1961), which presents the not too convincing theory that European thought changed profoundly between 1890 and 1914.

On diplomacy and imperialism, see *Sidney B. Fay, *The Origins of the World War* (2 vols., 2nd ed., New York, 1967), a standard diplomatic history of Europe from 1870 to 1914, which is excellent and easy to understand. See also *Stewart Easton, *The Rise and Fall of Western Colonialism* (London, 1964), a survey of European colonial expansion that includes a large bibliography.

CHAPTER EIGHT

The catastrophe of the Great War, which began the twentieth century, has been treated by countless historians. Three works in particular ought to be of great interest to the beginning student. *Barbara Tuchman, *The Guns of August* (New York, 1962), is a superb book on the follies and courageousness displayed in the first month of the war. It is beautifully written, and the student interested in modern warfare is urged to read it. For a general view of the war see *Cyril Falls, *The Great War: 1914–1918* (New York, 1959), which is quite good. On an individual campaign, see *Alistair Horne, *The Price of Glory: Verdun 1916* (New York, 1952), a compelling study of the appalling, purposeless carnage of Verdun and the criminal incompetence of most military leaders. Finally, the student would enjoy *All Quiet on the Western Front* (Boston, 1929), by Eric Maria Remarque, the best of the novels on the Great War.

On totalitarianism, the most popular of the postwar ideologies, there are numerous good books. *George Orwell, *Animal Farm* (New York, 1945), is a short, simple, and genuinely powerful fable on communism, depicting it clearly as a horror. In longer form, the same message can be found in *George Orwell, *Nineteen Eighty-Four* (New York, 1949). For a study of communism in the Soviet Union, see *E. H. Carr, *The Bolshevik Revolution: 1917–1923* (3 vols., New York, 1951–1953), an immense study quite favorable to the Communists. See also *Bertram D. Wolfe, *Three Who Made a Revolution* (New York, 1964), an excellent study of Stalin, Lenin, and Trotsky.

There is a considerable literature on the Nazi regime. One might begin with *Adolf Hitler, *Mein Kampf* (Boston, 1943), a long and disjointed essay on why Hitler believed the Jews were subhuman and how he was going to save the world. The best single book on the Nazi government is *Alan Bullock, *Hitler: A Study in Tyranny* (New York, 1964), a somber, powerful tome the student ought to read. One also ought to read Olga Lengyel, *Five Chimneys* (Chicago, 1947), a hideous tale, but necessary if one is to understand Nazism.

On totalitarianism in general, three books are particularly valuable for the beginning student. *Hannah Arendt, *The Origins of Totalitarianism* (New York, 1968), is an excellent but difficult book. *Erich Fromm, *Escape from Freedom* (New York, 1941), examines the psychological pressures that make people embrace a simplistic totalitarian cult; it is valuable also as an explanation for religious conversions. Finally, the student should read *Eric Hoffer, *The True Believer* (New York, 1951), a hostile examination of totalitarianism, written in a series of short, pungent observations.

On the democracies, whose various weaknesses played a large role in the success of totalitarian states, see *F. L. Allen, *Only Yesterday,* (New York, 1957), a clear and critical account of America in the 1920s. See also, *Robert Graves and Alan Hodge, *The Long Weekend: A Social History of Great Britain 1918–1939* (New York, 1963), which is bitterly critical of British society and politics between the wars.

Social and economic affairs played a large part in the politics and thoughts of everyone after the Great War, and they have been written up in some detail. See *John Kenneth Galbraith, *The Great Crash* (Boston, 1972), a witty and clear account of the beginning of the Depression, and *C. Northcote Parkinson, *Parkinson's Law, or the Pursuit of Progress* (Boston, 1957), a beautifully written little essay on the sad and dangerous nature of bureaucracy. See also *William Whyte, Jr., *The Organization Man* (New York, 1956), an extremely critical and acute commentary on the types of men who created the managerial aristocracy in America and who will ultimately do so elsewhere. Finally, the student should see *Joseph Schumpeter, *Capitalism, Socialism and Democracy* (New York, 1950), which we have previously described.

On war and politics, the best books are by Winston Churchill. See particularly his *The Second World War* (6 vols., Boston, 1948–1953), a striking and detailed account of how World War II began and how the British fought it—an indispensable work. See also, *Raymond Aron, *The Century of Total War* (Boston, 1955), a major book by an important French political theorist on the nature of modern politics and diplomacy. Finally, see *Fred J. Cook, *The Warfare State* (New York, 1964), an analysis of the American military-industrial complex, and, by implication, the military-industrial relationships among all the great powers. This study of the impact of total and permanent war on domestic affairs is quite pessimistic, and gives us an unflattering insight into ourselves.

Index

absolutism, France, 1600s, 153–154

Africa, European colonization, 1914, 307

agriculture: adjustments, 1300–1450, 19–25; mechanical changes, 247–248

Alexander II of Russia, 297

Algeciras Conference, 323–324

Algeria, war with France, 384–385

alliances and crises, pre–WWI, 321–324

Alsace-Lorraine: and French-German hostility, 321; German annexation, 275

Amalgamated Society of Engineers, 280

Amiens, Treaty of, 237

American Sugar Refining Co., 279

anticlericalism, Enlightenment, 206, 207–208

anti-Semitism, 346–347

Antwerp, economy, 1500s, 60–61

apprenticeship and guilds, 42

Arkwright, Richard, 249, 252

art and letters, Enlightenment, 198–200

artisans in urban society, 192

Asia, European colonization, 1914, 311–313

Assembly of Notables, 220

atheism and Enlightenment assault of Christianity, 206–208

Atlantic Charter, 377

atomic bomb, 377, 395–396

Austria: annexation of Bosnia, 324; collapse of empire, 328; defeat by Bismarck, 273–274; defeat in Italy, 268–269; Nazi annexation, 370; and partition of Poland, 172–173; reform of central administration, 1700s, 215; revolution, 1700s, 217; revolution, 1848, 264, 265; rise, 1600s, 166–168; and Seven Years' War, 170–171

Balkans in 1870–1914, 296

banks in industrial financing, 278

Battle of Britain, 374–375

Bayle, Pierre, 201, 205–207

Beckett, Samuel, 387–388

beer hall Putsch, 343–344

Belgium, industrialization, 1815–1914, 276

Beneden, Édouard, 399

Benoist, Élie, 205

Berlin Wall, 382

biology, scientific inquiry, Enlightenment, 202–203

Bismarck, Otto von: and German alliances, 321–323; and German constitution, 294; and German Empire, 270–275

Black Death, see plague

Bohemia: fall of monarchy, 89; Hussite Rebellion, 103–104; law and royal power, 93, 94

Bohr, Niels, 395

Bosnia, Austrian annexation of, 324

Russo-Turkish war of 1787–1792, 172

Salutati, Coluccio, 48, 49, 50
Savonarola, 102–103, 104
Scandinavia, decline of empire, 80–81
Schleswig-Holstein affair, 271
Schlieffen Plan, 325
Schumpeter, Joseph, 365
Schuschnigg, Kurt, 370
science: domination of, 400–401; and technology, Industrial Revolution, 251–253
scientific thought, Enlightenment, 202–203
serfs: in rural society, 194–195; Russian, emancipation, 297
servants, in Old Regime society, 192
Seven Years' War, 1756–1763, 170–171
sharecroppers in rural society, 195
skepticism, Enlightenment, 205
Smith, Theobald, 398
social change, 1450–1600, 26–29
social class and industrialization, 243–244
social Darwinism, 286
socialism: Marxian, 287–289; utopian, 286–287
social mobility and industrialization, 282–285
society: and government, Enlightenment, 208–211; industrial, 244–246, 275–289; Old Regime, 182–197; scientific, 1900s, 393–397
sovereignty vs. parliamentary government, 96–98
Spain: civil war, 1930s, 351, 369–370; colonial empire, 177–178; disintegration, 1600s, 157–158; economic crisis, 1600s, 146; exploration and trade routes, 54–57; and great war for empire, 180–182; law and royal power,

93; Napoleon's invasion of, 239; revolution and civil war, 1600s, 150–151
Spengler, Oswald, 387
Stalin, Joseph, 336, 338, 339, 377
state(s): dynastic, 84–90; and Lutheranism, 123–125; territorial, 80–81, 87–90
Stolypin, Peter, 299, 342
Strassmann, Otto, 395
subvention nationale, 219, 220
Sun King, *see* Louis XIV
superstition, Enlightenment assault on, 206–208
Sweden and Great Northern War, 1700–1721, 169
Syllabus of Errors, 300, 301

taxation: France, 1600s, 156–157; France, 1700s, 218; and monarchs' need for money, 95–96; Napoleon, 236; reform of enlightened despots, 215–216
technology: innovations and industrialization, 248–251; and science, Industrial Revolution, 251–253; WWII. 373
tenants in rural society, 195
Tennis Court Oath, French National Assembly, 223
Terror, France, 227–232
thought: European, crisis in, 1680–1700, 200–201; scientific, Enlightenment, 201–202; social and economic, and industrialization, 285–289
Tilsit, Treaty of, 238
towns: effect of economic changes on, 39–41; failure of autonomy, 74–77; quality of life before 1600, 43–52; *see also* cities
townsmen: and European expansion, 31–32; and trade, 35–38
trade: disruption of unity, 38–43; economic regulation, 36–38; and European expansion, 31–35; Great Britain, 1700s, 247; and